# THE
# SORCERER'S
# APPRENTICES

**Also by Peter Foster**

The Blue-Eyed Sheiks

# THE SORCERER'S APPRENTICES

Canada's Super-Bureaucrats
and the Energy Mess

PETER FOSTER

Collins Toronto

First published 1982
by Collins Publishers
100 Lesmill Road, Don Mills, Ontario

**Canadian Cataloguing in Publication Data**

Foster, Peter, 1947-
   The sorcerer's apprentices

ISBN 0-00-217025-6

1. Petroleum industry and trade — Government policy —
Canada. 2. Energy policy — Canada. 3. Canada — Economic
conditions — 1971- * I. Title.

HD9574.C22F682       333.8'2317       C82-095150-1

Printed in Canada

# Contents

"... the pigs had to expend enormous labours every day upon mysterious things called 'files', 'minutes', and 'memoranda' ... This was of the highest importance for the welfare of the farm, Squealer said. But still, neither pigs nor dogs produced any food by their own labour; and there were very many of them, and their appetites were always good."

ANIMAL FARM
GEORGE ORWELL

# Acknowledgements

As with my previous book, *The Blue-Eyed Sheiks*, the most important part of the research for this volume consisted of personal interviews. I spoke to many people in the oil industry, the government, the public service, the political parties, trade associations, the academic world and the consulting business. In most cases, these interviews were granted on a confidential basis. However, I also know that a number of people who were extremely helpful to me will disagree with what I write and therefore not wish to be named as collaborators. To all these people, nevertheless, I am deeply grateful.

First among those who can be named is my editor, Colleen Dimson, who was as skillful, conscientious and constructive as she was a pleasure to work with. Since Collins is the only publisher with which I have worked, direct comparisons with others are not possible. However, I believe that I could not find a more efficient and pleasant organization with which to deal. Once again, I must single out Margaret Paull for her efforts. Others I wish to thank for their help, encouragement, or just being themselves are Jane Cottrell, John Howse — my "reference point" — and his family, Richard and Cathy Osler, Nancy Colbert, Dave Yager, Delton Campbell, Jim Bagnell, Nigel Taylorson, Sarah Healy, John Scott, Sheila Farrell (for her excellent "paperwork"), Ashley Geddis, Jamie Deacey, Tom Kennedy, and Bob Foulkes, whose friendship I hope survives the publication of this book.

I have made references to a number of books in the text. However, one which I found very useful but to which I have not made reference elsewhere is *The Super-Bureaucrats: Structure and Behaviour in Central Agencies*, by Colin Campbell and George Szablowski.

# Introduction

*"Men born to freedom are naturally alert to repel
invasion of their liberty by evil-minded rulers.
The greater dangers to liberty lurk in the insidi-
ous encroachment of men of zeal, well-meaning
but without understanding."*
JUSTICE LOUIS BRANDEIS

When the Liberals defeated the short-lived government of Joe Clark in
February, 1980, they promised lower petroleum prices than the Conservatives,
Canadianization of the oil industry, and energy security through self-sufficiency
in oil. Two and a half years later, they had delivered the highest petroleum price
increases in Canadian history, a financially-crippled Canadian sector of the oil
business, and a more uncertain supply future than at any time since the first
OPEC crisis of 1973-74.

The Liberals' National Energy Program — introduced in the October, 1980,
budget — was one of the most revolutionary, controversial and, it can be
claimed, disastrous policies in Canadian history. Quite apart from its adverse
direct impact on the energy sector, the NEP helped to decimate stock markets,
severely damage the Canadian dollar and destroy the confidence of foreign
investors. It also caused the country's industrial future — in the shape of the
energy megaprojects — to be held to ransom, and injured Canadian-U.S.
relations more than any policy in living memory.

The question here is whether we are dealing with fraud, ineptitude or bad
luck. The answer is a little of each.

This book is about the NEP's roots, its creation and its results. But it is about
far more than a single policy, for the National Energy Program touches on —
and, indeed, is the culmination of — a number of critical trends in Canada
today: the growth of bureaucracy; the declining credibility and political influence of big business; and last, but by no means least, the economic illiteracy of
the general public, which — under a poll-obsessed, politically bankrupt,
Liberal government — has been used as a justification for radical — and
ruinous — economic policies.

Indeed, the first issue to be addressed is: just why did the public provide
such overwhelming support for such a disastrous policy? The answer seems to
be threefold: first, because they did not understand — and were misled —

13

about its true nature; second, because they supported the principle, but had no idea of the implications of the Canadianization of the oil business as proposed by the NEP; and finally, and perhaps most critically, because they held a dangerously skewed view about who has power and who provides wealth in Canada today.

Most of the public did not see the NEP for what it was — primarily a revenue grab. Indeed, it was seen — and sold — as a policy with two other primary objectives: Canadianization of the oil business and energy security. With regard to the latter objective, those who wrote the policy were well aware that they were — to a greater or lesser degree — sacrificing efficient and effective oil and gas exploration and production in order to take the business out of foreign hands and seize more revenue for government.

To claim that Canadians could enjoy — and afford — both secure supplies and a more prominent Maple Leaf flag over the oil business was perhaps less a fraud than a calculated risk taken by the NEP's authors. If the risk failed, then it would be the people of Canada who would ultimately have to pay.

Moreover, the revenue grab clearly worked against Canadianization by the private sector. This may have been no accident, for the NEP's authors were clearly in favour of putting a much larger portion of the oil business under the control of government rather than into private Canadian hands. The enormous tax increases of the NEP — designed to fill depleted government coffers — in fact, damaged the Canadian element of the oil industry far more than the foreign-controlled section. It was to prove one of the policy's greater ironies that the only companies readily able to withstand Ottawa's financial onslaught at a time of unprecedentedly high interest rates were the very multinationals it was meant to hobble.

If the taxation effects were, indeed, meant to be part of the process of achieving Canadianization, then the policy might be likened to that of an incompetent zoo-keeper who decides to get rid of his menagerie's elephants because they are not leaving enough food for the other animals. He resolves, therefore, to kill off the offending pachyderms by throwing a huge plastic cover over the whole zoo and then pumping in gas. The results of such action would be obvious to all but the most short-sighted. Before the elephants topple, virtually every other animal will have been exterminated.

The NEP claimed that Canadianization of the oil industry was justified, necessary and feasible; and that it should be carried out by discriminating against foreign companies. Nowhere did it make any kind of case showing that the dominant position of foreign-owned companies had damaged Canada's interests. Its case seemed to be based on the fact that foreign oil companies had been treated too generously. It also made the vague assertion that: "A more fully Canadian industry is likely in the long run to build a more dynamic energy sector, more responsive to Canada's goals."

Canadianization is a motherhood issue. There can scarcely be anyone in Canada who does not support the idea of a greater level of domestic ownership in the oil industry. However, the implications of foreign ownership are widely misunderstood, and its negative impact overestimated. Meanwhile, the enormous benefits to the Canadian economy of the foreign investment that led to present levels of outside ownership tend to be almost completely ignored.

In the early days of the post-war Canadian oil boom, there had been a large influx of foreign capital which, in the absence of financial enthusiasm from Canada's eastern bankers, had been the industry's seed money. Without that financial injection, the industry would never have grown. However, the NEP implied that corporate investment in Canada should be considered a one-way street. Once a mature company began to return capital to its overseas investors, it should then be considered fair game for expropriation.

The program, not surprisingly, was to do enormous damage both to Canadian-U.S. relations and to the confidence of foreign investors in general.

However, one of the principal criticisms of the NEP's Canadianization program was not that it reflected ingratitude, but rather that it involved a heavy price; a price concealed from the Canadian people when the NEP was announced, but which subsequently became readily apparent. The Liberal government successfully sold to the Canadian people the idea that the NEP, far from implying any economic damage to Canada, would in fact be good for investment and employment. Such was plainly not the case.

The quite separate claim that Canadianization was necessary was based on the assertion that if a grab was not now made for greater control of the industry, the "windfalls" from further increases in domestic oil prices related to further increases in the world price would go to foreigners. The basic premise of the NEP was that world oil prices would continue to rise in real terms. Once that ceased to be the case — even in the short term — the rationale for quickly grabbing foreign-owned oil companies then disappeared.

The world oil-price slump in the wake of the NEP meant that not only did Canadian companies financially cripple themselves in order to take over foreign-controlled companies, but they took them over at inflated prices.

It is frequently claimed, particularly in Ottawa, that the NEP has taken much unjustified blame for the condition of the oil industry. However, while it is true that economic recession would have hit the oil business in 1981 and 1982 even without the NEP, the fact remains that the NEP aggravated the recession and harmed the very companies it was meant to be helping. Moreover, the longer-term impact of the NEP — based on a discretionary system run by Ottawa bureaucrats — has not yet been seen. As it was, in the summer of 1982, while much of the Canadian oil industry was fighting for its financial life, it was also struggling with a labyrinthine new set of government rules and regulations that threatened, like some massive encrustation of barnacles on a ship's hull, to slow progress to a crawl.

The failure of the NEP was a matter of incompetence; not simple incompetence but highly complex incompetence, a far more dangerous kind. It reflects a much bigger problem in Canada today; that the system appears to be

15

increasingly out of control. The administrative machine created by Pierre Trudeau as Reason's response to the complex demands of modern society is appearing more each day like some vast contraption constructed by a mad scientist, whirring and clanking most of the time for no ostensible purpose and then, suddenly, lurching off in some radical new direction. One of the problems of the first two years of the 1980 Liberal government was that when the machine did lurch, its purpose appeared to reflect not the wishes of those meant to control it — the politicians — but those meant to serve it, the bureaucrats.

This book does not totally "blame" the bureaucrats who appear in its pages for the NEP disaster. The ultimate responsibility lies with Pierre Trudeau's Liberal government. The mandarins who created and nurtured the NEP were not wicked, or unintelligent or without social conscience. Their fault lay in their exaggerated views of their own abilities and the competence of the state. The Liberals' failure lay in supporting these beliefs all the way through to their injurious conclusions.

In the end, the men who framed the National Energy Program seem like nothing so much as Sorcerer's Apprentices, allowed to exercise powers they did not fully understand, could not control and which, in the end, were bound to overwhelm both themselves and their political masters. Unfortunately, the results of their inept tinkerings have to be suffered by the entire Canadian people. We have had to pay for the very expensive, practical education of a group of Ph.Ds who believed that their ivory-tower musings could be transferred to the real world. And we have not finished paying yet.

As this book goes to press, the infinitely flexible Liberal government appears to have pulled back from the arrogant nationalist interventionism of its first two years of office, retreating once more into one of its perennial "pragmatic" poses. However, it would be a mistake to regard this apparent change of direction as either repentance or reform. For many Liberals, pragmatism merely means a temporary abandonment of "ideals" in order to ensure the longer-term goal of maintaining power. Unless the "ideals" behind support for the NEP are clearly understood and clearly rejected, they are likely to resurface. As it is, the NEP has perpetrated an enormous shift towards a centrally-controlled economy where bureaucratic discretion takes precedence over personal or corporate initiative. Whatever the short-term posture, that seems to remain the Liberal ideal, and unless we understand both the economic and political dangers of such a shift, then the trend is likely to continue.

# PART ONE

## Business vs
## the Power Machine

# 1
# The Sheiks Revisited:
# The Oasis Dries Up

*"Is there a greater tragedy imaginable than that, in our endeavour consciously to shape our future in accordance with high ideals, we should in fact unwittingly produce the very opposite of what we have been striving for."*

THE ROAD TO SERFDOM
FRIEDRICH HAYEK

In 1979, the role model for Calgarian oilmen had been King Croesus. Three years later it was Icarus. The golden touch had been replaced by disintegrating balance sheets and plummeting share prices. To a degree, many Calgarians' problems stemmed, like those of Icarus, from having dared too much. They had tried to fly too high on shaky wings. But that did not reduce their bitterness towards a federal government that had encouraged them to take to the air and now seemed to watch indifferently as they struggled to stay aloft.

The whole of Canada, indeed the whole of the Western world, was staring at recession and perhaps far worse, but for Calgary and Calgarians it was different. Of all Canadian cities, Calgary, buoyed by the petroleum boom of the late 1970s, had been raised the highest. Now it had the farthest to fall.

The feeling had grown that this was the boom that would never end. In any case, people were far too busy getting a piece of the action to bother about macroeconomic projection. The opportunities were boundless. If you were hardworking, or smart, or lucky, then you just had to make it. If you were all three, millionairedom was almost inevitable.

The town had become a magnet for entrepreneurs, and it had brought out the entrepreneur in many of those already there. In a remarkably short time, a corporate hagiography had been compiled. Not only were Canadian entrepreneurs building empires that promised — if one could believe in zooming, linear projections — to match the size of the multinationals, but a whole raft of others with less exalted corporate aims were engaged in an exercise that still tended to arouse universal admiration and envy — they were accumulating vast sums of money in a very short time. While men like Jack Gallagher, the uniquely charming chairman of Dome Petroleum, and Bob Blair, his more combative counterpart at Alberta Gas Trunk Line (later to become Nova), seemed to seize

19

the initiative from the foreign-owned, major oil companies, the shares of other, much smaller companies took off in flights of stock-market fancy that made their investors happy and their founders wealthy beyond the dreams of avarice.

Three years ago, I had come to Calgary to write *The Blue-Eyed Sheiks*, a book about oil and oilmen. I returned in the spring of 1982 to see how the class of '79 was doing. The change was remarkable.

At first sight, things didn't seem that different, as I drove down the new highway from the airport towards the glistening towers that rise out of the foothills. Reaching downtown, you noticed that, once again, downtown had come out a little further to meet you. Block by block, storey by storey, the naked dimensions of the place continued to grow. In the previous three years, since the *Sheiks* first appeared, magnificent new additions had been made, and continued to be made, jostling each other for a view of the mountains or the plains. Bob Blair's panorama from the grey heights of Bow Valley Square had been spoiled, if not obscured, by the black-mirrored towers of Esso Plaza next door, but soon Blair was to move into an even more enormous, razor-sharp axehead of a building a few blocks west. Petro-Canada's redbrick head office, nick-named Red Square by the local inhabitants, sat on the west side of Esso Plaza, its modest size reflected in Esso's gigantic new black tower. But Petro-Canada was also soon to vault beyond and above Esso with its own twin towers. And in the middle of the city, the new Bank of Montreal building, the highest of all, was taking shape.

But something was wrong. Anyone aware of the economic and political background would realize that this was not a good time for the oil business. But there was more than a potential downturn hanging over Calgary. There was a change in psychology. It was when you got down to ground-level, to dinner-table level, to office level, to bar level, that you could really become worried about Calgary's future.

Indeed, after a few days of doom and gloom from the inhabitants, the city's architectural body began to resemble nothing so much as a freshly-dead corpse whose hair and fingernails continued to grow though its heart had stopped beating.

## The Biggest Boom

Calgary's status as an oil town goes back to the turn of the century, but it has only been since Imperial's classic find at Leduc in 1947 that it has been considered an oil town of global standing.

Since then it had known booms and busts as the excitement of new finds had swept through the city, or as markets waxed and waned. But it had witnessed nothing like the period from 1975 to 1980, when rising oil prices, soaring natural-gas prices and unprecedentedly generous tax provisions had created a hothouse atmosphere of growth and prosperity.

The economics and psychology of an oil boomtown are unique. I remembered that three years ago there had been a conference on economic projection at the Four Seasons Hotel, and some bang-up, Ph.D. economist from the Conference Board in Ottawa had got up and started spouting about general economic indicators for the coming period. And he had said that — based on his numbers — housing starts, a vital economic indicator, would be pretty static in the coming year. Well, everybody in the audience had just laughed out loud. They hadn't really meant to be impolite, but gee, the guy was just plain *dumb*. All you had to do was take a walk around to see that construction of all sorts was bursting at the seams. This was a town that wasn't going along with any shiny-assed economist's meek, little linear projections. It was just plain booming. And of course, they had been right and the Ph.D. economist had been wrong. It proved what they had thought all along about Ottawa's number-crunchers. They just didn't know from hell what was going on. Most of all they didn't understand that Calgary wasn't a place of nice, safe macro-economic projections and aggregates. It was a town of individuals where the psychology of success ruled.

But that was three years ago, back in 1979, and since that time, those shiny-asses in Ottawa had established that they didn't really give a damn for the psychology of success, or for entrepreneurial drive. What they gave a damn for was things like structural imbalances in the oil industry, and regional imbalances in revenue distribution. What that meant, translated into plain English, was that they thought the foreign oil companies were getting far too big and Alberta was getting far too rich.

So what those shiny-asses had set about doing was to take their centralist ideas, and their social consciences, and their Ph.D.s in economics, and their ignorance of the real world — with its dirty fingernails and its need to meet payrolls — and they had set about putting the whole thing straight. And what *that* meant in plain English was just screwing the whole thing up.

How could things have gone so wrong when three years ago they looked so *right*?

Of course, three years ago, Joe Clark had been in power and everybody had felt pretty damned good about that. In fact, with Joe Clark in power the whole attitude towards the East seemed to be changing. Stan Milner of Chieftain Developments, whose head office happened to be in Edmonton, but who was, nevertheless, one of the bona fide, self-made oil multimillionaires, had sat smiling behind his solid gold Rolex and said: "Y'know I feel so good about Joe Clark being in Ottawa that I'm going to Berlitz to learn *French*." Yes, attitudes were changing. It wasn't just that everybody was getting rich. Most of all, the national focus seemed to be shifting. The eastern bankers who had previously kept Albertan oilmen cooling their heels in outer offices before they told them "no" were now paying court to Calgary's new stars.

Once the trek east to Bay Street had been a nerve-wracking experience. Now the smooth men from the Big Five banks and the major brokerage houses would climb into their corporate jets and fly out to Calgary on the weekend if Jack Gallagher or Bob Blair looked as if he might need another hundred million or so. Everybody from the shiftiest eastern financial carpetbagger to the chairman of the Bank of Montreal seemed to be moving out to Canada's petroleum mecca.

Better than that, while good old Joe Clark was moving into office, the world situation made things look even rosier. The Ayatollah had sent shivers through the global oil market and prices had started to soar again. And where world petroleum prices went, it seemed that Canadian prices were sure to follow. Even when Joe Clark had been unceremoniously dumped by the electorate in February of 1980 and the old enemy, Pierre Trudeau, had returned from the electoral dead, the mood of optimism had survived, at least for a while.

But when the Liberals had returned, there had been a new, and different, emphasis on energy policy. In opposition, the Grits had asserted that Canadianization was a key objective. But so what? So had the Conservatives. Anyway, the Liberals had been talking about it for years. In any case, what had Calgary's new stars to worry about? After all, they were Canadian. Canadianization could only help them.

But then, on October 28, 1980, had come the bombshell, the National Energy Program. The program was aimed at wresting revenue from the big oil companies and Alberta, but its higher taxes were most damaging to the very part of the industry it was meant to help — that owned by Canadians. Activity began to grind down as money, equipment and expertise headed south of the border. The value of Albertan petroleum land sales, a key indicator of industry health, slumped 65% in the first half of 1981. Geophysical activity fell off by 25%, while 40% of the drilling rigs disappeared over the same period.

Nevertheless, "Canadianization" of the industry had started. Dome Petroleum and other companies, fêted as the pride of the domestic industry, dived in and loaded themselves to the gunnels with debt in order to buy out U.S.-controlled oil businesses. Meanwhile, there was still confidence that the National Energy Program's punishing taxes would be changed. After all, the industry still had one big ally in its fight with Ottawa: Peter Lougheed, the iron-willed Albertan premier. They might not always get along with him, but at least they knew that a healthy petroleum industry was the bedrock of his first concern, a prosperous Alberta.

Through 1981 they had waited as the federal and provincial governments squared off against each other at meeting after meeting. The Alberta side didn't appear to be consulting with the industry, but there remained an implicit faith that Peter Lougheed wouldn't let them down. Then, after months of negotiations and a final, six-day bargaining marathon in Montreal, Peter and Pierre had appeared together on September 1, 1981, clinking champagne glasses. A deal had been made. A collective sigh of relief was breathed. But when the agreement was examined in detail, when the companies ran the numbers through their computers, the numbers just didn't make sense. This deal wasn't much better than the NEP. In fact, in places it was *worse*. Its assumptions were all wrong; its revenue projections were pure fiction; it was

22

just a disaster. Either Alberta had been conned, or it had sold them down the river.

Other things, too, were going badly. Interest rates continued to hit unprecedented levels, so that all those companies that, like good Canadians, had borrowed up to the hilt to buy out foreign oil companies suddenly found themselves bleeding to death through holes in their balance sheets.

Meanwhile, the whole, world-market picture was changing dramatically. All at once, what had been pictured as a temporary glut on global oil markets appeared to be longer-lasting. Official world oil prices were falling, spot prices — for uncommitted oil cargoes — were plummeting. These developments had a dramatic impact on the financial viability of what had been considered Canada's petroleum ace in the hole, its huge reserves of "non-conventional" heavy oil and tar sands, the largest deposits of their kind in the world. During the struggle with Ottawa, Peter Lougheed had declared such synthetic oil projects hostages to an agreement. When an agreement had been reached, the two sides had believed that they had the right formula for making the tar sands and heavy oil projects economically feasible. But they hadn't. The projects had been postponed or cancelled.

## Staring into the Abyss

Suddenly a spectre appeared over the land of plenty, and just as suddenly, the psychology of success began to evaporate. Just as three years before it had seemed that there was no ceiling on the upside, now it appeared that there was no floor on the downside.

Calgary found itself staring into the abyss.

The golden age of vision and expansion in the Canadian oil business had turned into the era of creative accounting. In particular, an accounting wrinkle called "capitalization of interest" was sweeping town like the latest fad diet sweeping through some well-padded suburb. Only this wasn't really a fad, it was a fight for corporate survival. Capitalizing your interest expenses meant that you didn't show them in your profit-and-loss account; it meant they didn't come out of the cash flow figures you declared in your financial statements. But the problem was that those interest payments *were* a real drain on your resources, whether you showed them as such or not. Capitalizing interest charges may have made some companies appear healthier, but the actuality was cosmetic to say the least. Indeed, in some cases it was like applying make-up to a plague victim.

So now, companies were showing positive cash flows in their financial statements, only positive cash flows didn't actually mean that you had any *cash* to play with. And that seemed to be almost everybody's situation. The entrepreneurs had become awfully quiet, just sitting there and relying on the good grace of the banks to lend them some more money so they could pay off the interest on their *existing* loans. The increasingly less-friendly bankers, meanwhile, had no reason to feel too sanguine about the situation. In their eagerness to open their coffers to the new lords of Canadian business, they had exposed themselves financially to an unprecedented, and in some cases alarming, degree.

The banks were now a lot less free with their money, and the companies were really strapped. The drilling wasn't being done, and the bills were taking longer to get paid. And people were going under.

Within the new, plush, split-level 400 Club — where the working heart of the Calgary oil business gets together over a few drinks — the men with the calloused hands and good, solid expense-account bellies were having some pretty miserable conversations.

"You going broke, George?"

"Me? Hell no. Who told you that?"

"That's what I heard."

"Well, that's just plain *bullshit*."

And it might be bullshit for George, but it certainly wasn't for a lot of other guys around the patch. All over the club, from its big, ground-floor bar to the men-only sanctum on the top floor, most of the talk seemed to centre around who was in trouble, and who wasn't going to make it. And then, after a few drinks, the temperature would rise and the conversation would turn to Ottawa and to Peter Lougheed, and the air would begin to turn a little blue.

And it was the same at the Petroleum Club and at the Ranchmen's Club, where the corporate and financial elite did their lunchtime entertaining. The Petroleum Club, with its concentric circles of vice-presidents in the upstairs dining room buzzing like hornets, had always been a place, to put it mildly, for mutual reinforcement of views. There had never really been too much dissent on the excessive level of government involvement in the business. But over the previous year-and-a-half, the level of government activity had been sufficient to keep conversations at the paroxysmal level.

Perhaps the greatest irony was that the federal government's policies appeared to have achieved the exact opposite of their declared intentions. Those suffering the most were the home-grown stars of the 1970s, men who, at the end of the decade, had appeared ready to seize the mantle of leadership from big foreign-controlled oil; men who had led the way, at the government's behest, in taking over foreign-controlled oil companies.

Three years before, I had sat in the modest little third-floor office of Bob Brawn, president of Turbo Resources, and listened to him talk of his success and the success of his Canadian entrepreneurial peers in the oil business. Turbo had been raised up as a shining example because it was an integrated oil company — that is, its business stretched all the way from petroleum exploration and production to gasoline retailing out of its own service stations. It appeared to have successfully invaded the territory of the major oil companies. Brawn, a man with a square jaw and a record of 16-hour work days, took undisguised pride in his achievements. "If you spend all your time going to

24

Toronto," he had said, "then it's hard to get things done. I like the fact that this is becoming a centre of power."

Brawn was a future empire builder with a cordial disdain for his multi-million-dollar paper worth. Turbo was an all-Canadian company that had recently received the accolade of having its share price integrated as part of the Toronto Stock Exchange's key 300-share index. That share price, proudly displayed in the company's gas stations and even in the office corridors leading to the washroom, was doing its little bit to boost the "TSE 300". Now three years later it was doing its bit to depress it.

Toronto, in the shape of the banks and the Ontario Securities Commission, seemed to be exacting its revenge.

In the wake of the NEP, Turbo had joined the hunt for companies to acquire. In the summer of 1981, it had eventually come upon Merland Oil and, as if tempting fate, had offered $13.13 a share for 51% of the shares. The deal was to be part of a corporate reorganization under which Turbo would fold itself into its own 72%-owned subsidiary, Bankenko Mines, eventually to form a company with more than $500 million-worth of assets.

However, the problems arose when it came to making the follow-up offer to the remaining holders of Merland shares. Turbo wanted to swap their shares for equity in Bankenko Mines, but there was shareholder resistance as claims were made that the paper offer was not as generous as the cash offer, as Ontario Securities Commission regulations required. The deal became bogged down in litigation. As share prices fell, the share swap offer began to look less and less attractive. Meanwhile, mounting interest rates on the cash borrowed for the Merland purchase and for other corporate expansion was beginning to put a severe squeeze on profits. At the end of March, Turbo had to announce that its bid for control of Merland had failed.

Meanwhile, some of Turbo's banks were becoming a little nervous. By the end of March, 1982, Turbo was seeking to reschedule its debt as one of its lenders, the French bank, Crédit Lyonnais, expressed doubts about the company's ability to meet its interest payments. The company announced a $22 million loss for 1981. Turbo was struggling.

Three years before, Bob Brawn had said: "The trick is to spot the cycles and buy at the low point." In the spring of 1982, the quote was somewhat more poignant. It was: "There will be no fire-sale."

In the course of looking around for companies to take over, Brawn had in March, 1981, made a bid for CanDel Oil Ltd., a subsidiary of St. Joe Minerals Corp., which was at that time the target of an unwelcome $2 billion bid from the Seagram empire. But when the sealed bids had been opened on March 27, Brawn learned that he had lost to another of Calgary's high fliers, Gus Van Wielingen, the head of Sulpetro. Van Wielingen firmly believed, like so many of his counterparts, that the way to stay sharp was to keep control of one's corporate interests. He had bid $545 million.

Born and raised in Holland, Van Wielingen, a man with a patrician air, revelled in business at the highest and yet most personal level, clocking up hundreds of thousands of miles every year in his Learjet. Counting Peter Lougheed as a friend, cultivating federal politicians, doing deals with the likes of the ubiquitous and ultra-well-connected Maurice Strong — the tycoon and international do-gooder — Van Wielingen seemed like the very model of the new, aggressive, politically-aware Canadian oilman of the 1980s.

However, the CanDel purchase had taken the long-term debt of Sulpetro close to $800 million. Its net loss for 1981 was $31 million. It too was seeking to "restructure" its debt.

And so, moving from corporate office to corporate office, the sad stories had continued.

The eight game-fish, caught mouth-open in their terminal leaps by the taxidermist, still graced the wall of J. C. Anderson's office. Only now it looked as if they, like everybody else in town, were complaining.

However, J. C. Anderson, the next on my list of Sheiks to be revisited, saw some "hellacious opportunities" when all the smoke cleared.

Anderson, a bulky native of Nebraska, had been a company man with Standard of Indiana when he had been transferred to Calgary in 1966. In 1968 he had gone it alone and within ten years had built a private corporate empire worth more than $300 million, of which his share was worth more than $50 million. Three years ago he had been thinking about rationalizing all his interests and going public. He still hadn't. At least Anderson had lost none of his sense of humour or his salty turn of phrase in the three years since I had interviewed him for *The Blue-Eyed Sheiks.* He had a neat way of summing up the competence of some of those who had been responsible for the existing energy regime. "They wouldn't know how," he said, "to pour piss out of a boot if the instructions were written on the heel."

Nevertheless, Anderson seemed a good deal more cheerful than most, although he had common problems with interest rates. "Hell," he said, "we're paying the banks $5,000 an hour in interest and some hours we just don't *earn* $5,000." Nevertheless, perhaps fortunately, he hadn't gotten involved in the big-stake takeover game that had crippled so many of his colleagues. "Of the defunct companies in town," he said, with a twinkle in his eye, "we're in the best shape."

And so it went. Sheik after Sheik watched with amazement as their financial oases had been, if not dried up, then at least reduced to murky puddles.

The effervescent "Wee" Bobby Lamond was trying to cope with the drying up of the drilling funds that had provided the growth for Czar, his main company, and all the little satellites that he had helped set up.

There had been a saying around the oilpatch intoned by all the older oilmen, oilmen who had seen both boom and bust. It said: "I'd rather be lucky than smart." But Lamond, and a lot of those like him, had dared to tempt fate. "Luck," the little Scotsman had said, "is a myth."

Lamond still had his Rolls, and his Mercedes and his Lincoln and his Corvette, and they all sat outside his enormous mansion on Mount Royal, but the businesses weren't doing too well. Losses for 1981 had been almost $5 million, not including almost $4 million of interest that had been capitalized. Czar's Denver office had been closed; its oil reserves in Texas had been written down. Luck might well be a myth, but over-optimism, soaring interest rates and government taxation weren't.

For all the Sheiks, there was bitter irony in this state of affairs, for the NEP, less than two years previously, had maintained that its principal purpose was to confirm and encourage the shift of the domestic oil business into Canadian hands. Such an obviously worthwhile cause had attracted enormous public support, for there was a widespread public belief that control of the Canadian oil business by the giant multinational oil corporations was a "bad thing".

# 2
# The Dictatorship
# of the Polletariat

*"I remember it was with extreme difficulty that I could bring my master to understand the meaning of the word* opinion, *or how a point could be disputable; because* Reason *taught us to affirm or deny only where we are certain; and beyond our knowledge we cannot do either. So that controversies, wranglings, disputes, and positiveness in false or dubious propositions are evils unknown among the Houyhnhnms."*

GULLIVER'S TRAVELS
JONATHAN SWIFT

The Houyhnhnms were indeed a very different race from us poor benighted Yahoos. If we were to speak only whereof we were certain, then virtually the whole world would be as silent as a Trappist monastery. Swift, if he were alive today, would scarcely be surprised to learn that although free speech had been widely established as an inalienable right, there was no corresponding obligation to hold a coherent philosophy or even to be well-informed. However, he might find rich potential for satire in a system where highly valued specialists were employed specifically to gauge the public's "positiveness in false and dubious propositions", and where such misperceptions and delusions were used as the very touchstones of what was politically acceptable. What barbs might he fashion for a world ruled by the dictatorship of the "polletariat", where public opinion specialists were employed by political parties lest their leaders should, by mistake, mouth some truth unacceptable to the pattern of public ignorance?

Opinion polls are powerful and useful analytical tools, and political organizations and corporate marketers ignore their use at their peril. But they have also, in the past decade, emerged as the somewhat depressing symbol of political expediency, particularly in the latter half of the 1970s, when Pierre Trudeau's principal secretary Jim Coutts brought polls — and, in particular, pollster Martin Goldfarb — to the heart of the Trudeau machine. They established the depressingly pragmatic approach that ideals, truths and moralities were only as valid as the statistical analysis of reactions to them from ten thousand telephones.

Uneasiness at the new political world was poignantly expressed by Dalton Camp, the Tory political pro, who, speaking of himself in his book *Points of Departure*, said: "A generation of poll-takers had usurped his role. No man could afford improvisation in the face of so much confirmed opinion and when politicians abandoned private judgement and experience for samplings compiled from the rudimentary examination of strangers. Public opinion — a noxious phrase — had become the karma of men who dream of power in the concubinage of computers.

"But what sort of system is it in which the leaders follow and the followers lead? What is the role of the political parties, other than as claques? Who will test the firmness and the fervour of unfavourable public opinion if politicians only flinch before it? ... Elections are henceforth to be preordained, issues determined and strategy decided, out of the tabulations of the Teeters and the Goldfarbs."

Ironically, in 1968 Pierre Trudeau had himself expressed similar sentiments about public opinion in *Federalism and the French Canadians*. Speaking of the mass media, he said that "to the extent that they claim to reflect public opinion" there was a danger that they "constitute a vehicle for error, if not indeed an instrument of oppression. For my part, I have never been able to read newspapers without uneasiness, especially newspapers of opinion. They follow their customers and therefore are always lagging behind reality."

Jim Coutts was, however, to show Trudeau that any politician who failed to "follow his customers" was headed out of office.

In any democratic system, the winning and retention of power inevitably requires, at minimum, attractive packaging and convincing salesmanship of one's proposals. As with all salesmen, exaggerated claims are sometimes made. The frequent assertion that all politicians are liars is more a reflection of the demands of the democratic political system than of the natural mendaciousness of those who enter it.

However, the supremacy of public opinion and the tendency to "dress-up" policies between them open the door to dangers, particularly in a highly complex society. When the public does not understand something, or has widespread misconceptions about it, then its views should obviously not be used either as a guide or a justification for action in that area. Moreover, making a political package attractive is one thing. Selling a set of highly radical policy initiatives as something they are not is quite different, especially when it is accomplished by playing upon public ignorance and misconception.

## The Decline of Business

Each individual's understanding of the society in which he lives involves an inevitable simplification. One simplifies along the lines of one's psychological predispositions, upbringing, education and the prevailing moods and conventional wisdoms of society. Individuals who produce simplified frameworks blatantly out of sync with the more generally accepted truths about themselves and the world are treated as disturbed, psychotic or paranoid. However, if enough people concur with some deviation from objective truth, then such a belief becomes conventional wisdom. A man who thinks he is Napoleon would be generally regarded as mad. A man who thought he could fly would be considered self-delusive to a potentially disastrous degree. But a man who regarded all oil companies to be involved in a conspiracy to rip off the general public would more likely be considered a pillar of mainstream thought.

One of the root causes of the NEP disaster was an increasing divorce of popular belief from underlying realities. In particular, the conventional wisdom has long held that governments are competent and corporations are too powerful. This has inevitably led to a long-term trend to support the acquisition of more and more power and regulatory control by central government, and to an increasing tendency to ignore the voice of business.

If the whole concept of the opinion polls is seen as somewhat depressing for those who believe in political commitment before expediency, then the thought patterns the polls reveal with regard to business and its role and power in society should be almost horrifying to the corporate sector. Throughout the 1970s, business lost both credibility and legitimacy in the public mind. Despite the increasing encroachment of government into society, private enterprise remained the overwhelming producer of goods and services and the principal supplier of jobs and generator of wealth. Yet it was somehow possible for the populace to separate the concept of corporation from the goods, wealth and jobs it provided; to find the concept of corporations unattractive but take its benefits for granted.

That, however, is not to say that the public had no grounds for suspicions about how far business "packaged" its own messages to the public.

Most Canadians have doubts about the honesty of business advice. Indeed, the outstanding example may lie in energy. In the early 1970s, when Canada had been exporting more than a million barrels of oil a day to the petroleum-hungry U.S., the U.S.-controlled oil companies in Canada had told the government that the country's oil reserves were virtually limitless. When the U.S. petroleum hunger sparked the OPEC crisis soon afterwards, the very same companies announced that Canada was in danger of running out of oil within a decade without further price increases. Again, when the Arctic Gas consortium — dominated by the foreign-controlled oil companies who had discovered large amounts of gas in the Mackenzie delta — sought to build a pipeline for that gas down the Mackenzie Valley, they asserted that the gas would be needed for Canadian markets within a fairly short time because Albertan gas reserves were running out. Within a couple of years, the province's natural gas reserves were bursting at the seams.

These examples were viewed less as a natural tendency to marshal arguments that serve one's own purposes than as a fundamental perniciousness in the corporate sector that was ultimately counter to the public good.

The public's natural suspicions about big oil companies were heavily fuelled by the two OPEC crises of the 1970s. When oil company profits soared in the wake of each crisis, in 1974 and 1980, it was assumed that they must somehow have engineered the crises for their own ends. But such suspicions did not emerge out of the blue. They fitted well with a long-term uneasiness the public held against big corporations, the roots of which went back to the very origins of modern capitalism.

For many small-"l" liberals the whole concept of business is intrinsically linked up with the images of children forced to work down mines and in mills in 19th-century Britain and the robber barons who presided over the enormous growth of the U.S. around the turn of the present century. It is not merely that these are distasteful historical details; they indicate that all of capitalism is built on what can be considered the least noble of motives.

One of capitalism's prevailing problems with its public relations has been that it is, at root, based on personal fulfillment — or greed, as its detractors prefer — as a top priority. Adam Smith, the eighteenth-century Scottish philosopher, father of economics, and still the most oft-quoted guru of the *laissez-faire* system, said it all: "It is not from the benevolence of the butcher, the brewer, or the baker that we expect our dinner, but from their regard to their self-interest. We address ourselves, not to their humanity, but to their self-love, and never talk to them of our necessities, but of their advantages."

Smith of course stressed that the collective self-love so demonstrated produced a wonderful system, because the market, through competition, restricted the ability of capitalists to pursue their acquisitiveness to a socially harmful degree.

But Smith also said something else that is less often quoted by modern entrepreneurs: "People in the same trade seldom meet together but the conversation ends in a conspiracy against the public, or in some diversion to raise prices."

In this basically unpleasant — but, no doubt, largely valid view — of many small businessmen, Smith laid the ground for critics of corporate capitalism. It seemed obvious that if anyone could suppress competition, by cornering the market, or joining with others to fix prices, or whatever other means, then he would pursue his acquisitiveness "to a socially harmful degree". Once the market ceased to be a thing filled with atomistic units, and larger entities began to appear, then *caveat emptor.*

Adam Smith's intellectual legacy was not pretty. At its best it was based on greed; at its worst it led to oligopoly or monopoly. As the leading American economist, Robert Heilbroner, has written: "The acquisitive behaviour on which it is perforce based has suffered all through history from the moral ambivalence in which it has been held; all efforts to raise money-making to the level of a positive virtue have failed. The self-interest of the butcher and the baker to whom Adam Smith appealed in lieu of their benevolence may serve as powerful sources of social energy, but not as powerful avatars of the social imagination."

31

Although we are separated from Adam Smith by some two hundred years, it is his view of the market that forms most people's views of modern corporations. Not the part about the brewer's self-love, but the part about the conspiracy. Since the man in the street has little or no conception of what a large corporation actually *is*, he assumes that it is merely the tradesman writ large. He believes, at least implicitly, that with the growth of giant organizations, "the pursuit of acquisitiveness to a socially harmful degree" is now possible. In his view — to take the most-quoted example — the multi-national oil companies, now that they have reached Gargantuan proportions, are in a position to do what the butcher and baker — and probably he himself — would do if they got the chance, rip the public off in order to make excess profits.

Thus the public has come to believe that the corporate sector possesses far more power than it actually does, and that, in the case of the oil industry, this power expresses itself in an ability to get "more than its fair share" of the revenue from oil and gas. In an April, 1981 study carried out for the Canadian Petroleum Association by leading Tory pollster Allan Gregg, the public was shown to hold generally negative feelings about the oil and gas business, to regard it as very powerful and — although competent — selfish and callous. Of those polled, 47% thought the oil and gas companies got more than their fair share of oil and gas revenues, vs. 28% who thought the federal government received too much, and 17% who thought provincial governments received too much.

Moreover, there was, in the same poll, enormous support for the National Energy Program. Asked whether the government's move to make 50% of the business Canadian-owned by 1990 would increase or decrease the chances of running out of oil and gas in the near future, 52% of respondents thought it would decrease the chances. On balance, 84% favoured the move, 61% favoured even stronger measures, and 70% believed it would both increase the number of jobs available to Canadians and would help economic growth. One cannot argue with gut support for the program. However, the misguided beliefs in its economic benefits can only be attributed to either a great and unfounded faith in the wisdom of governments, or to a total misunderstanding of the structure and motivations of business in general and the oil business in particular. In most cases, it was probably a combination of both.

Again, in the wake of the Federal-Alberta petroleum pricing agreement of September 1, 1981, a poll by Gregg's Decima Research demonstrated that 40% of respondents thought that the petroleum industry would benefit most from the agreement, vs. 22% who thought that Ottawa would benefit most and 28% who thought Alberta would be the winner. This was a truly astonishing result, since the petroleum industry considered to benefit most had *no part* in the negotiations. Moreover, the agreement was actually disastrous for the industry, a fact testified to by the subsequent revision of the agreement by both Ottawa and Alberta.

These polls clearly indicated the ability of the Liberals to sell the NEP as a growth-promoter and a job-creator when it was exactly the opposite.

## Government by Gallup and Goldfarb

In a speech in early 1982, consultant Charles Perrault summed up the feelings of many businessmen towards the NEP and the support for it in the opinion polls. "Most disturbing to me," he said, "is what I call Government by Gallup and Goldfarb, the Machiavellian fashioning of policies which, as stated in their simplistic objectives, play on the emotions of Canadians and have their very broad support, while contributing directly to economic stagnation and unemployment. It reminds me of the way an unscrupulous undertaker can prey on the emotions of a widow to get her to spend far more than she should on her husband's burial.

"Ours is a nation of economic illiterates. Only one-third of Canadians can even choose the right definition of profit in a three part question, remember. The average Canadian is ripe for plucking — and Ottawa knows it . . . Most Canadians like the NEP, and applaud Canadianization. I like Canadianization too. But I think I can see the cost, and the cost is too high, and by the time the average laid-off worker realizes this, it's very late and much harm has been done."

Accusations of economic illiteracy are harsh, but they are true. Most people have no more knowledge of the workings of the economy or of large corporations than they do of the functioning of their own pancreas. It would be a bizarre society that suggested that leading surgeons took random samples of opinion as to the best way to perform operations before making their first incision. Nevertheless, public opinion is considered a quite legitimate basis for sweeping economic operations on the Canadian corporate sector.

As Wilbert Hopper, chairman of state oil company Petro-Canada, said at a Calgary conference one year after the emergence of the NEP: "I would like to preface my remarks by asking you to keep one observation in mind. In a recent survey of the Canadian public, by none other than the Canadian Petroleum Association, a full eighty-four per cent of Canadians expressed their support of the government's Canadianization program. Whatever comes of this conference, whatever observations and suggestions for improvement are made by various speakers, the reality is that the National Energy Program is a very popular policy. . . . In my estimation current governments — like all previous governments — will heed the overwhelming support given by the general public rather than the complaints of a narrow interest group. The National Energy Program is here, the government has clearly enunciated its goals, public support is overwhelming, the sky has not fallen. Calls for radical revisions by the industry, like the tilting at windmills by Don Quixote, may be satisfying to your soul, but not terribly effective."

Hopper was articulating perfectly the Ottawa attitude to business, that it was just "a narrow interest group" rather than the engine of wealth and growth in society, and that its bleats really didn't need to be listened to. Later in the same speech, Hopper said: "You know and I know that generally speaking the Canadian public does not trust the oil industry. This has been proven many times by reliable public opinion polls. Like Peter who cried wolf, the industry is just not believed any more."

## Where Business Failed

It sometimes seemed that business had resigned itself to that fact. If major companies were declining in popularity, and if their very legitimacy was being questioned, then they appeared to be doing very little to counter the trend. Business had a profound belief in the rightness and validity of what it was doing and believed that it had no case to make to the public. It continued to mistakenly believe that the way to get what it desired from the political system was by keeping up contacts with key politicians and bureaucrats. For ten years, the executives who sat on committees of the Canadian Petroleum Association talked about publicity campaigns, but to most of them it seemed like a great waste of money. "God," they'd say, "we deal directly with governments. What's the *point* of trying to get the public on our side?"

Opinion polls were acknowledged as a slightly distasteful means of gauging public ignorance, but why would anyone find such information useful? — except of course, in marketing one's products.

The men from the big companies had no doubt about their role as the engineers of growth and the producers of wealth in society. Increasing government red tape was a fact of life to be bemoaned and complained about behind closed doors but it was not a case to take to the public.

This attitude on the part of business was a terrible mistake. Its roots and its potential consequences were spelled out in a brief but incisive book, *Where Business Fails*, by Professor Jim Gillies, former MP and senior policy advisor to Joe Clark. From the very heart of the government machine during the brief Clark government, Gillies was able to experience at first hand the enormous power and ideological influence of the Trudeaucrats who remained from the defeated Liberals, and was to gain firm convictions about the dangers of excessive government control. But the main burden of his book was the argument that business had failed in its relations with government in the past decade, and that the implications were potentially very serious. In particular, Gillies pointed to a potential vicious circle in the present situation. The more government regulates and intervenes in the activities of business, then the less efficient business becomes. This in turn might lead to more demands to regulate and intervene in business, leading to yet further declines in efficiency. And on and on. "The challenge," writes Gillies, "of the modern business firm is how to contend in a society that turns increasingly to the political system for the resolution of both social and political problems . . . Furthermore, it is quite incorrect for businessmen to believe that elected officials and bureaucrats assign a privileged position to business in society. They do not. Indeed, if

34

anything, they perceive the power and role of business as substantially less significant than it was a few decades ago."

Things were to grow much worse when the Liberals returned to power in 1980. During the first two years of the 1980 Trudeau regime, the Liberal government and the business community were to represent virtually two solitudes.

# 3
# Galbraith the Guru

*"The need to rationalize the likes and dislikes
which, for lack of anything else, must guide the
planner in many of his decisions, and the necessity of stating his reasons in a form in which they
will appeal to as many people as possible, will
force him to construct theories . . . which seem to
provide a rational justification for the prejudices
which he shares with many of his fellows."*
THE ROAD TO SERFDOM
FRIEDRICH HAYEK

Dislike, distrust and fear of big business and the excessive power it supposedly wielded was not just a gut feeling among the populace. It amounted to an
ideology among the left-wing intellectuals who came to the fore when the
Liberals returned to power in 1980. This philosophy, rooted in the prevailing
liberal economic ideas of the 1960s and 1970s, had been particularly influenced by men like John Kenneth Galbraith. However, the bottom line of such
thinking was the very opposite of liberalism in its original form. For what
economists like Galbraith maintained was that corporate power was so large
that the state was forced to take countervailing powers to itself. Galbraith's
thinking amounted to a charter for centralist interventionism.

In George Radwanski's book *Trudeau*, the Prime Minister is quoted as
saying: "I can't say that I was much of an original thinker in government; I hope
I was in academic life. But what I've tried to do in government is be sensitive to
the institutional, ideological, and social realities, and to make sure that we are
responding to them. And whether it be Galbraith or Heilbroner, or Plato or
Aristotle for that matter, there are certain things that I believe to be right and
true, and I want to make sure that they are not neglected in the process of
government."

In 1975, according to columnist and author Richard Gwyn, Ian Stewart,
then Trudeau's economic advisor, gave Galbraith's recent book *Economics and
the Public Purpose* to Trudeau to read. Shortly afterwards, in his year-end
telecast, Trudeau made his famous announcement: "We haven't been able to
make it work — the free market system." Moreover, Galbraith, as the highest-
profile proponent of permanent wage and price controls, undoubtedly had a
profound influence on Trudeau's decision to reverse completely the party's
campaign position and introduce such controls. Indeed, Trudeau said: "I'm not

as wise and experienced as Galbraith, but there's no doubt that his thinking has permeated my thought."

Searching therefore, for the philosophical foundations of the modern Pierre Trudeau in particular, and of the Ottawa mindset in general, we might do well to examine just what John Kenneth Galbraith has had to say that made Pierre Trudeau think him so "wise". In particular, since the book obviously had such a profound influence, we might concentrate on *Economics and the Public Purpose.*

John Kenneth Galbraith is one of the world's best-known economists. Canadians, starved of celebrity, take some pride in the fact that he was born and raised in the little town of Iona Station, Ontario, and attended the Ontario Agricultural College in Guelph. The fact that he left Canada never to return — except to tower above podiums for a high fee — is not dwelt upon. To those who have never probed too deeply into what he has to say, he appears an avuncular figure, dispensing kindly wisdom from the top of his cranium, which stands some six feet and eight inches above the ground. Galbraith is witty and epigrammatic, the dismal science's answer to Oscar Wilde. His books have sold in the millions and he has had a widely-syndicated television series. These two last mentioned facts might be considered sufficient grounds for suspicion. The fact is that nobody has done more to bring modern capitalism and large corporations into disrepute and ridicule. It is a dubious distinction.

Galbraith dismisses all notions that giant corporations want to rip off their customers. His basic thesis is that their evil lies not in any desire for "excessive" profits, but in something far worse, their ability to subvert the system totally to their own ends. These ends are, for society at large, trivial and worthless. In John Kenneth Galbraith's society, corporations are in the business of making intercontinental ballistic missiles, genital deodorants and plastic grass [his own examples]. The men who run them have mundane desires and are self-delusive in their beliefs. Consumers of their products are manipulatable morons who, under the influence of sufficient advertising, could be persuaded to eat plastic sandwiches or ride about on motorized unicycles.

Lest anyone might think the above to be a parody of what such a well-thought-of and widely-respected economist thinks, let us allow Professor Galbraith to speak for himself. In particular let us examine what he had to say in *Economics and the Public Purpose,* the book that so impressed the Canadian Prime Minister's senior economic advisor and the Prime Minister himself.

The basic tenets of *Economics and the Public Purpose* are similar to those put forward by Galbraith in his other books, such as *The New Industrial State.* He takes a number of observations about the nature of the modern capitalist state — or, rather more specifically, about the USA — and with the help of some portentous jargon uses them as a flight of fancy into a world of massive corporate manipulation. His basic facts are that the modern corporation is a large technocratic structure dependent on committees of specialists; that its goal is growth; that it sets the prices for its products in the market rather than having them determined in any classic "market" fashion; and that it attempts to influence its market through advertising.

Then comes the sociological jargon. A company's desire for growth becomes "the affirmative purpose of the technostructure". Its more modest objective, to protect its corporate ass and not go broke, becomes "the protective purpose of the technostructure". The flight is now ready to take off.

Of central importance to Galbraith's thesis is the somewhat improbable assertion that consumer choice has ceased to exist. In the neo-classical view of economics, the consumer proposes and the producer disposes. Under the Galbraithian system the reverse is true. Moreover, the consumer can be persuaded to buy any rubbish, and what rubbish it is!

Pointing, in *The New Industrial State*, to the technostructure's attempt to maintain that the myth of consumer sovereignty still exists, Galbraith says that the corporate deceivers declare that: "Any interference with the exercise of choice leads to . . . a low level of satisfaction. Accordingly, government objection to lethal automobile design, disabling drugs, disfiguring beauty aids or high-calorie reducing compounds is interference with the individual's choice."

This is not to say, of course, that such despicable products have not actually appeared on the market — although, in a world that has in this respect quite rightly taken heed of Galbraith, such is less likely these days. The point is that in Galbraith's world, businesses seem to manufacture *only* dangerous or frivolous products.

Again, in *Economics and the Public Purpose*, Galbraith takes advertising and growth and turns both into extremely sinister concepts. The very large firm "must plan not only its own operations; it must also, to the extent possible, plan the behaviour of the people and the state as they affect it." Thus, the natural tendency to seek to influence forces that affect one's wellbeing — be "one" an individual or a corporation — becomes a devious plot to subvert all of society.

Again: "Such power — over prices, costs, consumers, suppliers, the community and the state — is best served by size, so growth becomes a top priority". Once again, a subtle perversion. Growth is not viewed as an indication of the successful manufacture of goods the public wants. It is primarily a sinister attempt to seek to control one's environment.

Galbraith's assertion that the needs of the technostructure dominate all are are often taken to absurd lengths. People do not, according to Galbraith, pursue higher incomes to have command over more goods and services. Higher incomes are *promoted* by the technostructure merely so that consumers have the wherewithal to buy its output. This inversion is rather similar to Panglossian logic of the kind that declares that we have noses so that we may have somewhere to put our spectacles! The principal difference between Galbraith and Voltaire's Dr. Pangloss, however, is that whereas, for the latter, this was "the best of all possible worlds", for Galbraith, modern society is a dismal thing indeed.

# The Corporate Clown

As for corporate executives, they are pathetic creatures, pursuing growth not merely for the enslavement of society but for their own petty aggrandizement. Says Galbraith: "And as sales, number of employees or the value of assets managed increase, so do salary, expense accounts and the individual's claim to non-salary income or privilege. The scale of his office and the excellence of his furnishings are enhanced; his access to private lavatory and company plane are assured. So is his reward for employee obeisance and peer group homage." Thus does Galbraith reduce corporate management to a laughingstock, whose likelihood of advancement, moreover, becomes greater the more ludicrous he becomes. "The marketing man who successfully persuades the public to buy some abnormally improbable artifact will, in consequence, be in charge of the resulting larger marketing operation."

Corporate management's inconvenient tendency to display social virtues that fail to fit Galbraith's view of social subversion are cleverly dealt with by making them seem farcical. Galbraith claims that after the pursuit of the principal targets of secure earnings, growth, technological virtuosity and higher dividends, the manager's other goals include: "Building a better community, improved education; better understanding of the free enterprise system; an effective attack on heart ailments, emphysema, alcoholism, hard chancre and other crippling diseases; participation in the political party of choice; and renewed emphasis on regular religious observance."

Meanwhile, it is not just the hapless consumer that the technostructure holds in thrall to its "improbable artifacts". The government, too, is its servant. As evidence of this, Galbraith points out that it is the large companies whose products are supported, not the small ones. "The government . . . contributes notably to inequality in development. Where the industry is powerful, government responds strongly to its needs. And also to its products. It gives the automobile industry roads for its cars, the weapons industry support for its weapons, other industries support for research and development." It indicates a true perversity of thinking to come to the view that roads are the gift of government to the automobile industry rather than to the public. Since, however, Galbraith has saddled himself with defending the concept of the all-powerful corporation, such are the logical somersaults he is forced to perform.

Galbraith is perhaps at his most unconsciously amusing when he attempts to establish that the technostructure dictates public taste, in particular in the world of art. "Good" art, according to Galbraith, is given a low priority in society merely because the technostructure cannot embrace the true artist. "Since the good artist cannot or will not be subordinate to the organization, the large, relatively immobile enterprise commands not the best talent but the most accommodating." Here, of course, Galbraith, like God on the Last Day, is standing in judgment on all art on the basis of whether its perpetrator works for a giant corporation or not. If he does, then he *cannot* be a good artist. As for the dolt of a consumer, he automatically assumes that all technological innovation — be it rug deodorant or the single-wiener rotissomat — is a "good thing" because he has been so conditioned. His lack of appreciation of new artistic trends is simply due to his lack of the "right" conditioning. "Accordingly," pontificates Galbraith, "the first impression of artistic innovation is almost invariably unfavourable. What is new is commonly thought offensive or grotesque. So it was with the Impressionists, the Cubists, the Abstract Expressionists, and so it is with the modern exponents of Pop Art . . . The technostructure embraces and uses the engineer and the scientist; it cannot embrace the artist . . . Engineering and science serve its purpose; art, at best, is something which it needs but finds troublesome and puzzling. From these attitudes come those of the community and government. Engineering and science are socially necessary; art is a luxury."

This series of statements is astonishing not merely for its overweening intellectual arrogance but also for its stupidity. The consumer, according to Galbraith, is merely an automaton whose objection to having wallpaper designed by Jackson Pollock, or whose lack of "appreciation" of a pile of bricks lying on the floor of some national art gallery, is merely due to his conditioning. It never seems to occur to Galbraith that those who swoon over such works of art are themselves subject to the much more perverse conditioning of terminal trendiness.

## Crusade without a Destination

But although it is easy to make fun of this point, it is here that we must consider what is most sinister in Galbraith's theory or at least what has the most sinister implications. If our beliefs and our attitudes are shaped by the corporate technostructure — the so-called planning system — and they are worthless, then who is to give us our new values? What is the true "Public Purpose" and who will decide it? What is to be the shape of this new Millennium? What are to be its aims?

The answer is an anticlimax. Galbraith sets out to destroy the modern capitalist system but has nothing but liberal tinkering and a latter-day civil rights thrust to put in its place. "The reasonable goal of an economic system is one that allows all individuals to pursue socially benign personal goals regardless of sex." Nevertheless, such vague goals are to be pushed forcefully. "The need for remedial action to align the use of power with the public interest can no longer be escaped. And such remedial action ceases to be exceptional but becomes, instead, an intrinsic need." The Crusade must set sail at once. Its destination, however, is somewhat uncertain.

What are to be the specifics of this plan to take us somewhere else from where we are? First, says Galbraith ringingly, must come "emancipation of belief". This means, presumably, accepting the Galbraithian view of things. "Until this has happened, there is no chance of mobilizing the public on behalf of its own purposes in opposition to those of the technostructure and the planning system."

But then comes the dangerous activist nub of Galbraith's thought. The planning system must be bridled. "This means restricting resource use in the areas of overdevelopment . . . Redirecting the resources of the state to serve the public." Galbraith presumably means something more here than mere product safety regulation, or the application of product standards. We can probably take for granted that the banning of plastic grass and genital deodorants is high on his list. However, his thinking leads into somewhat dangerous territory, that of central economic dictatorship.

The first moves of such a system are not to be positive ones; they are to amount to an economic pogrom against those ludicrous individuals, the corporate executives, those devious manipulators of the system and purveyors of "improbable artifacts". "There is no evidence and no reason to suppose that the supply of executive talent requires the stimulation of present prices (*i.e.,* wages). Accordingly, the present analysis supports the most vigorous use of the progressive income tax as an instrument for promoting equality. And it refutes the case for special treatment of what, with much license as applied to higher salary levels, is called earned income. And it similarly denies the need for special pecuniary incentives to executive performance."

Galbraith wants more than higher taxes, however; he wants permanent wage and price controls. And wage controls are not merely to be used as an instrument of controlling inflation, indeed they are not *primarily* to be used as a method of controlling inflation. Wages are to be dictated by central authority. " . . . once wages and salaries are subject to public action," says Galbraith, "nothing excludes the next step which is to narrow by public action the differential between those who do the unpleasant work and those who like their work . . . Men of talent, even at lower levels of compensation, would prefer the executive offices to the shop floor."

Within the overall economy, strong government support is to be given to the so-called "market system", that part of the economy outside the planning system — those small businessmen unable to bend markets to their will. Perhaps Galbraith's most astonishing recommendation for the market system is that "self-exploitation" should be ended. In other words, Galbraith wants to curb the desire to work hard, " . . . limiting hours and conditions of work for self-employed entrepreneurs, notably in service industries, retailing and manufacturing". What has always been considered among the most admirable of basic human motivations is treated not only as a form of delusive "self-exploitation", it is also to be outlawed.

Perhaps the most surprising thing about John Kenneth Galbraith is that he has been taken so seriously. The roots of Galbraith's thought lie less in objective analysis than in a basic, and very moral, distaste for modern society and all its trappings. Galbraith is not at heart a visionary, he is an old curmudgeon. As a social satirist, Galbraith is brilliant, and — if classified as

41

such — would rank with Swift. Unfortunately, his skill in laying bare the more obvious excesses of modern capitalism has been confused with the ability to recommend a sweeping, and in some objective sense, preferable alternative. Instead of being treated merely as a witty iconoclast, he has been hailed by many as an economic guru.

At heart, Galbraith loves mankind no more than Swift. The view of the public as manipulatable morons in thrall to giant corporations is little removed from Swift's Yahoos. And yet he feels compelled to save humanity from itself. If the present edition of mankind is unsatisfactory, it is merely because man, like putty, has been moulded into a form which does not reflect his essence, but the worthless desires of an evil technostructure. He believes, unlike Swift, that beneath the Yahoo lies the Noble Savage. Such is the conceit of all socialist reformers.

## The Fatal Flaw

The reason Galbraith's approach cannot work — and is, in fact, highly dangerous — is clearly stated in Galbraith's own analysis, and yet, he is apparently blind to it. Quite apart from the vague nature of Galbraith's brave new world, the key question is: who is to set its standards and administer it?

Galbraith's whole analysis is based on the fact that organizations tend to serve their own interests before those of anyone else. " . . . the problem of power derives not from *private* organization but from organization [my italics]. All organization excludes interference from outside or above; its goals are those which serve the interests of its members."

We are left then with two problems: Where are we to get the all-seeing agents of goodwill who will administer Galbraith's program, and how — since they must inevitably work in a large organization — can they possibly maintain their purity of purpose? Galbraith's thinking inevitably leads us down a cul-de-sac where we can only swap one — as even Galbraith admits — "comfortable" servitude for another which is much less certain and potentially far less pleasant.

Such thinking, at best, leads us into a world of overblown government bureaucracies. At worst it leads into totalitarianism. And yet Galbraith still receives enormous support and is, in particular, the darling of the undergraduate set. To witness his reception — vs. that given to William F. Buckley — in a debate at Harvard in early 1982, was to comprehend the way the winds still blow in academe, whatever might be happening outside in the ugly world of Reagonomics. However, the fact is that the ugly world of Reagonomics is, to a major degree, the *result* of the bureaucratic consequences of liberal, Galbraithian thinking.

Galbraithian thinking is embraced by the young, the academic and the naive because its motivations seem right. Surely, if you are bright enough and of good heart, they say to themselves, then it must be possible to erect a system that is better than one based on mere *greed*. Such a driving force is treated not as an ineluctable truism of human nature, but merely as an unacceptable motivation.

It would be nonsensical to claim that Galbraith is the guiding force of Ottawa's thinking. In many respects, Galbraith's system is peculiarly American, although he claims that this is only because the most powerful techno-structures exist in the U.S. Canada has no equivalent to the Pentagon and the Canadian parliamentary system does not lend itself to the type of powerful political lobbying carried out by corporations in Washington. However, it is less the specifics of his system than his overarching condemnation of capitalism, and his belief in the ability of some "public planning authority" to define and effect a superior "public purpose", that are embraced by many of Ottawa's power elite.

When you suggest to such people that they are acting beyond their powers, they look affronted. What, then, are they to do? Accept the imperfections of society? Do nothing? That was not the spirit that heralded in the golden age of Trudeau and the Trudeaucrats. To them, a problem perceived was a problem to be solved, and the force of reason could solve all problems. This was to be the age of hope.

The spirit of liberal reform was summed up by Heilbroner. In his history of economic thought, *The Worldly Philosophers*, he wrote: "The questions which face us in the future are not the purely economic ones of whether corporations will naturally grow larger or whether we will suffer from inflation or unemployment, but the moral ones of whether we will let corporations grow unchecked and whether we will allow inflation or unemployment to develop unchecked. Government planning, environmental protection, efforts to establish the responsibility of large enterprise — these are the tools of the anti-economic, moral impulse. To the extent that this is true, to the extent that we no longer let the game of economics proceed unhindered to its natural outcome, we are going beyond the economic revolution. After two centuries of sailing almost as the winds directed us, the tiller of society is again in our grasp."

But Heilbroner's words contained the same implicit question as Galbraith's. "The tiller of society" might be considered to be in "our" grasp, but just who were the steersmen to be? Where, in this brave new world, would power lie? Just who were "we"?

# 4
# Do Something!
# The Growth
# of Ottawa's Power

*"A minister is like a surfer riding the wave of bureaucratic advice. If he stays on top of the wave, he can look very good. Sometimes, as under the most recent Liberal government, the wave can bring him crashing, but one thing is certain — if he attempts a course different to the one dictated by the wave, he will certainly wipe out."*

The nation's capital is a distant and dimly-understood city for most Canadians. Certain facts are thought to be known. It is the place where Pierre Trudeau rules and politics happens. It is also the place where a horde of underemployed and overpaid public servants sit in bloated, Kafkaesque government departments gazing absently over the Ottawa and Rideau rivers. This latter "fact", the growth and increasing inefficiency of the public service, is firmly established in the conventional wisdom. The Canadian public has frequently been enraged by Pierre Trudeau, but they are never quite sure how mad they should get. He is a complex and charismatic man and thus often given the benefit of the doubt. It is easy, however, to get mad at the bureaucracy. Almost everybody has either personal experience of, or has known someone who has been subject to, some piece of flagrant ineptitude or unfair treatment. It is always possible to relate such tales to sympathetic listeners who invariably add some favourite bureaucratic vignette of their own. There is a general presumption that this is the long-term state of affairs with which we live; almost a cosy truism.

That an idle lump of man-years exists is not to be doubted, but what the public should perhaps be more aware of, and concerned about, is not the unproductive many, but the hyperactive few. They have never had to face an election, but they are the men who, in many respects, run the country.

When the Trudeau inheritance is assessed, his years of power will surely be seen as years of frustration and failure. In terms of his principal objective, national unity, Trudeau can survey only a history of increasingly poisoned federal-provincial relations — with Alberta, with Quebec, with Newfoundland. The "Rule of Reason" was eventually to bog down in economic recession and a series of clashes over revenue sharing and resource jurisdiction. The Constitution was brought home to become the principal source of growth in demand for the services of the legal profession — a doubtful political monument. The 1980 government's great new thrust of the National Energy Program became a disaster.

However, the principal legacy of Trudeau to the Canadian political system was the introduction of a new style of government and a new structure of bureaucracy. The stars of this new firmament have been called many names: super-bureaucrats, subjective bureaucrats, policy entrepreneurs, or power brokers. But whatever they are called, they were truly Trudeau's children, the chosen few, the analysts, agents and expeditors of Reason. They were to reach a position of unprecedented power during Pierre Trudeau's fifth term of office.

Ottawa has had a long history of powerful bureaucrats wedded to the Liberal governments who dominated the post-war period. But Trudeau's new men were very different from the classical bureaucrat, a disinterested specialist operating within a strict hierarchy and steering clear of political involvement; a man who received his policy mandate from above and then faithfully worked out the program for its implementation. The new elite were *involved*. They were innovative, they took risks, they bent the rules.

When Pierre Trudeau came to power he was well aware of the dangers of bureaucracy. In *The Practice and Theory of Federalism*, he stressed " . . . there are physical limits to the control which may be exercised over the central bureaucracy by the people's representatives and by the judiciary. The executive power may tend to increase its control by increasing the number of ministers; but the Cabinet will quickly reach that size beyond which deliberation becomes useless and decision impossible . . . The legislative power can increase its control over the bureaucracy by increasing the length of the parliamentary session, but there again British experience shows that the entire year proves too short . . . In time, it is hoped that administrative law will be expanded and perfected, that Parliament will learn to use the committee system with greater effectiveness, and that other devices will be developed to *protect democracy against bureaucracy*." [my italics]

But when Trudeau thought of bureaucracy and its faults, his principal concern was its tendency to seek its own purposes, to oppose government policies it found inconvenient. The solution lay not with control by politicians at all. It lay with the creation of his own super-bureaucracy, an elite group who would not only help him control the bureaucrats but provide the analysis and advice for his new rule.

But reform was also needed for other reasons. The system was being made subject to new demands with which it was increasingly less able to cope.

## Growth by Public Demand

Historically, the growth of government has been due both to external and internal factors. Apart from government's fundamental tasks of defence, the enforcement of law and order and provision of requisite public amenities, it has long been accepted that the state should intervene to regulate and control aspects of trade and the environmental excesses of unbridled industrial development, as well as to legislate on a wide range of areas of public interest, from safety on the job to speed limits on the highway.

In addition, in the decades following the Great Depression of the 1930s, and largely due to the influential writings of British economist John Maynard Keynes, it became universally accepted in the Western democracies that the government held responsibility for overall economic management — for stimulating growth, maintaining employment and controlling inflation. This trend was firmly entrenched by the greatly increased level of government intervention necessitated by the Second World War. It was also enforced by the great post-war economic boom which led to the belief that the government had not only the responsibility but also the ability to deliver growth, full employment and stable money. Thus, whenever a glitch appeared in the increasingly affluent lives of Canadians — and, indeed, of the inhabitants of other industrial democracies — it became the norm to demand that the government "do something". The public seemed to see nothing contradictory in simultaneous complaints that the government was "too big" and that it was "not doing enough".

More recently, as growth has slowed, unemployment increased and inflation mounted, there have been doubts cast over the ability of governments to deliver. The general belief continues to exist, however, that they *should* deliver. Their failure is more often seen as a reflection on their competence than as an endemic problem in the system. That the growth of government might itself be a critical part of the problem is seldom considered. The cry merely goes out: "do something".

Eventually, in an attempt to respond to so many demands, the government machine begins to develop an internal logic of its own. Every wave of legislation requires further legislation to cope with the problems that it has itself created, and this further legislation leads to yet further legislation. Moreover, once government becomes big enough, then a critical — and enormously demanding — part of its function becomes management of itself. Are its policies, programs and expenditures effective and efficient?

In Canada, there has been little ideological opposition to government intervention. Canadians are considered pragmatists and government involvement in the economy has been almost an imperative of Canada's existence. Insofar as Canada is a geopolitical anomaly, effectively a great east-west strip of population attempting to assert itself collectively against the north-south pull of economic logic, government involvement has been essential. Apart from tariff and other general regulations, it has also led governments into great projects such as the CPR and the TransCanada PipeLine, the giant natural-gas artery from Alberta to its eastern markets.

The most enormous growth in the public sector has taken place since the Second World War. Direct economic activity undertaken by government has increased from less than 4% of all goods and services in the immediate postwar period to about 16% at the beginning of the 1980s. Between 1950 and 1980, the proportion of total gross national expenditure attributable to government increased from 27% to 48%. In money terms, government spending increased more than fivefold between 1970 and 1982, to around $70 billion.

The sheer volume and complexity of the government's business has meant that the whole parliamentary system has become more and more out of line with the demands of policy analysis and implementation. The tourists and groups of schoolchildren who, heads a-swivel, tour the ornate Gothic corridors of the Centre Block and strain to get a glimpse of question period, nudge each other at the sighting of anyone who looks at home in the building and ask: "Is he important?". What they probably mean is: "Is he a politician?" The answer, however, is that if he is a politician then he almost certainly isn't important. There are legions of bureaucrats far more significant in the decision-making process than average MPs, who, as Pierre Trudeau once so candidly observed of the opposition variety, are "nobodies".

As Jim Gillies put it: "The problem of Parliament is that there is a deep confusion between form and substance. Committees meet and therefore it is presumed that they are effective; question period is colourful and therefore it is assumed that it is a useful way to extract information from the government; speeches are made because so many days are allocated for a bill and it is believed that they are relevant."

Bureaucratic power is much greater than that of Parliament but has no such grandiose trappings. There are not — and are unlikely ever to be — guided tours around the Department of Energy, Mines and Resources, or the current Privy Council Office. There is little to see. But it is in these places that the real power lies. And real power wants no business with the nescient masses.

It is not just the average MP who is becoming increasingly irrelevant to the exercise of power. Under the Trudeau regime, with its heavy emphasis on exhaustive technical analysis, the already proliferating piles of paper reached mountainous proportions. Cabinet ministers who spend their entire lives on the run — attending cabinet committee meetings, dealing with increasingly disgruntled MPs at parliamentary caucus, answering questions in the House, looking after their constituencies, making public appearances — have less and less time for "homework", the crucial examination of issues and policy alternatives. More and more they have had to rely on their bureaucrats to distill issues for them down to comprehensible proportions, to whittle down the mound of briefings to a few "tight" pages. Politicians inevitably choose alternatives rather than pursue an issue from analysis to decision. Bureaucrats provide both the information and the policy alternatives. It would be a strange public servant who did not make his own preferred alternative appear the most attractive. Those who analyse a situation and reduce it to manageable proportions are effectively making the decision. That is not automatically to imply that the resulting decisions are bad; just to acknowledge that in modern government, the memorandum is the message.

## Keeping Power out of Sight

Indeed, it is virtually impossible for a minister to go in any direction but that chosen for him by his bureaucrats. Even to attempt to do so would be seen as perverse. A minister is like a surfer riding the wave of bureaucratic advice. If he stays on top of the wave, he can look very good. Sometimes, as under the most recent Liberal government, the wave can bring him crashing, but one thing is certain — if he attempts a course different to the one dictated by the wave, he will certainly wipe out.

Senior mandarins tend to privately rejoice in — but publicly deny — the extent of their power. It is in their interest to perpetuate the myth of their merely advisory function because acknowledgement of greater power would invite public scrutiny and more strident — and possibly even effective — calls for accountability.

But if anybody is going to blow the whistle on the bureaucrats, it isn't likely to be the politicians.

Senior politicians are of course reluctant to admit just how much they rely on non-elected officials. Nor will they admit that the system is in any way slipping from their grasp. To appear to be master of the situation is obviously the required pose for a cabinet minister. Even to suggest to a member of cabinet that his department is a quite separate entity from himself is to raise hackles.

The accepted view of the relationship between the Liberals and the senior bureaucrats is that the two have become virtually inseparable. As Jeff Simpson wrote in *Discipline of Power*: "There was nothing sinister nor partisan in this affinity of perceptions; politicians simply felt comfortable with advice tailored to their own way of thinking and so favoured those who could provide them with such advice. The affinity was reciprocal; not only did the civil service see the country through a Liberal prism, the Liberals accepted the assumptions of the civil service."

This view seemed to be powerfully supported when Joe Clark came to power in 1979 and — among his many other problems — appeared to have such difficulty bringing the bureaucracy to heel, particularly at the Department of Energy, Mines and Resources. The bureaucracy was portrayed as old dogs unable to perform the policy contortions demanded by their new masters.

However, perhaps the Clark period more accurately showed that the bureaucracy felt themselves quite independent guardians of a set of values generated within their own ranks. The main thrust of the National Energy Program, for example, was developed within the department of Energy, Mines and Resources under a Tory government quite unsympathetic to it. Equally important, the Liberal government itself had in the previous decade proved unreceptive to the kind of interventionism espoused in the NEP. The bureaucrats under the Tories were not pining for their previous Liberal masters as much as for more reasonable ones.

# 5
# All the Sun King's Men

*"For at this point of cabinet development (be-
tween 20 and 22 members) the whole committee
suffers an abrupt chemical and organic change.
The nature of this change is easy to trace and
comprehend. In the first place, the five members
who matter will have taken to meeting before-
hand. With decisions already reached, little remains for the nominal executive to do. And, as a
consequence of this, all resistance to the committee's expansion comes to an end. More members
will not waste more time; for the whole meeting
is, in any case, a waste of time."*
PARKINSON'S LAW
C. NORTHCOTE PARKINSON

By the summer of 1982, Pierre Trudeau had assembled the largest cabinet in Canadian history, with 35 members. This might well be considered a size, as Trudeau himself said, at which "deliberation becomes useless and decision impossible", but the key reform that Trudeau had implemented was to take deliberation and decision-making effectively out of the main cabinet and into a system of interlocking committees, a change in fact instigated under Trudeau's predecessor, Lester Pearson. These formed a number of more or less important inner cabinets, by far the most important of which was the Priorities and Planning Committee, which was of course chaired by Trudeau.

The ostensible purpose of this reform was to create a more efficient process of cabinet review and decision-making. Its effect, once an administrative system had been set up to serve the committees, and bureaucrats had been brought into committee meetings, was to transfer much effective power out of the hands of the cabinet members altogether. The power remained in the cabinet meetings, but it subtly shifted from the elected politicians to the expert advisors.

Trudeau could indeed claim to have strengthened the cabinet system, but in the process he probably weakened the cabinet. This is frequently viewed as a perverse side effect of Trudeau's original purpose. It may well, however, have been a central part of Trudeau's intention. Trudeau arrived to herald the Rule of Reason, and cabinet ministers were not always Reason's most obvious agents.

The part of the bureaucratic structure that was to grow most in power under Trudeau's system was inevitably that part which served him and his new cabinet system, the so-called Central Agencies: the Prime Minister's Office, the Privy Council Office and Federal-Provincial Relations Office, the Treasury Board Secretariat and the Department of Finance. The most powerful men in Ottawa under Trudeau either worked, or had worked, in these elite agencies which served the policy and personal needs of the Prime Minister, the administrative needs of the various cabinet committees, and the management needs of the whole civil service.

The two most powerful of these central agencies in the Trudeau regime were the Privy Council Office and the Prime Minister's Office. The role and power of the PMO changed according to the nature of the man who led it. However, the power of the PCO slowly but surely increased after Trudeau's close friend and long associate, Michael Pitfield, became Clerk of the Privy Council in 1975.

## The Jealous Guardians

The men and women in the Prime Minister's Office, a tight-knit group who operate from the Langevin Block across Wellington Street from Parliament, are the jealous guardians of Pierre Trudeau. They determine who has access to the Prime Minister and are the custodians of his public image. They concern themselves with every aspect of Pierre Trudeau's life, from the organization of his travel schedule, through to the selection of the right tie for his television appearances. They are the Prime Minister's switchboard, sifting through the huge mound of letters and telegrams which arrive each day to decide which are important, and which select few will reach the attention of the Prime Minister himself.

The head of the PMO is Pierre Trudeau's principal secretary, potentially a very powerful man. Two in particular of the five men who have served in that position have been recognized as such. The first, Marc Lalonde, the forceful lawyer who held the post between 1968 and 1972, used it as a springboard to become the strongest minister in Trudeau's cabinet. Significantly, it was he who presided over the creation of the National Energy Program. The other, Jim Coutts, who held the post from 1975 to 1979, became Trudeau's political right hand. Recognized as the High Priest of Pragmatic Politics, Coutts, a cherubic, Harvard-trained Machiavelli, embedded the somewhat uncomfortable notion of the supremacy of the public opinion poll at the heart of the Trudeau Machine, and became known as the great manipulator.

Again significantly, Coutts was close to the heart of the push for the National Energy Program. Coutts, who left the job in 1979 in a bid to enter the political mainstream to acquire the appearance as well as the substance of power, was succeeded by Tom Axworthy, who is both less ruthless and less powerful than his predecessor. However, Axworthy, a disciple of Walter Gordon, the patron saint of economic nationalism, was also a key force in the push for the NEP.

If the power of the PMO at any time depends very much on the character of its principal secretary, the power of the Privy Council Office is firmly embedded in its position at the heart of the cabinet system. It is PCO officials who make the cabinet's agenda and thus decide what will reach it for discussion. They oversee the documentation of proposals and have the responsibility for recording decisions. They sit in at virtually all sessions of cabinet and its committees.

The PCO's head since 1975, the tall, professorial Michael Pitfield, is considered to be the most powerful public servant in Ottawa, the acknowledged master of Trudeau's mandarin machine. He hires and fires not only the 200 members of the PCO who staff cabinet meetings, advise the Prime Minister on policy and oversee the rest of the civil service, but he also has the principal influence on the salaries, promotions and shufflings of the government's top 100 or so officials — the deputy ministers and their equivalents who head departments and other agencies. Pitfield is not a man in the public eye. He wields his powerful influence within cabinet meetings, at his daily briefings with the Prime Minister, and as head of numerous standing and ad hoc committees.

The last of the seven children of Ward C. Pitfield and Grace MacDougall, Pitfield had a well-heeled Montreal upbringing similar to Trudeau's and his relationship with Trudeau and Trudeau's power elite goes back a long way. He came to Ottawa with a law degree from McGill in 1959 to be an aide to Conservative Justice Minister Davie Fulton, joining another young lawyer named Marc Lalonde. He consulted with Trudeau when the latter was a law professor at the University of Montreal. When, in 1964, a team of Quebec francophones led by Trudeau* wrote their landmark tract on their anti-nationalist, rationalist-functionalist view of government, it was Pitfield who translated it into English. Once again, one of the document's signatories was Marc Lalonde. When Trudeau came to power in 1968, Pitfield — who had been among those who had persuaded him to run — was, at 29, already an assistant secretary to the cabinet. In 1971, Trudeau made him deputy secretary to the cabinet and in 1975, secretary, Clerk of the Privy Council.

Significantly, when Joe Clark came to power in 1979, the only public servant he fired immediately was Michael Pitfield. Equally significant, when Pierre Trudeau agreed in December of 1979 not to retire and to return and fight the 1980 election, one of his first calls was to Pitfield, who had gone into exile at Harvard, to make sure that he would come back.

When Lalonde had been at the PMO between 1968 and 1972, he had ranked as the new regime's top political administrator, bringing his stern hand to bear on inter-departmental squabbles and keeping a tight rein on the bureaucracy. However, when Coutts became principal secretary, the PMO

---

* The group centred around the magazine *Cité Libre*, a moderately left-wing publication opposed to the ardent Quebec nationalism of Maurice Duplessis.

became much more political, more election-oriented. The role of master of the bureaucratic system passed to Pitfield.

Under Pitfield, the power of the PCO, which was already considerable, was further beefed up. Ian Stewart, who so profoundly influenced the Prime Minister's economic thinking, achieved that position of power after being brought to the PCO as chief economic advisor. When Jean Chrétien was finance minister, Pitfield tried to install Stewart as deputy minister of Finance, perceived as the most powerful deputy ministership in government, but Chrétien had opposed it. It was Pitfield who in 1979 placed Stewart in the deputy ministership of the Department of Energy, Mines and Resources — a move which turned out to be of great importance, since most of the analytical foundation of the NEP evolved during that period — ironically under the Tory government. Pitfield at last had his way and Stewart was installed as Finance deputy minister when the Liberals returned in 1980. It was Michael Pitfield who nursed the controversial NEP through its many cabinet drafts and redrafts. Such legislation could never have been passed without his whole-hearted support.

If the new bureaucrats were Trudeau's children, then Michael Pitfield was their godfather. Frequently the best and the brightest were brought straight into the PCO to become thoroughly acquainted with Pitfield's system before being moved out to promote its ascendancy elsewhere in the bureaucracy. Pitfield's Committee of Senior Officials each year chose a short list of high fliers for special training and attention. If you wanted to go anywhere in the system, Michael Pitfield had to know your name. If you were going anywhere, he did.

## Taking Charge

This bureaucratic elite had a new style and a new approach. The most important characteristic of the new men was their academic and professional backgrounds which tended to be in economics and law. Ph.D.s abounded. If they had actually worked, they were likely to have been lawyers or academics. In line with the shifting demands of politics, the elite tended to move from policy area to policy area rather than sticking in any one department. They did not look upon government as a career or a vocation but as a job in which they could advance very quickly and exercise far more clout than in any private sector job. The brightest graduate to enter Imperial Oil soon becomes aware that it will take him thirty years of very hard work to get to the top. In government, within five years a bright individual could be making policies that had far more importance to Imperial's future than anything the company's chief executive was likely to do. We shall shortly meet one such individual, Dr. Edmund Clark, who actually did.

There was enormous competitive spirit among these people. The game was to get to the key policy areas and come up with the bright ideas. They often treated ministers as equals, although they undoubtedly regarded many as intellectual inferiors. They were not subordinates, they were colleagues and they believed they were needed, not to serve politicians so much as to help them come to the right decisions. Moreover, since they were involved in long-term strategy, they often looked with disdain on the sort of short-term ad hocery that the need to be re-elected forced on their political masters. Indeed, they frequently had to step in to try and stop the government from performing irrational "political" acts. Not, of course, that they were unaware of the political implications of policy options. Indeed, since they were deeply involved in the promotion of various policies, they developed a keen interest in making such policies appear politically attractive. For Michael Pitfield and his stars, the line between bureaucracy and politics was very vague.

They developed a feeling of elite intimacy, regarding those outside the policy process as powerless and unimportant. They loved the idea of an intellectual scrap, of using Machiavellian means to gain the high ground. Like Joel Bell, another of the supermandarins with whom we shall soon get acquainted, they quoted Aristotle: "Strategy is the art of winning." They liked to win. And they knew they were winners.

They revelled in power, the ability to make people jump to attention, the knowledge that when they called — "this is so-and-so from the PCO" — politicians and other bureaucrats came to the phone quickly, or returned calls A.S.A.P. But what they didn't like was getting calls from those outside the network, the charmed first circle of policy. Then they got spooked. They were secretive by nature, partly because they felt very much part of cabinet's closed decision-making process, partly because they felt journalists and other probing outsiders almost certainly wouldn't be able to comprehend the complexity and value of what they were doing, and partly because they had a vested interest in hiding their own power from outsiders. This, they felt, was almost certain to be misinterpreted.

And slowly but surely, Pitfield's men were elevated within the system to the key deputy ministerships of the important ministries. The most important means of controlling the bureaucracy is to have men whose ideas reflect your own in the key positions of power. And once you had reached a senior position in a large or powerful department, such as Finance or Energy, Mines and Resources, then you were sure to have one of the most prized possessions of the senior mandarins — a voice in cabinet. Of course, it wasn't your own voice, it was the analytical voice of your department and thus, of your minister. When the deputy ministers and other bureaucrats were allowed into the cabinet room, the heart of power, the potential for a vast increase in their influence was handed to them. It was their intrusion into this inner sanctum that established their power most completely.

Compared with a minister who not only had nowhere near their level of academic or professional training, but who also had to spend most of his time dealing with the unfortunate trivia of modern politics — sitting in the House and dealing with the caucus and the constituency — the bureaucrats shone. More than that, since some ministers were on as many as eight of the twelve

53

cabinet committees, they simply couldn't find time to keep abreast of all the issues involved. As a result, they sent their officials along to pinch-hit for them. The substitutes were frequently a lot more skillful than the originals. Asked for their views, they would of course stress that they were not putting forward *their* views but those of their ministers. They pointed out that if they were raising objections, then these were the objections that their minister would have raised. Their own feelings on these issues were, they claimed, irrelevant.

Cabinet ministers inevitably had to have a somewhat ambiguous attitude to what they perceived going on around them. On the one hand they realized they needed the bureaucracy simply to stay on top of things; on the other they were aware of them as a growing independent force among them. What they may not have realized was the extent to which they were falling under their thrall.

Former cabinet member Robert Andras was quoted in Richard Gwyn's *The Northern Magus* as saying: "There was no evil intent on anybody's part, and indeed it was a benign kind of growth. The problem is that in that impossible job, in which you spend your days submerged in paper, it becomes progressively easier and easier to reach out to the familiar, to your aides and civil servants, who speak the same kind of decision-making language as you, and whom you know that when you say, 'give me a paper on such and such' will produce the kind of paper that meets your decision-making needs. As a result you reach out less and less to the unfamiliar, to the real outside world, to people."

But it was more than that. It was sometimes difficult to see where Trudeau ended and his machine began. "Whenever you were dealing with the PCO or PMO," another former cabinet minister told me, "you had to ask yourself: is this question really coming from Trudeau or is it coming from Pitfield?" Just how much was being delegated and who was in charge?

## Losing Control

The suggestion that the government is out of control is far from novel. Indeed, the Lambert Royal Commission on Financial Management and Accountability reported in 1979: "After two years of careful study and consideration, we have reached the deeply held conviction that the serious malaise pervading the management of government stems fundamentally from a grave weakening, and in some cases an almost total breakdown, in the chain of accountability, first within the government, and second in the accountability of government to Parliament and ultimately to the Canadian people."

Financial accountability is one thing, political accountability is another. Mandarins will nod gravely at what Lambert said and emphasize the need for more financial control, but when it comes to accountability for their role in the political process their attitude is quite different. How can you be accountable to people who can't possibly understand or appreciate what you are doing? It's not, they might claim, that they are off on any power trip; their assumption of power has nothing to do with being power-hungry; they have had power forced upon them.

Modern policy-making is highly complex, and they believe, indeed, they know, that they are the best-equipped to carry it out. They have large brains, elaborate educations and, most important of all, access to the facts. Interference by those with anything less than all these qualifications is considered not just a waste of time but also potentially dangerous.

John Kenneth Galbraith has reached the analytical heart of the matter: "What is called bureaucratic arrogance reflects, in fact, the need to exclude the even more arrogant individual who does not know what he does not know . . . Group decision-making is authoritarian because, by sound instinct, it must protect itself from poorly informed outsiders, including those who are nominally in positions of power."

Again, with his usual satiric emphasis, he points out that: "In public bureaucracies there is, perhaps, a special skill. Presidents, Secretaries of Defence, Prime Ministers and Ministers are elaborately briefed on matters which they do not comprehend. This is but rarely to allow them to decide. Rather it is to give them the impression, and allow them to give others the impression, that the decision is theirs. So believing, they are somewhat less likely to feel the need to assert their authority which, being uninformed, would be dangerous or damaging."

Within this set-up, the most powerful ministers became those who were technocrats themselves, men like Lalonde, who knew how to "work the system". It has frequently been said that the bureaucracy became politicized under the Trudeau regime. That is true, and is almost certainly inevitable under any long-serving regime. Perhaps more accurately, however, politics became bureaucratized. Strong, independent ministers, particularly those with a leaning towards free-enterprise, men like Robert Andras, John Turner, Donald Macdonald, disappeared. Ministers weren't required to come up with original thoughts. That's why the bureaucracy was there. Roles were reversed. The ministers were there to push through the policies evolved by their mandarins. Indeed, the bureaucracy became politicized not so much in that it absorbed the political priorities and objectives of the Liberal Party, but in that it set them.

There was no mandarin plot to seize power. It's just that power, like nature, abhors a vacuum. The fewer the ideas the Liberals had about policies, the more they relied on their bureaucrats to provide them, and when they returned to power in 1980, the Liberals had very few ideas indeed. The bureaucracy in the Department of Energy, Mines and Resources, however, had a lot.

# 6
# The Energy Mandarins

*"Jack Austin was the bureaucratic wave of the future, and the vessel needed to ride that wave, he firmly believed, was a state oil company."*

Ottawa's bureaucracy is organized into shifting empires of mandarin power. During the Trudeau era, as has been explained, power in general shifted towards the central bureaucracy created around the cabinet, in particular to the Privy Council Office dominated by Michael Pitfield. The importance of line departments, like Industry, Trade and Commerce, or Energy, Mines and Resources, depended on the importance of their particular area of policy at any one time, or on the prevailing view of bureaucratic organization promoted by Michael Pitfield. An example of the latter type of re-organization was the massive interdepartmental shuffle promoted by Pitfield in January of 1982, when regional development responsibility was moved to the Ministry of State for Economic Development and the trade functions of Industry, Trade and Commerce were shifted to External Affairs. Such changes, although they cause sleepless nights in Ottawa, are of little import to those outside the capital.

The growth of EMR, however, was much more a matter of external developments combining with forceful intellects and egos to create an enormously powerful internal momentum.

Trudeau's super-bureaucrats tended to move around in response to the policy needs of the time. Status was very much attached to being in the policy hot spots, and these men had an unerring nose for knowing where the action was likely to be next. They also had an unshakable faith in their own purity of purpose and their capability for intellectual firefighting.

For a super-bureaucrat, to be in a department where no major policies were being made was to be a soldier in peacetime. These men not only enjoyed the intensity of the policy-making process, they had a voracious appetite for it. It gave them the opportunity to influence outcomes, to mould society for the public good, and, in the case of economic programs, to play God with the allocation of what could sometimes amount to hundreds of billions of dollars. It was a fix of power unparalleled in the field of business, about which these men tended to know little, or in the academic world, about which they tended to know a lot.

To be in the middle of a key policy-making group, to sit in intellectual rivalry and co-operation with men one regards as one's intellectual peers, to rub shoulders with ministers as equals, to appear in cabinet and put one's ideas forcefully — these were the super-bureaucrats' fondest wishes and highest achievements.

There had been a period of magic once before in EMR. It had occurred in 1973 and had been all the more pleasurable because nobody had seen it coming. The situation had been perfect: a fast-developing external crisis that created the need for new and complex domestic policies, and a brilliant team of young bureaucrats gathered around an equally brilliant catalyst. The catalyst was Jack Austin.

## The First Energy Czar

Jack Austin was obviously a little apprehensive that spring day in 1970 as he waited by the main door of the Centre Block on Parliament Hill. Although only in his late thirties, he had already enjoyed considerable success as a resource and labour lawyer, and had also been involved as an investor and manager in the hectic world of Vancouver mining. His academic qualifications were impeccable: a Harvard fellowship and a doctorate in international commodity arrangements from Berkeley. But the reason he was standing that day waiting for Pierre Trudeau to emerge from the House was that earlier in his career he had been bitten by the political bug. Art Laing, who was to be a cabinet minister in the Pearson government, had heard Austin speak at the University of British Columbia and had been so impressed he had asked him to run his campaign in Vancouver South. Laing had won and taken Austin to Ottawa with him as his assistant. In 1965, Austin had run unsuccessfully for the seat of Vancouver Kingsway, and had then returned to law and the mining business. But he had never forgotten the heady world of Ottawa. And Ottawa had not forgotten him.

In Ottawa, he had impressed a number of senior civil servants, including the dean of the bureaucracy, Gordon Robertson, then clerk of the Privy Council. In 1970, persuaded by his advisors that he needed more outside experience in the public service, Pierre Trudeau decided to recruit some private sector representatives to senior positions. Austin's business experience was hardly of the corporate variety, but his other qualifications were perfect. Moreover, he was "politically acceptable", an essential qualification for appointment to the position of deputy minister, the most senior bureaucrat in any department. Deputy ministerships were Order in Council appointments and ultimate approval rested with the Prime Minister himself, and that was why Austin had been told to be at the Centre Block that day. Eventually, Trudeau appeared, and the two men shook hands and climbed into Trudeau's limousine, which was heading to the airport for a waiting Jetstar. Austin had not originally intended going along, but in the end he climbed into the government jet and flew with Trudeau to Toronto. The job for which Austin was being considered was that

57

of deputy minister in the Department of Energy, Mines and Resources, a fledgling ministry formed just four years before by grafting responsibility for energy onto the mainly mining-and-water-oriented Ministry of Natural Resources.

EMR, however, was very far from being a policy-oriented department. It was packed with scientists and technical Ph.D.s, with earth physicists and mineral geologists who spent their days carrying out surveys and making maps and working in the laboratory.

Insofar as the government had an energy policy arm, it was the National Energy Board, the regulatory and advisory body set up by the Diefenbaker government ten years before. However, the NEB wasn't an independent policy-making body. It came to its findings on the basis of the submissions from the oil industry and the figures of the Alberta Energy Resources Conservation Board, which was itself closely identified with the industry. Like most regulatory agencies, it had, over the years, become closely associated with the companies it was meant to regulate, but in 1970 that seemed to present no great problem. Despite Walter Gordon and the economic nationalists, the prevailing view still held that what was good for Imperial Oil was good for Canada.

Given this state of affairs, Austin was obviously concerned about the amount of influence he might hope to have at EMR. What job did Trudeau want done?

Trudeau replied that the government wanted to understand the role of energy in Canadian society. Who operated it and how, and was the public interest being served? "Were there," asked Austin, "any specific objectives?" "None," replied Trudeau. The government wanted to know whether Canada had enough resources in the short, medium and long-term, and at what prices they could be brought into production. The conversation proceeded along general lines, until Trudeau asked Austin what particularly interested him in the energy field. "A state presence in the oil industry," said Austin. Trudeau, although he appeared to show no great enthusiasm, nevertheless said he had an open mind on the issue.

Thus, in an interview in the clouds, was the seed of Petro-Canada planted. The seed was to take six years to sprout into a hostile world, but as Austin left Trudeau in Toronto he was satisfied that he would be able to "build and take the big picture" within EMR. But it must be remembered that when Austin moved to the department — which was, because of its boffin atmosphere, affectionately known as the Carling Street Institute of Technology — energy was not considered a pressing problem. Somewhat astonishingly, in the light of what was to happen just three years later, finding a market for the large Alberta surplus was considered the main problem with oil. Delegations from Calgary were, in 1970, visiting Pierre Trudeau and begging him to build a pipeline to take Alberta oil into Montreal for the sake of national security. He was advised to tell them, however, that they should seek a market for their oil in the U.S.

Austin's main priority, meanwhile, was a state oil company, a self-imposed mandate that had as yet virtually no support within the Cabinet, and indeed, was a concept stoutly opposed by certain sections of it.

Inevitably, Austin's arrival in Ottawa was to ruffle many feathers. The National Energy Board saw his appointment as an implicit criticism, while any outsider pushed into a deputy ministership aroused resentment in the rest of the bureaucracy. Within EMR, Austin was at first treated with a combination of suspicion and awe. His commitment to delve into the world of policy was seen by some in the department as a challenge, but many regarded it as a threat to their scientific purity. What, they asked themselves, was this part-academic, part-lawyer, part-businessman, part-Liberal backroom man doing in the role of senior bureaucrat, and moreover heading a department whose primary task was to be a knowledge base for pure and applied science?

But Jack Austin was the bureaucratic wave of the future, and the vessel needed to ride that wave, he firmly believed, was a state oil company.

## Making a Run for Home

Just months after he assumed office in Ottawa, Austin perceived a golden opportunity to gain a state oil company the "easy way". Home Oil, which had been the Dome Petroleum of the 1960s, was to be sold because of financial trouble. Jack Austin pointed out to his minister, Joe Greene, that unless the government intervened, it might easily fall to an American oil company. He asked permission from Greene to seek out Home's head, Bobby Brown, and find out what he was contemplating.

Bobby Brown was an oil promoter in the classic tradition. He had been bitten by the oil bug in the Turner Valley in 1936, when he had helped his father and another legendary Calgary entrepreneur, Max Bell, drill in what turned out to be the biggest field in the British Empire.

In 1950, Brown had gained control of Home Oil through a complex corporate pyramid of holdings. Under Brown's leadership Home enjoyed a switchback ride. His successes were many, including the discovery of the large Swan Hills field in Alberta, but so were his unsuccessful gambles, and towards the end of the 1960s, he made his greatest, and last, big gamble, in the North Slope of Alaska after the huge find at Prudhoe Bay. When the Prudhoe bubble burst in 1970, Home's shares plummeted from $81 to less than $10. Brown, the man who flew everywhere in a $3 million Grumman Gulfstream II that featured bathtaps in the shape of gold-plated dolphins, and whose health was now ruined by alcoholism, saw his empire crumbling and knew he had to sell.

It was then that Jack Austin came to call.

Austin told Brown that the Liberal government did not want Home to fall under foreign control and that it might even be prepared to buy it out. Brown subsequently held extensive negotiations with a number of Canadian companies, although his preferred purchaser was Ashland Oil of Kentucky.

Just before Christmas, 1970, a key meeting was held in Ottawa between

Brown and a powerful government group that included not only Austin but also Deputy Finance Minister Simon Reisman and Deputy Secretary to the Cabinet Marshall Crowe, who was later to become head of the National Energy Board. Brown told them that none of the Canadian companies with whom he had negotiated had been able to come up with an acceptable offer. He also pointed out that because of preferential tax treatment in the U.S., a U.S. company could afford to pay more for Home, and that he obviously wanted the best price. He left the meeting with the impression that the government had no more interest in acquiring Home. But if he also left with the idea that the Liberals might let it fall under U.S., or indeed any foreign control, he was very mistaken.

Brown signed a deal with Ashland on January 18, 1971. The following morning, when he presented the deal to Joe Greene in Ottawa, Brown received a rude shock. The Energy Minister told him that Ottawa had no intention of allowing such a deal to go through. The government might not actually *have* legislation at that moment to stop the deal, but such legislation was pending, and Greene told both Brown, and Ashland's president, Orin Atkins, that the Liberals planned to use it.

By now, the issue was beginning to surface in the press. Tommy Douglas, the NDP's fiery leader, was trying to get a special debate in the House on Home's sale. Why, he asked acting Prime Minister Mitchell Sharp, had the government not moved decisively to block the sale? The answer, of course, was that the government still had no legislation under which it could do so. But Douglas eventually got his debate and on February 18, 1971, the morning of the day the sale was to be finalized, the federal cabinet decided that, legislation or no, they would block Home's sale to Ashland. An announcement to that effect, made in the House at 11:30 P.M. by Joe Greene, took the wind out of the NDP's sails.

Jack Austin saw things once more going in his favour and he continued to push forcefully behind the scenes for a government takeover. In early March, it seemed that he had won the day. The cabinet gave approval for a purchase, to be made through Eldorado Nuclear. On March 5, Austin phoned Brown in New York and told him to present himself with his advisors in Ottawa the following day. The government intended to purchase Home. The disgruntled Brown arrived in Ottawa for a weekend of discussions. The following Monday, March 8, he flew to Toronto to meet Greene and try to put the case once again for an Ashland takeover. He was unsuccessful. Bobby Brown was now a very sick man. He had had several heart attacks and was in generally very poor health. His financial position was almost as poor as his health, but something deep down made the idea of a sale to government stick in his throat. After eleven days with the lawyers, a deal was worked out. Brown flew to Ottawa for the momentous signing. However, as Joe Greene waited to make an announcement to the House of Commons, Brown, sitting before the document that would mean a momentous change to the oil business in Canada, had a change of heart. He suddenly thrust it to one side and declared: "I've come too damn far in life to sign everything away in half an hour. Tell them I won't sign today. I want the weekend to consider it."

The whole of Canadian business breathed a sigh of relief when Brown returned a couple of days later from Toronto and dropped a bombshell, declaring in a written statement: "After careful and thoughtful consideration I have decided I would prefer to deal with the private sector . . . I now intend to try to put a consortium of Canadian and American companies together to see if I can accomplish my desires and still keep Home's control in Canada."

After another month of negotiations, Home's new Canadian "saviour" emerged as another Toronto-based gas utility, Consumers' Gas. On April 22, 1971, Joe Greene was able to rise in the House and tell the Canadian public that the Liberal government had made sure that Home did not fall into foreign hands. For Jack Austin, however, Home's takeover by Consumers' was marked by a tinge of regret. He had almost had it. A state oil company.

For the Liberal government, a buy-out of Home would have been a very significant move. There had been small-scale direct intervention in the oil business before — providing help with the construction of the TransCanada PipeLine and taking a stake in the Panarctic Oils consortium that was drilling in the eastern Arctic — but the buy-out of an oil company was still a move considered with some trepidation, not to mention ideological opposition, in the Liberal cabinet. Jack Austin was way ahead of the politicians he was serving. The outbreak of the first OPEC crisis, combined with pressure from the NDP, who held the balance of parliamentary power, was, within a couple of years, to send them scuttling after him.

## Forming the Nucleus of Policy Power

Austin now set about putting together the analytical team that would both make the case for a national energy presence and provide a comprehensive review of the whole energy picture. External events were making such a review essential. In particular, the world market for oil was tightening rapidly. U.S. domestic oil production had peaked, but demand had not, and so it was sucking in an increasing amount from outside sources, including Canada, which, in 1972, was exporting an astonishing 1 million barrels a day south of the border.

Amid mounting suspicions of a sell-out, pressure increased both on new Energy Minister Donald Macdonald and his deputy Austin to come up with some answers, and some policies. It was under these circumstances that Austin was to assemble under him at EMR a small, tight-knit team that was to prove a dominant influence on Canadian energy policy for the next decade.

Austin had asked a friend at the Harvard Business School to recommend a Canadian who might carry out a comprehensive study of national oil companies for him. His friend came up with Bill Hopper's name. Hopper's credentials seemed ideal. A geologist by training, he had worked for Imperial Oil and as a consultant before doing a stint between 1961 and 1965 as senior energy economist with the National Energy Board. Then he had gone to work for leading consultants Arthur D. Little in Cambridge, Mass. When Austin first heard of him, he was working there on a study of the Algerian state oil company, Sonatrach. Hopper undertook to carry out a study for Austin and in 1972 he joined EMR as senior advisor on energy policy.

As senior economic advisor, Austin recruited Ian Stewart, a brilliant academic economist at that time working as a project analyst with the Treasury Board. With an original degree from Queen's, Stewart had gone on to Oxford as a Rhodes scholar and then Cornell before returning to teach firstly at Queen's and later at the American Ivy League college, Dartmouth. Stewart had come to Ottawa in 1966 to work for the Bank of Canada as an econometrician, a practitioner of perhaps the most arcane branch of the dismal science. From there he had been recruited to the Treasury Board by Doug Hartle, the head of its planning branch. Stewart came to Austin's attention because he was working on a study of Atomic Energy of Canada Ltd. (The study's conclusions were quite erroneous, but what threw them off was the side-effects of the OPEC crisis with which Stewart was now to develop an intimate acquaintance.)

The third key member of Austin's team was Joel Bell, perhaps the archetypical, Ottawa policy entrepreneur. Austin had been impressed by Bell when he had met him in connection with the Gray Report, the review of foreign ownership that led to the Foreign Investment Review Agency. Austin was a member of the inter-departmental committee of deputy ministers that reviewed the legislation and Bell was the report's chief researcher and principal author. Although only in his late twenties, he had already become firmly plugged into the policy circuit, and was a perfect example of the sort of "altruistic technocrat" attracted to "Athens on the Rideau" by Pierre Trudeau.

The son of an affluent Montrealer, Bell had read law at McGill and then gone into practice for a while before moving on to Harvard for a post-graduate degree in law and economics. While still working at Harvard, he began commuting north to Ottawa to consult first with a task force on reform of labour legislation and then to do work for the Economic Council of Canada and others. He then worked with Ron Basford, Minister of Consumer and Corporate Affairs, on new competition laws before moving to the Gray Report.

Bell had had nothing to do with energy before, but Austin admired his intellect and his flexibility. He was an economist but equally important, he was a lawyer, and no bureaucratic team could afford to be without at least one lawyer.

There were a number of other senior bureaucrats involved in the pre-OPEC deliberations of the department, men like Tom Tuschak, who worked on the department's background econometric model of the economy, Gordon McNabb and Ralph Toombs, but the heart of the analysis lay with the minister, Macdonald, and with Austin, Hopper, Stewart and Bell, men with a whole phalanx of legal qualifications and economics degrees, professional problem solvers who relished nothing so much as a big problem.

During 1973, the quartet of Austin, Hopper, Stewart and Bell would get together at EMR when everyone else had gone home and let their intellectual hair down, shooting out, and shooting down ideas, revelling in the exercise of reason upon an increasingly important problem. From the post-NEP ruins of Canadian energy policy in 1982, Joel Bell looked back upon this period with undisguised nostalgia. "It was a very freewheeling kind of set of discussions," he says. "There was no room for bureaucratic deadweight. We had to respond quickly and we did. The government was well-served."

In June, 1973, EMR produced its preliminary analysis, *An Energy Policy for Canada — Phase One.* The report caused more controversy behind the scenes than it did in public. The NEB, in a huff that anybody should be giving policy advice apart from itself, had refused to cooperate with the report. The Department of Finance, meanwhile, was miffed at the econometric forecasts of the report — an area it considered to be its exclusive domain — and also with the "gloomy" projections on energy prices. Indeed, one of the document's most controversial elements was a forecast that Canada might face "substantial price increases for energy", perhaps "double or triple present levels by the year 1990". They were actually to rise fourfold by Christmas of that year.

The most controversial aspect of *An Energy Policy,* however, was its recommendation of a Canadian state oil company, Austin's chief policy goal. Ironically, the study that Hopper had produced on international oil companies had not been as gung-ho in favour of a Canadian energy company as Austin had hoped, and Austin had beefed up that section for early drafts of *An Energy Policy.* However, the Cabinet — in particular its "right wingers", Bud Drury, Mitchell Sharp and Robert Andras — had opposed the notion completely, as had Simon Reisman, the deputy finance minister and one of the most forceful and powerful bureaucrats in the capital at the time.

In the latter half of 1973, however, the national oil company was to take a back seat to the fast-breaking drama of the OPEC crisis. After *An Energy Policy — Phase One,* the plan was that Austin and his team would move on to the policy recommendations, phase two. But they were overtaken by events. On the energy front, oil prices had been raised on four occasions in the first eight months of the year and the New Democratic Party, which held the balance of federal power, was calling for price controls and the movement of now-cheaper Alberta oil into Eastern Canada. Faced with rapid price escalation in other key commodities and a crippling strike, Parliament was recalled and Austin's team spent the Labour Day weekend thrashing out energy problems. In the event, the decisions taken that weekend were to revolutionize control of the Canadian oil industry. In the following three months, the basic structure of Canadian energy policy for the rest of the decade was to be evolved by Austin's team.

## Seizing Control as Tempers Flare

In a controversial move, Austin and his team recommended that prices be frozen temporarily to prevent windfalls as the Canadian domestic price chased that of OPEC. The industry was stunned by the move. If they could have basted Austin on a spit, they would have done so immediately. But the industry's days of calling the energy policy tune were numbered.

In those hectic final three months of 1973, as the world price of oil prepared to take off against the background of the Yom Kippur war and the Arab oil embargo, the lights hardly ever went out at EMR. The unfolding OPEC situation demanded not only a massive rethink of domestic policies but also those on energy relations with the U.S. Domestically, Albertan oil suddenly developed new charms when compared with the increasingly expensive and unstable foreign variety, not merely because it was secure, but because it could also be bought cheaper. That Albertan oil should at last be pumped via a new pipeline into Montreal was a cause for happiness in the Albertan government and within the oil industry. That it should be done so at a controlled price was not. Furthermore, Austin's team decided that the world price had to be charged for exports of oil to the U.S. This caused an uproar south of the border, and an equally large uproar in Alberta when Ottawa announced that it would cream off the difference between the domestic price and the world price in order to subsidize more expensive imports.

In purely logical terms, the move seemed to make sense, but insofar as the oil Ottawa was pricing belonged constitutionally to Alberta, the stage was set for the outbreak of a protracted energy war.

Lougheed called the export levy, which was a mere 40¢ a barrel when it was first imposed: "the most discriminatory action ever taken by a federal government against a producing province in the entire history of confederation . . . We have to protect the Alberta public interest — not from the Canadian public interest — but from Central and Eastern Canadian domination of the West."

American reaction was similarly indignant. The first word of Ottawa's decision to charge world prices was given by Austin to Julius Katz, at that time the major interface on trade between the U.S. and Canada, in the ritzy surroundings of the Polo Club in Paris. When Austin, accompanied by Canadian ambassador Peter Towe, outlined the main points of the government's new energy policy to Katz, the American took great and instant objection, a stance that was to be reflected throughout the U.S. for many months. The State Department, in particular, regarded the charging of world prices for exports as an "unfriendly act" and sent a stiff diplomatic note to that effect.

The main thrust of EMR's thinking on energy policy was to appear in a speech given in the House by Pierre Trudeau on December 6, 1973. In the speech, authored mainly by Austin, Trudeau announced: the creation of a national oil company, Petro-Canada; an oil pipeline to be built from Sarnia to Montreal to carry Albertan oil into Quebec, which had previously been served by cheap imported crude; federal funds for research into oil sands development; and Ottawa's approval for the Mackenzie Valley pipeline to bring natural gas from Prudhoe Bay in Alaska via the Mackenzie Delta, where gas from Canadian discoveries would be piggy-backed onto it.

There was a widespread perception, particularly with regard to the Liberals' espousal of a national oil company, that the policy was introduced to maintain the support of the NDP. The NDP, which made enormous political capital out of the OPEC crisis, had for some time been suggesting a single, subsidized price for domestic Canadian oil, and that Albertan oil should be pushed into Montreal. But their most strident calls were for the nationalization of Imperial Oil, a move which, in some unexplained way, was to be a panacea for Canadian energy problems. The Liberals' announcement of a national oil company was seen as a response to this call.

Many Ottawa observers saw the Liberals' energy policy as an example of the NDP tail wagging the Liberal dog. For example, the *Financial Post*'s respected Ottawa bureau chief, Clive Baxter, wrote: "For a man as contemptuous of muddled thinkers and political cowards as Trudeau used to be, last week's experience of having to rush a mishmash of barely digested new policies before Parliament and then a press conference (in which he had to duck most questions of substance) must have been a profoundly unsettling experience. But clearly it was the price his advisors said must be paid to avoid defeat this week at the hands of the New Democrats."

In the wake of Trudeau's speech, Tory back-benchers had brayed: "Will the real David Lewis (leader of the NDP) please stand up."

However, to view the announcement of a national oil company primarily as a sop to the NDP would be to misread the situation. It represented at least as much Jack Austin's personal vision of the national interest.

# 7
# Petro-Canada
# Gathers Momentum

*"I have never known much good done by those
who affected to trade for the public good."*
WEALTH OF NATIONS
ADAM SMITH

Behind Jack Austin's enthusiasm for a state oil company was the unspoken assumption that he should be the company's first chief executive. He had moved to the Prime Minister's Office as Pierre Trudeau's principal secretary in 1974, but he badly wanted the call to head Petro-Canada. However, in 1975 a number of press reports accused him of a conflict of interest in his business dealings. The accusations were taken up in the House. Against this background, Donald Macdonald told him that it would be very difficult to make him the first chief executive. Austin was deeply disappointed and eventually, the heat over his former business life also forced him out of the PMO. He was offered, and took, a Senate seat. A super-mandarin had been sidelined.*

Macdonald still had to find a suitable head for the new Crown corporation. One of the first that sprang to mind was Jack Gallagher. Gallagher, already a regular visitor to Ottawa, was particularly known to the federal government because Dome had drilled the first well for the Panarctic Oils consortium of which the federal government was a partner. However, when Macdonald approached Gallagher, Gallagher politely told him that "he just didn't believe" in Petro-Canada. In any case, Gallagher felt that he had bigger tasks in front of him.

Another prominent Canadian in the oilpatch was Arne Nielsen, head of Mobil Canada. Nielsen was universally popular, and was something of a local hero, not merely because he was given the credit for the discovery of the giant Pembina field, but also because he was the first Canadian to head up one of the Calgary subsidiaries of one of the world's major oil companies. At the time, Nielsen was known to be having problems with the New York-based Mobil's high-handed, branch-plant mentality, and expressed some interest in the job. However, there was a problem with salary.

---

* Austin's star was to rise once more in 1981 with his appointment to the federal cabinet as Minister of State with special political responsibility for reviving the Liberals' sagging fortunes in the West.

In the end it was Pierre Trudeau who suggested Maurice Strong, one of the most fascinating and elusive figures ever to bridge the gap between private entrepreneurship and public service. Strong, who came from a poor background in Manitoba, had worked his way up the corporate ladder, around the world and eventually into the United Nations in a dazzling display of career acrobatics. He had been in the investment business, worked for Jack Gallagher, started his own oil and gas company, headed the Power Corporation, and then switched to the Canadian International Development Agency in Ottawa before being invited to the U.N. as executive director of their environment program.

Strong seemed to have a perfect background for the job, but it was this perfect background that made many people anxious about him. What made Maurice Strong run? Was it altruism or ambition? Donald Macdonald, uneasy with the idea of Strong, pointed out to Trudeau that ideally what the government wanted was someone who would stay in the job for five years. Macdonald was well aware that Strong, on his breakneck ascent to whatever vision of personal apotheosis drove him on, had never stayed five years *anywhere*. However, Strong had powerful friends in Pierre Trudeau's government's new "important places". In particular, Jim Coutts thought he should have the job. Macdonald was at this time moved to Finance and Alastair Gillespie was shuffled to the Energy ministership. Gillespie was asked by Trudeau if he would be able to "live with" Strong, and the cabinet was given a further opportunity to discuss the issue. However, everyone realized that Strong was the man Trudeau wanted and, since the appointment of deputy ministers (which Strong effectively was) was the prerogative of the Prime Minister, the issue was closed.

Gillespie, however, like Macdonald, was also uneasy about Strong. He knew that Strong would be useful as chairman and organizer, but someone was still needed to run the company day-to-day, the sort of mundane activity which Strong would soon find tedious.

Bill Hopper, who had been appointed assistant deputy minister at EMR in 1974, was high on the list of cabinet choices for an executive position with the Crown corporation. He knew the industry well and had had a central role in the evolution of the Liberals' energy policy. However, he had no hands-on experience of management and was felt by many who knew him to be a "perennial consultant". Nevertheless, he went with Strong as executive vice-president. The other key men to go with Strong and Hopper were Joel Bell, who saw in Petro-Canada an appealing mix of policy and the chance to manage a corporate entity — a novelty for him too — and David Scrim, yet another bright young bureaucrat who had done "backroom" work on the *Phase 1* energy policy. It has now passed firmly into the corporate mythology of the national oil company that these four men set up shop in the International Hotel in Calgary early in January, 1976 with nothing more than a taxi-cab account, a mandate and an authorized capital limit of $1.5 billion.

PetroCan had been given the federal government's direct interests in the

67

petroleum business — its 45% stake in Panarctic and its holding in Syncrude — but its top priority was obviously to develop a more powerful corporate presence. A competent staff, and an acquisition, were the primary requirements.

Don Axford was hired from Mobil Canada to head up exploration, and Don Wolcott from Dome Petroleum to take care of operations and transportation. Axford, like Nielsen, was upset with the "down" that Mobil's head office had developed towards Canada. Wolcott, a brilliant and visionary engineer, was unhappy because he felt that Dome — where his natural-gas liquids schemes formed the basis of the company's cash flow — had never recognized his achievements.

## Growing in a Hostile Environment

The first couple of years of the Crown corporation's existence were marked by numerous clashes of egos as the new management attempted to accommodate not only to each other but to the extremely hostile Calgary environment. Calgary looked with a mixture of distaste and amazement at the strange and new forms of life presented to it by the Crown corporation. Strong knew both the corporate world and the oilpatch intimately but his style was alien to the Calgarians. He arrived with his Scandinavian mistress and bought a ranch — an honour for which the locals considered sufficient cash not the most important qualification. He brought literate — and even literary — executive assistants like John Ralston Saul (who was to write the bestselling novel *Birds of Prey*) whose very urbanity was taken as something of an insult by the locals. He brought *French*-speaking consultants and advisors like Marie Choquette, a woman around whom mystery swirled, and who seldom failed to point out the differences between Montreal and Calgary. Why, the switchboard even started answering the phone "Good morning, Petro-Canada, Bonjour", and that didn't go down *at all* well with the corn-flake box psychosis in the local community. Eventually, the new company took up residence in a red-brick building on 4th Avenue and some wag, in record time, renamed it "Red Square". And all the while the local press sniped away and employees were welcomed into the Petroleum Club with all the enthusiasm that a leper might attract. And that was just the flak from *outside* the bunker at Red Square.

The internal clash of personalities started at the very top. Strong and Gillespie had never hit it off, and the situation didn't improve when Strong continuously tried to circumvent the official chain of command. It might not even have been circumvention. It was just that Maurice Strong moved in mysterious ways, and that included his management style. He had always assiduously avoided the idea of being tied down within a structure. His preferred method of operation was through personal contacts, which, in Maurice Strong's hectic and accelerated world, was absolutely essential when you just had *so much to do.*

When Strong wanted something, he tended to go straight to the place he perceived he could get it, the Prime Minister's Office. That fact said a lot about the realities of the very personal power structure Trudeau was building. However, such a mode of operation found very little favour with Alastair Gillespie.

The other main internal tension surrounded the relationship between Bill Hopper and Don Axford. Axford was a firm believer in the potential of the East Coast, in particular Sable Island (a belief that was subsequently to be vindicated) and one of his first acts as Petro-Canada's exploration head was to persuade Strong to negotiate a farm-in with his old company, Mobil Canada. The deal that Strong did with Arne Nielsen — in which Mobil Canada farmed out some of its Sable Island acreage — was a very tough one on PetroCan, committing the national oil company to heavy financial obligations from which there was no contractual escape. Hopper didn't like the deal at all. And he already didn't get along with Axford.

Nevertheless, despite these internal tensions, the top priority, once a basic staff organization had been set up, was to find a takeover candidate which would provide landholdings, production income and further staff expertise.

The candidate selected from the hit list was not a surprising one. The activities of Atlantic Richfield had been curtailed by its heavy investments in Prudhoe Bay — one of the main reasons why it had suddenly withdrawn from Syncrude in 1974 and forced a government bail-out of the project. Atlantic Richfield Canada, Arcan, was another victim of the cash squeeze, but its sale was also an obvious potential source of cash for its strapped parent. After initial approaches to Bob Anderson, Arco's colourful head, Bill Hopper carried the brunt of the negotiations that brought Arcan into the fold for $342 million. Arcan was transformed into Petro-Canada's principal operating subsidiary, Petro-Canada Exploration. It provided PetroCan with 300 or so staff and cash flow of about $50 million a year from production of 30,000 barrels of oil and liquids a day and 90 million cubic feet of gas. It also had a net interest in undeveloped exploration acreage of some 11 million acres as well as tar sand leases on 1.2 million acres. Strong appointed Axford head of the operating subsidiary, but shortly afterwards, Ottawa decided that Hopper should be president, and Hopper in turn decided to shuffle Axford aside. Then he shuffled him out of the company altogether. Hopper was obviously keen to put his own stamp on PetroCan and hired Andy Janisch, a top-flight but low-key operating man from Gulf Canada, to run the company.

After a relatively short period of operation, it became apparent to Petro-Canada's management that its mandate to explore in the frontiers and act as catalyst rather than competitor to the industry was becoming expensive. Arcan's operating base was nowhere near big enough to pursue their corporate ambitions unless they were to trek year after year back to the government for new injections of funds. The solution was seen to be a further, and larger, acquisition. The target selected was Husky Oil, a Canadian incorporated company with huge, heavy-oil landholdings in the Lloydminster region but whose headquarters was situated in the picturesque little town of Cody, Wyoming, where it was run by the man who started it, Glenn Nielson, and his son Jim. The takeover attempt was to leave egg on PetroCan's, and in particular Bill Hopper's, corporate face.

Frustrated in an attempt to work out a farm-in arrangement with Husky, PetroCan had decided on an all-out takeover attempt in early 1978. However, sloppy security led to a stock-market leak that sent Husky's share price soaring. On June 8, 1978, PetroCan was forced into revealing its intention to make an offer for Husky stock. The Crown corporation had to launch its bid without the assistance of its top legal brain, David O'Brien, who had become seriously ill a few weeks before. But its most serious miscalculation was its belief that the Nielson family would be amenable to an offer.

The following three weeks were to witness one of the most fascinating takeover battles in Canadian history.* The Nielsons managed to elicit a counterbid from the almost legendary head of Los-Angeles-based Occidental Petroleum, Armand Hammer — an octogenarian who had counted both Arab kings and Lenin among his friends. Petro-Canada and Occidental spent two weeks attempting to outbid each other against the background of a heated political debate about the merits of foreign vs. state-ownership. In fact, Petro-Canada was calmly confident that the Foreign Investment Review Agency would never let the Occidental bid go through.

However, in the third week, Bob Blair, the brilliant, nationalist head of Alberta Gas Trunk Line entered the fray in an unexpected, subtle and devastating way. The key to his victory was that, as the battle between Hopper and Hammer progressed, more and more Husky shares had fallen into the hands of the New York arbitrageurs, a group of high-rolling investment dealers who snap up shares in a takeover situation when it looks as if there will be counter-offers and thus higher share prices. After two weeks of battle there were such large blocks of Husky shares in New York that it was possible for Blair to go in and buy a controlling interest of Husky in the open market. The move was regarded as a stroke of corporate genius.

Blair's victory was a debacle for Petro-Canada and a stinging personal defeat for Hopper. Hopper was in PetroCan's Ottawa office when he heard the news of what Blair was doing, and frustration drove him to the point of tears. He felt that he had been royally screwed. It wasn't just that he had lost the prize. He had lost face as well.

American observers were aghast at the Crown corporation's handling of the takeover attempt. The word that recurred most often was "amateurish". First, PetroCan had been naive enough to imagine that they could approach Husky with a "friendly" offer. Then they had underestimated Husky's ability to make a counter-offer. And then, finally, when it had seemed that the scales were tipping in PetroCan's favour as a result of what many considered the "unfair" advantage given it by FIRA, Blair had stepped in and blasted the national oil company's bid out of the water.

---

* For a full account, see *The Blue-Eyed Sheiks*.

Despite assurances from Blair that he had in no way intended to outsmart Petro-Canada, and the brave face put on the whole affair by Bill Hopper — who claimed that it would make no difference in the previously close relations between the two companies — the temperature between Blair's head office and PetroCan, just two blocks away, dropped to zero.

Friendships between Petro-Canada and Husky employees were actually broken up over the affair and some of PetroCan's executives felt, in the words of one of their number, like "the gang who couldn't shoot straight".

Within a couple of months, however, Hopper had drawn a bead on an even larger and more attractive prize than Husky, Pacific Petroleums, which was 48%-owned by Phillips Petroleum of Bartlesville, Oklahoma. Suspecting that the leak that had forced their hand on Husky might have come from the finance houses they had used for the takeover, PetroCan decided to make the Pacific takeover an in-house job.

The company pursued a much tighter battle plan and the scheme was to a large degree masterminded by Joel Bell. Alastair Gillespie had been uneasy when Bill Hopper had suggested that Bell be made vice-president of finance. What, he thought, did Joel Bell know about finance? What training had he had? However, Bell was to win his spurs with the Pacific takeover. PetroCan not only managed to pick up Phillips' stake, but the key move by Bell lined up sufficient minority shareholders to take ownership over 50% and thus achieve effective control.

However, the Pacific move was to create even more controversy than either the Arcan takeover or the aborted attempt on Husky. Arcan had been strapped for cash and "sitting on its hands"; Husky controlled a key natural resource of heavy oil and was widely considered to be poorly managed; but what rationale could PetroCan offer for its takeover of Pacific? Pacific was considered to be well-managed and although the major shareholding lay in the U.S., it was controlled locally. What did a Petro-Canada takeover achieve apart from self-aggrandizement? Petro-Canada had decided that it didn't like engaging exclusively in all the expensive frontier exploration that represented an enormous drain on resources and no prospect of returns for a decade or more. It wanted to get into the ring with the rest of the players in Western Canada, to get its hands on some of the "cream".

But there was another rationale. An election was due early the following year. The Liberals were slumping in the polls and the Conservatives were making threatening noises about disbanding the national oil company. PetroCan's senior management were well aware that the larger PetroCan became, the more difficult it would be to disband. Not surprisingly, no such rationale was offered to the public.

But there was also a split in the cabinet over the desirability of the Pacific takeover. It was rumoured that Gillespie and other more "right" leaning, cabinet ministers, such as Robert Andras and Jean Chrétien, were less than keen, realizing that the Pacific takeover would increase PetroCan's autonomy and thus reduce government control over it. There was a fear that PetroCan was beginning to betray the inevitable tendency of all organizations: to serve its own purpose, chiefly survival, before any others. There were also concerns over the cost. However, Joel Bell, who was in charge of the financial projections, produced an attractive set of figures to support the deal's attractiveness. But the most important support for the Pacific takeover came from Pierre Trudeau himself. And thus it was approved. The cost was $1.5 billion.

The Pacific takeover, completed by March, 1979, marked a turning point in PetroCan's history. It was now in the big leagues. Combined production of Arcan and Pacific made PetroCan the seventh largest oil and natural-gas liquids producer in Canada, and second only to Shell Canada as a natural gas producer. Pacific also brought a very attractive land position in Western Canada, as well as more than 400 retail and wholesale marketing outlets. PetroCan was now integrated. But it wasn't just the size and scope of operations, it was the whole orientation of the company that was changing, from a mere arm of government policy to an entrepreneurial entity. This shift had a lot to do with Bill Hopper's personality.

Hopper had never fitted easily into the conventional model of the bureaucrat. Those who took a less hostile attitude towards PetroCan recognized him as a "free enterpriser at heart". But free enterprise means competition, and Bill Hopper was just *itching* to compete with the rest of the industry. They all sat around in the Petroleum Club and spouted *laissez-faire* economics out of the eighteenth century, boasting about how clever they were to make so much money, when Hopper knew that it was a combination of OPEC, generous government regulations and being in the right place at the right time that was really the cause of their success.

And all the time, in Hopper's view, they weren't really competing at all. They just got together in cosy consortia, sitting on their vast acreages and farming-in and farming-out to each other and slapping each other on the back in an orgy of self-congratulation. But what hurt most was the jibes, the suggestions that Hopper just didn't belong. He wasn't an *oilman*.

He had to sit back and take all the stuff about PetroCan's unfair advantages and its playing with monopoly money, and it not finding a drop of oil or a whiff of gas. That really riled Bill Hopper and made him more determined than ever to take on the industry toe-to-toe and just *rub their noses in it*. Many believed that he had a complex about filling Maurice Strong's shoes, and Husky had hurt him deeply. But now he had Pacific.

The problem, of course, was that, under PetroCan's mandate, the Crown corporation wasn't meant to be a competitor; it was meant to be a catalyst, to go boldly where the industry didn't want to because of the expense. With the Pacific takeover, all that changed.

In little more than two years, PetroCan had become a significant force in the Canadian petroleum industry. It was the largest Canadian-owned oil company, and although it was still smaller than the integrated majors — Imperial, Gulf, Shell and Texaco — it had certainly made its presence felt. The strength of that presence, however, was soon to be severely challenged. On May 22, 1979, the Clark government was elected. However, Petro-Canada had friends in high places, and the highest was the state oil company's cradle, the Department of Energy, Mines and Resources, which, as the Tories assumed power, was once again becoming the place to be in Ottawa.

# 8
# The Second Coming of Energy, Mines and Resources

*"The statesman who should attempt to direct private people in what manner they ought to employ their capitals, would not only load himself with the most unnecessary attention, but assume an authority which could safely be trusted to no council and senate whatsoever, and which would nowhere be so dangerous as in the hands of a man who had folly and presumption enough to fancy himself fit to exercise it."*
                    WEALTH OF NATIONS
                    ADAM SMITH

In the fall of 1978, two very different men in two very different places moved to new jobs. One arrived in triumph from exile in France to the holy city of Qum in Iran. The other, somewhat more mundanely, transported his papers from Ottawa's Place Bell Canada, home of the Department of Finance, to 580 Booth Street, the newly-built, black tower of the Department of Energy, Mines and Resources. The former, the Ayatollah Khomeini, an aged and thunder-browed Islamic fundamentalist revolutionary, had just seized power from the fallen Shah. The latter, Dr. Edmund Clark, a bright-eyed economist in his early thirties, was moving to EMR as assistant deputy minister of economic and policy analysis.

Inevitably, the passage of the Ayatollah took place amid domestic fanfare and worldwide media attention. The move of Dr. Clark was noticed only in Ottawa, where a gossipy network transmits word of any subtle shift in the bureaucratic power structure with the excitement of a jungle telegraph. Nevertheless, although Dr. Clark's passage was not widely noted at the time, his subsequent role at EMR, combined with his own very personal commitment to nationalist reform, was to make a considerable contribution towards a policy revolution in Canada.

The two men are linked because the accession of the Ayatollah led to the withdrawal of Iranian oil supplies from the world market, providing the background to a further surge in OPEC prices. This, in turn, led to the critical reassessment of Canadian energy policies — in which Clark played a key part

73

— and which was to form the basis of the 1980 Liberal government's National Energy program.

The analytical work at EMR was carried out under the short-lived Conservative government of Joe Clark. The fact is significant because it was neither initiated by the Clark government nor by the Liberals that had preceded it. However, it was eagerly seized upon by the 1980 Liberal government, whose hunger for a return to power considerably exceeded the size of its policy platform.

The second coming of the Department of Energy, Mines and Resources should perhaps be traced back to the arrival at the department in April, 1978, of Marshall "Mickey" Cohen as deputy minister. A 43-year-old Toronto lawyer, Cohen had clearly established himself as a high flier in the Department of Finance. He had practised law for ten years in Toronto when he was brought to Ottawa in 1970 to be a special tax advisor. In 1971, he became the department's assistant deputy minister of tax policy, and three years later, was also given responsibility for federal-provincial relations. Cohen had a key backroom role in the difficult federal-provincial negotiations over oil pricing that had so soured Ottawa-Alberta relations in 1974, and had played a critical part in the evolution of other key policies, such as the review of social security and the anti-inflation program.

Michael Pitfield had been enormously impressed by Cohen, as, in turn, had Pierre Trudeau. It wasn't just Cohen's brainpower; his unassuming and affable style made him part of the key group that wielded powerful influence within the cabinet's mystical force-field. He demonstrated an uncanny ability to handle bureaucratic egos and territorial jealousies both within Ottawa and in his dealings with the provinces. Smooth, brilliant, articulate, he was described by a colleague at Finance as "Trudeau's type of guy".

Cohen in fact was only to stay at EMR until the end of 1979, when he moved over to the Department of Industry, Trade and Commerce as deputy minister. However, he was to return to EMR as DM when the Liberal government defeated the Tories in 1980, and he was to preside as the senior bureaucrat in the formulation and implementation of the National Energy Program, and in the protracted and bitter negotiations with Alberta that surrounded it.

However, his move to EMR in April, 1978, was important in that it signified that the department's policy side was once again being beefed up. His arrival also marked the beginning of an influx of a number of key players from the Department of Finance who would lay the groundwork for the NEP. By far the most important of these was Ed Clark.

## Bureaucratic Enfant Terrible

Of all the public servants connected with the NEP, none was to become better known than Clark. He was to be seen, particularly in Alberta, as the epitome of Ottawa's anti-business, interventionist bias, and as a key force in the resurgence of the fiercely nationalist sentiment espoused by the returning

Liberals in 1980. Clark was to assume, in Calgary in particular, a notoriety never before accorded any public servant. An almost mythical view of him was to trickle down even as far as the roughnecks. But Clark was rightly a controversial figure, for he typified the enormous influence that a non-elected public servant — in the absence of, and sometimes despite, firm political guidance — can have on the formulation of policy. His background was highly academic and theoretical, and he had no experience of industry, yet he was the intellectual leading edge of a policy that had more effect on the oil industry than any other in Canadian history.

Ed Clark had an outstanding academic background although, under the Trudeau regime, this became the rule rather than the exception. After an economics degree at the University of Toronto, Clark went to Harvard, where he earned his Master's degree in 1971 and his Ph.D. in 1974. During 1972 and 1973, he was team leader of the University of Toronto Tanzania project and his doctoral thesis, "Public Investment and Socialist Development in Tanzania", as a result of his notoriety, became one of the best-known academic dissertations in the Calgary oil patch.

In the wake of the NEP, literally hundreds of copies of the thesis, which had been published by the University of Toronto Press, were photocopied and passed around Calgary's Petroleum Club, with "selected quotations" high-lighted in an angry yellow, felt-tip pen. "The study," read one such passage, "is seen as part of the larger effort by scholars everywhere to turn their attention to the issue of how to build socialist societies. It is my belief that socialist scholars in particular should devote more of their energy to analysing the problems of socialist societies and the problems of transition to socialism, and somewhat less to criticizing capitalist societies. While anti-capitalist critiques can take us part way towards understanding how to build a socialist reality, they are not sufficient."

Such statements inevitably caused mild apoplexy in the Petroleum Club, and generally high levels of blood pressure throughout the oil industry's corporate suites.

Clark was a product of the post-Vietnam and Watergate era, a watershed for the ethical credibility of big government and big business. He was an active member of Harvard's Union for Radical Political Economists, and colleagues remember him as a forceful proponent of left-wing views, who brooked no contradiction. His move to the Department of Finance in 1974 as a whiz-kid surprised some of his former academic colleagues, one of whom said: "I expected to find him leading a revolution somewhere in the jungle rather than sitting in an office in Finance."

From the beginning, Clark impressed people. He had all the latest buzz-words and analytical concepts at his disposal, but most of all he had ideas, the currency in which Ottawa marks a man's worth. He joined Finance as a special advisor in the Economic Analysis Division, and in 1975 he became the chief of the Regional and Sectoral Analysis section of that department. Clark first came to prominence in Ottawa at the time of the Anti-Inflation Board. The concept of wage and price control was clear enough, but implementation was a problem. Clark came up with many of the answers as deputy director-general of the Prices and Profits Branch of the board, where he served during 1975 and part of 1976. Significantly, Mickey Cohen, Ian Stewart and Joel Bell all had a hand in the formulation and implementation of the A.I.B. program. At that time, it was the place to be.

Clark returned to Finance in 1976 as director of the Long-Range and Structural Analysis Division. It was there that he got to know Mickey Cohen better. Although Cohen was generally considered to lean to the right in his political views and Clark was clearly inclined to the left, when the two men had worked at Finance, they had walked to work together and a friendship had formed. Therefore, when Cohen was moved to EMR his former colleague Clark seemed an obvious choice for the department's policy arm. Clark agreed to go to EMR as assistant deputy minister with responsibility for overall energy policy development and the administration of the sector's energy programs. He went about his new task with a will. Many of the old-style bureaucrats were moved aside, and there was a purge in the Fiscal and Policy Analysis section.

Since the hectic 1973-74 period, energy policies had evolved at a more normal rate. Oil prices, under a 1977 agreement with Alberta, were rising by $1 a barrel every six months and, towards the end of 1978, seemed to be closing in on the world price. Natural gas was priced at 85% of oil's price. In addition, a wide variety of new programs — such as taxes on gas-guzzling cars and grants for home insulation — had been introduced to encourage conservation.

But most important, under the Liberals' policy of "need to know" and also partly as a reaction against the severe fiscal regime imposed on the industry during the federal-provincial fight in 1974, both Ottawa and Alberta had created generous incentives for reinvestment of profits and to induce private individuals to invest in the oil business. The industry had responded with an exploration boom, of which the principal result was a large increase in discoveries of natural gas. Particularly generous incentives had also been provided for frontier exploration.

Clark's arrival, however, was to change EMR's orientations considerably.

The move of Clark and Cohen to EMR marked the beginning of an enormous surge in the department's power. In the following two years, until the emergence of the National Energy Program in October, 1980, it was *the* place to be in the great Ottawa bureaucratic structure, the place where *key policy was being made.*

Clark and his team were models of the Trudeaucracy, as much leaders as followers of political thought. While at the Department of Finance, Clark had examined the impact of higher Canadian energy prices and concluded that the implications for Canada were negative and needed to be rectified. Because of the predominance of Alberta as a petroleum producer and the dominance of high-energy use in the manufacturing industries of the East, principally Ontario and Quebec, Clark believed that Canada should be considered rather as if Saudi Arabia and Japan existed within one country. Rocketing world oil prices had obviously led to a redistribution of wealth in favour of Saudi Arabia and against the non-energy-producing but high-energy-consuming Japan. The same thing had happened in Canada, with a redistribution of wealth in favour of Alberta — and to a lesser extent Saskatchewan and B.C. — and against petroleum-consuming provinces of the East. This, in Clark's macroeconomic world, created an imbalance which the federal government had the responsibility of correcting. Higher oil prices created what were considered by Clark and other economists as "windfall" profits, "excess" economic rents that should be taxed away and then reinjected into the East to compensate for the higher petroleum prices the consuming provinces were forced to pay. However, the Liberals, in Clark's belief, had failed to do that adequately.

Clark believed that EMR under Macdonald and then Gillespie had developed a mindless supply-side mentality and an obsession with self-sufficiency. This meant that too much cash was going to a dominantly foreign-controlled industry. Clark considered this an extremely undesirable development, for as well as being a staunch believer in strong, centralist macroeconomic control, Edmund Clark was also a very strong, economic nationalist. He believed that Canadian corporate managers were weak. More important, he believed that the only answer to the "problem" was state intervention. Clark was soon to receive a powerful ally in those beliefs.

## Pitfield Shufflings

At the end of 1978, the bureaucracy experienced one of its perennial "Pitfield shuffles" with the creation of the new super-ministry, the Ministry of State for Economic Development, to the senior mandarin's post of which the enormously powerful Gordon Osbaldeston was appointed. Osbaldeston was a public servant in the classic mould, an administrator concerned more with the overall excellence of information and policy advice available to ministers than with promoting any ideological view. When powerful bureaucrats move, there is an inevitable tendency for them to take along some of the best talent from their previous department. Such talent is obviously only too willing to move in the wake of a man "on the way up". That was the case with Osbaldeston, who had previously been deputy minister at the Department of Industry, Trade and Commerce. The move of Mickey Cohen to ITC at the beginning of 1979 was seen as a re-establishment of Industry's status which would provide a counterweight to the powerful new bureaucratic warlord at MSED.

Equally important, however, Cohen's temporary departure from EMR cleared the way for the arrival of Ian Stewart. As economic advisor in the Privy Council Office, Stewart had enjoyed enormous influence on Pierre Trudeau's economic thinking in the previous four years. Indeed, it was believed that if the Liberals were to fall and Stewart were to survive, he would have to move out of the PCO, where his close association with central policy-making might make him vulnerable to the axe.

Stewart was not widely considered an ideologue. Rather he was thought of, and preferred to think of himself, as a synthesizer of ideas. He was, however, a firm believer in the healing powers of government. His social concerns were profound; so profound, in fact, that he put in fourteen-hour days agonizing over decisions. Stewart was a man without personal enemies, a rarity in Ottawa's hyper-competitive atmosphere. He was described by Robert Collison in *Canadian Business* as "something of a Canadian Andy Hardy, grown up, immensely successful, exceedingly decent."

Ed Clark had enjoyed an excellent working relationship with Mickey Cohen, and was to do so again, but the meeting of minds between Clark and Stewart was much greater. Both were brilliant academic economists, and both shared profound social, and, to a significant degree, socialist convictions.

At about this time, other key players also arrived from the Department of Finance to make up the team that was to evolve the main thrust of the NEP. George Tough, an American born in Charlotte, North Carolina, had spent his early years mineral prospecting in Canada before going to the University of Western Ontario and graduating at the top of his class in geography. He had taught high school for a couple of years before moving on to the University of Calgary to pick up an M.A. in geography. He had joined EMR's mineral resources division in 1968, when the department was still dominated by scientists, but had moved to Finance in 1970. Like Ed Clark, he had experience in the Third World, having been seconded to the Ford Foundation in 1973 for a two-year stint as mineral policy advisor to the government of Botswana. When he returned, he became assistant director of resource programs back at the Department of Finance. Early in 1979, a few months after Ed Clark moved to EMR, Tough followed him to become director-general of energy strategy.

Another key figure from Finance was to be Dr. Len Good, who had worked with Clark in the Long Range and Structural Analysis Division between 1976 and 1978. Good was another economist who had been at the University of Toronto at the same time as Clark. He had taught economics at the University of Prince Edward Island for a couple of years and then picked up a Ph.D. from the University of Western Ontario. However, his thesis, "An Econometric Model of the Canadian Cable Television Industry and the Effects of CRTC Regulation", although a good deal more relevant than most doctoral theses, was not to achieve the notoriety of that of his new boss in EMR's Economic and Policy Analysis sector.

As far as the Liberals were concerned, the last six months of their rule in late 1978 and early 1979 was not the time for sweeping new policy initiatives on energy. Fear of shortages dominated the winter months. The election dominated the spring. But in any case, it is uncertain how far the Liberals would have been immediately amenable to the main thrust of the analysis of Stewart, Clark and their new policy team. For the main thrust of that analysis was that the Liberals, in their energy policy, had given away the farm.

That was the message that Clark and Stewart were determined to give to the new Tory government. However, the fit between left-wing bureaucrats who believed in the need for more state intervention, and who regarded Alberta as similar to Saudi Arabia, was bound to be somewhat uneasy with a pro-business government that stressed its ability to get along with the provinces and wanted to disband Petro-Canada.

# PART TWO

## The Roots
## of the National
## Energy Program

# 9
# Joe Clark Meets
# the Reason Machine

*"All with experience of large-scale business or
government know the amount of time that informed juniors spend on considering how to contend with ill-informed superiors."*
THE NEW INDUSTRIAL STATE
JOHN KENNETH GALBRAITH

When Joe Clark came to power, the Trudeau government had ruled for
eleven years. Not only was the seam between the government and the bureaucracy invisible, but few people outside the worlds of academe or political
administration thought the issue of bureaucratic power a matter of more than
passing interest.

If the Conservative government can be said to have accomplished anything,
for at least a brief period it turned over a great garden stone called Ottawa,
under which new and fascinating life-forms had been developing for eleven
uninterrupted years. The creatures did not appear hostile. Indeed, they even
thought themselves ready to serve. If they appeared a little cerebral and somewhat short-sighted, that was no surprise — it is after all, dark under a stone.

The Trudeau era had built a bureaucratic machine that was the embodiment of rationalism or, at least, thought it was. To any one problem there could
ultimately be only one "best" rational solution, hence the system had become
monolithic in its thinking. It believed that it was the guardian of the "right" way.
Any new government which came along with a different set of policies could
only have done so because they had not sufficiently analyzed the situation.
Their thinking was woolly. They needed to be educated.

The bureaucracy's attitude towards the Conservatives' energy policy took a
number of forms. Some of them looked upon it with sympathy; some looked
upon it with the attitude an English butler might display towards a used diaper:
it was a dirty business, but somebody had to clean it up. The struggle over
policy during the brief Clark era provides a fascinating insight into the
workings of modern government in Canada, but it is important to remember
that that was not the reason for the Tory government's fall. Indeed, the Clark
government would have done better, arguably survived, if it had followed more
closely some of the bureaucracy's advice.

The simple fact is that the Clark government fell, or rather tripped, onto its own sword.

As in all tragedies, the Conservative party had one fatal flaw that led to its undoing: it forgot that it was a minority government. In classical tragedy it is often hubris, a too lofty view of one's own powers, that is the route to self-destruction. Pride cometh before a fall. In the case of the Conservatives, what came before the fall was energy policy. When the Conservatives had come to power, energy policy had really seemed like such a small priority. Their energy platform was a thin thing indeed. Cobbled together quickly in parliamentary backrooms, it consisted of just three elements: self-sufficiency in oil by 1990 — a piece of political one-upmanship on the Liberal's more modest "self-reliance", a vague commitment to the motherhood of Canadianization, and a promise to dismantle Petro-Canada. The last item was not really a piece of energy policy at all, but rather an article of free-enterprise dogma that was increasingly to appear out of place in the turbulence of the petroleum business. In the end it was to become the Conservatives' policy albatross.

## The Shadow of OPEC

The Conservative government was ill-starred because it was born in conjunction with the second OPEC crisis. Joe Clark's pedestrian march to glory in the spring of 1979 was matched, step-by-step, by global events of much greater import. The small swell that washed him to electoral power was accompanied by a global wave of enormous economic and political significance that was ultimately to help sweep him out of office.

As the 1979 election was called, the revolution in Iran that drove the Shah from power was in full swing. While Clark flew and bussed doggedly across the country, presenting his earnest message in schools and community halls, clandestine meetings were taking place in the opulent surroundings of the Hôtel du Rhône and Hôtel Président in Geneva between the world's largest oil dealers and representatives of governments — such as South Africa and Israel — that had been embargoed and were desperate for oil. Coverage of Clark's campaign on the evening news vied with stories of lengthening lines and fraying tempers outside gasoline stations in the U.S. While he wrapped up his election bid, oil cargoes were changing ownership, and sometimes course, in mid-ocean. As voters went to the Canadian polls, giant tankers, paying $35,000 a day in dues, sat off Kharg Island in the Persian Gulf, where Iranian oil is loaded. Their nervous captains watched the new revolutionary government divert the oil they were meant to receive under long-term contracts to the higher-priced spot market. In the week before and the two weeks after Clark's victory, the world spot price for oil doubled, to almost $40 U.S. a barrel. As he attended his first economic summit conference in Tokyo the following month, word arrived that OPEC had increased the official price of oil from a floor of $14.55 U.S. to a range between $18 and $23.50. Clark even became a bit player in the global drama as the Iraqi National Oil company threatened to cut off oil to Canada in response to Clark's promise to move the

Canadian embassy in Israel to Jerusalem. Backing away from that commitment was to be Clark's first painful lesson in the world of oil-fuelled politics.

These developments raised new questions about Canadian energy, although the farsighted would have seen the writing on the wall at the time of the Iranian revolution. For a start, they placed an enormous additional financial burden on a country subsidizing imports of 450,000 barrels of oil a day. The Geneva increase alone would add about $1 million a day to Canada's import subsidies.

As far as Conservative policies were concerned, increased world prices were actually a great help to the policy of self-sufficiency. To the extent that these increases were allowed to domestic companies, exploration and production could be stimulated and consumption would be depressed. Indeed, it was only the second OPEC crisis that made self-sufficiency possible. However, world oil turmoil, in particular that part manifested on television screens in the summer of 1979 as the gasoline line-ups reappeared south of the border, was disastrous for the policy of disbanding Petro-Canada. For the key question that arose from — or rather was underlined by — the second OPEC crisis was: who does, and who should, control oil?

The Clark government's approach, insofar as the policy had been thought through at all, was that things should be left up to the industry. Free enterprise was best. Disband Petro-Canada. The Clark government mistakenly thought that their election indicated a concurrence in these views by the electorate. Nothing could have been further from the truth, as they were to discover to their cost.

That the senior mandarins did not go along with the Conservatives' Petro-Canada policy came as no surprise to Joe Clark and his advisors. They saw the bureaucracy's attitudes as a natural desire to protect their own, combined with a certain mental inertia.

However, the Conservatives had misjudged both the bureaucracy's independence and viewpoint. They were not interested in defending Liberal policies. In fact they disapproved of them. They felt themselves to be the guardians of certain principles, many of which certainly coincided with Liberal thinking, but many of which also went beyond it. Indeed, the message that they gave the Clark government was that, under existing conditions, the energy policies of the previous Liberal government, with the exception of Petro-Canada, were poor ones. The Liberals, claimed the public servants, had constructed a system which effectively transferred financial power to the foreign-controlled oil industry and the provinces. The EMR bureaucracy, which had strong left-wing, centralist views, powerfully opposed both those trends.

In the eyes of the mandarins, the whole of energy policy needed a re-think and they — not the Tory party's policy makers — were the obvious people to do it.

## Seizing the Policy Initiative

The mandarins' principal concern was the flow of petroleum revenues in Canada, a three-pronged river of cash where the provincial and industry streams were at full flood while that which flowed into federal coffers was little more than a trickle.

The renewed OPEC crisis and soaring world prices meant that higher prices in Canada were inevitable. However, under the existing system, this would cause industry and provincial revenues to almost burst their banks, while the federal government would be left with a parched riverbed!

The existing system had arisen from the federal-provincial battle in the wake of the first OPEC crisis. The real weapons of the battle had not been words, but the sometimes blunt instruments of taxation and royalty collection. The federal and provincial governments had hacked away at the oil industry's income like muscular apprentice butchers. But the problem was that they hacked to the bone and companies started to leave the country for the less hostile regime south of the border. Fairly soon, both governments realized that there would be little point in divvying up the golden egg in advance if the goose was either deceased, or had flown south. So they reversed the process and, like amateur plastic surgeons, began grafting revenue back onto the creature in the form of allowances and incentives.

The result of all this hacking and grafting, when combined with subsequent budgets, produced a tax structure which seemed like a misshapen monster of fiscal ad-hocery. But it wasn't the complexity of the beast to which the mandarins at EMR objected. After all, the macro-management to which the bureaucracy subscribes always produces systems encrusted with myriad measures to counteract the side-effects of the original legislation.

What the mandarins objected to was the results of the system, its so-called, structural "spillover" effects. When they looked at the results of the bureaucratic fight of the preceding four years, they discovered that they had lost! Not only was Alberta bursting with funds, most notably in the form of the Alberta Heritage Fund, the biggest piggy bank in Canada, but the oil industry, too, had enjoyed an unprecedented boom. Worse, the part of the industry which appeared to benefit most from the complex system of tax incentives was that containing the foreign-owned majors, who had become the objects of fear and loathing in the corridors of power.

Even if the second OPEC crisis had not emerged, the bureaucracy would almost certainly have pressed the new government to "rectify" these tendencies, which offended their sense of equity — that is, equity based on convictions of strong central power and inclinations towards interventionism and away from private enterprise. How much luck they would have had with a ruling party that was pro-business and pro-provincial is another matter. However, given the likelihood of much higher domestic prices, the bureaucracy's concerns became obsessive. If the prevailing system was to be maintained, then not only would the rich — in the shape of Alberta and the oil companies — get richer, but the poor — the federal government — would have to shell out more in equalization payments to almost everyone but Alberta. And of course the federal government would — to the extent that higher oil prices promoted inflation and slowed growth — be called upon to provide counteractive economic measures.

Given a centrist, anti-business bureaucracy and a federalist, pro-business government, friction of some sort was inevitable, but what raised the temperature of the affair was that the whole game was suddenly being played for much higher stakes.

Of course, the very idea of a "clash" between a government and its bureaucracy seemed like a contradiction. The bureaucracy, after all, is there to serve the government, to advise it, to provide programs for its policies. However, the Conservative government proved that such is far from the case.

In the ideal world of executive-bureaucratic relationships, the new government would simply have sent its policies along to the mandarins who would, dutifully and whatever they thought of them, have gritted their teeth and set down to penning programs that would implement them. But such was not the way of modern, ultra-sophisticated bureaucracy — a committed bureaucracy that serves what it perceives as the national interest before it serves the ill-thought-out policies of a fledgling government.

The mandarins immediately set out to squash the government's first energy policy element — self-sufficiency — on grounds of impracticality, and its last objective — the dismantling of Petro-Canada — on grounds of undesirability. Canadianization they liked, but not just a wishy-washy motherhood kind of Canadianization. The big, foreign-owned oil companies, because of the tax system, were just getting bigger and bigger. That had to be stopped and stopped quickly.

Thus Joe and his advisors found that when they pulled the levers of the energy machine to make it go one way, it persisted in going the other. Mandarins, after all, are not Zulu warriors to be marched off a cliff to show their obedience. They believed that Joe Clark's energy policies were all wrong, and thus they felt it was their duty to change them. Were they not, in the end, doing Joe a favour?

That idea still causes the dethroned members of Joe's court to seethe. Bureaucrats, they point out, are meant to be there to find ways of carrying out the government's policies, not seeking ways to convert the government to their own.

The Clark era raised some crucial questions about the relationship between government and the bureaucracy. First, there is absolutely no doubt that the Tories came to power with a slim and ill-thought-out energy policy, although in their defence it was framed when it seemed there was no particular reason to make energy a high priority. OPEC was to change that. Given that situation, and a professional bureaucracy which understood energy issues much better than their political masters, it was inevitable that the Conservatives would change their policies as better information became available to them. However, the issue to be considered is whether the mandarins pushed policies that went beyond objective analysis into the field of ideology and political preference, particularly interventionism and nationalism. How far did the bureaucracy succeed in bending their political masters, and just how did they do it? Due to the "open" nature of the Clark government — another feature for which the public should be thankful — it is possible to examine these questions as it never was under the preceding Trudeau regime.

## Joe Clark's Policy Phalanx

It has become a truism of political analysis that Pierre Trudeau lost the 1979 election because he had allowed himself to become isolated by the Praetorian Guard of the Prime Minister's Office. Ironically Joe Clark, once in power, assembled an even tighter phalanx around him. It was that phalanx, in particular Clark's senior policy advisor and intellectual mentor, Jim Gillies, that was to clash so strongly with the bureaucrats at EMR. Once the bureaucrats had persuaded the new energy minister, the hapless Ray Hnatyshyn, of the correctness of their views, that clash became internecine warfare within the party itself.

Something of a rarity in the ranks of the Conservatives, Jim Gillies had at least the academic qualifications for the senior mandarinate. Educated at the University of Western Ontario, Brown University and Indiana University, Gillies had spent fourteen years on the faculty of the Graduate School of Management at the University of California in Los Angeles. From 1965 to 1972, he had been the founding dean of the Faculty of Administrative Studies at York University. But Gillies was more than just a Ph.D. economist, he was a self-confessed intellectual. During the 1979 campaign, while the boys were playing cards in the back of the plane, Gillies whiled away the hours reading Tacitus's *The Annals of Imperial Rome*, once reportedly being sufficiently embarrassed to hide the book inside a copy of *Playboy*. He also possessed social graces, and his tall professorial figure, during his period as MP for Don Valley between 1972 and 1979, was often sighted on the Rockcliffe diplomat-and-mandarin circuit.

But Jim Gillies wasn't a mandarin. His bearing marked him as a patrician, a member of an elite to be sure, but one whose politics were all wrong for the Ottawa bureaucracy. Gillies was a committed, even devout, free-enterpriser. The bottom line of his politics was Jeffersonian, but the idea that the best government is the least government was diametrically opposed to that of the bureaucracy, perhaps even to the times in which we live. His attitude to business was summed up when Dalton Camp was assessing his suitability for the riding of Don Valley. He was, said Camp, "the natural candidate for a constituency that was very nearly the locus for the opinion that government ought to be run like Brascan."

But also, Gillies was accused of having a short span of intellectual interest. He was an innovative thinker, but once he had the grand concept in mind, once he had come to what he believed was the correct strategy, he found it hard to concern himself with the matter further. Gillies believed that he shouldn't have to bother himself with details; these things should be delegated. But that was not the mandarin way. The mandarin way was thinking things through, analyzing and agonizing until every last implication of policy had been dissected. Gillies belonged to the school that said that the best chief executive was the one with nothing to do; that anybody who couldn't have his desk cleared and be out on the tennis court by five-after-five was managing his time badly. Nothing could be further from the scheme of values in Ottawa, where anybody not at their desk at seven P.M. *obviously wasn't involved in key policy making.* Gillies' approach to politics was that the system should be manned by gifted amateurs, people who had something to bring from some other walk of life. He had once suggested to John Diefenbaker that people shouldn't be allowed to become either professional politicians or bureaucrats. No view could have been more of an anathema to the intellectually-honed, deeply-committed squadrons of Trudeaucrats.

To the mandarins, such a dilettante approach was not only mistaken, it also indicated a lack of earnestness, and Gillies certainly did nothing to allay their fears. He found it very difficult to take some parts of the great game seriously. For example, during his first few weeks as senior policy advisor sitting in the room next door to Clark, he noticed that in his in-tray every morning were briefing documents whose import he often found hard to comprehend. He noticed that these documents were headed with a number of initials of whose meaning he had no idea, but he didn't like to confess his ignorance. However, he eventually decided to broach the subject with the mandarinate. What were all these documents with the initials at the top? Why, he was told, they were the overnight cables sent to embassies around the world. The initials stood for London and Hong Kong and Auckland. Moreover, as copies of these cables went to very few people in government, he was honoured to receive them. "Well," replied Gillies, "they're no use to me so I want you to stop bringing them to me."

There was quiet shock. Here was a man with privileged access to the overnight cables, to information — no matter how much of it useless — that was the lifeblood of power in the system. And he didn't want them. Mandarin heads were shaken.

Again, while he was with Clark at the Tokyo summit, the Prime Minister asked him to work on a speech for him. A senior bureaucrat, brow knitted, leaned over his shoulder as he was typing the draft. "But what will they think in Moscow?" asked the mandarin. "They won't read it in Moscow," replied Gillies. Indeed, reflected the civil servant, here was a man who just didn't take the whole thing seriously enough.

Would he like more staff? they asked him. Surely, with the immense pile of work that he *must* have, he needed a few more people to help. "God no," Gillies would say, "I'm not really that busy myself." And mandarin eyes would roll heavenwards.

Clark had two other key advisors, Bill Neville, his chief of staff and principal "fixer", a pudgy, hard-driving, former journalist, Liberal aide and lobbyist; and Lowell Murray, his top party pro, described as an "existential Celt" from Cape Breton, home of that political breed. Murray, a man given to taking retreats in faraway places, was supposed to see the political implications of policies. In this he clearly failed.

It was this trio that guided Clark in his thinking, and stiffened him in his resolution, on energy policy. They all appeared on the front cover of Canadian *Weekend* magazine on November 17, 1979, which featured a piece by columnist and author Richard Gwyn on "Ottawa's new rulers". There was Murray on the left, his short stature disguised by the broad field of the lens; Gillies to the rear, egg-headed, arms folded in a posture of quiet confidence; and Neville to the right, looking tough. Sitting between them, one bird-like hand quivering on his knee, the other hovering a thousandth of a millimetre above his shiny desk, trying so hard to look friendly and human, sat Joe Clark. The team may not have been terribly photogenic, but it was an open team. There had been no cosy shots of Pierre Trudeau sitting smiling between Michael Pitfield and Jim Coutts. But Clark's team had trouble within. And it had particular trouble in energy policy.

# 10
# Putting the
# Tories Straight

*"Everything had always come easily to Hnatyshyn, who was considered one of the party's rising stars. But nothing had prepared him for what he had to face at EMR. Hnatyshyn's task, according to a former colleague, was a little like trying to learn the lead in Hamlet after the curtain has gone up."*

The struggle between the bureaucracy and the Tory party pros centred around Jim Gillies and Ian Stewart. As a Galbraithian interventionist, a workaholic and someone who believed in taking the broadest view of any issue, it was obvious that Stewart's relationship with the Prime Minister's senior policy advisor would be a testy one. Gillies was a staunch advocate of *laissez-faire* and of achieving one policy objective at a time. Gillies regarded Stewart, with his fourteen-hour days and his six- or seven-day weeks, as hopelessly ill-disciplined. Stewart regarded Gillies as a dilettante.

Along with Stewart, Gillies saw Dr. Edmund Clark as his main "adversary" within EMR. What annoyed Gillies more than anything was that these two super-mandarins did not see their job as simply "doing what they were told". They insisted on pursuing the implications of energy policy through to its impact on every area of national life, from overall economic management to the outcome for federal-provincial revenue sharing. This, fulminated Gillies, was none of their business. If any bureaucrat should be concerned with these issues of broad economic management and revenue sharing, it should be those in the department of finance. But there was another reason Gillies didn't like their advice: they were telling the Tory party that it had a lousy energy policy.

Gillies tried very hard to have Stewart fired but Stewart had, in the first few weeks of Tory rule, established his value through his broad knowledge of key policies. To a government desperate to grasp the system as quickly as possible, a man like Stewart, who gave "the best briefing in Ottawa", was invaluable. Stewart impressed initially at a briefing he gave to cabinet on energy policy. His lucid and articulate presentation, backed up by the inevitable flip-charts, was considered a *tour de force*. Others did not fare so well. Bill Hood, the deputy minister of finance, by contrast, gave a stumbling and bumbling display. Gillies had him fired.

Stewart also went to Tokyo with Clark, where he gave briefings that impressed Clark enormously and, insofar as they helped the Prime Minister to perform creditably, further convinced him of Stewart's indispensability.

Energy policy also received a higher priority after the Tokyo summit, where OPEC activities had forced it high on the agenda. Along with the other summit nations, Clark had made specific commitments to control oil imports. He had agreed that Canada would reduce net oil imports by about 100,000 barrels a day by the fourth quarter of 1979, and that imports would be held at that level during 1980.

But there was another, more immediate, problem facing the Clark government in the summer of 1979; the possibility of oil shortages in the coming winter. The country had just squeaked through the preceding winter but now there were genuine fears that, at last, the reality of the energy crisis — in which the Canadian people stoutly refused to believe for the quite plausible reason that they had never personally experienced it — would be brought home.

Eastern refiners, particularly companies like Ultramar and Petrofina, were having severe problems because of the disruptions in supply from Iran and Iraq; companies like Gulf Canada were being financially hit because their imports were more expensive than other companies'; Western Canadian production was proving to be lower than expected; the oil sands plants of Syncrude and Great Canadian Oil Sands were performing badly, and pipeline capacity was limited. As a result, supply was tight and inventories low from coast to coast.

In the event, the country once again squeezed through the winter without crisis and the Tokyo summit commitments were soon to lose their relevance, due to a dramatic turnaround in the oil market to a position of oversupply. However, going into the autumn of 1979, these additional problems compounded what was already a very complex energy situation. The Tories had to negotiate a new pricing arrangement with Alberta and review the whole revenue-sharing issue against the background of OPEC turmoil; they had to struggle with their policy on disbanding Petro-Canada; and all the while they had to learn how to govern the country. The atmosphere inside the department of EMR was, during that six months, like a pressure cooker.

## The Minister Meets the Mandarins

The man who had to assume the energy hot seat was its new minister, Ray Hnatyshyn, a bright and personable lawyer from Saskatchewan. Everything had always come easily to Hnatyshyn who was considered one of the party's rising stars. But nothing had prepared him for what he had to face at EMR. Hnatyshyn's task, according to a former colleague, was a little like trying to learn the lead in Hamlet after the curtain has gone up. He was chosen energy minister primarily for geographical reasons. Harvie Andre, the Calgary MP, had perhaps been first choice but had been put out of the running by his role as a director in Abacus Cities, a Calgary development company that had gone

92

bankrupt amid accusations of mismanagement and worse. Clark, however, felt that he needed someone from the West. A native of Saskatchewan was preferable because Saskatchewan was an oil producer — and thus Alberta would feel that it had common cause with it. At the same time a Saskatchewan MP was likely to make the consuming provinces of the East less nervous than an Albertan.

But this was not the right time for a man with little background in economics and no background in energy to be taking on the most demanding portfolio in government. Hnatyshyn might have been bright but he never grasped the nettle. During the first few weeks in office a steady stream of mandarins — assistant deputy ministers and director generals — came through his office to give briefings on the various parts of the complex energy picture. And Ian Stewart was always there to expand a point, to add a note of clarification, to provide a summing up. But after just a few of these very demanding three-hour sessions, the word began to trickle down: the information didn't seem to be going *in*. The Minister just wasn't *applying* himself sufficiently hard. The Minister was going home at *five o'clock*. And every Friday lunchtime, the Minister would take the plane back to Saskatchewan, to be with his family. And sometimes he'd come back on Sunday, and sometimes he'd come back on Monday, and nobody could hold down this kind of cabinet post with a three-and-a-half day week.

Hnatyshyn was first and foremost a politician. He wanted to keep his constituents happy and stay popular. He always made sure that any calls that came to the Minister's office from Saskatchewan were answered right away. He worried about what people thought of him. But style was of little use when it came to coping with a three-hour briefing on the energy tax pyramid; charm held absolutely no place in comprehension of oil industry economics; popularity didn't help sort through myriad mandatory schemes to control the consumption of oil. So pretty soon the word spread from the briefings on the twenty-second floor of EMR that the Minister wasn't "coping with the paper", he wasn't cutting the mustard.

As executive assistant, Hnatyshyn had a bright, young ex-Imperial Oil employee, Harry Near, who had done work in Ontario for the successful Clark campaign in the 1979 election. Near had been suggested by Paul Curley, another Imperial employee who was Conservative party national director, and was joined in Hnatyshyn's office by yet another Imperial man, Pat Howe. This seeming mass transfer of employees from Imperial's head office on St. Clair Avenue in Toronto was inevitably brought up by the Opposition as proof that the party was kowtowing to Big Oil. The irony, however, was that the Big Oil position certainly didn't emerge from Hnatyshyn's office. It came from that of the Prime Minister.

The mandarins regarded the presence of the Imperial employees with more than a little apprehension. But Howe found himself with too many other things to do to get involved in policy, while Near had to attempt to vet the department's policy documents — drafts of which came wave after wave from the hum of Ph.D.s below — while at the same time organizing the Minister's busy schedule.

Near, the mandarins soon noticed, seemed to apply himself a good deal harder than Hnatyshyn. They made a little joke of it. They started calling Near "The Minister" and Hnatyshyn "the Minister's assistant". Behind their backs, of course.

But Hnatyshyn did learn. Unfortunately, what he learned, and learned to see the sense of, was the view of his senior advisors, and this was the view that he took to cabinet. Unfortunately for Hnatyshyn, that was not the view that Joe Clark and his senior policy advisors wanted to hear. Gillies believed that Hnatyshyn had been brainwashed by his senior mandarins, and his advice, like Stewart's, was, therefore, treated with suspicion. Tragically for the Conservatives, the source of the advice stopped it from being considered on its merits.

Joe Clark had returned from Tokyo realizing that energy had to become a higher priority. Asked for solutions, Ian Stewart wrote a memo which went to Clark under Hnatyshyn's signature on July 12. It pointed out the political importance of finding energy solutions, but also the particular problems added by inter-provincial and federal-provincial relations, and the public's lack of understanding on energy issues. It stressed the importance of oil pricing as a central pillar of policy and concluded, "Perhaps only an heroic approach in a defined and urgent time-frame has a reasonable chance of success."

Heroic seemed a rather strange word. Was it meant to appeal to Clark's self-image? Or did it reflect a rather romantic, bureaucratic view of the importance of their work? In the end, perhaps, the Clark government's energy policy could be considered heroic. However, it also proved suicidal.

It is important to remember that the central, and some would say fatal, element of Tory energy policy was the one over which they had least real control — higher prices.

As Clark's energy policy unfolded, and was finally announced in the December 11 budget, there was widespread misapprehension that the Conservatives were adopting radically different pricing policies to their Liberal predecessors. After all, were the Tories not — in their "final" offer to Alberta — suggesting increases of $4 a barrel for oil for 1980 and $4.50 thereafter vs. the Liberals' $2 a year? But the fact was — as the Liberals were only too clearly to show when they returned to power — that the determining factor of the Clark policies, the rapidly rising world price of oil, was one that the Liberals had not had to address before they fell from power.

However, although the Conservatives may have had little choice but to raise oil prices, what they did have control over — or at least were in a position to fight for — was what happened to the higher revenues from price increases. When the Tories came to power the last thing they imagined they would be doing was slugging it out toe-to-toe with Alberta or trying to cream off funds from oil companies. But that, according to the mandarins at EMR, was what they had to do.

The Tories believed that if they gave the oil industry the funds — in the form of higher prices — the oil industry would then come up with the goods. It was simple supply-and-demand. That Alberta would become richer through the higher royalty and tax revenues it would receive was not considered a problem either. Alberta, after all, was part of Canada.

The mandarins subscribed to neither of these views and set about educating their new masters in short order. Alberta, too, was to show the government that its thinking was naive. Clark's inner cabinet had asked the department for "a comprehensive review of the energy situation, including pricing and revenue-sharing options and an assessment of the role that prices could play in achieving the objectives of self-sufficiency." In response, the Tories received their first rude awakening to the complexities of Canadian energy, and to a bureaucracy with very firm ideas of its own.

A simple response to their question about prices and self-sufficiency was expected by the market-minded Tories. It was the response of classical economics: the price goes up, supply rises, demand drops. The Ph.D. economists manning the great black tower of Booth Street needed little reminding of the first law of economics, but their approach was quite different: prices go up and, under the prevailing tax and revenue scheme, the oil companies and the province of Alberta get richer; the consumer, and perhaps more important, the federal government, get poorer. Their concern with what the Tories considered the central issue, energy itself, was secondary.

## A Dressing Down from EMR

The EMR bureaucracy's thinking was outlined in a confidential discussion document, under the name of the Minister, issued to the cabinet on August 16. Entitled "Background to Energy Policy Choices", it pointed out that the government faced "critical choices" to which there were "no easy solutions". The paper started out by outlining the immediate problems facing the federal government: meeting the commitments on reduced oil consumption that Clark had made at Tokyo, and the prospects for oil shortages in the domestic market in the coming winter. Then it went on to summarize the renewed OPEC crisis and the differences between Canada's situation at the present and during the first crisis six years before.

But then the bureaucracy got down to the nitty-gritty — telling the Conservatives just what was wrong with their policies and with the system they had inherited.

They informed their political masters that self-sufficiency in oil by 1990 was out of the question. Higher prices as a result of OPEC might help keep the demand side of the equation down. As for supply, the bureaucrats didn't believe the industry could find more conventional oil, and they certainly weren't prepared to risk giving the oil companies more money to find out if they could.

The oil companies, said the bureaucrats, were far too rich already, as were the producing provinces, in particular Alberta.

The whole fiscal energy scheme, they said, was skewed. The federal government was pulling in only 10% of petroleum revenues while the producing provinces and the oil companies were more or less splitting the remainder. This was swelling Alberta's Heritage Fund — a particularly sore point with the federal bureaucracy — to the point where by 1985 it would be worth $25 billion and have revenues at two-thirds the level of the Canada Pension Plan, revenues, moreover, that would be growing much faster than those of the CPP.

All that excess cash in the coffers of big oil was merely serving to drive up payments for land — thus making Alberta even richer — inflate other costs too, and allow the companies to diversify.

The analysis painted a picture of a pernicious and predatory oil industry muscling out smaller Canadian companies while spreading its tentacles outside the oil business through diversification.

In particular, the bureaucrats seemed to be obsessed by Imperial Oil and Shell Canada. As an example of Imperial's tendency to throw its weight around, the study quoted the company's "acquisition", through its subsidiary, Esso Resources, of Canadian Hunter. In fact, the statistics were all wrong and the implications quite unfounded.

Esso Resources had not acquired Canadian Hunter. It was to earn the right to just 12½% in Canadian Hunter's properties at Elmworth, where it had made a major gas find, and 17½% of the company's other properties in return for carrying out $150 million-worth of exploration work, with an option to carry out another $29 million-worth at a later date. Virtually the whole oil industry considered Canadian Hunter to have made a very smart deal and Imperial a dumb one. But for the bureaucrats this was yet another example of small Canadian companies being pushed aside by the multinationals.*

Again, on imports, the majors got it in the neck: "Perhaps inadvertently, a system has been established which provides easy access to reasonably-priced domestic oil for strong, integrated companies such as Shell and Imperial and leaves weaker companies such as Golden Eagle totally exposed to the international market."

The reason that Golden Eagle was "exposed" was because it had never explored for or discovered any domestic oil. Shell and Imperial had, and the source of their relative strength was being treated as an almost reprehensible activity.

Big oil was also accused of holding up tar sands development. "In some cases," said the report, "both supply and conservation efforts are hindered by

---

* An additional irony was that, once the Liberals returned, and, aided by a willing bureaucracy, formulated its National Energy Program, John Masters, the president of Canadian Hunter, was one of its most vociferous critics, engaging in a highly personalized slanging match with federal Energy Minister Marc Lalonde.

technical, psychological and institutional constraints. Some of the problems are of governments' making; others arise due to hesitation on the part of the private sector. One example of the latter may be the pace of oil sands development. Here, decisions by two companies — Imperial and Shell — are the determining factors. Both companies are aware of the technical challenges, and wish to learn from the experience of Syncrude and GCOS; both companies are also cognizant of the relationship between rate of investment and the working of the tax system. For example, the effective cost of investment in an oil sands plant rises substantially if the investor cannot write-off the investment immediately because it is making other investments that use up the tax shelter."

Shell and Imperial, in other words, were portrayed as virtually holding the country to ransom because they were acting in a normal commercial fashion.

The bottom line of all this thinking was soon to be revealed. EMR had consulted with both the provinces and representatives of the industry on energy policy proposals, although obviously more willingly with the former than the latter. All the provinces had agreed, they claimed, as far as the producing companies were concerned, that "no further incentive in the form of prices or taxes appeared justified. They agreed that the pace of supply development could only be further accelerated by direct government actions, since the scope for indirect actions, including work requirement regulations, was virtually exhausted." The statement didn't mention Petro-Canada, but it really didn't have to. It was telling the government that its policy on disbanding the national oil company was quite wrong. This wasn't the time to be getting out of direct involvement in the oil industry. It was the time to be getting in much deeper.

One last dig at the major oil companies was to be made before the paper moved onto its policy considerations. "All provinces — and the producing provinces in particular — stressed the country's dependence on the major oil companies and the technology they possess, and said that unless these companies were satisfied with the conditions for investment in Canada, they would not 'deliver the goods'." Once again, the oil companies' inevitable tendency to either act or not act on a commercial basis was portrayed as economic blackmail.

The paper then moved onto its policy considerations, the first two of which effectively squashed two of the three legs of the Tories' energy tripod. The first conclusion was that oil self-sufficiency by 1990 would be difficult and expensive "barring happy surprises". The second was that, given "considerable monopolization of supply options", the only way to speed up developments was through direct involvement or "chosen instruments", or in other words, Petro-Canada.

Perhaps the most bizarre aspect of the analysis was that it was effectively telling a "free-enterprise" government that the previous Liberal government had been too soft on the big oil companies. The bureaucrats were suggesting that the Tories shift to the left!

The paper delivered two final slaps to the Conservatives' collective face. First it said that they shouldn't even be considering self-sufficiency. That wasn't what was important: "The key question . . . ," the paper lectured, "is not whether Canada can achieve oil sufficiency, but whether polices can be devised that support that important objective while improving, rather than worsening, the other problems associated with energy."

The second slap was that energy policy should not, and could not, be looked at in isolation. "The clear message from the provinces, however (whose view we share) is that we cannot take an issue like oil prices for example, and decide it in isolation. Instead, price decisions should come only as part of a fresh look at the system, including the distribution of benefits and costs."

The Tories had asked for a discussion paper and what they had received was a dressing down. But the mandarins also had a very pressing specific policy on which to put the Tories straight: Petro-Canada.

# 11
# Swimming against the PetroCan Tide

*"And now they were in power. No thoughts of backtracking. The time had come to deliver the goods. They moved quickly. Even before they had requested EMR and other departments to review the "immediate privatization of Petro-Canada", Ray Hnatyshyn, in one of his first acts as Energy Minister, sent a letter dated June 15 to Bill Hopper instructing him to reverse immediately steps to absorb Pacific Petroleums."*

For a suitable historical precedent to the Conservatives' commitment to dismantle Petro-Canada, we might have to go all the way back to King Canute — the English monarch who demonstrated the limits of regal power by sitting at the seashore and commanding the tide not to come in. Joe Clark was attempting to set an ill-thought-through ideological stance against a global wave of government intervention in response to OPEC-induced uncertainties. The consequences were more than wet feet.

Petro-Canada provided yet another painful lesson for the Tory government. It is a rash party — particularly one in a minority government — which allows either ideology or election promises to stand in the way of political expediency. It is an even rasher one that allows itself to appear to be opposing the sweep of history.

Petro-Canada was one of the major shoals on which the Tory government foundered. And yet, when it had all started, the policy had seemed so logical. The Tories were, after all, the party advocating less, and more effective, government. PetroCan had somehow become the focus of their plans to Get Government Off the Backs of the People — always a ringing phrase. It had become the centre-piece of their promise to "privatize" Crown corporations. The word "privatize" had most recently been used by the Liberals, but the Tories had adopted it because it had just *sounded* so right.

But the policy was to misfire disastrously. The debate about PetroCan was meant to take place within the context of a fight against bloated governments and overextended bureaucracies. Instead, the electorate saw it as an attempt to disband the nation's security blanket against the cold winds of international energy uncertainty.

At a time when the Ayatollah's baleful stare was appearing almost every night on the television news, and the withdrawal of Iranian supplies was causing the world spot price of oil to soar, Joe Clark seemed eager to hand the nation back into the clutches of big, foreign-controlled oil.

The emergence of OPEC as a powerful force in 1973 had raised searching questions about the control of oil and the role of the major oil companies. At first sight it appeared that the OPEC nations had won and the oil companies had lost. But it soon became apparent that the oil companies had not lost as a result of the OPEC crisis — in fact, their profits soared as never before. Now that the producing countries of the Persian Gulf and Africa and South America and the Far East held the upper hand, it seemed that the oil companies had no difficulty in identifying themselves — very profitably — with their interests. The only clear loser, it seemed, was the petroleum consumer.

There had of course been suspicion about the roles of the Seven Sisters — the world's largest oil companies: Exxon, Shell, Texaco, Mobil, British Petroleum, Standard of California and Gulf — during the first crisis. But when the second crisis emerged at the beginning of 1979, the powerlessness — or, implicitly much worse, lack of desire — of the oil majors to moderate the situation led to an unprecedented surge of demands all over the globe for governments to "do something".

Anthony Sampson, author of the classic study *The Seven Sisters*, summed up the wave of feeling in an article in *New York* magazine in July of 1979:

"All the companies have been convinced that they must be responsible for the future of energy.

"But they cannot be. It would be absurd to blame the companies for engineering the current crisis. But they played a large role in the evasion of responsibility that preceded it. And they are in no position to rescue the world from the present dangerous scramble.

"*Only governments can ensure that the West does not become the victim of this kind of energy casino.* For even though a bigger price may eventually encourage greater energy investment and reduce oil consumption, the interim will be far too dangerous to be left to the companies. The retreat from the chaos of Rotterdam or Geneva will call for far stricter government control and far more effective international agreement. And if the voters cannot face up to that challenge, when it is so urgently presented, then they deserve what they get."

In Canada, the challenge of greater government control was one that the citizens seemed quite prepared to face. Attachment to pragmatism rather than ideology had always been a prominent feature of the Canadian people as a whole. With no prevailing myths of class oppression or social revolution, Canadians liked, above all, simply what worked. When things didn't work, they expected the government to step in and do something about it. The Canadian electorate read disquieting news stories of war and oil embargoes in the Middle East; they looked at the gas line-ups in the U.S.; they saw what appeared to be "huge" oil company profits; and they worried about the possibility of freezing in the dark. In energy, it seemed, things just weren't working, so the natural demand was to seek action from the government. In response, the government of Pierre Trudeau had come up with Petro-Canada. The national oil company was not an interventionist whim; it was a government response to the demands of the electorate. Amazingly, the Tories never analyzed the situation in this way. In particular, they never realized the powerful reinforcing effect that the second OPEC crisis in 1979 would have on the electorate's desire for an energy security blanket. The opinion polls, however, soon began to tell them the story.

The 1979 July Gallup poll showed that 48% of Canadians were opposed to selling Petro-Canada shares while only 22% supported it. Perhaps even more significant, a poll taken in the heart of oil country by the *Calgary Herald* in mid-August showed that although 80% of the survey favoured selling shares, 81% also favoured retention of the Crown corporation.

The Conservatives had never been as closely wedded to the opinion polls as their Liberal foes. Indeed, there existed a current of thought within the party that such instruments bordered on the immoral. The feeling was most clearly expounded by Dalton Camp, one of the party's more cerebral, and most literate, spokesmen, who wrote that public opinion was a "noxious phrase" and he spoke for a large body within the party. Polls not only denied the logic of strong personal initiative in politics, they placed the system in the hands of men like Jim Coutts, Trudeau's personal secretary and the most avid of poll-followers, who, many believed, had turned his master into a political chameleon, ever-forced to blend with the shifting numbers of electoral analysis.

Polls for Camp meant that any attempt at paternalism — albeit that such an approach was inevitably elitist — was doomed. Henceforth you could not go where the electorate, as verified by the pollsters, had no intention of following. Polling was the ultimate instrument of populist demagoguery. You whipped up the people by throwing their own misconceptions back at them.

Camp articulated what was equally deeply felt throughout the party, particularly by elitists like Jim Gillies. Gillies was a throwback as far as the political system was concerned. He still held faith in the idea that it is enough for men of good will to decide what is right and then press through with it regardless. This feeling pervaded Clark's immediate advisors. Bowing to the polls was seen as an indication of a lack of resolve, an absence of moral fibre.

Perhaps the greatest irony, however, was that, in Allan Gregg, the Tories had at their disposal one of the country's smartest political pollsters. Gregg, in his early thirties, given to wearing long hair, jeans and an earring, might not obviously fit the Conservative party's image, but he provided Clark with analyses that offered the purest insight. Indeed, in retrospect, Gregg could only be compared with Cassandra, the daughter of the King of Troy who was gifted with foresight but doomed never to be believed.

Gregg went straight to the heart of the Tories' problems with PetroCan. In the face of the OPEC crisis, said Gregg: "Our action . . . is being presented through the opposition and the media as fueling the uncertainties of the future. In other words, in the face of an impending 'energy crisis' and excessive profits by multinational companies, we are seen to be dismantling the only *Canadian* entity standing between the people and the problem. We must therefore, when explaining these changes to Petro-Canada, present something more than a knee-jerk commitment to free enterprise."

The words, however, seemed to fall on deaf ears. By now the whole issue had become disastrously entangled with pullbacks from other 1979 election promises, in particular the move of the Canadian embassy to Jerusalem and the commitment to a stimulative budget. Moreover, it was making Gillies mad that the mandarin machine wasn't asking "how high?" when he said jump. The more trouble Clark's closest advisors had in getting the bureaucratic system moving, the more determined they became to cut PetroCan down to size, in fact, to cut it down to no-size at all. The men at the policy centre of the government, Joe Clark and Jim Gillies, had both spoken in the great Petro-Canada debate in 1975, as had Harvie Andre, who now had considerable input into Tory energy policy. When Jim Gillies had spoken, it had been the very voice of the Free Market, the embodiment of *laissez faire*. "The best way to assure a high standard of living," he had said, "is not for the government to move directly into the production and distribution of goods and services. The evidence is all too clear that in those areas where the government moves in directly, the efficiency of operation is something less than maximum." This understatement caused smiles and knowing nods on the Tory side of the House; the sentiments drew long applause.

The young back-bencher, Joe Clark, as a good Albertan, also spoke against the bill, although his theme was accusatory. "If the Government sees something moving in the country," he said, "it wants to get into the act, not as a mediator, not as a regulator or in the traditional way that the federal government and governments as a whole have operated, but as a controller. It wants power. It is prepared to extend its influence and its activities by intruding upon the jurisdiction of the provinces, by moving into the private sector whatever the consequences. It is preoccupied with extending its own power and influence whatever the cost. That is the real reason why we have this piece of legislation before us tonight." Again, the picture of creeping socialism and power mania drew angry agreement and long applause from the Conservatives present.

## Zap, You're Frozen!

And now they were in power. No thoughts of backtracking. The time had come to deliver the goods. They moved quickly. Even before they had requested EMR and other departments to review the "immediate privatization of Petro-Canada", Ray Hnatyshyn, in one of his first acts as Energy Minister, sent a letter dated June 15 to Bill Hopper instructing him to reverse immediately steps to absorb Pacific Petroleums. The Tories knew that part of the rationale for that acquisition had been PetroCan's desire to become so big that it would be virtually impossible to disband. Well, thought the new cabinet, if that was the plan, we have to stop it as soon as possible. Earlier that same week, PetroCan

102

had informed Pacific Petroleums' creditors that it had applied, under the Canada Business Corporations Act, to dissolve Pacific and fold it financially into Petro-Canada Exploration, its wholly-owned operating subsidiary. The transfer was to be completed on June 30. To stop the dissolution seemed like a symbolic act to the Tories. In imperious tones, the letter to Hopper explained that the "new Government of Canada will want to review the future role of Petro-Canada and, accordingly, until this review is completed, the corporation should refrain from altering its current corporate and asset position."

It was as if the Tories were borrowing a phrase from their arch foe, the man whose political career they had just ended. "Zap," they were saying to PetroCan. "You're frozen." Unfortunately for the Tories, both Petro-Canada and Pierre Elliott Trudeau showed remarkable recuperative, even reincarnative, powers.

But at the time, the letter added further depression to the gloom that had already settled over "Red Square" after the May 22 election. Now the phones stopped ringing as the rest of the industry saw no point in dealing with a doomed company. At the Thursday bi-weekly executive committee meeting after the leak of the Hnatyshyn letter, Donald Harvie, vice-chairman of the board and son of the great Calgary millionaire and philanthropist, Eric Harvie, got up and attempted to give a rallying speech, saying how much the board was behind the management team. But Harvie is not a good speaker, and his gesture fell flat, increasing the gloom if anything.

In the immediate aftermath of the victory, the public servants on the company's board most closely associated with the Liberals, men like Bill Hood, deputy minister of finance, Tommy Shoyama, former deputy minister of finance, and Ian Stewart were concerned with their own necks. That their necks were in danger was clearly shown by the subsequent experience of Bill Hood, whom Gillies had successfully axed in favour of Grant Reuber.

Any paranoia Ian Stewart might have had was heightened by the fact that he read about Hnatyshyn's letter to Hopper on Pacific in the *Globe & Mail*, where it had been leaked to energy reporter Jeff Carruthers. Stewart was the deputy minister at EMR and they hadn't even *told* him about the letter.

But if there was confusion among the board members, there was something much worse in the executive suite, where an internal split appeared. Of the senior officers, the Liberal appointees, Bell and Hopper, the "Ottawa men", would obviously be the first to go. They weren't just public servants. They had had a hand in virtually the whole Liberal energy program throughout the 1970s. But for the remainder of the senior management, all of whom came from the private sector, privatization held no real horrors. In fact, some of them positively welcomed the idea. That was inevitably to be the cause of considerable friction. In the end, Hopper and Bell survived, and it was some of the corporate suite's staunchest "free-enterprisers" who got the chop.

Hopper and Bell were regarded as Liberal sympathizers, and the organization was obviously "politicized" to a significant degree before the Tories came along. In the weeks before the election, Petro-Canada had been conspicuously involved in two exploration successes — one at Sable Island off the coast of Nova Scotia and one at Whitefish in the Arctic Islands — which were declared to be of great significance. Brought to you by the Liberal party. The announcements, one made by Pierre Trudeau, looked a little obvious, even to the least cynical of observers. Dalton Camp, in *Points of Departure*, merely noted of the final weeks of the campaign: "Trudeau has suddenly begun to campaign. . . . Furthermore, Petro-Canada had been a party to a gas find in the high Arctic, a timely happenstance suggesting divine intervention." Or that of Jim Coutts. However, with the election of the Tories, the organization became much more politicized. Those who believed that Petro-Canada had to survive in its present form to be effective now began in subtle ways to direct it against the external threat to its existence, Joe Clark. Journalists were courted as they had not been before and fed stories embarrassing to the Clark government and the rest of the industry.

But a picture of Petro-Canada as the Liberals' most worthwhile creation, it seemed, might not be enough to save them, and on May 23, the day after the federal election, an air of foreboding fell over PetroCan's Calgary headquarters. Here they were, a huge and growing agglomeration of departments and divisions, seemingly like any other company. They were pumping oil and gas all over Alberta; they had exploration crews throughout Canada; they had chains of gas stations and a balance sheet full of solid production and processing facilities. But where they were not like other companies was that they were joined together by unsubstantial stuff, political will. Or at least, on that morning in May it seemed dangerously insubstantial.

In the event, however, PetroCan was to show that political will can be the strongest of adhesives, as long as it is mixed with its vital additive, public support. Political will without that essential ingredient, as Joe Clark discovered to his cost, can, in the absence of a parliamentary majority, be the most self-destructive of indulgences.

# 12
# Dismantle Petro-Canada?
# You Can't Get There
# from Here

*"They had asked for a review of privatization, and what they had got was a series of options which ignored total privatization completely and merely recommended a sale of unnecessary assets."*

Of all the Tory policies that the bureaucracy opposed — and there were many — perhaps the dismantling of Petro-Canada was the least popular. Petro-Canada was the brainchild of the senior mandarins. It was the thinking man's big oil company; at once a workhorse of the people and a window on a much mistrusted industry. Joe Clark's threat to disband it could only have been hatched in the innocence of pure ideology, and the mandarins — once sure that their opinions weren't going to lose them their jobs — lost no time in persuading the Clark government of the error of its policy ways.

On June 21, Clark's inner cabinet asked EMR — in consultation with the departments of Justice and Finance, and also the Treasury Board and the Privy Council Office — to undertake "an extensive and detailed review" into the immediate privatization of Petro-Canada. What the cabinet got two months later was two documents that amounted less to a program for achieving the stated government policy than a masterly assembly of legal, financial and political arguments to establish that the government's chosen course of action could not possibly be followed. Dismantle Petro-Canada? You can't get there from here, they said.

The principal author of the document was David Scrim, the young mandarin who had spent a couple of years with PetroCan. Scrim firmly believed in the necessity for a national oil company, but also had some beliefs of his own about PetroCan, including the conviction that a number of the assets it had acquired from Pacific just weren't necessary for it to fulfill its mandate and that its financial controls were too loose. Hopper and Bell waited with trepidation. Did Scrim want any help? No, he replied. Could they oblige him with any facts or data? Maybe, he said. And then he sat down to write.

An examination of the resultant documents, in particular the secret reference discussion paper "Privatization of Petro-Canada", provides fascinating insight into the skills of bureaucracy when it wants to guide policy. In fact, the

Petro-Canada policy was doomed for political reasons, but while the Gallup polls were showing the Tories the errors of their policy in the public arena, EMR was quietly, but just as devastatingly, pointing out its shortcomings in private.

For a start, the document acknowledged that due to the issue's high political profile, "It would appear that some action is necessary in response to the party's election promise. However," it continued, "it is also of importance that the more fundamental priority of energy self-sufficiency not be obscured." The Tories, the document implied, had to get their priorities straight and cleverly, but quite spuriously, it linked Petro-Canada with self-sufficiency.

The policy lecture began by pointing out that the Clark approach to Petro-Canada was out of step with the entire world. "The role of state corporations," it said, "has become an almost universal element of energy management both to combat the concentration of power in the hands of a relatively few multi-nationals as well as to provide an alternative to other more direct government stimulative action and to promote a better understanding of energy operations."

Moreover, disbanding PetroCan would damage the government's own energy policies. It could attempt to pursue these policies through additional regulatory or tax changes, but — as all the other weighty policy documents that had landed on the cabinet's desk indicated — there were limits to the use of these indirect measures.

PetroCan had done sterling work in the frontiers and, if the government wanted to accelerate heavy oil and tar sands development — the only way to reach self-sufficiency by 1990 — then it could only do so through an instrument such as PetroCan. As for foreign ownership, another of the government's priorities, disposition of PetroCan's assets would probably accentuate the trend to foreign control. Make a condition of sale that it could only be sold to Canadians? The document had an answer for that too. It said that such a provision would mean that the government would receive less from any sale because of the restricted market.

Whether they liked it or not, said the document, the era of greater government involvement in energy had arrived. The government needed a "window on the industry", but it also needed an active instrument for investments such as Sable Island and Panarctic Investments, something that the proposed Energy Bank just couldn't provide.

The financial considerations, too, were filled with pitfalls. The government might realize between $2 billion and $3 billion from an asset sale, but the taxpaying corporations who would most likely buy the assets would then be able to make tax deductions to offset the purchase. The government would be gaining cash from the sale but losing it in tax revenue.

And if there was no PetroCan, who would do all that costly work in the frontiers? Further incentives could be given, but they too represented a cost to government "with no control and without the benefits of future profits to compensate the initial risk undertaken".

As for the provinces, Alberta might never have been politically supportive, and British Columbia had its eyes on PetroCan's holdings in Westcoast Transmission for its *own* provincial resource company, British Columbia Resources Investment Corporation. However, all the other provinces tended to favour PetroCan. The industry too, although its initial reaction was hostile, now "actually supports Petro-Canada on the grounds that they are an attractive partner for financing purposes and on the basis that if government is to be actively involved they prefer dealing with a corporate rather than a bureaucratic entity."

And then, of course, there was public support for Petro-Canada, perhaps the most important point of all, at least politically. "The general public tends to have a distrust of large multinational enterprises and a concern over the wealth distribution accruing to producing provinces. As a result it is almost certain that the concept of a government energy corporation has the general support of most Canadians. A recent Gallup poll indicated that Canadians were in favour of Petro-Canada being maintained by more than a two to one majority."

The document then moved onto an examination — or rather dissection and logical destruction — of the privatization alternatives. First came privatization by sale of assets. This would take place in a "fire sale atmosphere" where there would be "a dilution of worth caused by the disintegration of operations and the probable loss of personnel." There would be a "substantial reduction in the stimulative role of direct government investment." Moreover, the cash used to take over PetroCan's assets would be "diverted from the search for and development of new resources." (This argument was, of course, to be brushed aside after the announcement of the National Energy Program fourteen months later when opponents of the NEP pointed out that a buy-out of foreign companies in Canada also diverted cash from exploration and development.)

The document acknowledged that state-to-state trading could be carried out by some other government organization, although the author cast a sly dig at his own caste in saying: "It will be important, however, that these negotiations be carried out by persons with operating experience and not by diplomats or bureaucrats."

PetroCan's "window" too would be difficult to replace. "Specifically," it said, "Petro-Canada's management and operating personnel have, on a number of occasions, provided timely and important advice on energy policy issues."

An asset sale, in brief, was, in the eyes of David Scrim and EMR, not a terribly good idea.

What then of a sale of shares? This path, said the document, was blocked by a complex barrier of legal and financial problems. "It is clear that the pursuit of such an option would require a highly technical review of the existing corporate entities as well as the consultative assistance of financial intermediaries." Complexity, of course, is usually meat and drink to the bureaucracy, but in the case of PetroCan, a positive Gordian Knot of difficulty was portrayed. And of course there were myriad other difficulties. It would be the biggest underwriting the Canadian financial community had ever attempted; the market would also place a high discount on the shares. Then, of course, there were the policy implications; the possibility of foreign ownership increasing; the possibility of the "goals of the new owners" not matching the programs being pursued by the company. Indeed, a widely-held company could prove a rudderless ship. One thing for sure, Petro-Canada could no longer be a policy instrument, even if the government maintained a minority stake.

What about maintaining the company but cutting off its special status? Well, PetroCan itself wouldn't have minded losing the privilege enabling it to "back-into" federal leases, so that was possible. However, any attempts to cut off PetroCan's call on the Consolidated Revenue Fund or to change its status as an agent of Her Majesty could have dire financial consequences. It was these features that had allowed PetroCan to borrow so easily on capital markets. Withdraw them and clauses in creditors' contracts stipulated that debts had immediately to be repaid. This could mean that the government would have to find $1.7 billion. "This repayment requirement," Scrim said darkly, "may have serious financial implications for the government and/or the corporation."

The final alternative discussed was that of partial privatization. "Specifically, the government could order the sale of such items as Petro-Canada's portfolio investment in Westcoast Transmission, a portion of its Syncrude interests and other selected parts of its operations." This alternative obviously held some appeal for the document's author. It suggested selling off the pipelines, foreign producing properties and refining and marketing outlets acquired as part of the purchase of Pacific. "None of these assets appear to have an essential function in terms of assisting Petro-Canada to fulfill its policy mandate."

"From an energy policy point of view," it said, "it would be desirable to make a decision now in favour of privatizing Petro-Canada by selling off those assets which should be in the private sector." The clear implication, of course, was that the rump of PetroCan was to be left behind, and not privatized at all. This point was made explicitly a little later. "There seems no reason to question our party's commitment to privatize Petro-Canada. What this means specifically in terms of assets which go into the private sector and those which should be retained in some public body for strategic reasons is still a question." That a considerable body of PetroCan's assets should be maintained in a public body — be it Petro-Canada or Petro-Canada by another name — was not considered a question. The inquiry had been subtly shifted so that by the time it came down to its final recommendations, the idea of a complete sale of assets or sell-off of shares had been totally rejected.

There were, said the cabinet document, three options. The first option recommended that the Minister appoint a board of trustees to evaluate the privatization alternatives and the assets of PetroCan "to recommend the process for disposing of those assets whose operations would be more effectively carried out in the private sector consistent with our energy objectives." It also recommended that "the Board would consider the role Petro-Canada might have in Canada's future energy policy, and in the government's overall approach to achieving oil self-sufficiency." The Minister would then "recommend to Ministers what course of action he advises as to the future role of Petro-Canada."

The question of its existence was taken for granted. The issue was merely to be that of its "role".

The second option was identical to the first, except that the board would be required to present its findings by September 15, whereupon the ministers would make their decision and then send it back to the board for detailed recommendations on the process of privatization which was accepted.

The third option was that ministers "agree in principle to the privatization of those assets of Petro-Canada whose operations would be more effectively carried out in the private sector consistent with our energy objectives *leaving Petro-Canada with sufficient assets to carry out its appropriate role in energy policy and provide it with sufficient cash flow to carry out that role except in the case of major development projects.*" [my italics]

Under this third option, a board would be appointed to determine the PetroCan assets "whose placement in the private sector would better meet our energy needs." The board would also determine how much of the proceeds would go to Petro-Canada and how much to the Consolidated Revenue Fund. Finally, it recommended that Petro-Canada be forced to submit a five-year forecast of capital requirements to the government.

The document's Parthian shot was that the government had made a mistake in stopping the financial integration of Pacific Petroleums into Petro-Canada, since it had already been operationally integrated. It also pointed out that integration would not influence any of the alternatives set forth and might ultimately enhance the financial value of the corporation.

When Clark's closest advisors saw these recommendations they were furious. They had asked for a review of privatization, and what they had received was a series of options which ignored total privatization completely and merely recommended a sale of unnecessary assets. The issue of whether Petro-Canada should survive was not even addressed.

The Scrim document's terms of reference for the board of trustees — which would henceforth become a Task Force — caused intense and heated debate at the cabinet's policy get-together in Jasper at the end of August. Ironically, the polls may now have caused views on privatization to harden within Clark's immediate advisory group, for a poll by Gregg in August indicated that the people thought that the Conservatives were not keeping their promises. In Lowell Murray's analysis, keeping the election promise on Petro-Canada was absolutely imperative, and he delivered a rousing speech in Jasper to that effect. But there was now considerable opposition within the cabinet to the policy, which was clearly a political liability. Hnatyshyn had, by now, been totally converted by the mandarins. John Crosbie and Flora MacDonald — having recently been exposed to the full blast of global energy concerns at a meeting of the Organization for Cooperation and Development in Paris — believed that PetroCan was necessary, while others like Roch LaSalle, Walter Baker and John Fraser thought the poll's message about PetroCan's popularity more important than Murray's call to keep the faith.

Ian Stewart — whose encyclopaedic knowledge Joe Clark liked to have on tap — was present at Jasper and was asked to frame the Task Force's terms of reference in a way that would reflect government policy more than Scrim's. However, Clark and his trio of advisors still considered that these terms were framed so as to leave Petro-Canada intact. So in the end, it was decided that the Task Force would be charged with "advising as to the procedures for transferring Petro-Canada to private ownership, which of the existing assets of Petro-Canada might most beneficially be returned to the private sector, as well as means of broadening Canadian participation and ownership in the petroleum industry." And they wanted the job done quickly. There was no doubt that Scrim's analysis that the Task Force was seen by most observers as a way of buying time was correct. But now Clark wanted to move ahead quickly. The Task Force was to report by the middle of October. The most pressing problem, however, was deciding who was to be on it.

## Task Force in a Tangle

"Petro-Canada should have a large picture of Joe Clark in their boardroom," says one senior mandarin, chuckling at the delicious irony of the situation. "Without him, they might have ended up as just another, medium-sized company."

The irony is indeed great, for Joe Clark's attack on Petro-Canada served merely to accentuate the public's regard for it. This, in turn, confirmed to the subsequent Liberal government that the time was ripe for a revolutionary new policy of interventionism and discrimination in the energy field, the National Energy Program. Petro-Canada was, in turn, to become that policy's first great beneficiary.

But if there is to be a large portrait of Joe Clark, there should also be miniatures of the members of the Conservatives' Petro-Canada Task Force, for it was that unfortunate group that — as it sought to fulfill a difficult mandate — raised the public outcry that eventually ensured Petro-Canada's survival, even if the Tories had not fallen from power.

Who were these unfortunate men?

The Task Force's chairman, Donald McDougall, more or less fell into the job as he simultaneously fell out of the presidency of Labatt's Breweries after a personality conflict with John Labatt's chief executive Peter Widdrington. McDougall knew virtually nothing about oil but he was a senior corporate executive, a good party man and a friend of Lowell Murray, so he seemed to fit the bill.

McDougall was joined by three other appointees. Ross Sykes was a senior chartered accountant from Halifax and devoted party worker over the years. Roland Giroux was the Quebec representative. Powerfully connected in Ottawa and throughout the business community — he was a director of Power Corp., Consolidated Bathurst and the Bank of Montreal — Giroux was also known as a "great mind".

Syd Kahanoff, the final member of the panel, was an oilman, in fact an oilman's oilman, the man who had built Voyager Petroleums in Calgary from nothing to a company sold in 1978 for $200 million (from which Kahanoff collected $55 million). Kahanoff was a legend in a hard-working industry, and was famed for starting work at breakfast meetings at 6:30 A.M. His connections throughout the oil patch and within Alberta were enormous, and his politics were, not surprisingly perhaps, well to the right.

In addition to the members, financial teams from three investment houses — Dominion Securities, Burns Fry and McLeod, Young, Weir — were hired to look at the financial complexities of share issues or asset sales. Other key figures were Paul Little, a business executive and party worker who was the group's executive director, and Ralph Hedlin, a well-known Toronto-based oil consultant, who did most of the report's writing.

The group had a big job to do and a ridiculously small amount of time — five weeks — to do it. They had to establish that the Conservatives' privatization of Petro-Canada could be carried out. Nevertheless, the group started with a feeling of euphoria. McDougall even talked about getting the report out in less time than they were given. They set up twin "shops", one in the offices of EMR in Ottawa, and the other within Red Square in Calgary, where — whether they were called trustees or any other name — they were greeted with all the joy that receivers would attract at any company.

That is not, of course, to say that they ever met with any discourtesy. Some of the executives seemed to go right along with them, particularly those who had been recruited from outside industry. Despite the fact that they had freely joined Petro-Canada, they just couldn't get used to the idea that anything that was "non-commercial" could immediately be justified as "in the national interest". It meant that you could do *anything*. They were uncomfortable with a world where the touchstone of return on investment — despite the lip service paid to it — ultimately meant nothing. Meanwhile, Bill Hopper just bent over backwards to help the Task Force, particularly when it appeared that, whatever else privatization meant, it might just mean that *he* kept his well-paid and exciting job. Yes, Bill Hopper quite firmly committed himself to give them all the help they wanted.

But of course, that didn't meant that the frostiness, or the difference of perspective between the Task Force, the mandarins, and the public servants on the PetroCan board, didn't show through. In the first week, the members met in Ottawa with some of the senior mandarins, including Ian Stewart, Ed Clark, and David Scrim. Everything was very polite but the bureaucrats just couldn't avoid letting their views on the structural problems of the oil industry come through.

Afterwards, Syd Kahanoff, who knew more than a little about the impact of higher petroleum prices on exploration and production — it had been the huge gas price increases of the 1970s that had made him, and his company, such an enormous success — said, "These guys just don't believe in elasticity of supply." But it was not so much elasticity of supply that the mandarins didn't believe in, but the fact that to test it you had to raise prices and give more money to the oil companies, most of whom were foreign-owned. This distinction in nationality meant little or nothing to Kahanoff, who had in the formative years of his company trekked east for good Canadian money but had been turned down by the financiers of Toronto. In desperation, he had had to go to New York, where he, like so many Albertans, had found his seed capital. In Kahanoff's eyes, if there had been no American investment, there would have been hardly any Canadian oil industry. He didn't go along with the mandarins' thinking at all.

In the Task Force's first week, Joel Bell led a presentation on Petro-Canada and its achievements. It was a *tour de force*, comparable perhaps to Ian Stewart's presentation to cabinet on energy policy. Almost everyone was enormously impressed, but old Syd Kahanoff just looked at Petro-Canada's frontier acreage and he almost drooled. "Just give me that acreage and a telephone," he said afterwards, "and I'll get it drilled."

And then there was the PetroCan board. In the second week of the Task Force's existence, Don McDougall and Paul Little attended a PetroCan board meeting in Ottawa, where the atmosphere, if it could not afford to be hostile was certainly chilly. Tommy Shoyama, who had given long and loyal service to the Liberal government as one of the first circle of the bureaucracy, just couldn't contain himself. He didn't say it was dumb to privatize Petro-Canada in so many words, but he just repeatedly questioned the whole concept. And McDougall could just say, well, that's not our mandate, we're not here to see *whether* we should do it; we're here to see *how* we should do it. And Senator John Aird and Don Harvie, two of the outside directors, smoothed things over and kept the temperature down, but the public servants were thinking, well this whole concept just hasn't been *thought through* properly. These guys just don't know what they're doing.

Meetings like this were uncomfortable, but the Task Force felt that it had to touch *all* the bases. Paul Little, the executive director, had an uneasy day all alone with Saskatchewan's petroleum mandarins, but for the most part, those with whom the Task Force felt they had to touch base were on their side. They visited the industry associations in Calgary, and Don McDougall met with B.C.'s premier, Bill Bennett, who was pretty keen to get his hands on PetroCan's one-third stake in Westcoast Transmission, and Paul Little went to see the people at Westcoast Transmission, who were just *dying* to get out from under PetroCan.

But then there were the meetings that weren't meant to be uncomfortable, or at least not as uncomfortable as they turned out. A meeting with Ontario's energy minister and senior energy officials almost turned nasty. Ontario liked PetroCan, or at least they realized their electorate liked it. They, too, thought that privatizing it was dumb.

More disquieting still, leading members of the industry were now saying that Petro-Canada wasn't such a bad thing. Jack Armstrong, chairman of Imperial Oil and at the pinnacle of petroleum's corporate elite, was actually saying that Imperial could live with Petro-Canada. Some Conservatives considered that this amounted to a stab in the back. And the politically astute were saying to the Task Force members: just watch out, you're in a minefield. But if they were, they had to stay there. Their mandate demanded it. And they still had the rump of the party rooting for them. Go get 'em, they said.

There were a few companies who even wanted to start picking over Petro-Canada's bones before the intended *coup de grace* was delivered. Anthony Hampson, head of the Canada Development Corporation, came along to the Task Force and said he was more or less prepared to start rolling PetroCan into the CDC right away. Bob Brawn and Ken Travis, the multi-millionaire duo who headed Calgary's Turbo Resources, came into the belly of the beast at Red Square and said that if any breaking up was going to go on, then they wanted to make a bid for PetroCan's service stations at once. But McDougall had to make it clear that he couldn't do that.

By the end of the first week in October, the Task Force was ready to start writing, and they spent all the following week running through draft after draft, working late into the night so Joe Clark could table the report in the house on October 15. At times the drafting process was a little tetchy. One night Sykes, who liked to hide his steel-trap mind behind a kind of downhome way of talking, said to Hedlin: "Ralph, you use far too many semi-colons." And Hedlin said: "Well I know how to use semi-colons and I think I use them very well." So Sykes came back and said: "Well, in my firm I've *fired* people for using too many semi-colons." "Well," replied Hedlin, "you've probably fired some pretty good people."

And that was that.

It was perhaps inevitable that, given the amount of time they had to do such a complex job, the Task Force would produce a less than satisfactory report. As it was, however, they had their work torpedoed before it saw the light of day. Paul Little was horrified to learn from a house-guest arriving at his front door that federal NDP leader, Ed Broadbent, was reading their report over the radio on Sunday, October 14, the day before it was due to be tabled in the House. What's more, whatever the shortcomings of the report itself, Broadbent destroyed its credibility by making it appear to be something it was not, a recommendation to dismantle Petro-Canada. That was all a public still spooked by the prospect of energy shortages in Canada wanted to know.

But in any case the report was not clear in laying out its recommendations. Moreover, it was couched in classical free-enterprise terms that seemed strangely out of place given the temper of the times and the mood of the electorate. The philosophy was pure eighteenth century. "Government, *per se*, must be responsible for public interest activities designed to assure secure domestic supplies of energy for Canadians. But the Government must not pre-empt activities that are more efficiently and effectively served directly by citizens, whether citizens act in their individual right or organize together as company or co-operative."

The report went on to attack Petro-Canada's dual role as a profit-making corporation and an instrument for achieving national objectives. This, it said, placed managers "in a constant state of uncertainty," and meant that accountability was impossible. Mismanagement would be difficult to spot.

113

However, these arguments, couched in the terms of mainstream *laissez faire*, had little appeal to a general public which demanded security before any vague notion of economic efficiency.

Then the Task Force moved onto its recommendations. PetroCan should be split into two parts, one a private sector company called Petro-Canada, the other a government agency. The private company would act like any other oil company. The investor would have "a democratic right to influence policy through the annual meeting of the Board or, as an alternative, to dispose of his investment." The view was that of what might be called the classical Utopian capitalist, of a nation of shareholders each reviewing his portfolio of shares constantly and spending his time doing nothing else but turning up at board meetings to ask intelligent questions, or else working through the market, buying and selling to ensure the optimum allocation of resources.

The government agency would do the dirty work, the frontier exploration and high technology development, those "non-commercial" activities previously vested in Petro-Canada in its role as an instrument of public policy. The report gave no detail of the division of assets between the two entities, so although in fact the vast bulk of assets would have remained in the private company, this was not made clear, and although the report claimed that Petro-Canada should not be dismantled, it certainly appeared like a major split of the company.

The report then gave details of the broad areas of the government agency's responsibilities plus recommendations on the ways dubiously commercial assets, like Petro-Canada's 48% of Panarctic Oils and its 25% share of the Polar Gas project, should be shared between the two entities. The broad sweep of the proposal was that everything likely to cause a cash drain should be dumped on the government and ultimately the taxpayer.

The private entity, meanwhile, would pick up all the juicy parts of PetroCan, while all public servants would be thrown off its board. However, the report did indicate that the government might retain a 25% stake for an "interim stage".

And how was Petro-Canada finally to be privatized? An ordinary public share issue could, said the financial advisors, not raise enough money. Moreover, the goal of broad distribution would not be achieved that way. Giving people rights to purchase shares at a discount was considered, but that, too, was regarded as unsatisfactory. It was considered that they might give away some of the shares and sell others, but this, too, was relatively expensive and gave no guarantee that money could be raised. A piecemeal selling off of assets was out of the question. So what could they do? The "solution" finally emerged from the lips of Roland Giroux. "The only answer," he said, "is to give the whole damn thing away."

And that, in the end, is what they decided to do.

## Long Live Petro-Canada!

As soon as the report came out, Bill Davis leapt to the attack. "Our government believes," he said, "the present national responsibilities of Petro-

114

Canada should be retained and that the federal Government should retain ownership of Petro-Canada as a national publicly-owned petroleum institution."

Joe Clark's Conservatives now appeared in a worse mess than ever over PetroCan. Far from buying themselves time, they had, as David Scrim had predicted, merely appeared indecisive. Moreover, the Task Force's recommendations, as leaked by Broadbent, created a general impression that the government was disbanding the Crown corporation. They were certainly stopping the commercial part of it from being an instrument of public policy. Moreover, the recommendation to give the corporation away while absorbing its debt seemed quite out of step with a party claiming that it was making a bold stand for fiscal responsibility.

As for the mandarins, they just looked at the report and concluded that their impressions of Tory thought processes might, if anything, have been overgenerous.

After the report came out, Don McDougall had the thankless task of going on a coast-to-coast tour attempting to "sell" it in a series of speeches and radio and television appearances, but he was doomed to failure. The Tory party now had to attempt to salvage something from the ashes. Ray Hnatyshyn, who from the beginning had, or wanted, very little to do with the Task Force, was deputed, along with Michael Wilson, Minister of State for International Trade, to co-chair a special cabinet committee to rescue something from the Task Force debacle.

During the last two months of his administration, PetroCan became the largest single thorn in Joe Clark's side. He came under constant attack in the House and, since he still had no clear policy, found it inevitably hard to defend. In the event, the Clark government was to fall before it had its chance to perform its final *volte face* on Petro-Canada.

In the first week of the campaign, Joe Clark revealed his "final" Petro-Canada policy, a Frankenstein-monster stitched together from ill-fitting limbs of public policy, political expediency, and a rump of obeisance to the market. The monster was not only to be as big and powerful as before, it was promised that it would become even bigger. It would be publicly traded, with half its shares given away, another 20% sold and the remaining 30% held by the government.

The Tories would "contract" with the company to engage in country-to-country oil trade, non-commercial frontier exploration and special research and development. Somewhat sheepishly, the Tories were turning to the PetroCan executives and saying: you can have it all back and more. But some of the shrewder and more politically-aware executives weren't too interested any more in what the Conservatives had to say. They knew the Conservatives' days were numbered.

# 13
# Falling Out
# with King Peter . . .
# And the Electorate

*"But if they decided on confrontation, warned the
bureaucrats, it was critical that the federal government see it through. It might involve the declaration of an emergency, possibly the takeover of
Alberta's oil and gas production, and, as a last
resort, Royal instruction to the Lieutenant-
Governor of Alberta to disallow provincial legislation — a move considered even by the federal
officials to be 'incredibly' provocative."*

One aspect of the bureaucracy's advice that the Tories found particularly
disquieting was that they would have to be prepared to do battle with Peter
Lougheed for the fruits of higher oil prices. Such a prospect hardly seemed to fit
in with Joe Clark's brave words about Canada as a "community of communities".

The bureaucrats at EMR had done battle with Peter Lougheed and his
cohorts before. They understood their psyche. They knew that every time the
world price of oil rose, their counterparts in Edmonton would calculate the
additional amount of Alberta's "subsidy" to the rest of the country, and that
Peter Lougheed's feelings of self-righteousness rose with the volume of that
multi-billion dollar figure. If Joe Clark had in any way anticipated any concessions from a "fellow" Tory premier, he was in for a rude awakening. To Peter
Lougheed, there were some things far bigger than party affiliation. The biggest
was Alberta.

In a way, Joe Clark's presence as federal Prime Minister may have strengthened Peter Lougheed's commitment to the primacy of Alberta. Lougheed had
been pressed hard to run in the February, 1976 Tory leadership convention, the
convention where a strange alchemy had turned Joe Clark into a party leader.
But Lougheed had decided not to run. Many believed that it was because he
had analyzed himself and found himself wanting in his ability to cope with the
Quebec issue. But after that final ballot, Lougheed had been astonished to see
the elevation of a man who had once been a political footsoldier in the ranks of
the Alberta party.

That, more than anything else, perhaps convinced Peter Lougheed that he could have won. Several days after the convention, Lougheed was asked by a reporter if he thought he could have won the convention on the first ballot. "No," he is said to have replied, "we would have won it on the second ballot."

Peter Lougheed is not a man to carry petty grudges — big ones, against the Eastern establishment, certainly — but the fact that he was now to renegotiate his province's rights against someone whose job he had effectively turned down in favour of his commitment to Alberta cannot have made him any less determined to drive a hard bargain.

But in any case, it looked at first as if Joe was going to hand him his demands on a plate.

Part of the Clark election platform had been a claim that he would be able to get on better with the provinces than the Trudeau government. Joe's view of the nation was less centralist than Pierre's and so Canada would be given a chance to live as a "community of communities". It was a nice phrase, but energy was once again to throw Joe a curve ball in federal-provincial relations. The OPEC increases and their inevitable pull on Canadian prices was to reveal naked provincial self-interest such as had not been seen since the great petroleum battle of 1973-74. Between Ontario's demands for price restraint, and Alberta's demand for higher prices and more revenue, Joe Clark's community of communities met a fate that not even the glibbest of election phrases should suffer.

## Girding Joe's Reluctant Loins

The relatively low-key 1977 federal-provincial agreement on petroleum pricing did not run out until July 1, 1980, but events in the world market forced an earlier reassessment of domestic pricing, of which federal-provincial sharing was an essential part. The senior mandarins at EMR had left the Clark government in no doubt as to their feelings about Alberta's excessive wealth as a result of earlier arrangements.

And now Peter Lougheed and his own group of advisors and bureaucratic knights saw their duty to their province calling once again. That wellspring of Western resentment, fed by mythologized history and memories of wrongs and snubs from the East, began to flow in the hearts of the Alberta court. And even in some of Edmonton's hard hearts, there was almost sympathy for the opposition. How could Joe Clark even aspire to joust with King Peter? How could the ignoramus Hnatyshyn match the hatchet face and hatchet mind of Merv Leitch, a man who had been through the wars and knew the score? And yet there appeared a barrier to sweeping victory. The hated Trudeaucrats at EMR remained.

Lougheed regarded them as no less enemies to the legitimate ownership rights of Alberta than their previous Liberal masters — indeed, he regarded them as all being cut from the same warped cloth.

It is not certain if Joe Clark or Ray Hnatyshyn had any idea how bitterly

Alberta would fight, but the bureaucrats did. And they were not disappointed. Given the assault they were planning on Alberta, they knew that a violent reaction was inevitable.

EMR outlined its negotiating stance in a document accompanying the "Background" paper that had poured cold water on self-sufficiency. The document stressed that there would be conflict also with Alberta over revenue sharing, and that there would be no solution "without Alberta believing that we were prepared to take them on in a major confrontation if they refused to compromise".

As for specifics, the bureaucrats recommended an excise tax increase of up to 50¢; that oil should jump $18 a barrel over the coming three years, but that the federal government should take *all* of the industry's and most of the province's additional revenues.

Ontario was shown the proposals and, predictably, didn't like them. Nevertheless, they formed the basis of the package that the Tory cabinet took to Jasper at the end of August for their first, and last, massive policy get-together in power. Joe Clark met with Lougheed after the session on August 31, but the package was not officially presented until September 13, when officials led by the new Clerk of the Privy Council, Marcel Massé, met with their Albertan counterparts. The package had been toned down in some areas but beefed up in others, and it was to prove far from palatable to Peter Lougheed.

The package presented on September 13 consisted of a trebling of oil price increases, to $6 a barrel per year, over the coming three years; a call for relatively cheaper natural gas for new domestic markets; a new windfall profits tax equal to 50% of the revenues accruing above the existing increase levels of $2 a year for oil and 30 cents a thousand cubic feet (mcf) for natural gas; and finally the creation of two new institutions, a "Stabilization Fund" and an "Energy Bank".

The federal government was to put 10% of its revenue from the new federal tax — which was effectively a windfall profits tax — into the Energy Bank and the other 90% into the Stabilization Fund.

But then came the elements of the proposal that raised Peter Lougheed's blood pressure. The federal government wanted Alberta to put 50% of its incremental revenues (that is, above those of the old agreement) into the Bank as loans at cheap rates and 50% into the Fund as grants. They also suggested a Royal Commission on Revenue Sharing.

The federal government was effectively recycling Alberta's oil revenue for it, telling the province what to do with *its own* money. Peter Lougheed was furious.

The federal government was left in no doubt about Alberta's view of the proposal at two subsequent meetings, one between Hnatyshyn and Leitch, and a particularly acrimonious one between Lougheed and his advisors and Clark and his team — Hnatyshyn, Crosbie and Gillies — on Thanksgiving Day, October 8.

When Lougheed saw the federal proposals, he saw the hand, not of the federal Tory policy-makers, but of his old foes at Energy, Mines and Resources. On October 8 he almost threw the federal proposals on the floor. This was the *same old stuff* he had got for years under Trudeau's Liberals. And he told Joe so. He just wasn't going to stand for it.

As a result of these meetings, things seemed to be going very much in Lougheed's favour, to the chagrin of Ian Stewart and his officials at EMR. The issue of selected federal excise taxes had now been broached and accepted by Alberta but the Stabilization Fund had to be dropped. Alberta said that concessional loans, or equity, to the bank were out of the question, and balked at cheap gas for new markets. At the Thanksgiving Day meeting Lougheed laid out his take-it-or-leave-it concessions. He said he would commit more funds to the tar sands and allow the federal government more revenue from these projects. He offered to change the tax structure on existing wells to encourage "enhanced" production (by pumping water or solvents into the well). He said that he would lend $2 billion to the Energy Bank, at prime rate, and that he wanted a $4-a-barrel increase in the first year and subsequent increases of $4.50 up to 90% of the "Chicago" price, taken as the prevailing competitive price for oil in the U.S. market. Lougheed ended the Thanksgiving meeting by stomping off, an old Albertan negotiating trick which never failed to impress.

However, by the middle of October, with or without justification, the federal side seemed to believe that an agreement was close at hand. On October 15, a memorandum was delivered to cabinet entitled "Outline of a National Energy Strategy". This document was accompanied by an 11-point plan that was meant to be the basis of the federal strategy. The oil pricing agreement it contained was for: $4 annual increases subject to 90-95% of Chicago average price; international prices for synthetic and upgraded heavy oil; and a joint Federal-Provincial-Industry paper to study the feasibility and effectiveness of higher prices for enhanced recovery, newly discovered oil and gas and so called "tight" natural gas production — that is, gas that needed expensive stimulation. Existing gas was to continue to be priced at 85% of the parity with oil; incremental gas was still to be 65% of the crude parity; and there would be an extension of the system to Quebec City at subsidized rates and discussion of the appropriate tariff for extension of the gas distribution system eastwards beyond Quebec City. The Energy Self-Sufficiency tax (50% of revenues above $2 a barrel for oil and 30¢ per mcf for gas) was maintained, as were the excise tax proposals and the Energy Bank. There would also be other measures to stimulate conservation, gas substitution for oil and increased participation in the industry by Canadians.

When this package was laid before cabinet, a deal with Alberta was considered to be imminent. The following week, on October 22, Joe Clark was due to appear on television to give a major speech on energy and announce the excise taxes that would go into effect that night. All that remained, it seemed, was for Hnatyshyn to meet with Leitch on the intervening Wednesday to settle the final package. There — out of courtesy — Leitch would be shown the

119

relevant sections of Clark's speech. As an additional concession, Alberta was offered a review of pricing on July 1, 1980, to see that the world price had not moved too far ahead of the Canadian price, in which case there might be room for additional increases.

But whether the federal Tories were excessively optimistic, or had their wires crossed, no agreement emerged. When Leitch met Hnatyshyn the following Wednesday, he told him that the $4 with a clause for review wasn't sufficient. What Alberta wanted was $4 *plus* a formula that would allow the closing of the gap with the Chicago price with an overall half-yearly cap on the increase of $3. Although Alberta was prepared to stick to the $4 for 1980, the formula meant that annual increases could be back up to $6 subsequently. Alberta wanted the formula tied down; they didn't want the vague promise of a review.

EMR, harking back to its original "Background" discussion paper, did not like the idea of world prices as a reference point, considering them artificial and arbitrary — also far too high. They considered that a far more rational price level to aim for was that which was sufficient to bring on the required additional Canadian supplies. They didn't like the mechanism of the market. They thought that a rational approach was far superior.

Alberta had other ideas. Leitch told Hnatyshyn that he didn't like the idea of an annual review and he particularly didn't like the idea of a ceiling tailored just to the Canadian market. What, said Leitch, if there were some great oil or other energy breakthrough in the next few years? Then the consuming provinces would not want to buy from Alberta and the province would be stuck with Syncrude and the other non-conventional projects and have to bail them out. It seemed like an unlikely scenario, but Leitch seemed to take it seriously enough.

Leitch then laid out the province's position on natural gas prices. They both agreed that existing gas flows should continue to be priced at the equivalent of 85% of the domestic oil price. However, Leitch told Hnatyshyn that Alberta itself was negotiating with Ontario and Quebec with regard to a lower, incentive price for new volumes. If there were concessions to be made, Alberta wanted it to be clear that *it* was making the concessions, and not being forced to do so by the federal government. Leitch indicated, however, that Alberta was prepared to go to a parity of 70% from its present incentive level of 75%.

Then Leitch went over various other concessions, some of which had already been discussed in phone calls between Clark and Lougheed. Alberta was prepared to adopt a royalty formula for Alsands that was more favourable to the federal government than that applied to Syncrude; they were prepared to support the concept of a permanent tar sands construction workforce; they were prepared to spend an additional $800 million up to 1990 on tar sands research and development, as well as providing grants and incentives for new enhanced oil-recovery techniques; Alberta wanted a statement of support from the federal government on additional gas exports; they were prepared to discuss joint ventures in such areas as extension of the gas system east, strategic oil storage in Atlantic Canada, development of Sable Island and possibly the western electric grid; Alberta would invest on a regular commercial basis in Imperial's Cold Lake heavy-oil project, the Shell consortium's Alsands plant and the Alaskan Highway gas pipeline. Finally, Alberta didn't want the excise tax to be a tax across-the-barrel and it didn't want to impose an Energy Self-Sufficiency Tax that would turn the industry off.

EMR didn't consider these to be very large concessions.

The key point remained oil pricing, and the main thorn in the federal government's side remained Ontario. Bill Davis inevitably placed his own electoral neck before that of Joe Clark so he obviously could not be seen to acquiesce to the "enormous" price increases being considered. Davis, aware that an election was on the horizon, gave a series of speeches denouncing price increases in which he embraced the wishful-thinking school of economics. "There is no honest consensus," he said, "that significant oil price increases, by themselves, lead effectively to reduced consumption."

In a memorandum that Hnatyshyn sent to Clark after his October 20 meeting with Leitch — sent incidentally on October 22, the day Clark was meant to go on national television to announce the new energy program — Hnatyshyn said: "Alberta appeared to want to make a deal as soon as possible to lay the whole matter to rest. Ontario appears to want to stall the whole matter as long as possible but will be critical of whatever we do whenever it is announced."

As it was, the gaping differences in the ranks of the provincial and federal Tories were to be laid bare at the meeting of First Ministers held on November 12. As Jeff Simpson wrote in his book, *Discipline of Power*, for the federal Conservatives, it was "the political equivalent of self-immolation."

Lougheed and Clark met two days later in Saskatoon, but Lougheed was not budging an inch. Alarmed, the federal bureaucrats tried to stiffen Clark's resolve. They felt he was crumbling and in danger of giving it all away. As it was, Lougheed agreed to a price ceiling for oil of 85% of the Chicago price but still wanted the basic annual $4 plus the formula to "close the gap" that was likely to take it to $6. He said he was prepared to go along with an incentive natural-gas price of 75-80%, but only if Clark publicly committed himself to higher natural-gas exports, which he did.

But Lougheed insisted that there be no federal tax on petroleum revenues at the wellhead. Lougheed suggested that if the federal government wanted more revenue it should look at reducing incentives; take it out of the industry instead, he said.

In the minds of the mandarins at EMR, it was now the time for decision, and six days after the Saskatoon meeting with Lougheed, they outlined the federal position, and the alternatives open to the federal government, in a series of briefing papers.

It had become clear to the federal side that Alberta had not moved in any substantial way from the position it had taken when official negotiations had started the previous month. Nor did it appear that they were prepared to do so.

In the eyes of EMR, Alberta thought that it held all the cards and that the federal government couldn't afford to risk a major confrontation. But if the federal side gave in, then the package would not only be bad, it would be disastrous. Alberta's Heritage Fund could grow to more than $30 billion by 1985 and its surpluses by 1990 could amount to $100 billion. "The picture," said EMR, "is one of destructive fiscal imbalance, an imbalance threatening to the basic integrity of the nation."

The federal picture, by contrast, was growing ever more desperate, because it derived its revenue from the non-energy sector, whose revenue was being damaged by higher petroleum prices. There might be political reasons for doing a deal but it would be a *bad* deal, said EMR. Faster price increases would leave less room for the excise tax, which might have to be phased out; eliminating incentives instead of imposing the Energy Self-Sufficiency Tax would only provide half the revenue and would damage investment; additional taxes on resource profits as an alternative were not feasible; the reduced gas incentives would reduce substitution and thus aggravate a situation in which there was a surplus of gas and a shortage of oil. Finally, if the federal side gave in, then they were unlikely to be able to pursue other elements of their energy package, such as Canadianization.

And there were broader implications. If the federal government lost any right to explicitly recycle Alberta's swelling energy revenues, then the principle that Alberta had any obligation to the rest of Canada would have been lost. Moreover, the central government's authority and credibility would be damaged.

But if there was to be an impasse, what could the federal government do? There were a number of options, said the bureaucrats, depending on how tough the federal government wanted to appear. They could reveal that there was an impasse but that there was no cause for despair, announcing that the old agreement did not run out until the following July while at the same time imposing the excise tax. They could — as they, in fact, did — announce an impasse but spell out a package in the budget, although this of course left open the massive question of how they could spell out a package when there had been no agreement; or finally — they could impose a solution. They could pull out the big stick. This, of course, would politically damage their image of the government-that-could-get-along-with-the-provinces. Nevertheless, they would be shown to be strong, shown to be a federal government committed to federal responsibilities and not some half-baked notion of "community of communities".

EMR pointed out that the road would not be easy. It would have to be made clear that in default of a solution — that is, provided the Albertan government was to be given one last chance — Ottawa would then use the powers under the draconian Petroleum Administration Act, introduced during the first OPEC crisis, to establish the inter-provincial price for oil and gas. But that, acknowledged the EMR paper, meant a real fight. "In blunt terms," it said, "it would be a mistake to start this process unless the government were prepared, and considered itself able, to pursue the issue to the end . . . it would have to be prepared for an onslaught by Alberta" which would threaten to set prices, or increase royalties or cut back on oil production.

However, if there was going to be all-out war, advised the federal officials, then Ottawa might as well also consider adjusting the package further in their own favour. They might consider a two-price system, one for old, and one for newly-discovered oil; they could impose higher excise taxes; modify the Syncrude levy (in effect a tax on oil at the refinery gate); or they could establish new mechanisms to blend imported and domestic oil prices.

How far was Alberta prepared to press its claims? Was Peter Lougheed bluffing? Moreover, there were risks from curtailed industrial activity if the oil companies thought that a replay of 1974 — when the dispute had caused them to head for the border — was coming.

But if they decided on confrontation, warned the bureaucrats, it was critical that the federal government see it through. It might involve the declaration of an emergency, possibly the takeover of Alberta's oil and gas production, and, as a last resort, Royal instruction to the Lieutenant-Governor of Alberta to disallow provincial legislation — a move considered even by the federal officials to be "incredibly" provocative. The matter would finish up in the courts but the Ottawa mandarins, who, like master chess players, had thought the whole thing through many moves in advance, believed that they would ultimately win.

Two letters to Peter Lougheed were drafted. One, described by a federal official as the "Super Doomsday" letter, told the Albertan Premier just where he could go. The other, which was sent, was described as a "modified screw-you" and took a somewhat toned-down line that nevertheless left Lougheed in no doubt about the federal government's resolve. EMR it seems, had finally galvanized their political masters.

A few days later, a reply was received from Peter Lougheed. "In examining your position," it said, "I find considerable symmetry between your position and the one advanced by the Government of Ontario." He said that he saw the threat of unilateral action in Clark's letter.

Insightful as ever in their political analysis, the EMR mandarins had warned the Clark government of Alberta's likely response to a hard line. "Alberta presumably doubts," they had warned, "that this government, committed to amicable relations with the provinces and more cognizant of provincial rights than the previous government, would make such a dramatic move against the interest of a province. Thus, Mr. Lougheed could be doubly upset at any suggestion of unilateral federal action."

He certainly was.

So in the end, Joe Clark's government chose a course that almost certainly held the potential for further confrontation with Alberta. Its energy package was announced in its budget of December 11. Although it had to leave many details out, it was nevertheless, certainly not a package that capitulated to Peter Lougheed. As the budget was tabled, there were rumours that an agreement with Alberta was close, but such rumours had been around since negotiations started.

It has been traditional for finance ministers in Canada to announce their budgets in new shoes. John Crosbie, loved by the press for his wry sense of humour, decided to announce his budget in a new pair of mukluks. But the outcome of the budget on December 11 was to be less than amusing for the Tories: it was to be their fall from power.

## The Fatal Budget

Crosbie announced that, although there was no agreement with the provinces, the federal government was "prepared . . . to permit" oil price rises of $4 a barrel in 1980 and $4.50 thereafter, subject to further adjustment after 1982 if necessary. Thus Peter Lougheed was not to get his formula on shifting the price closer to the Chicago level. New gas would be priced at 65% discount to the parity with oil, again lower than Lougheed had wanted to go. Moreover, there *would* be a revenue tax to take "amounts roughly equal to half" of revenue increases in excess of $2 a barrel and 30¢ an mcf, although the technical details would still have to be worked out "in a co-operative effort". The one tax over which there was no immediate problem, the excise tax, set at a level of 18¢ a gallon, was announced to take effect at once.

But relations with Alberta were soon to enter the realm of the hypothetical. The Liberals, in particular Jim Coutts, an avid poll-watcher, knew that this unpopular budget — with the 18¢ excise tax its most detested and misunderstood measure — was being brought down by a government already floundering in a morass of unpopularity. The budget gave the Liberals a good chance of bringing down the minority government. The polls told them they could win a subsequent election.

At the Liberal caucus party the day after the budget, the feeling that they could, and should, vote down the government's budget grew by mutual reinforcement. Pierre Trudeau had already announced his resignation and the party seemed in disarray, but the chance was there, the chance to seize back power. And being in power was all that mattered.

On the morning of December 13, concern began to surface in the Clark camp. In particular, Nancy Jamieson, Clark's assistant, warned Clark's morning meeting that the government did not have the numbers. "Her warning," wrote Jeff Simpson, "was treated as a minor joke, an excessively skittish reaction to a tight but manageable parliamentary crisis."

But they did not have the numbers, and that night the Tory government fell. Joe-of-259-days was electorally beheaded because of the party's fatal flaw — it forgot it was a minority government. But perhaps no minority government could have successfully dealt with the economic pressures which that revolution ten months before and half a world away in Iran had unleashed, a force scarcely comprehended by the Canadian electorate which found it difficult to look beyond its next visit to the gas pump.

# 14
# Liberal Flexibility: Whatever Policy It Takes

*"Now I will tell you the answer to my question. It is this. The Party seeks power entirely for its own sake. We are not interested in the good of others; we are interested solely in power. Not wealth or luxury or long life or happiness: only power, pure power ... We are different from all the oligarchies of the past, in that we know what we are doing."*

1984
GEORGE ORWELL

The ideology of the Liberal party is difficult to sum up because it is almost impossible to pin down. Take, for example, the startlingly — and obviously quite unconsciously — frank assessment of Pierre Gimaiel, Liberal MP for Lac St. Jean, quoted in the *Globe & Mail* on March 1, 1982.

"To be a Liberal does not mean to fight for a province called Quebec, or a country called Canada, to fight for NATO or the Warsaw Pact. To be a Liberal is first and foremost to be an elected representative, a person whose leitmotif, whose supreme will, is to provide opportunities for development and progress for all Canadians.

"In such a situation, anything can be justified. If the development of individual Canadians is to be achieved through socialization, the Liberal party can turn socialistic.

"If the development of individual Canadians is to be achieved through a turn to the right through a strengthening in the industry, the Liberal party can move to the right.

"If in order to promote our development the Liberal party thinks we have to be communistic, we shall be communistic. This is what it is all about to be a Liberal. To be a Liberal is to be open to all ideas."

Jeffrey Simpson, in *Discipline of Power*, expressed a similar view of the Liberals' chameleon approach to policy, although in somewhat less heroic terms. Writing of Jim Coutts, at that time Pierre Trudeau's manipulative alter ego and cherubic hatchet-man, he said: "Coutts viewed policy from the exclusive perspective of its political utility in enhancing the Liberal Government's popularity; any Liberal policy could be changed, or any Conservative or NDP policy stolen, as long as it furthered the popularity of the Liberal Government."

125

In the wake of the Liberals' return to power in 1980, the emergence of the National Energy Program was touted as evidence of a much firmer commitment to political philosophy on the part of the party. This new ideological shift to the left was portrayed as the result of a soul-searching reassessment of eleven years in power with no political monuments, eleven years of political adhocery. In fact, it could be seen as the greatest adhocery of all. The Liberals did not bring down the Clark government because they felt they had pressing policy commitments for the good of the country. They had a more basic belief. It was that *they* were for the good of the country. The bungling performance of the Clark government convinced them more than ever of their divine right to rule. Equally important for some of them, in opposition they were suffering withdrawal symptoms from the fix of power. Their ministerial staffs of ten or more had been replaced by single aides; no longer could they summon the limousine to take them to the waiting Jetstar; they no longer had access — at least in theory — to the bureaucracy and its resources.

Under these circumstances, more than one former cabinet minister was heard to mumble that he wished that he'd lost his seat the previous May. Being in the opposition was discovered to be worse than being out of politics altogether. The party rank-and-file, meanwhile, were attributing their government's fall from power either to Trudeau's tendency to surround himself with "intellectuals who ran the government like a post-graduate course in public policy", or to the excessive power and influence of Jim Coutts, who was thought to have somehow isolated their guru from contemporary realities. Whoever's fault it was, Trudeau had become remote, and unpopular, and the party had paid the price. More important, however, the Liberals appeared bankrupt of ideas, as had become abundantly apparent at a policy convention in Winnipeg in November, 1979. The party seemed to be at its nadir.

On November 21, 1979, Pierre Trudeau had announced his resignation to a tearful Liberal caucus. An era, it seemed, had ended. Trudeau, the man whose election in 1968 had appeared to herald the age of reason and hope in Canada, was now departing amid disillusion from a lame-duck party; going not with a bang, but a sniffle from his back-benchers. However, Liberal fortunes were about to change with astonishing speed. Within three weeks of Trudeau's resignation, Tory ineptitude had suddenly opened the door to their possible defeat over an unpopular budget.

The Liberal opposition had few policies; it had no leader; but none of that mattered. Leaders and policies could be decided later. The all-important goal for the parliamentary party was to seize power once more, to reassume their self-perceived birthright. And its attendant perks.

Feelings among the party's rank-and-file, however, were at once less selfish and more complex. The party, according to prevailing grassroots opinion, needed time to regroup and heal its wounds, to find a new direction and select a new leader. Moreover, in opposition the party members had far more influence over the caucus than they had when it was in power. There was a feeling that a period of opposition could well prove salutary for re-establishing closer links between the parliamentary Liberals and the party nationwide. That was not the perception at the core of the parliamentary party. Opposition hurt, and it was not too difficult to whip the caucus into a see-nothing frenzy about the necessity of defeating Joe Clark. The ostensible reason for bringing Joe Clark down was his budget, the most unpopular aspect of which was an 18¢-a-gallon hike in the excise tax on gasoline. The real motivation for many of them was a simple lust for power.

For the Conservatives, the combination of the 18¢ increase, a minority position in Parliament and an electorate incapable of thinking beyond its next visit to the gas station was inevitably disastrous. The November Gallup poll had already shown the Conservatives a stunning 19 points behind the Liberals. The excise tax was hardly likely to narrow the gap. If the Liberals could force an election, all they had to do was go through the motions of a campaign and let the momentum of Joe Clark's unpopularity carry the Tories over the brink.

Pierre Trudeau, presented with the prospect of almost certain victory, was "persuaded" to return. Trudeau maintained his personal agenda of keeping Quebec within confederation — an issue of growing importance with the following spring's referendum — and patriating the constitution. But these issues, as Trudeau's key advisors knew, were not "sexy" politics. They had to have at least one specific policy in an area of widespread concern and interest. The choice was obvious. It was energy.

## Call for Walter Gordon

The Tories' brief period in power demonstrated to the Liberals the two key areas on which a "winning" energy policy had to be predicated. One, the promise of lower prices, was obvious. The other, the popularity of Petro-Canada, had come as something of a surprise, even though the Crown corporation was the Liberals' own creation. PetroCan's public support was mirrored by a corresponding increase in suspicion about multinational oil companies in the wake of the Iranian crisis. The implication was obvious: it was time for some economic nationalism.

The Liberal party's infinite flexibility was partly due to the broad range of political views embraced by its members. The ascendancy of particular factions, or ministers, depended on the demands of the moment. In the summer of 1979 it was time for the dull red star of Herb Gray, unwavering champion of economic nationalism, to move into the ascendancy. At another time and place, the lumpen Gray might well have done dogged duty as manager of a collective farm in the Ukraine. He was the very antithesis of political sex appeal, but he was the locus of where Coutts and the party pros thought the Liberals ought to be.

Gray's economic nationalism was a throwback to the days of Walter Gordon, the former Liberal cabinet minister who, in the 1960s, had ranted about the dangers of American domination of Canadian industry. Gordon —

the economic nationalist who had his shirts and shoes made in England and who did not hesitate to take American money into his own holding company, Canadian Corporate Management, or to sell subsidiaries to American companies when financially expedient — had always been an outspoken critic of multinational oil companies. He called them "international pirates". Gordon still lived in an age when Bill Twaits, the crusty little firebrand chief executive of Imperial Oil, would go and tell energy ministers what their policies should be. That age now appeared to have ended but the name of Imperial was still enough to raise Gordon's blood pressure. He continued to believe that the company should be nationalized rather than taken over.

And that, basically, was why Gordon had always been regarded as a politician who went too far out on a limb. He advocated extremist measures that were quite impractical unless Canada was planning to sever all links with its main trading partner. But Gordon's extremist stance was also based on a quite rational analysis of the situation with regard to foreign-owned oil companies in Canada. The nation simply couldn't *afford* to buy a significant number of them out at anything approaching a market price.

That was just one of the critical issues to which the Liberals' National Energy Program failed to address itself adequately.

Nevertheless, Coutts and leading political pro, Senator Keith Davey, as well as Tom Axworthy, brother of Lloyd and the man who would take over from Coutts as Trudeau's principal secretary, were all old friends of Gordon. Coutts and Axworthy were subsequently rumoured to embrace economic nationalism, as opposed to acting only out of political expediency.

In addition, however, although economic nationalism seemed the electoral policy for the times, there also appeared to be some reason to believe it was a more feasible policy than it had been at the time when Gordon was in government. This new factor was the emergence in Alberta of what appeared to be a viable alternative to the multinationals, a group of entrepreneurs who appeared to have seized the initiative from the major oil companies in the turbulent seventies. Jack Gallagher had successfully promoted frontier exploration in the Beaufort Sea. Bob Blair had beaten out the pride of the foreign-owned oil establishment in winning regulatory approval to build the Alaskan Highway gas pipeline from Prudhoe Bay in Alaska through Canada to the lower 48 states. Meanwhile a significant number of other Canadians had built sizable companies through success in gas exploration in Alberta or through servicing the province's booming exploration activity.

Gallagher and Blair had been particularly adept at selling their pet schemes to the federal government. Their skill, combined with the Foreign Investment Review Agency — which by its very existence had deterred the majors from attempting any large, oil-company takeovers for most of the 1970s — had already created a much more nationalistic environment in the oil business. Although it is uncertain if the existence of these "new nationalists" was a factor during the making of energy policy for the 1980 campaign, they were subsequently seized upon by the Liberals as the potential springboard for their proposed increase in Canadian control of the oil industry. Dome in particular was to emerge as the "chosen instrument".

Nevertheless, economic nationalism was still a subject that caused considerable unease in the Liberal party, not least to Pierre Trudeau himself.

Trudeau had always been a staunch opponent of nationalism, both on economic and ideological grounds. One of the constants of his political career had been his unswerving fight against Quebec nationalism. "A nationalistic government," he had said, "is by nature intolerant, discriminatory, and when all is said and done, totalitarian." As long ago as 1965, in *Federalism and the French Canadians*, Trudeau had written: "A sound economic policy must never be based on the assumption that workers would be ready to accept a drastic lowering of standards of living for the mere pleasure of seeing a nationalist middle class replace a foreign one at the helm of various enterprises."

He had berated René Lévesque's notions of nationalizing private power companies within the province, because the money involved "would simply buy in Quebec's name properties that already existed in Quebec."

If all these arguments applied to Quebec within Canada, then surely they applied equally to Canada within the broader international community. Nationalistic economic policies at the national level would be "discriminatory"; they would bear a cost; and they would, in the end, merely buy in Canada's name properties that already exist in Canada.

In the past, Jim Coutts had attempted to get Trudeau to display just a "little bit" of economic nationalism when he had been due to meet with the editorial board of the *Toronto Star* — the most rabidly nationalistic newspaper in the country — but Trudeau had refused.

Moreover, in an interview with the *New York Times* some years before, Trudeau had clearly distanced himself from the Walter Gordon camp, saying: "I think the problem of economic domination is somewhat inevitable, not only of the United States over Canada but perhaps over countries of Europe as well ... These are facts of life and they don't worry me ... If the whole country became nationalistic in an economic sense, it would soon find itself trying to eat its pride, you know, but you don't go far on a proud stomach."

Trudeau had here clearly indicated that he was aware of the adverse economic consequences of a nationalistic trust, and he was to be proved absolutely right.

Nevertheless, as Coutts no doubt pointed out to Trudeau when he persuaded him to return and fight the election, if the Liberal leader wanted to defeat the separatists in the Quebec referendum, and he wanted to patriate the constitution, then he first had to win the election. PetroCan's popularity proved, in the oil industry at least, that economic nationalism was sexy. And the Liberals didn't have too many sexy policies ready to pull off the shelf.

But if energy was the policy to promote, Gray was not the man to advance it. His political leanings might be correct, but his charismatic shortcomings and his focus were all wrong. As MP for the motor town of Windsor, he was a manufacturing man, a proponent of centralist industrial strategy. He was also clearly tied to the cheap energy aspirations of Ontario's Golden Triangle — a potential burden if they were to sell the policy as one in the national interest. No, Herb Gray wasn't the man. The man was Marc Lalonde.

## Marc Lalonde: The Divine Wind

Lalonde was already energy critic when the Tories fell, and if there was to be a new policy that required getting tough both with the industry and the producing provinces, then he was the man to implement it.

Lalonde had enjoyed a position within Trudeau's inner circle for longer than almost anyone else in Ottawa. His roots — ninth generation farming stock from Île Perrot, west of Montreal — were very different from Pierre Trudeau's well-heeled Montreal upbringing but, as a student, he had met the ten-years-older Trudeau and their paths had since mixed and mingled. A devout Catholic, his early education had been with the Holy Cross Fathers, a somewhat less rigid order than the Jesuits who moulded the young Trudeau.

After receiving his B.A. from Laurent College in 1949, Lalonde went on to the University of Montreal to pick up an M.A. in law. He also picked up three scholarships, which he used to enrol at Oxford to study for another M.A., this time in economics and political science. He then returned to teach law and economics at the University of Montreal. He practised law for a number of years and did a further stint as a teacher at the University of Ottawa, as well as briefly, in 1959 and 1960, acting for the Progressive Conservatives as special assistant to Davie Fulton in the same office as Michael Pitfield. Like Trudeau, his federal political affiliations came fairly late. Nevertheless, by the time he had gone to help Fulton, his stance on Quebec was very clear, and that was when the political bond with Trudeau had begun to grow.

In particular, he had been involved with Trudeau in the magazine *Cité Libre*, although he had a lower profile than Trudeau, who was one of the magazine's intellectual spearheads.

In 1967, his reputation established as a brilliant young lawyer, he became policy advisor to Liberal Prime Minister Lester Pearson, and played a critical role in persuading Trudeau to run for the leadership when Pearson retired. When Trudeau was swept to power in 1968, Lalonde became the principal secretary in the Prime Minister's Office, and was largely responsible for the enormous concentration of power in the PMO in the following four years. It was during that period that he developed his skill, and his reputation, as a political expeditor, the man who could make things happen.

In 1972, he ran for, and won the seat for Outremont, and has, ever since, been at the heart of Trudeau's tight-knit cabinet committee system, first as minister for health and welfare, becoming minister responsible for the status of women in 1974, then as minister of state for federal-provincial relations in 1977 and then, seven months before the Liberal government fell, as minister of justice in 1978.

Lalonde's affinity with Trudeau was not an emotional one. They were not so much friends as allies in a number of commonly perceived battlefields: the fight against Quebec separatism, the promotion of social justice and, through all, a rational system of decision-making in Ottawa. Lalonde was the perfect Trudeaucrat, with an incisive legal mind and a thorough knowledge of the workings of Ottawa. But there was also a powerful combatant strain within him, as there was within Trudeau. His ego, based on profound convictions about his own powers, was huge, and he did not brook fools easily.

Lalonde shared with Trudeau a profound lack of sympathy with business and the corporate establishment. It was compounded by the fact that, like Trudeau, he believed he understood what businessmen were all about.

Dalton Camp, as ever, put it most succinctly. "Mature politicians," he wrote, "secretly believe board chairmen and company presidents to be political cretins and would as soon take their advice as harken to a herd of mandrills." Lalonde, Trudeau and many others like them believed that most businessmen were woefully narrow in their views and, worse, that they were intellectually inconsistent. One day they would be trumpeting the joys of free enterprise like so many latter-day Adam Smiths; the next, if their business was in trouble, they would be rushing cap-in-hand to the government for aid. Every time they saw a government policy with which they disagreed, they would claim the sky was falling in; whenever government policies helped them get rich — as had certainly been the case for the oil industry in Alberta between 1974 and 1979 — they would assert that it was due exclusively to their own two-fisted entrepreneurial skill. The Liberals — indeed most Canadians — also held profound concerns about the honesty of business advice.

The decline of what were considered pro-business forces in Cabinet — the departure of the likes of John Turner and Donald Macdonald — was not considered problematic. Indeed, it may well have been considered the removal of an unhealthy bias. Trudeau had said: "I'm told the business world thinks that they don't have a real spokesman in Cabinet or in the party; well, I'm not going to go and get one elected artificially in order to say we have a spokesman. If business thinks it should be more interested in politics, let it send some people."

The business view wasn't really felt to be important. When they weren't being devious, businessmen were considered to be just like so many Pavlovian dogs who salivated when the bell was rung and whimpered when the stick was raised. This had led to the opinion — possible in Ottawa's rarified, ivory control-tower atmosphere — that it wasn't really business who was doing things; it was government policies. Such a line of thinking was obvious in the opposition energy policy document subsequently formulated under Lalonde but never published.

Under a section of the paper marked "Supply of Hydro-Carbon Energy Resources", it declared: "As a result of the taxation and pricing policies implemented by the past Liberal Government, Canada's known and recoverable reserves of oil and gas have increased enormously." It was not oil companies or entrepreneurs who had found the oil and gas; it was zombies reacting to the ineluctable stimulus of all-wise government direction.

This in turn had led to an even more misguided belief: that anything business could do, *government could do just as well if not better*. As Richard Gwyn pointed out in *The Northern Magus*: "Interventionism . . . came naturally to Trudeau because he has scant respect for the entrepreneurial ability of Canadian businessmen, and a great deal of respect for the ability of his government and himself."

In particular, Trudeau had great respect for the technocratic skills of Marc Lalonde. Lalonde believed that the government had made a mistake in taking as much notice of industry views as it had in the 1970s. In his opinion, this was part of the reason why the Liberals were looking back at eleven years without significant historic achievement. Petro-Canada was one of the few Liberal creations that had emerged so far as an unqualified popular success, and yet if business had been listened to, the Crown corporation would never have been created. So now, when the Liberals came back, the strategy would be to choose a course and then stick to it, not listen to the carping advice of industry — whose huge support staff could always nickel and dime you to death.

And that was another very good reason why Lalonde was the man to do the energy job. Unlike Trudeau, who tended to agonizing and indecision, Lalonde, once he had the task laid out before him, was iron-willed. Lalonde's years in the PMO had honed his skills as fixer to Trudeau's philosophy. Once he was convinced of the fundamental rightness of what he was doing, the combination of his charisma, his ego and his knowledge of the system formed a juggernaut of political momentum.

Moreover, his single-mindedness was aided by the fact that he was uninterested in winning popularity contests. He had no desire to be, or at least realistically acknowledged that he could never be, Prime Minister, an aspiration for which at least a degree of both Albertan and business support would have been necessary. Indeed, as a man whose family came clearly first, he had no real qualms about leaving politics. He was the ideal political kamikaze, an unimpeachably pure Divine Wind of political change prepared to sacrifice himself for the greater good of the nation and the party.

Not surprisingly, his appointment to the energy portfolio made the more perceptive members of the Albertan government and the oil industry more than a little nervous.

# 15
# Promises, Promises: The Liberals' Creaky Energy Platform

*"But I can tell you this, the 'Made in Canada' price will result in lower prices to consumers than the one proposed for the next four years by the Clark budget."*

PIERRE TRUDEAU
From a campaign speech
in Halifax, Jan. 25th, 1980.

After the May, 1979 election defeat Pierre Trudeau announced the formation of 21 caucus groups of Liberal MPs who were to develop policy for the new Parliament. In the general mood of Liberal depression, only half a dozen or so of these committees took off. One that did was Lalonde's Energy and Environment group.* An internal party document at the time stressed a needed emphasis on lower prices, defence of Petro-Canada, a strategy for tar sands development — public ownership was considered an alternative — a decision as to whether Canada should participate in efforts to break the OPEC cartel, and the need for a "solar and renewable energy corporation". There were also nuclear, conservation, hydro and environmental issues to be resolved.

One would think that such a massive policy review would require significant resources. The resources brought to bear amounted to one policy researcher. Barbara Sulzenko had been working in the research bureau of the Liberal party when Herb Gray had suggested she go and see Marc Lalonde, who was looking for a researcher. "I hear you're an energy expert from New Zealand," Lalonde had said as she walked into his office. In fact, there had been some confusion. Sulzenko was an American with an M.A. from New York University and a background in consumer advocacy. She was not an economist. She had no background in energy or knowledge of the Canadian oil industry. Within a week she was helping to write energy policy for the Liberal party.

Sulzenko, a serious young woman, was typical of a whole raft of loose-floating policy groupies within the nation's capital, young people with extended

---

* The group's other members were Charles Caccia, the party's environment critic, Lloyd Axworthy, Jean-Jacques Blais, Pierre Bussières, John Evans, Maurice Foster, Jacques Guilbault, Roméo LeBlanc, Bernard Loiselle, Gary McCauley, Paul McRae, Art Phillips and Roy Marcel.

educations, refined social consciences, and limited experience of the world. Their urge towards centralist economic control comes from a combination of a desire to do good at the broadest level, and a highly dangerous economic naieveté. Lack of an economics degree is not the critical factor. Indeed, if anything, economics degrees tend to make these young people more dangerous. They do not trust market economics; they do not trust large corporations; they feel distaste at the selfishness of entrepreneurial motivation, and they have an unshakable belief that they can improve the world.

They are potentially dangerous because their position gives them a disproportionate amount of power with politicians who constantly seek for new and electorally "saleable" ideas but whose tight schedules give them virtually no chance to generate ideas themselves.

Sulzenko's view of the economy was that there should be a multiplicity of government bodies each monitoring their industrial sector and responsible for approving price levels and dictating the acceptable level of return on capital. That was the view she brought, with Lalonde's full approval, to her policy proposals.

Sulzenko had only been working for Lalonde for a couple of months when the Tories were defeated on their budget. Since the Tories had fallen on energy, in particular their price-increase proposals and their Petro-Canada policy, it was obvious that a Liberal platform would be based on lower prices and a strengthened Petro-Canada. However, the chief party pros, in particular Coutts and his former mentor, Keith Davey, realized that the party was unhappy about being thrust again so soon into an election. It was necessary that the party feel that it was being included in the formulation of policy for a new Liberal government.

After the election was called, Coutts and Senator Davey therefore decided to assemble a "platform committee" consisting of 20 members of the Liberal caucus and 20 party members from across the country to "bring policy suggestions for the Liberal campaign from a broad cross-section of the Party and of the country". The committee was chaired by Allan MacEachen with "co-chairpersons" Lorna Marsden, a professor from the University of Toronto and MP Céline Payette. The remaining party representatives consisted of an assortment of political pros, academics, consultants and at least one oil-company man, Jim Higgins, an executive with Dome Petroleum. Higgins was, as a result of his somewhat outspoken stand at the meetings, to find himself temporarily exiled to Dome's British subsidiary!

Some of the party members may have had some naive idea that they were genuinely present to make policy suggestions. When they arrived in Ottawa to discover that all 40 of them were to meet for just two days, December 29 and 30, to go through a two-inch-thick policy agenda — the result of the work of the 21 caucus groups — their views changed. Many of them also discovered the existence of *another* committee, the "strategy committee", which was obviously the *real* decision-making body with regard to the policy platform. The strategy committee consisted of Trudeau, MacEachen, Coutts, Davey, Lalonde, Don Jamieson and party pro, Kathy Robinson.

It became increasingly apparent to the platform committee members from the party that their presence was more window dressing than genuine consultation. In particular, a number of them believed that Allan MacEachen was there more to remind them of the limits of their mandate rather than its scope. They felt they were a rubber stamp. However, once they found out about the existence of the strategy committee, a number of party people successfully pressed for a second meeting of the platform committee so that the resolutions of the first meeting could be reviewed and commented upon by the strategy group. The second meeting took place on January 5 and 6.

Although there were a large number of policy items on the platform committee's agenda, energy, as the issue that was going to bring Joe Clark down, dominated the proceedings. It was obvious that MacEachen, Bob Andras and Don Johnston were all concerned about fiscal policy and the government deficit. This issue was to be closely linked to energy, because the federal Liberals realized that the one large potential source of additional revenue for Ottawa lay in a financial grab for a greater part of Canada's petroleum income, the bulk of which was now flowing to Alberta and the oil companies. They also realized that the more oil and gas prices increased, the more potential revenue there was for them. However, this was not the time to stress such appealing economic realities. This was the time to stress how successful the Liberals would be at keeping petroleum prices down. It was pricing that dominated the platform committee's debates.

The platform committee split more or less along regional lines, with the consumers of the east, led by Lalonde, speaking for low prices, and the pro-producer western group, led by Bud Olson, recommending, at the minimum, higher "incentive" pricing for new production.

Several representatives from Eastern provinces — guiltless of economic education yet unashamed of making sweeping economic prescription — held a somewhat moral tone, objecting to oil companies' "windfall profits on oil that was costing pennies to produce". They could not specify exactly where this oil was being produced, or by whom, but they were sure that they were being ripped off. Their modest proposal, therefore, was that — along the lines suggested by Sulzenko — all oil should be subject to public utility pricing; that is, that the price of oil from any well or facility should be determined by its cost of production plus a "suitable" percentage of profit. Regardless of the fact that such systems had failed disastrously throughout history and that utility pricing would require an army of competent bureaucrats who simply did not exist, this proposal was seen as being indisputably "fair". And that, to the bright young political pros of the Liberal party, was all that mattered.

Those in favour of utility pricing realized that their approach was somewhat interventionist, but they argued that the system of regular and automatic price increases instigated by the previous Liberal government was arbitrary, the worst of characteristics for those with a supremely rational, Ottawa-can-regulate-all view of the universe. The Liberal government's price increases had been set without public hearings and without a study of all requisite data. It was absolutely essential that the people's tribunals should sit on such issues. Barb Sulzenko, for one, was simply not prepared to allow automatic price increases for conventional oil.

When Jim Higgins, the executive from Dome Petroleum — at that time one of the great Canadian corporate success stories of the 1970s — heard all this, he just couldn't contain himself. Higgins had been a long-time Liberal party worker in Alberta, an outside interest encouraged by Jack Gallagher on the basis that all connections with Ottawa in these politicized times were valuable. However, Higgins' one problem was that he found it hard to keep quiet when he heard what he considered to be some of the impractical suggestions coming from his innocent colleagues. When Higgins heard the term "utility pricing", he went for his verbal gun, rose angrily to his feet and said that the suggestion was just *bullshit*. Marc Lalonde was heard afterward to suggest that Higgins should be locked in a cupboard and the key thrown away. Ever obliging to federal Liberal wishes, Dome management sent Higgins to its London subsidiary for a year.

In the end, the powerful personality of Marc Lalonde, aided by a general realization of what was politically expedient, won the case for low prices.

What subsequently became the other key energy items from the platform — the target of 50% Canadian ownership of the oil industry by 1990 and a stronger Petro-Canada — were both motherhood issues. The concept of 50% Canadian ownership had been hanging around the party's platform since 1974. The platform, however, as had always been the case, had few convincing means of achieving the level. There were suggestions that approval of new energy projects should be based on sufficient Canadian content, that PetroCan should continue to encourage Canadian partners and that federal land legislation should ensure Canadian presence in frontier development. There was also some talk of tax incentives to encourage the purchase of shares of Canadian-owned vs. foreign-controlled oil companies, but that did not figure in the final policy document. Perhaps it smacked too much of capitalism.

The final Liberal energy policy document was never published, but a copy has fallen into the author's hands. It is, to say the least, somewhat embarrassing to read in the light of what the Liberals were to do to energy prices over the ensuing two-year period.

The document rejected the Conservatives' proposed 18¢-a-gallon excise tax and the extension of the gas tax to commercial users and public transit systems because such measures would "impose a heavy burden on low and middle-income Canadian families; they would raise the price of food and other essential goods and push the over-all inflation rate to double-digit levels."

That is a perfect description of what the Liberals were, in fact, to do.

Speaking of the party's proposed emphasis on conservation and proposed energy alternatives, it declared: "A Liberal Government . . . will reject reliance on price increases as the main instrument for maintaining balance between energy supplies and consumption."

Such a high price strategy, far from being rejected, was soon to form the main thrust of government policy.

No specific price levels were mentioned in the document. However, it declared that the domestic price would be "Made in Canada" — a ringing term supposedly coined by Roméo LeBlanc. What this meant was the actual price would be a "blended" price, a weighted average of Alberta conventional oil, higher "incentive" priced tar sand and frontier oil, and imports. But there was a problem here, as the economists on the platform committee were quick to point out: such a "blended" system, if it were introduced immediately, would mean a price increase far greater than the Tories', an immediate jump of perhaps $8 a barrel, not accounting for any further increases in the world price, the incentive price, or that for conventional Albertan oil.

The document, to cope with this point, said: "The Government of Canada will (continue to) subsidize the import component of the "Made in Canada" price for the period of time that is necessary to ensure that price increases are gradual and do not result in hardship for consumers and businesses."

In the event, the import subsidy was phased out very rapidly within eighteen months, imposing unprecedented price increases onto consumers just as the country was moving into a recession.

## A "Brilliantly Cynical Campaign"

It is true that the Liberals had no control over the import element of the blended price, which was to continue to rise dramatically as they moved once more into power. But, even without those precipitous increases, those who ran the numbers on the "blended" price found it hard to see how the Liberals would keep the price below the Conservative level, especially since there would be enormous pressure from the financial experts to phase out the increasingly expensive import subsidy. Lalonde decided, nevertheless, to go ahead with the politically attractive commitment that the Liberals' increases would be, overall, less than those of the Tories'.

Subsequently asked by a reporter how the prices of conventional and non-conventional domestic oil would compare to the international price, Lalonde replied: "If the price of conventional is X, you will have a price of X plus Y for the non-conventional oil, and then the international price — you know what that is — but we have indicated we will continue to subsidize the price . . . So what you would end up with would be a mix of these prices."

One might have been forgiven for believing obfuscation was afoot.

While all this backroom policy-making was proceeding, the Liberals were mounting what Senator Keith Davey later described as a "brilliantly cynical" campaign. While the Liberals' platform committee argued with fervour about future directions for the party, the strategy committee knew that the solution was not to announce new policies, but to announce as few as possible while focusing on the Clark government's inadequacies and keeping Pierre Trudeau's profile close to the ground. Very few policy speeches were made by Trudeau but two key ones — or at least so subsequent events established — were delivered towards the end of the campaign by the once-and-future Prime Minister. They were delivered in Halifax on January 25 and in Toronto on February 12.

In Halifax, Trudeau lambasted the Tories for their 18¢ excise tax on gasoline, suggesting, somewhat deviously but effectively, that the revenue was to be used to pay for the Tories' policy of mortgage interest deductibility. "And that tax," he declared, "is particularly onerous on you Nova Scotians. Because many, many in this province have to use their cars to get to work."

Trudeau went on to reveal in its most skeletal form some of the key aspects of the energy platform formulated by Sulzenko and Lalonde and pushed virtually *in toto* through the platform committee. He spoke of a seven-point program "to achieve energy security, at a fair price for all Canadians". The seven points were: a "Made in Canada" oil price; energy security through accelerated domestic development and insuring offshore supplies; the substitution of natural gas and other energy forms for oil; a strengthening and expansion of Petro-Canada; a new emphasis on conservation and the promotion of alternative energy; ensuring Canadian ownership and control of the energy sector; and finally, a plan to make energy the core of industrial and regional development.

"The Government of Canada," he said, quoting verbatim from the energy document, "will continue to subsidize the import component of the "Made in Canada" price for the period of time that is necessary to ensure that price increases are gradual and do not result in hardship for business and consumers."

Trudeau announced that a Petroleum Pricing and Auditing Agency would be set up to investigate and report on industry costs, profits and operations as a basis for price increases. The actual level of price increases was not known, because that depended on the agency's findings. "But I can tell you this," said Trudeau, "the 'Made in Canada' price will result in lower prices to consumers than the one proposed for the next four years by the Clark budget."

On 50% Canadianization, Trudeau said: "Petro-Canada, Federal land regulations, and tax allowances" — the final element added to the policy document — would make it happen.

In his Toronto speech, Trudeau returned to similar themes and spoke in addition of a greater role for the Foreign Investment Review Agency as an instrument for increasing Canadian control of the economy in areas other than energy. But first came the politicking. "The Clark Budget," he said, " . . . would have jolted Ontario with such a sharp increase in energy costs as to bring economic growth to a virtual standstill." It represented, he declared: "the strongest assault against Ontario since the War of 1812."

The Liberals, said Trudeau, would countenance no such thing.

## The Tories Lose Their Grip on the Energy Machine

The Tories meanwhile, who had struggled for six months to get their hands on the reins of bureaucratic power and a grasp on the complex demands of making policy, suddenly discovered that they may have learned new and valuable lessons but had forgotten a basic one: a minority government cannot hope to introduce unpopular policies, however realistic, and survive. Now, as they were forced back on the election trail with the polls showing that they were lagging behind the Liberals, the bureaucratic machine threatened to get out of control. In particular the one at EMR.

One aspect of energy policy that Ian Stewart and Ed Clark had found particularly objectionable as the international price of oil had rocketed by more than $10 in the previous year, was that this price was automatically paid to the Syncrude partners, the largest of which was their *bête noire*, Imperial Oil. This, to Stewart and Clark, was totally inequitable and indicated very significant and quite unjustified windfall profits for the companies involved. Under the original Syncrude agreement, the world pricing provisions could be revoked in exceptional circumstances under a *force majeure* provision. During the heat of the campaign, Ian Stewart managed to get Ray Hnatyshyn to sign a cabinet request to invoke the *force majeure* clause, which was then actually passed by a distracted cabinet. When Bill Neville, Joe Clark's chief of staff, and Harry Near, Hnatyshyn's assistant, discovered this they were shocked and livid, because the international price for synthetic oils was part of their election platform. To invoke *force majeure* would look both inconsistent and inept. Before the clause could be enacted, Neville had it sent back to cabinet and revoked.

Henceforth, Neville and Near had to make sure that they kept a careful eye on the department. But if Stewart and Clark had lost that round, they knew that it would not be long before the Liberals — who were more likely to see the "inequity" of the Syncrude situation — would return and do their bidding.

Until they fell from power in 1979, the Liberal government was the only government a great many Ottawa bureaucrats had ever known. It was inevitable that a bureaucracy would have evolved that fitted its political masters ideologically. Many close acquaintances and friendships had been formed, and these obviously did not disintegrate when the Tories came to power. It may be illegal for the bureaucracy to give policy advice or information to an opposition party, but such legislation is virtually impossible to enforce.

It would be a mistake to imagine that the bureaucrats at Energy, Mines and Resources were pining for the return of their previous Liberal masters. It is important to remember that the analytical documents that came out of EMR during the Tory administration contained an implicitly critical view of previous Liberal policies, policies that had effectively given too much away to both the provinces and the foreign-owned oil industry. But if the Liberals had been at times misguided, the Tories were proving in some cases to be just plain *thick*.

So when the bureaucrats met with their old political masters, or with Liberal advisors, they spoke with frustration about just how *incompetent* the Clark government appeared. They were taking so long to *learn*. Of course, they pointed out, they were *loyal* to the Tories, and they didn't like to appear disloyal by pointing out what a *mess* they were in, but it was really too bad. Just look at poor Ian Stewart, they would say. Why, because they're so slow-witted, they've almost pushed him to a nervous breakdown.

But ironically, close to the end, the Tories finally seemed to be catching on. Joe Clark was at last persuaded that he had to get tough with Peter Lougheed over energy before Alberta's wealth, and Ottawa's penury, forced the whole federal fiscal system to topple over. He finally accepted that he just couldn't dismember PetroCan. He eventually realized that he had to deal with the foreign ownership of the country's leading industrial sector. But then the fool had gone and got himself defeated.

So now, when it was obvious that the bureaucracy was going to get its old masters back, it became a matter of priority that those once-and-future masters started to think along the right lines.

It wasn't really anything sinister. It was just that people talk about ideas, and ideas, as the main currency of Ottawa, tend to get snapped up. Politicians are often quite prepared to pirate others' policies and claim them for their own, if they will win votes, but the bureaucracy is far more interested in promoting the *right* policies. Credit is not required. In fact, in most cases it is assiduously avoided.

When it was clear that the Liberals were going to return, EMR began, in the terminology of Ottawa, to become very "leaky". Sometimes they would speak to Liberals or their policy advisors directly; sometimes they would just float an idea where they knew it would be picked up. Thus "blended" prices and "Made-in-Canada" policies were being discussed in the department for some time as part of Tory policy before they mysteriously appeared as key elements of the Liberals' energy platform.

For the bureaucracy to give advice to the Opposition might have been illegal, but it was not illegal for an employee of a Crown corporation to do so. Advice on energy policy, however, might well be considered somewhat irregular when the Crown corporation involved was Petro-Canada. But then that wasn't the sort of conflict recognized by Joel Bell, PetroCan's senior vice-president.

For Bell, the Conservative reign had been a nightmare. And even though the Tories had now staged an about-face on PetroCan, moving to a position where its power would actually be increased, their views on using it as a policy instrument were still very different from his. Bell also, as the most "political" of senior employees — a long-time Liberal advisor and author of many Liberal policies — was unlikely to continue to keep his job under a Tory government. In fact, many observers marvelled at the fact that he had kept it for so long.

Now, however, with the prospect of a Liberal return, Bell could once again assume the dual role of policy advisor and policy implementor that he believed was PetroCan's unique mandate. In fact, he reassumed the advisory role before the Liberals had been returned to power, going through the Liberals' energy platform at meetings with Lalonde and Sulzenko in December of 1979 and January of 1980. From Lalonde's point of view, Bell was not only an extremely knowledgeable advisor but also important as a senior executive in the company which would be one of the main instruments for the government's new nationalistic initiatives.

Bell, however, certainly didn't agree with everything Sulzenko was proposing. In particular, he strongly disliked the notion of a Petroleum Pricing Information Agency as a monolithic monitor of industry activities. He also —

and with some vested interest since Petro-Canada was an oil company — disliked Sulzenko's reluctance to believe that any price increases should be allowed to oil companies until they had been "justified".

If no price-agreement had been reached with Alberta by July of 1980, it had been decided that an interim $2-a-barrel price increase would be allowed. Bell wanted $1 of this to go to the producers, and the remainder to be split between Alberta and the federal government. Sulzenko, however, wanted to cut the oil companies out of any increase unless such increases could be justified. Sulzenko's politically appealing view prevailed and the final, unpublished, Liberal energy document declared: "The amount of the increase which will be available to producers will be determined following an examination of the revenue requirements that will ensure continued development of oil reserves."

Bell and Sulzenko also argued over what the new research organization for alternative energy proposed in the energy platform should be called. After the second platform committee meeting, Bell met with Sulzenko and Lalonde to go through the final proposals before Sulzenko wrote them up. Bell wanted the new alternative energy entity — which would initially operate under the aegis of PetroCan — to be called Energetech or Enertech. Sulzenko believed the name was, as she wrote in a subsequent memo, "too technocratic to capture the imagination of the nation". She liked "Alternate Energy Corporation of Canada". Bell, smiling, told her that since it would be a subsidiary of PetroCan, he was sure of having *his* name approved in the PetroCan boardroom. However, since Sulzenko was writing the document, she stuck to Alternative Energy Corporation of Canada. Eventually it was decided that another name would better "capture the imagination of the nation", and the alternative energy corporation eventually became Canertech.

Bell's main objective, however, the survival and strengthening of PetroCan as an instrument of national energy policy, was something on which there was little argument.

That Bell should advise an opposition party while a senior executive with a Crown corporation clearly appears to be a conflict of interest. Nevertheless, Bell's attitude is typical of the modern senior bureaucracy. They are rule-makers who consider themselves unbounded by rules, individuals so convinced of the oneness of the national interest and their own convictions, and so self-confident of their own abilities, that they feel almost compelled to lead the policy process rather than follow it.

After ensuring that the returning Liberal party was thinking along the right lines, Bell, like Stewart and Ed Clark, now patiently waited for their election and the role they knew they would — and should — play when it was time to put some flesh on the Liberals' skeletal policies.*

---

\* Barb Sulzenko was to miss the *annus mirabilis* of energy policy leading up to the National Energy Program. Lalonde decided not to take her with him to the Department of Energy, Mines and Resources, and she went instead as executive assistant to Herb Gray, who became Minister of Industry, Trade and Commerce.

# 16
# A Policy Star Is Born

*"The thing that socialists have learned to
nationalize best is socialism."*
PAUL HENRI SPAAK

Shortly after the Liberals returned to power, Mickey Cohen, the smooth lawyer who had returned to Energy, Mines and Resources as deputy minister, indicated in meetings with leading members of the Calgary oil industry that the government had moved *sharply* to the left. Don't blame us, he seemed to be saying, what's about to happen to you is *government* policy. In one way, of course, he had to be correct. Nothing ever got legislated in Ottawa that wasn't government policy. However, in another way he was somewhat disingenuous, for the rationale and momentum of the National Energy Program came as much, if not more, from within EMR as it did from the Liberals. In total, it was the extraordinary combination of political ego, ideological backing from the heart of Trudeau's power machine, and bureaucratic commitment — all supported by polls reflecting the public's misgivings about major oil companies — that was to provide the motive force for a policy package of revolutionary implications.

However, the priorities of the electorate were far different from those of Ottawa's power elite and over the ensuing two years, it was the electorate's priorities that were to be jettisoned.

The voters of Canada, insofar as they had voted for anything in the 1980 election, had voted for lower energy prices, security of supply and some vague notion of Canadianization — embodied in their support for the security blanket of Petro-Canada. The bureaucrats wanted higher prices, and they were quite prepared to put longer-term security of supply at risk in pursuit of their top priority — further central regulation, and public control, of the oil business.

The policy was bound to wind up being much more controversial than it looked when the Liberals returned to power, but if departmental muscle was needed to push it through, Energy, Mines and Resources was the department that had it. Once the Liberals returned, EMR appeared to take over much of the role of the Finance Department as well. Any interdepartmental fighting that this might have caused was alleviated by the fact that Ian Stewart had been moved over to Finance as deputy minister, and he was fully in sympathy with EMR's objectives. There thus grew a nexus between EMR and Finance such as had never existed before.* It was not surprising that when the National Energy Program was announced, it was announced not just simultaneously with the budget. It *was* the budget.

Never had such a sketchy political platform been transformed into such a muscular policy.

## EMR Runs with the Policy Ball

1980 was the *annus mirabilis* for the policy-makers at the Department of Energy, Mines and Resources. Beneath EMR's black tower at 580 Booth Street, on and around Dow's Lake, the skaters and ice-sculptures of February gave way to the joggers and cyclists of spring, and then the little sailboats of summer, as the policy-makers worked day after day, and late into each night, formulating their revolutionary new schemes for Canada.

The more important the policy, the greater the power fix for the bureaucracy involved. Within EMR there was full recognition that this was the single most important and sweeping policy initiative on which most of them would ever work.

They were working on far more than a mere energy policy. It was a policy which would radically change both federal-provincial financial relationships and the whole structure of the Canadian oil industry.

The Liberals had given them the ball, and now they were running with it. But of course, like good mandarins, they were running close to the ground.

When Cohen told the oilmen of the government's move to the left, they were obviously disturbed, but they remained unsure of the origins of this leftward thrust. By nature Cohen didn't seem a revolutionary to oil industry executives. He seemed to be an easygoing, ultra-smart corporate lawyer who found himself working for the government. About Ed Clark, however, they weren't so sure. He too had always seemed *pleasant* enough when they had met him during the Tory government, but they had had severe doubts about exactly where he was coming from. Of course, they had seen lots of bright young bureaucrats with leftist leanings. In fact, to some of them, *all* bureaucrats had leftist leanings. But Clark was about as left as they'd seen. And he didn't hide it.

Their unease was increased at meetings with the new Energy Minister, when he indicated to them that the Conservatives had broken *their* campaign promises, but the Liberals had no intention of doing the same. The oil men were advised to re-read the campaign speeches given in Halifax and Toronto by Trudeau, speeches in which he had outlined the new energy strategy.

Through the spring, summer and early autumn of 1980, consultation with the oil industry dropped to an all-time low. There were desultory meetings, but

---

* During the formation of the NEP, the critical bureaucratic group was a joint committee of senior mandarins from EMR and Finance. It was known as the "Enfin" committee. Enfin, in French, means "at last" and there is little doubt that the double meaning reflected the mandarins' view that they were getting on with a job that had needed doing for a long time.

the industry men had the distinct impression that they were cosmetic, and that the politicians and bureaucrats had objectives that were carved in stone.

Committed bureaucracies do not change their views for governments, and the Liberals, when they returned, were presented with analytical documents virtually identical to those which the EMR mandarins had given to the Tories. With the change of government, however, the mandarins found themselves with a much more appreciative audience.

The analysis of EMR appeared so rational, so unemotional. A national energy program wasn't just politically expedient, it was economically necessary. It was Reason's answer to the nation's lopsided distribution of petroleum resources and oil industry power: far too many resources beneath the soil of Alberta; far too much industry in the hands of foreigners. Unless these inequities were righted, Ed Clark and his minions pointed out to their new masters — as they had pointed out to the Tories — the fiscal structure of Confederation would become disastrously skewed and Canada's leading industry would fall farther and farther under foreign control.

They knew that they had to negotiate with Alberta, but both Ian Stewart at Finance and Michael Pitfield, who had returned from the academic oasis but political wilderness of Harvard to be Clerk of the Privy Council once more, agreed with Ed Clark that it was essential to get more revenue from Peter Lougheed, even if it meant an unprecedentedly bitter fight.

On the foreign oil companies, by contrast, they knew they could impose their will. Again, the analysis done by Clark and Stewart provided powerful analytical tools for the Liberals to move where the electorate told them. The analysis of Clark and Stewart was meant to be well-removed from Walter Gordon's bogeyman view of the big foreign-owned oil companies.

There was, however, felt to be one potential problem. Clark and Stewart believed that they had developed the perfect rationale for the modified expropriation of foreign-controlled oil companies. However, where their case was a little sticky was in terms of *justification* for such moves.

This absence of any comprehensive case against the foreign-owned, big oil companies was to prove somewhat problematic for both the Liberals and the bureaucracy. In the end it was addressed through the release, just before the announcement of the NEP itself, of a report by the Petroleum Monitoring Agency, the freshly beefed-up section of EMR meant to keep a close eye on industry financial performance. The report drew a series of comparisons between the foreign-owned and Canadian segments of the oil industry, and, without indicating the very large differences in the size, nature and investment requirements of the companies within the two groups, presented an "analysis" highly unfavourable to foreign companies. It implied that the foreign companies were paying out too much in dividends and resultantly investing too little, while the more virtuous domestic companies were incurring heavy debts in their promotion of the oil business.

The report pointed out that, in fact, there had been a significant reduction in foreign-controlled assets between 1971 and 1979. In 1971, 89.6% of oil industry assets had been held by companies with a majority foreign-ownership. By 1979, this figure had fallen to 63.8%. However, in publicizing the report, EMR used revenues to indicate that a large proportion of the oil industry was still under foreign control. By this measure, the revenues of companies under foreign control still amounted to 81.7% of the total in 1979, although the comparative figure for 1971 had been 94.4%.

Nevertheless, when the report was released, Lalonde clearly indicated what the oil companies could expect.

"As positive as this trend toward reducing foreign ownership may appear," he said, "I continue to regard the current levels as excessive. The Government is committed to increasing Canadian participation in the industry and the current situation will be taken into account in the formulation of our new national energy program."

Oil industry misgivings, which had grown throughout the summer, were confirmed by the obvious bias of the Petroleum Monitoring Agency's report. The PMA had not represented merely a statistical analysis; it was obviously laying the groundwork for discriminatory legislation against the foreign-owned oil companies.

At the beginning of August, shortly before the PMA report was released, Jack McLeod, a senior executive at Shell Canada and then chairman of the Canadian Petroleum Association — the industry group dominated by the big oil companies — and Ian Smythe, the CPA's executive director, paid a visit to Ottawa. Smythe, a former mandarin himself, had been hired by the CPA because of his knowledge of Ottawa and its arcane ways. Throughout the 1970s the industry began to realize that it needed to know what made Ottawa tick. Just how little the industry understood the capital's thinking was soon to become apparent.

A visit to Mickey Cohen was a high priority for the men making the rounds of their Ottawa network. There were clear indications that the Liberals were about to introduce a tough energy policy. In particular, McLeod and Smythe wanted to sound out Cohen on exactly what was likely to happen with regard to Canadianization.

Neither man imagined there was much chance of changing the general thrust of the government's policy. However, they believed that it still might not be too late to have some influence over the policy's implementation. McLeod casually suggested that the CPA might still be of assistance in helping the government achieve a workable scheme.

Cohen thanked him but said that help wasn't necessary. The policy had already been written.

A last-ditch attempt to divert the government from any precipitate action was made at an exclusive dinner in Calgary shortly before the NEP was released. Marc Lalonde and his executive assistant, Mike Phelps, met with the president of the Alberta Liberal party, Darryl Raymaker, and three of the most respected voices in the Calgary oil community: Al Ross, Louis Lebel and Arne

Nielsen. Al Ross was then chairman of the Calgary Chamber of Commerce and had recently left the presidency of Pembina Pipe, the pipeline and resource subsidiary of the enormously wealthy Mannix family's empire. Louis Lebel was Chancellor of the University of Calgary and a former head of Chevron Standard, the Canadian subsidiary of Standard Oil of California, one of the Seven Sisters. Arne Nielsen was head of Canadian Superior and former president of Mobil Canada, another subsidiary of one of the Seven Sisters. Both Ross and Lebel were long-time Liberal party members, a rare breed in the province.

The oilmen told Lalonde and Phelps that if what they *heard* about upcoming policy was correct, then such a policy would increase Western alienation and upset U.S. relations. Lalonde and Phelps were as ever polite, but the Albertans could not mistake the resolve in Lalonde's attitude. The federal Liberals had charted a course and Marc Lalonde appeared to stand firmly at the tiller. His self-confidence arose from the fact that the course had been charted by some of the best brains in Ottawa.

Marc Lalonde had very much wanted to introduce the National Energy Program himself. He had been intimately involved with it since the Liberals had returned to power and, as its final drafts went through cabinet, considered it now more than ever his brainchild. He had been there at a number of the intense policy sessions at EMR in the summer of 1980 where, although he had many other political chores, he had joined Mickey Cohen and Ed Clark and George Tough in framing key parts of the document. They had all sat around, tapping inexpertly at typewriters, or writing out key paragraphs in longhand — which sometimes presented a problem since Ed Clark's handwriting was almost illegible. Then Lalonde and his bureaucrats had taken these ideas to cabinet where their forceful analysis and his forceful personality had carried the day against any doubts his colleagues might have had.* This was no time to let pusillanimous spirits stand in the way of the policy that was to be a credit to the Liberals and a personal monument to Lalonde.

For Lalonde, the success of the NEP was particularly important. He wanted it to erase the memory of the other key policy area in which he had been frustrated, that of reform of social security. As minister of health and welfare back in 1973, he had set out to develop "a comprehensive, logical and hopefully imaginative approach" that would embrace "the whole sweep of social security". Aided by a team of enthusiastic young technocrats, Lalonde had laboured for two years to produce such a scheme, but by the time he had evolved his plan, the government discovered that it could not afford it, while the provinces had lost interest.

The NEP would be different. It would be a great success and the public would be left in no doubt about the Minister responsible for it. But, in the end,

---

* When Ed Clark gave his first presentation on energy policy to the new Liberal government's cabinet, Pierre Trudeau was so impressed that he stood up and applauded.

Lalonde was to be frustrated again. He would become totally associated with the policy in the public mind, but the association would not prove a joyful one.

But Lalonde was not to have the honour of announcing the policy. Since the NEP contained so many, and such sweeping, new tax measures, it was considered virtually a budget in itself. It was therefore considered appropriate that it be announced as part of the budget. It was left to Allan MacEachen, the finance minister, to reveal the NEP to the Canadian public on October 28, 1980.

## Ed Clark's Catch 22

The NEP in its entirety was released as a separate document, written, not in the usual heavy prose of government policies, but in a far more readable style. Its pages were broken up with informative little boxes, carrying titles like: "How Fluidized Bed Combustion Works" and "What is Enhanced Oil Recovery?". It had obviously been written with a great deal of enthusiasm.

Lalonde's introduction to the document declared that its objectives were "security" of supply, "opportunity" for Canadians to participate in the energy industry, and "fairness" in energy pricing and revenue sharing. In its weighty three-pronged objectives it thus linked itself to the revolutionary doctrines of the past. As France had once resounded with *Liberté, Egalité, Fraternité*, and America had rallied to Life, Liberty and the Pursuit of Happiness, now Canada would surely respond to Security, Opportunity and Fairness.

The document began by dismissing the sheer irrationality of world oil prices and the anomalies of the existing federal-provincial petroleum revenue-sharing arrangements. "The Government of Canada," it declared, "believes that the present system is inappropriate and unfair. It believes that more appropriate arrangements must be made, so that the national government, which is accountable to all Canadians, gains access to the funds it needs to support its response to national needs."

The document then moved on to the issue of industry ownership. It pointed out that the enormous increases in prices to oil and gas producers over the preceding decade had meant, since most of these producers were foreign-owned, a "wealth transfer . . . away from Canadians". It continued: "In general, price and tax policies have provided the industry with the cash flow necessary to finance its expenditures. This means that the oil consumer and the Canadian taxpayer have financed virtually all of the substantial expansion of this industry."

Thus, by reinvesting its profits, the foreign domination of the industry had increased.

However, continued the NEP, foreign companies were also exporting capital. "Concern is often expressed over Canada's need for foreign capital in the energy sector. Such a need is often cited as the basis for accepting the large degree of foreign ownership that exists in the oil and gas industry. Yet, the oil and gas industry, far from drawing in foreign capital, has — since the 1974 oil

147

crisis — been a capital exporter . . . Moreover, the prospect is for these capital exports to grow. The continued increase in oil and gas prices that will occur means a further large foreign wealth transfer from Canadians to foreign shareholders. By ignoring the problem of foreign ownership in the past, Canadians have lost a significant share of the benefits of having a strong resource base. If we fail to act now, Canadians will lose once again."

The argument seemed impregnable. The thinking dated back to EMR under the Tories. It could be called Ed Clark's Catch 22. Foreign-owned companies were bad if they reinvested profits, because that meant they gained an even stronger control of the industry. But if they didn't reinvest them, if they paid them out as dividends to their overseas shareholders, then they were even *worse.* Such companies should obviously be bought out now. "A further delay will put the value of companies in the industry so high as to make the cost prohibitive, leaving Canada with no choice but to accept a permanent foreign domination by these firms."

The problem, declared the NEP indignantly, was enormous: "Of the top 25 petroleum companies in Canada, 17 are more than 50 per cent foreign owned and foreign controlled, and these 17 account for 72 per cent of Canadian oil and gas sales. This is a degree of foreign participation that would not be accepted — indeed, simply is not tolerated — by most other oil producing nations."

In any case, it continued, the degree of private sector participation in the petroleum industry was too high. What was needed was "more companies like Petro-Canada".

The "Problems" section of the NEP closed with a message of hope. "If a way can be found to share more equitably the benefits of Canada's energy resources, it may be possible to insulate Canada from some of the shocks emanating from the world economy, and to build upon this energy strength an industrial base in all parts of Canada that will provide for sustained economic growth."

The route to the solution of energy problems clearly lay in giving more petroleum revenue to Ottawa, where it would be used in the national interest.

The document then moved onto the actual program itself, the system of prices, taxes and grants that would achieve "security, opportunity and fairness".

Pricing, for the average consumer, was the most immediate concern. The "blended" price system first suggested by EMR under the Tories was now instituted by the NEP. Under this system, different prices would be paid for conventional oil, tar sands oil and "tertiary recovery oil", that is, additional oil from conventional reservoirs that needed so-called "exotic" stimulation. These different prices would then all be "blended" with the higher costs of imported oil. For the consumer, this of course looked like, and indeed was, a complex system. What did it mean at the bottom line, at the gas pump? This was not clearly spelled out, and indeed was surrounded by double-talk. At one stage, the NEP said: "There is broad national consensus that oil prices in Canada should rise substantially." That, however, had certainly not been the consensus of the electorate which had voted out Joe Clark and believed in Pierre Trudeau's promise of lower prices. However, later in the NEP, Trudeau's promise was, it seemed, reiterated, stressing " . . . the government of Canada rejects the simplistic 'solution' of dramatic price increases for gasoline". Certainly the basic, wellhead price increases for conventional oil outlined in the document appeared lower than those of the Tories.

However, the crucial difference with the Tories' scheme was that the Liberals, via a new Petroleum Compensation Charge, PCC, planned to fold the cost of imports into the consumer price. This would inevitably make consumer prices higher. There was already a precedent for the PCC in the Syncrude Levy of $1.75 a barrel, an additional charge made on oil prices so that Syncrude producers could receive the world price for their output. The NEP would add 80¢ onto this charge immediately and add a further $2.50-a-barrel in each of the ensuing three years. In addition, the NEP declared that this charge might be increased in future as a source of revenue for government. The NEP announced yet a further charge on gasoline in the form of the Canadian Ownership Account, of which Petro-Canada was to be an enormous beneficiary. This charge, levied on petroleum consumers, would go straight to finance increases in public ownership.

The government, while appearing on one hand to reject dramatic gasoline price increases, on the other talked about levying two new charges. Nevertheless, there was to be a ceiling on the domestic price of 85% of either the international or the average U.S. price, whichever was lower. Natural gas prices would continue to rise, although at a slower rate than those of oil.

But perhaps too much time should not be spent mulling over the pricing proposals of the NEP. Within twelve months they had all been abandoned in an unholy grab for more revenue.

## A Paragon of Fine-tuning

The central part of the NEP was its new taxation and grant scheme, a self-confessed paragon of economic fine-tuning. "The National Energy Program establishes a new system designed to provide adequate incentive to the industry, while avoiding unfair windfall gains. The system will provide ample — but not excessive — cash flow from existing reserves, offer substantial investment incentives for exploration, and attract new sources of Canadian risk capital." Here indeed, with the wisdom of Solomon, many objectives were carefully balanced and all without the benefit of consulting the industry itself.

In order to bring this well-balanced economic model about, the first new tax proposed was a Natural Gas and Gas Liquids Tax (NGGLT) of 30¢ per thousand cubic feet. However, the principal new tax was the Petroleum and Gas Revenue Tax (PGRT) which effectively sliced 8% straight from the top of operating revenues, and, moreover, was itself not deductible when working out corporate and other tax liability. In addition, one of the most important forms of tax relief, the Earned Depletion Allowance, was to be phased out for conventional oil in provincial lands.

These new taxes and the removal of earned depletion were of course resented by the whole industry. However, the NEP innovated a discriminatory grant system, the Petroleum Incentives Program, under which the government would give back money to oil companies depending on their degree of Canadian ownership. They would also receive considerably more for drilling on federal rather than provincial land. A company that was 75% or more Canadian-owned would receive no less than 80% of approved exploration payments in the form of a grant from the government for drilling in the Beaufort Sea or off the East Coast.

The NEP also featured sweeping new regulations on Canada lands, that is, those over which the federal government holds jurisdiction. Henceforth a 25% interest in every right on such lands would be reserved for Petro-Canada or some other Crown corporation. In addition, a minimum of 50% Canadian ownership would be required before production would be allowed from such lands. To ensure that Canadians were benefitting from oil and gas activity, applicants for drilling rights would have to demonstrate that their operations would bring "industrial and employment benefits to Canadians". And finally a Progressive Incremental Royalty would be established depending on the profitability of each new producing field.

The bottom line of these preferential taxes and regulations was, of course, Canadianization of the industry. This general target contained three specific goals:

"• At least 50 per cent Canadian ownership of oil and gas production by 1990;
  • Canadian control of a significant number of larger oil and gas firms;
  • An early increase in the share of the oil and gas sector owned by the Government of Canada."

Of course, this third objective was not Canadianization as much as it was nationalization. To emphasize this point, the document continued: " . . . the goal of the Government is to increase the proportion of the oil industry owned by Canadians, through their national government, by acquiring several of the large foreign-owned firms."

In order to further squeeze the foreign-owned companies, the NEP announced that preference would be given to Canadian firms when it came to natural gas licences, that the ownership of non-conventional oil projects would be monitored, and that the Foreign Investment Review Agency would be used to prevent foreign-owned oil companies from either diversifying outside the oil and gas business, or buying "already-discovered oil and gas reserves".

The finances for the nationalization of companies would be provided through the Canadian Ownership Account, whereby funds would flow straight from gasoline-station cash registers to Petro-Canada and any other Crown corporations that the government cared to designate. Such a financial arrangement, by a somewhat unusual definition, was declared "self-financing".

For those who did not agree with this program, declared the NEP, there was an alternative. "The Government of Canada recognizes that the National Energy Program represents a fundamental departure, in many instances, from the current policy environment. Despite the fact that the policies will maintain, even enhance, the relative position of the oil and gas industry, some firms may regard the new conditions as unsatisfactory. The Government's acquisition program provides an answer to them. The Government of Canada is a willing buyer, at fair and reasonable prices."

Or, put more succinctly: if foreign companies didn't like it, they could sell out.

The NEP then went on to a long list of "Direct Action Programs" concentrating on increased supply, reduced demand and "rapid substitution" away from oil to more plentiful, Canadian, energy sources. These included grants for switching home-heating fuels, grants for switching to propane and compressed natural-gas transportation systems, refinery modifications, aid for expansion of natural-gas pipelines, and a greater role for renewable energy.

According to the NEP, there would now be great benefits for the oil and gas producers of the West. "The new incentive system for oil and gas exploration and development will foster accelerated efforts, and enhanced prosperity, among Canadian companies and individuals in the West. By ending the biases against Canadian involvement, the Program opens the doors to the large number of Canadian entrepreneurs already active in the industry, and gives them access to new large-scale sources of capital."

Albertans would benefit because "The Program creates the basis for prosperity that will endure into the foreseeable future." Indeed, all the western provinces would benefit. To demonstrate the government's largesse, however, Ottawa would set up — with its enormous new resource revenues — a $4 billion Western Development Fund. In addition, it would spend over $8 billion up to and including 1983 on new initiatives, $2 billion on the Western Development Fund and $3.4 billion on other ongoing energy projects. "This," it pointed out, "is an unprecedented level of expenditure for this sector, but one which faithfully reflects the national government's assessment of the stakes involved in putting right Canada's energy and economic future."

"The National Energy Program," the document concluded, "means making more efficient use of our energy for Canadians and by Canadians. It means bold decisive steps, not generalities; practical programs, not just ideas; rapid and concrete measures to resolve problems, not pious hopes. It means security, opportunity, and fairness."

One can almost imagine tears welling in the eyes of the lucky bureaucrat given the task of penning those final words. It had meant months and months of fourteen-hour days, but now they had produced the program that was to "put right" Canada's future.

# PART THREE

## Reality Intrudes

# 17
# Fear and Loathing in Calgary and Washington

*"My message is simply this. We really do mean it. We know what we are doing."*
MARC LALONDE
Statement made at *Financial Post*
conference in New York three weeks
after the announcement of the NEP.

The announcement of the National Energy Program created a furor both at home and abroad, particularly in the U.S. It was almost universally condemned by the business community, but, since this group was considered in Ottawa to be unenlightened and short-sighted, this came as no surprise. Perhaps what did come as a shock to its authors was that the most vociferous criticism of the program came from the very group that it was meant to help — the small Canadian oil companies. Indeed, immediately after the NEP announcement, the Independent Petroleum Association of Canada, the voice of the smaller, Canadian-owned petroleum companies, placed a nation-wide newspaper advertisement. Addressed to Marc Lalonde, the ad declared of the NEP: "It will make Canadians more dependent on expensive, insecure foreign oil.

"It will cost Canadians more for gasoline and heating oil in the long run.

"It will delay essential frontier exploration, oil sands plants, and heavy oil development.

"It will cost thousands of jobs that could be created by the oil industry across Canada.

"Canada must achieve oil self-sufficiency. We are the companies your program was supposed to help — the independent Canadian companies. It doesn't help us — it has stopped us in our tracks. We urge you to reconsider this program for the good of all Canadians."

The level of personal vituperation between Lalonde and some of the Calgary independents reached almost unprecedented heights of unpleasantness. Earl Joudrie, president of IPAC and of Voyager Petroleum, and John Masters, president of the highly successful Canadian Hunter, both became involved in slanging matches with the Minister. Masters said of the NEP: "I think it's the same kind of tactics the Nazis used to drive the Jews out of Germany. They ran through the streets and smashed store windows and then told the German businessmen to buy them out. Now, Trudeau and his people are smashing in

155

the U.S. oil companies and actually advising the Canadian companies to buy them out. It's so disreputable, I can't believe it."

The verbal battle with Masters was becoming so personal at one time that Lalonde had his assistant, Mike Phelps, call the president of Canadian Hunter and suggest a truce. "Why didn't the Minister himself call?" asked Masters. "Oh, that would be out of the question," said Phelps. "No deal," was Masters' reply. The dispute with IPAC was, one year later, to lead to the very public withdrawal of Petro-Canada from the organization.

Nevertheless, far from shying from exchanges over the program, Lalonde seemed to take delight in them. Indeed, he almost seemed to seek them out.

## The Minister Stiffens His Stride

This was partly due to his profound belief, supported by his bureaucratic henchmen, that what he was doing was for the good of the country, but it was also a reflection of Lalonde's combative and arrogant character. On podium after podium throughout Canada and the U.S. he declared the government's resolve and, from the lofty heights of EMR's superior analysis, poured scorn on critics. "To these people (who doubt the government's resolve)", he declared at a *Financial Post* conference in New York three weeks after the NEP's announcement, "my message is simply this. We really do mean it. We know what we are doing."

The clear implication was that critics either hadn't grasped the full import of the program or simply didn't know what they were talking about. Lalonde's approach was given in an interview in EMR's internal magazine *Intercom* in March, 1981: "To think you can do something that will be met with unanimous favour is just dreaming. That's not how our system works, so you have to be philosophical about it, develop a good tough skin, stiffen your stride and, if it gets tough, look in the other direction and go ahead."

Lalonde certainly had to stiffen his stride when it came to press criticism. The *Globe & Mail* wrote: "This is a shattering new direction for the Government to take, one that will alienate the producing provinces, the major part of the industry and quite possibly the United States where most oil companies originate."

The *Financial Times of Canada*, describing the program as "irresponsible", declared: "Never has the Government stated so emphatically its intention to force economic nationalism on what has been a highly successful and responsible segment of the private sector — the oil and gas industry."

Under a headline "Wildcat Canada resigns from the World", the respected British magazine, *The Economist* said: "Canada's new energy programme, the centrepiece of the Liberal government's first budget since it regained power, takes a giant leap away from the rest of the world."

Some of the harshest words, perhaps not surprisingly, came from the *Wall Street Journal*. " . . . this is the sort of program you'd expect to find south of the North-South dialog, rather than in a key democracy in the industrialized world.

156

Canada is trotting out all the Third World arguments, asking oil companies to try to imagine how America would feel if 82% of its oil and gas revenues were to go to foreign-controlled companies. But the key point is that 82% of Canada's oil and gas revenues wouldn't have amounted to enough to put in your eye, hadn't foreign investors taken the risk and put their capital to work there."

Press condemnation was not universal. *The Toronto Star*, one of Canada's most fiercely nationalist newspapers, described the NEP as a "superb energy plan . . . a monumentally important energy program designed dramatically to increase Canadian control over this vital sector of our economy."

Nevertheless, the generally adverse nature of the NEP's reception, combined with Lalonde's determination to "look in the other direction and go ahead" made the Energy Minister almost impervious to outside advice and even to the most obvious evidence of the policy's adverse impact.

After the NEP's announcement, the Canadian Petroleum Association began a series of trips to Ottawa to attempt to get the government to modify its policy thrust. At one of the first of these meetings, Lalonde welcomed a heavyweight group including Clem Dumett of Union Oil, Arne Nielsen of Canadian Superior, Fraser Allen of Amoco Canada and Harry Carlisle of Gulf Canada. The Minister smiled and told them they would always be welcome in his office, but before they could make any submission or suggestion, they were told that there would be no change in the NEP. They all realized that they might as well have terminated the meeting right there. Lalonde was dead set. Leading business journalist Sandy Ross, reflecting on an interview with Lalonde for *Canadian Business* magazine, summed it up. "I . . . got the impression he'd never once considered the possibility that he might be wrong."

Nevertheless, if there were few self-doubts at EMR, there was an awareness of the impact of adverse publicity on public support for the policy. Every day stories were appearing in the business press about the curtailment of exploration and development programs and the movement of drilling rigs over the border into the U.S.

## Good News from the Holy Trinity

By the end of January, 1981, even Marc Lalonde became aware that some good news was needed. Perhaps inevitably, the good news was dutifully provided by the "blessed triumvirate" of nationalist oil companies that had dominated the Canadian oil scene in the 1970s, Alberta Gas Trunk Line (now renamed Nova), Dome Petroleum, and Petro-Canada.

The first week of February was a good one for Marc Lalonde and EMR. Bob Blair announced that — against the ebb tide of oil industry investment — Nova would increase its budget by $30 million; Petro-Canada announced that it had arranged to buy out Petrofina Canada (71%-owned by the Belgian Petrofina S.A.) for $1.46 billion; and Dome revealed that it was going to create a giant new Canadian-owned subsidiary to increase Canadian presence in the oil industry (but more importantly to take advantage of the enormous new Petroleum Incentive Payments' grants).

Dome's move, perhaps typically, seemed the most innovative. The creation of Jack Gallagher and, latterly, Bill Richards, had been considered one of the most "Canadian" of Canadian oil companies, but in the wake of the NEP, the somewhat embarrassing fact had emerged that Dome Petroleum didn't qualify for PIP grants because its foreign ownership was too high. The government lowered initial levels of ownership requirements and introduced other modifications in return for commitments on the part of oil companies to increase the level of Canadian ownership. However, this still left Dome short of the massive cash infusions it would need for its Beaufort Sea activities and which it had previously found available in the uniquely generous provisions of "super-depletion".

The solution was the creation of Dome Canada, 52% of which was sold to the general public in March for $400 million, making it the largest equity issue in Canadian history. The remainder of the company would be held by Dome Petroleum, whose "payment" for the major portion of its interest was the transfer from Dome Petroleum to Dome Canada of half its 47% interest in gas-transmission giant, TransCanada PipeLines. The result of this complex arrangement was to make Dome Canada 75%-Canadian owned and thus eligible for 80% PIP grants in frontier exploration.

Of course, one of the multinationals would never have been allowed to get away with such a move. Indeed, subsequent provisions were introduced to make sure that they couldn't. Dome Canada's activities were entirely under the control of Dome Petroleum — which still had too great a level of foreign ownership according to the NEP. However, the fact that Dome was allowed to create this new entity clearly showed that it wasn't the letter, but the spirit of the NEP that counted.

Jack Gallagher asked Lalonde for a letter laying out the government's attitude towards Dome Canada. Lalonde replied and gave permission for the reply to be reprinted as an addendum to the Dome Canada prospectus. Both Dome's management and its underwriters were only too aware of the weight added to any prospectus's credibility by a letter from a federal minister. Lalonde, meanwhile, by giving permission for the letter to be reprinted — although it was in fact guarded and largely technical in nature — thus firmly appeared to be tying himself to the fate of Dome.

Petro-Canada's announcement of its takeover of Petrofina, meanwhile, was to herald a six-month buying spree of foreign oil companies, a spree that was at first to delight Ottawa, but eventually to cause the federal government to seek means to stop it. The partly federal-owned Canada Development Corp. acquired 75% of Aquitaine Co. of Canada from its French parent, Société Nationale Elf Aquitaine for $1.2 billion. Nova's subsidiary Husky Oil bought Uno-Tex Petroleum Corp. from Allied Corp. of the U.S. for $371 million, and there were half a dozen or so other significant deals. But then, once again, the biggest deal fell to Dome Petroleum. In what was perceived as a brilliant corporate manoeuvre, it snatched the 53% of Hudson's Bay Oil & Gas owned by Conoco of Stamford, Connecticut for a massive $2 billion.

However, only then, and for the first time, did the government seem to realize what the impact of these acquisitions would be on the Canadian dollar. The sale of Canadian dollars to buy U.S. dollars to make foreign purchases, combined with diminished confidence from overseas investors, was causing the currency to nosedive. Between 1976 and the end of 1978, the Canadian dollar had taken a hammering on international markets, falling from a value of more than U.S. $1.02 to about 85¢. It had shown some relative strength through the period of Joe Clark's government, but the rot had set in once again under the Liberals, and the NEP exacerbated it. Between mid-1980, before the NEP was announced, and mid-1981, in the wake of six months of furious takeover activity, the dollar slumped from 87¢ to 81¢, and it was to slide even lower. Finance Minister Allan MacEachen had to give a directive to the banks to halt their lending for takeovers of foreign oil companies.

Said Marc Lalonde: "Canadianization has exceeded the government's most optimistic expectations. We're the victims of our own success." Nevertheless, continued Lalonde: "The message is still Canadianize. The Canadianization program has the full endorsement of the Cabinet and the Minister of Finance. It's a matter, over the next short while, of pacing ourselves a little bit better than we have in the last few months."

However, it wasn't only the government that suddenly appeared to be the victim of its own success. Interest rates suddenly began to climb precipitously, and the Canadian companies that had boldly carried out the NEP's mandate suddenly began to find themselves seriously strapped for cash.

The NEP's authors, meanwhile, were discovering that their estimates of the costs of the PIP grant program were grossly inadequate, and in fact, billions of dollars out. Thus the NEP, for all its bold and self-confident claims of "putting right Canada's energy and economic future" suddenly seemed to be putting it all wrong. It had not only underestimated the program's cost, it had also severely underestimated the impact of its tax proposals on the industry and the impact of takeovers on the already shaky Canadian dollar. It had also underestimated, or perhaps failed to take into consideration, another enormously important factor in the nation's economic welfare, but one to which Canadian nationalists inevitably turn a jaundiced eye — the reaction of the U.S.

## Uncle Sam Takes Offense

The first moans of complaint over the NEP's impact on Canadian-U.S. relations came not from the U.S. but from Ottawa's own Department of External Affairs, livid that such an internationally controversial policy should have been pronounced without fuller consultation with them. However, the EMR elite and the chosen few outsiders from the PCO and Finance who had made up the magic policy circle of the NEP in the summer of 1980 had no desire to hear the warnings of those prepossessed by international diplomacy. They knew they were creating a controversial policy, and they were quite prepared that Canada pay the price, whatever that price might be.

The inevitable adverse reactions from the U.S. seemed to reinforce this attitude. Indeed, there seemed to be a certain satisfaction in some quarters, on the basis that any Canadian policy that the U.S. objected to had to amount to a piece of valuable national self-assertion. Walter Gordon and his fellow nationalists made pilgrimages to Ottawa just to shake Pierre Trudeau's hand.

Both Pierre Trudeau and Marc Lalonde maintained that U.S. complaints were, in any case, merely due to the power of the oil lobby in Washington. However, the Canadian government was well aware that U.S. concerns went well beyond those undoubtedly heightened by the voice of big oil in Washington.

Washington regarded the NEP not only as an example of "uncivilized" behaviour but also as a dangerous precedent that might be followed by other countries. In the U.S., the Canadian attack on big oil was regarded as a blatant attempt to capitalize on a widespread nationalist sentiment; sentiment of the kind that should be ignored by responsible central governments.

Harald Malmgren, an influential Washington-based consultant, told a Canadian audience in 1981: "There have been many occasions when congress felt just the way the present Canadian cabinet does — but the impulse to be popular and to encourage nationalistic sentiment was curbed by the broader knowledge that the ultimate damage to world trade relations, and even to political relations, would grossly exceed the momentary thrill of having a bash at foreigners."

Nevertheless, the thrill of having a bash at the U.S. appeared to be a highly pleasurable one. At first, the U.S. administration was guarded in its response to the NEP, seeking reversal through quiet diplomacy, but when that failed, and public statements became harsher, these statements seemed, if anything, to strengthen the resolve of the NEP's promoters, and to involve less rabid nationalists in a kind of knee-jerk defence of the Canadian position.

In September, 1981, following an unproductive meeting between Pierre Trudeau and Ronald Reagan, where quiet diplomacy had apparently failed, there were powerful statements from two high State Department officials, Undersecretary of State, Myer Rashish, and Assistant Secretary of State, Robert Hormats. Rashish spoke of "the perception, virtually rampant in Washington, that . . . relationships are sliding dangerously towards a crisis."

Pierre Trudeau expressed a sublime indifference to these strong words, managing at the same time to cast aspersions on the independence of the entire U.S. administration. At the end of September, he declared during a press conference: "What I wanted to ensure in my exchange with the President is that his administration wasn't, shall we say, being used by the oil lobby as a mouthpiece, and I have a conviction that it wasn't . . . But (when) the congressmen or the media or the odd official makes some noise, it doesn't really worry me."

Many Canadians of course pointed out that the U.S. stance could be considered humbug, since "buy American" and U.S.-preference policies were enshrined in many state laws, as well as in federal laws covering areas such as defence procurement, shipping and transportation. However, this drift towards a stance of counter-accusation tended to detract from what should have been the central concern of any examination of the NEP: was it in Canada's long-term interests? This consideration obviously had to take into account the possibility of U.S. retaliation.

One measure of retaliation considered by the U.S. was the enforcement of a provision of its Mineral Lands Leasing Act that required foreign companies' home countries to provide reciprocal facilities for U.S. oil companies. However, the Reagan administration decided in February of 1982 not to enforce this provision. This announcement was treated as a victory in Ottawa. However, in March the U.S. took its objections to the discriminatory agencies of the Canadian Oil and Gas Lands Administration (COGLA), and the Office of Industrial and Regional Benefits (OIRB), to the General Agreement on Tariffs and Trade, the Geneva-based international trade organization, where the issue was being decided as this book went to press.

Concern over the NEP was not restricted to the U.S. Objections were also raised by the European Economic Community and the Organization for Economic Cooperation and Development, where the NEP was viewed as a piece of beggar-my-neighbour national preference with potentially dangerous implications in a global climate of recession.

However, these international objections and possible repercussions were to be of secondary importance in the wake of the NEP. Ottawa knew, after all, that with respect to companies operating in Canada, whether domestic or foreign-owned, it had the legislative power to do its will. The potential destructiveness of that will was another matter. Where its legislative power led into a somewhat more problematic area was, however, with regard to the provinces, in particular Alberta.

# 18
# Alberta Turns Off the Taps

*"The meetings between the federal and provin-
cial sides during 1980 amounted, in the view of
both groups, to non-negotiations, mutual monologues. They squared off like two animals in a
jungle clearing, conspicuously displaying fangs
in the hope that the other side will back down."*

When the Liberals returned to power on February 18, 1980, the Albertan
government had experienced severe, and justified, misgivings. Pierre Trudeau
had stared into the jaws of political oblivion and returned. Marc Lalonde, the
new Energy Minister, was a man very much in the Trudeau mold, superficially
charming and yet with a cold heart and strong centralist convictions. Lalonde
had been at the heart of the Trudeau power machine for a long time. To the
Albertans, his appointment confirmed what they had suspected: that they were
in for a tough fight.

If Lalonde was viewed as the archetypal Trudeaucrat, his opposite number,
Merv Leitch was a role model for Albertan cabinet ministers. A former lawyer
with the establishment Calgary law firm of Macleod, Dixon until his election in
1971, Leitch had been Attorney General and Provincial Secretary, then Provincial Treasurer and, after the March, 1979 election, had been appointed to the
Energy and Natural Resources portfolio.

Leitch was square-jawed, taciturn and, most said, to the right of his premier.
Lalonde had the Gallic charm and looks of a statesman from a more Machiavellian age, and, most said, stood to the left of the Prime Minister. Leitch had
developed the qualities of technical analysis, linear thinking and good administration prized in a wealthy province where re-election was no problem. As one
Edmonton observer pointed out, if Leitch had to go from A to Z, he went in 25
steps. Lalonde, of necessity, was a politician with the broader range of vision
needed to keep the large and battered federal ship of state afloat.

There was little love lost between the two negotiating teams of bureaucrats.
Natural suspicion of the opposition in such negotiations was heightened as far
as the Albertans were concerned by what they considered the duplicity of their
federal counterparts in the past. The federal side, meanwhile, scarcely disguised their conviction that their own mission was a national one, while
Alberta's was inevitably more narrow and — by implication — more short-
sighted and selfish.

However, the Albertan public servants considered themselves to be fighting for far more than narrow, provincial interest. They saw themselves as an outpost against the dark forces of federal interventionism and centralism.

## The Provincial Team Prepares for Battle

On top of the traditional Western resentments regarding central economic domination and lack of political power, many of the Albertan negotiators had personally experienced Ottawa's high-handedness. Most were veterans of the 1974 campaign and harboured bitter memories of the Liberals and their bureaucrats. They remembered when Energy Minister Donald Macdonald had appeared to agree to an oil price increase schedule and then had been forced to renege by his federal cabinet. They remembered Simon Reisman, the powerful deputy minister of finance, sitting there, puffing his cigar and telling them — as if they were so many adolescents — that they just didn't know how to handle money of the magnitude thrown up by soaring domestic prices.

These experiences tended to make Albertans pretty humourless on the topic of federal-provincial relations. Alberta's senior bureaucrat was Barry Mellon, deputy minister of energy, who had been brought into public service with his Ph.D. in geology back in the early 1970s by the then Minister of Energy, Bill Dickie. Mellon was a "heavy" and sometimes seemed to find it difficult to restrain himself in the face of what he saw as Ottawa's duplicity. During the Clark government, when Marcel Massé, Clerk of the Privy Council, had made the first presentation to the Albertan team on a pricing agreement, Mellon had gotten out of his chair, gone to the blackboard in the room, and proceeded, like a stern schoolteacher with a retarded pupil, to demolish Massé's arguments and figures. The other members of the Albertan team just sat there and silently rooted him on, waiting for their chance to face down one of the opposition.

Then there was Wayne Minion, head of the Alberta Petroleum Marketing Agency, the effective "tap" for cutting back Albertan supplies. Minion, big, broad and bespectacled, was a veteran engineer, M.I.T. educated, who had worked for Brascan and B.C. Hydro. Now he was the provincial expert on markets and prices. Minion was in the front line and seemed to take a scarcely-disguised pleasure in the prospect of "leaning on" the federal government. Once, when he was asked how far the Albertan government should go in cutting back production, he suggested that there was "nothing magic" about Lougheed's subsequently declared ceiling of 180,000 barrels a day. Minion's feeling was that the province should just "keep cutting".

The province's main numbers man was Myron Kanik, assistant deputy minister in the Energy department with responsibility for policy analysis and planning. Kanik was a veteran of the oil patch, having spent a total of fifteen years with Pan American (which had subsequently been taken over by Amoco) and Chevron. Kanik's work on developing a common data base with the federal bureaucrats was to prove absolutely essential to the agreement that finally emerged.

Merv Leitch's executive assistant was Tom Wood, an old warhorse of federal-provincial battles. Wood had been executive assistant to Don Getty, the former Edmonton Eskimo star quarterback, one-time provincial cabinet pin-up, and Leitch's predecessor. Wood had been there during the eyeball-to-eyeball confrontations between Getty and Donald Macdonald back in 1974. He knew the federal-provincial score.

Finally, among the full-time negotiators was Jim Seymour, a boyhood friend of Peter Lougheed's who had moved from running the premier's Calgary office to manning his Ottawa outpost during the Clark government. A big, amiable man, there was something about Seymour that made him stick out in Ottawa, much as if John Wayne had been parachuted unwillingly into the middle of a bi-sexual hippie commune.

Once the initial perfunctory pleasantries between the federal and provincial sides had been exchanged in the spring of 1980, it soon became apparent that they were as far apart as they had ever been on their intentions for a new revenue-sharing arrangement.

The federal side's articles of faith were that the Canadian price system had to be "made in Canada", as they had promised during the election campaign, and that oil prices had to be divorced from "irrational" OPEC pricing. More important, however, they insisted on a higher share of revenue for Ottawa's empty coffers. In particular, they zeroed in on the huge flow of funds to the province and producers from gas exports. Throughout the 1970s, emphasis had always been placed on oil as the key commodity. However, it had been natural gas that had been the real beneficiary of the OPEC crisis and that had created most of Alberta's personal fortunes in the latter half of the decade.*

Throughout the 1970s, natural gas revenues had increased at a much faster rate than those of oil. By 1980, Alberta's income from natural gas and natural gas by-products, at about $8 billion, was to surpass its income from oil.

In federal eyes, however, the "windfall" from gas exports to the U.S., which in 1980 were being sold for twice the domestic price, was an obvious source of additional revenue for Ottawa. Peter Lougheed had other ideas. He described the federal government intentions towards natural-gas revenues as tantamount to a "declaration of war". The battle of words had begun.

The meetings between the federal and provincial sides during 1980 amounted, in the view of both sides, to non-negotiations, or mutual monologues. The

---

* This situation arose because of the way natural gas was priced in Canada. Its price was determined for major Eastern markets at the "Toronto City Gate". At the beginning of the 1970s, more than three-quarters of this Toronto City Gate price was represented by the cost of pipeline transportation. After it was determined to link the domestic natural-gas price to the price of domestic oil, there was a rapid escalation. The average consumer price increased about two-and-a-half times between 1970 and 1977. However, since the regulated transportation charge rose much more slowly, and had been such a large element to start with, the amount flowing back to the producer increased much more rapidly over the period, by a factor of about ten.

sides squared off like two animals in a jungle clearing, each conspicuously displaying fangs in the hope that the other will back down.

There was a suspicion on the Albertans' part that the federal side wasn't negotiating in good faith; that since the federal team was operating from such a weak base — that is, the existing taxation and revenue-sharing system — that it felt it had to change the ground rules unilaterally before real negotiations could get under way. That proved to be the case. The federal government's existing share of petroleum revenues was less than 10%, with the remainder more or less evenly split between Alberta and the producing companies. Lalonde and his team said they wanted 25%, and certainly no less than 20%. Alberta said no way!

By mid-July, Pierre Trudeau seemed to display scarcely concealed contempt for the Albertan position. Indicating that there would be no oil-constitutional trade-off, he nevertheless suggested that he might have "more" for Lougheed. Asked what this "more" entailed, the Prime Minister replied sarcastically: "More money." And if that didn't work, he said, "I think I'd offer him again more. At some point he'll say, 'Enough, enough'. I don't want the Canadian consumer to be strangled just to give a few more billion dollars to Alberta."

On July 1, 1980, the old agreement on petroleum pricing expired with no new agreement in sight. Shortly afterwards the two sides, who declared themselves "far apart", both announced that there was no point in further discussions. On August 1, Alberta unilaterally increased the price of its oil by $2 a barrel and that of its natural gas by 30¢ an mcf. Nevertheless, since Ottawa had already offered that increase to Alberta as part of a package, the action was not treated as excessively belligerent by Ottawa.

However, the action about to be taken by Ottawa was to be viewed as more than belligerent by Alberta: the announcement of the National Energy Program on October 28 was considered the economic equivalent of Pearl Harbour. Most of the provisions outlined in the NEP had been revealed to the Albertans in the course of talks throughout the summer of 1980. However, the depth of the federal government's resolve to impose them was still in doubt until a final meeting in September between Premier Lougheed and Prime Minister Trudeau. Then it became clear that the Liberals were prepared to take unilateral action. Less than two weeks before the NEP announcement, Lougheed sent Trudeau a letter warning that Ottawa and Alberta seemed to be "approaching a serious confrontation over national energy policies". However, the letter was conciliatory in tone and the Albertan premier offered to fly "within hours' notice" to Ottawa if Trudeau thought "anything constructive would result".

But the Liberals were set on their energy initiatives. The NEP may not have come as a surprise to the Albertan government, but that did not moderate the province's howls of anguish at what Merv Leitch called: "a massive and discriminatory attack on the resources of the people of Alberta". The federal budget, said Leitch, was "as bad as anything we could have expected". Alberta treasurer Lou Hyndman meanwhile said, not inaccurately: "In its budget,

Ottawa is attempting to move the power of decision-making (on energy prices) from Alberta to Ottawa, permanently." The NEP, he said, was "more like a thistle than an olive branch".

Peter Lougheed appeared on provincial television to tell Albertans that the Liberals' energy plan was like "having strangers take over the living room". The reason for the analogy was that the federal government was, like the Tories before them, trying to tax oil and gas revenues at the wellhead, thus assuming a fiscal prerogative that Albertans believed was constitutionally theirs alone. Also, the Liberals were proposing a multiple-price system based on the type of oil production involved. All the prices, in Alberta's opinion, were too low. Finally, the federal government wanted, in Alberta's opinion, to renege on tar sands pricing agreements.

The oil industry was fuming. The Albertan government was beside itself. There could, announced Peter Lougheed, be no further negotiations with the federal government until there were "significant" changes from the NEP.

## Facing Up to Ottawa's False Gods

In December, the powerful Albertan triumvirate of Mellon, Wood and Kanik headed east like missionaries off to confront the heathen masses. In particular, they were going to debunk the pagan Liberal deities that ruled in Ottawa. These false gods were, in the opinion of the Albertans, spreading figures around that quite misrepresented the results of the NEP in terms of revenue sharing. In Toronto, Barry Mellon seemed in danger of losing his cool, declaring that "those people in Ottawa are nuts". The federal government's new energy proposals, he said, were worse than draconian.

The two sides, Mellon pointed out, were using quite different sets of figures with different assumptions. Each side had a different view of what should be included in their revenue streams. Ottawa counted land-lease sales as part of Alberta's petroleum revenue, while Alberta didn't think they should be counted; the Liberals lumped Alberta in with B.C. and Saskatchewan, which, since the other two provinces taxed the oil industry more heavily, made Alberta provincial tax revenues appear higher than they actually were. Ottawa was also much more optimistic than Alberta on its projections for gas export revenue. Flying off the handle, Mellon declared that the Liberals' figures amounted to "unmitigated fraud".

However, the pricing arrangements of the NEP were still merely a bargaining stance, in that Alberta had not agreed to them. The key issue remained Alberta's constitutional ownership of the oil and gas. The federal government held the right of setting the price within Canada, but Alberta had the ultimate right of deciding whether it wanted to sell at that price.

The Albertan government had only two weapons at its disposal; weapons that were really the two edges of the supply sword. On the one hand, they could cut back conventional production; on the other, they could hold up approval of non-conventional oil megaprojects, most notably the Shell Canada-led proposal

166

for a third tar sands plant and the Imperial Oil scheme for a huge, heavy-oil production and upgrading facility at Cold Lake.

On television just after the announcement of the NEP, Lougheed announced that the time had at last come to reluctantly draw his weapons. Between March and September of 1981, he announced, oil supplies would be cut back in three, 60,000-barrel chunks to 85% of their existing level. However, oil was a weapon that had to be used carefully, for as Lougheed knew, the federal government had emergency measures that theoretically enabled it to seize producing facilities in times of crisis. Lougheed had, therefore, to assert that he was not promoting any kind of national disruption and that the taps would be immediately turned back on if foreign oil was not available. The Albertan Premier also announced that synthetic project approvals would be held up. With regard to the cutback, Lougheed was aware of other dangers, the severest of which was that the oil companies whose production was shut in would be less than enthusiastic. "We sense," he said, "that it will be part of Ottawa's strategy to turn Albertans against their government." And then, with more foresight than he knew: "Yes, we're going to have a storm in this province."

As expected, Marc Lalonde responded that such unilateral action on oil production might force the federal government to invoke the Petroleum Administration Act, introduced in 1974 and giving Ottawa sweeping powers of control in time of crisis.

The key weapons of both sides had recoils that were potentially lethal to their users. Ottawa of course realized that invoking the P.A.A. was not an action to be toyed with lightly. But Lougheed, too, was aware that his cutbacks would be enormously controversial both inside and outside the province.

So concerned was Lougheed to emphasize that the cutbacks would not harm consumers that Wayne Minion's Alberta Petroleum Marketing Commission sent a team to New York to visit oil brokers and ensure that imports were available to match the domestic cutbacks.

The cutbacks were designed to show the federal government how much more expensive imported oil was than that from Alberta. However, this ploy misfired because, under the National Energy Program, the Liberals had shifted the burden for subsidizing expensive imports from their own treasury directly onto the consumer via the Petroleum Compensation Charge. Marc Lalonde was therefore able to up the domestic oil price at the retail level to compensate for additional imports and then call the extra burden the "Lougheed levy".

Nevertheless, March 1, the day the first Alberta cutback of 60,000 barrels went into effect, seemed like a bleak day for Confederation. Alberta felt so alienated that it had to respond like a militant OPEC against a previous foreign oppressor. The day so long feared had come finally to pass: the oil weapon was actually being used within Canadian borders.

Behind the scenes, however, the bureaucrats were hard at work attempting to lay the groundwork for eventual agreement.

# 19
# Pie in the Sky

*"Those are the only economic alternatives available to an interventionist state. It can confiscate; it can redistribute what it has confiscated; it can spend more money than it possesses by borrowing and printing baseless money. There is only one thing it cannot do: produce wealth."*

A Time for Truth
William Simon

On the evening of April 12, 1981, four men sat down for a drink in the bar of the Winnipeg Inn. An observer would have perhaps noticed that the social intercourse was a little uneasy. After a while, however, things began to warm up and — if the observer had also been able to listen in — he would have heard the men talking about a subject close to Canadian hearts: hockey. In particular, the four men talked about the recent Stanley Cup series in which Edmonton had defeated the Montreal Canadiens. One thing an eavesdropper would not have heard the quartet talking about was a topic they were all very eager to avoid — oil and gas — for the four men were Merv Leitch and his executive assistant, Tom Wood, and Marc Lalonde and his top aide, Mike Phelps. This was strictly a "get-reacquainted" session and oil and gas was considered no matter for small talk. The occasion was the eve of the first full-scale negotiations between Ottawa and Alberta since the NEP's announcement six months before.

The federal side at Winnipeg, as well as containing Lalonde, Phelps, Ed Clark, George Tough and a team from Energy, Mines and Resources, also contained Robert Rabinovitch from the PCO, an archetypal bureaucrat all the way from his Ph.D. to his well-honed social conscience, and Sid Rubinoff from the Department of Finance. Rabinovitch was there as secretary of the all-powerful Cabinet Committee on Priorities and Planning, the elite political group headed by Pierre Trudeau, while Rubinoff's presence indicated the inevitable interest of the country's financial mandarins in a deal worth more than any other in Canadian history.

Winnipeg was home territory for Mike Phelps, although the location of the meeting had in fact been chosen by the Albertan side. After the morning session on the 13th, the federal side had decided to get out of the hotel for lunch. Phelps took Lalonde, Cohen, Rabinovitch and Rubinoff to the sparsely-furnished Oscar's deli in the city's north end. The bill came to $14.50. Cohen joked that the accounting people wouldn't accept it and perhaps they should add a nought to the total!

There were to be many noughts discussed that day, for what the two sides were haggling over was one of the largest internal-revenue sharing arrangements in the history of the world, worth literally hundreds of billions of dollars. Conceptually, it was simple. The negotiations had two distinct elements: first the size of the pie had to be determined, then it had to be sliced up. Providing that assumptions about world pricing, future demand and industry activity were correct, the key determinant of the size of the petroleum pie was the schedule of future price increases.

Of course the industry had to be left a large enough slice so that it could actually carry on its activity. After all, the industry was effectively the baker. But that consideration tended to be treated almost as an afterthought, something that tended to be relegated to the back of the well-stocked minds of the bureaucracy. Nevertheless, if the baker did not get a big enough slice to make his effort worthwhile, the whole pie could suddenly disappear, or at least shrink to a much less mouth-watering size. Under these circumstances, the fact that nobody invited the baker to the meetings that thrashed out both the recipe and the plans for divvying up the result seemed somewhat bizarre.

In Calgary and Toronto, the oil companies had access to the most powerful computers and the most up-to-date models in the world. They offered their services to Alberta, but Alberta wasn't interested. Whether it was because the provincial mandarins thought they could do the job themselves, or whether it was because they mistrusted the industry is uncertain. All that is certain is that they failed to avail themselves of the industry's information and for six months locked themselves into a rarified world of economic assumption and bureaucratic, computer projection with their Ottawa counterparts.

The bureaucrats were truly slicing up pie in the sky.

## Searching for a Common Computer Ground

To the public, the dispute between Ottawa and Alberta might have seemed primarily a battle about federal and provincial aspirations, where agreement was held up by the conflicting visions of Peter Lougheed and Pierre Trudeau. But there was another massive barrier to agreement that was far from obvious, indeed incomprehensible, to the average citizen. It was the sheer complexity of the revenue-sharing scheme that already existed. Indeed, it had become increasingly clear in the wake of the NEP that the two sides had no common base for their calculations. It was not simply that each side inevitably attempted to bend the figure to its own ends. It was that the system of royalties, taxes, grants and allowances had grown so enormously complex in the previous decade that few people understood them in their entirety. When combined with the two sides' differing assumptions about other key variables relevant to revenue sharing — future domestic demand, world prices in the 1980s, etc. — there was virtually no basis on which the two sides could even begin talking.

169

It was important that a common data base be developed so that the opposing sides could at least speak the same numerical language. Neither side agreed either on projections of revenue to be shared, or the impact of any particular fiscal move on the portions of the pie. Rectifying that situation was a prerequisite of any agreement.

Thus the two sides delegated their senior number-crunchers, Myron Kanik for Alberta and George Tough for Ottawa, to develop a common data base. It took almost three months for the two teams headed by Kanik and Tough to come to an agreement, a fair indication of just how complex the tax structure had grown.

Kanik and Tough developed a respect and admiration for each other during their months of work together. Their sense of achievement injected a new and positive feeling into the Winnipeg meeting on April 13 that had not been present at previous meetings.

Building computer models gives scarcely less pleasure to top bureaucrats than building model planes or boats gives to small boys. The purpose is the same: it is to recreate on a smaller, more manageable, scale the key features of the real world. For the bureaucrat it represents the opportunity to play God, to find out the crucial question: "What would happen if . . . ?" The advantage for the general population is that as long as academics or bureaucrats are playing with computer models, they are not experimenting with the real world. The disadvantage is that, insofar as the same people think they have created a valid model of the real world, they will expect the computer's inputs and outputs to be faithfully recreated in reality. "This works in the computer model, so let's put it in the budget." And there, of course, lies the rub.

The data base at which Alberta and Ottawa eventually arrived — their numerical vision of the world — was achieved by negotiation; it was a melding of the world as seen by Alberta mixed with the world as seen by Ottawa. The views, however, were far from disinterested. To the extent that one side could put over an assumption advantageous to itself, it could manipulate the ultimately agreement in its favour. However, at the same time it would skew the data base farther and farther from reality. It has subsequently been suggested that Alberta was outsmarted by the federal side, that Ottawa knew the damage that would subsequently be done to the industry by the agreement but figured Alberta would be left carrying the can. That may be crediting the federal side with too much foresight and Machiavellian deviousness, but the fact remains that the projections and assumptions so painstakingly agreed upon by the two sides were wrong. The impact on the industry was severely underestimated. Alberta *was* left carrying the can.

After the informal meeting the night before, a key part of the official meetings on April 13 was the joint presentation by Kanik and Tough that demonstrated to the ministers that both sides were working with the same set of numbers. Henceforth the issues were to be packaged up so that they could be offset against each other. The negotiators could say: "We'll give you your way on items one, three, six and ten, if you will accept our view of the remainder." Then the two ministers would send off their numbers men to run the figures and come out with the magic revenue sharing figure.

The Winnipeg meeting allowed the federal party to restate principles and indicate possible areas of compromise. They were not to make a firm offer.

The NEP had of course represented a major initiative by the federal side that had desecrated a number of Alberta's sacred tenets. The NEP had suggested a multi-tier price system for oil that flew in the face of Lougheed's assertion that there would be one (preferably world) price for Albertan oil. Under the federal proposals of the NEP, "old" oil, that is oil already discovered, would receive relatively low prices, while future discoveries would receive higher prices. At the Winnipeg meeting, the federal side indicated that it might consider higher prices for old oil if Alberta would consider accepting a two-price system.

As far as revenues were concerned, the federal side had effectively already made its grab via the new taxes announced in the NEP, principally the Petroleum and Gas Revenue Tax and the Natural Gas and Gas Liquids Tax. The extremely contentious issue of export taxes had been buried, although not made less objectionable to the Albertans, by the fact that *all* gas sales were now subject to tax by the federal government.

Finally, the federal side thought that Alberta should lower its royalty take in order to leave some more for the industry, which was wailing and gnashing its teeth about the onerous new federal taxes.

The Alberta side acknowledged the federal government's apparent new flexibility and promised that it would come forward with a proposal at the next meeting, whose time and place was to be fixed at a later date. With that, the provincial group left to return to Alberta and consider their position.

Two weeks later, on April 29, senior Alberta bureaucrats and cabinet ministers met for a three-day think tank at Jasper Park Lodge, where they decided on a key concession. They would allow the prices of old and new oil to be split, although they had no intention of letting "old" oil be sold cheaply. Over the following weeks the Alberta mandarins worked to fine-tune a package that would be presented to the federal side at the next meeting.

The site of the next meeting was chosen by Mike Phelps after negotiating with his counterpart, Tom Wood. When Wood heard Phelps suggest Banff he said that the Edmonton team would rather not meet in Alberta. Phelps pointed out that Banff wasn't *in* Alberta; it was a federal park. The point was made with Phelps' unerring nose for diplomacy. Wood took no offence and so it was decided: the next meeting would take place amid the scenic splendour, granite fireplaces and oak-panelled luxury of the Banff Springs Hotel on June 10.

## Friendships Form among the Foes

As at Winnipeg, the formal meetings of June 10 were preceded by informal get-togethers the night before. Leitch and Lalonde spent two hours together while Phelps met with Wood.

From Ottawa's point of view, the June 10 offer from Alberta represented significant progress. The federal group still considered that Alberta wanted too much for conventional oil, but it had accepted the principle of two-tier pricing and also a fixed-price schedule that did not automatically track the world price of oil — something that had always been regarded as an article of faith for the province.

The province still disliked Ottawa's new taxes intensely but refused to back off on its royalties in order to restore some of the industry's funds.

At the end of the meeting, the federal party boarded the twin Otter with a new and positive feeling. Indeed, the only misgivings were those of Mickey Cohen, who didn't relish the tight flight down the Bow Valley. The Albertans, too, felt that things were going well. Despite their opposing stances, friendships were blooming between the two sets of officials. Although the situation was hardly that of an interrogation or a hostage-taking, the federal-provincial negotiations were producing a phenomenon similar to that observed in both of those antagonistic situations — when you are forced to spend a long time with someone, whatever the circumstances, you begin to like them. After all, weren't all these officials after the same thing, the well-being of their constituents? Their constituents were different, although one side's theoretically contained the other's, and the negotiators had different views of the world, but they were all well-trained, rational men. They were all super-bureaucrats armed with powerful computers. They could work it out.

The two sides agreed to meet in Toronto on June 29 so that Ottawa could respond to Alberta's formal offer. In the intervening four weeks, the key Ottawa players, Cohen, Clark, Phelps and Tough, at meetings chaired by Lalonde, thrashed out their offer. Theoretically, at these meetings Lalonde and Phelps would address themselves to political stances and implications, while the bureaucrats would address the purely technical details. But of course these men were all in it together, all fighting for the same rational, federalist solution. Inevitably, lines became blurred. Cohen's acute political senses were much prized by the politicians. Clark could not fail but express himself on issues of equity which were, in reality, political in nature.

At the June 29 meeting in the Harbour Castle, the federal side still proposed a relatively low price for conventional oil — as ever with an eye to their election promise — but said they were prepared to go to higher prices for tar sands and new conventional oil, thus giving Alberta the let-out of a link to world prices. Alberta meanwhile, although it opposed the NEP and its particularly discriminatory methods of Canadianization, agreed to take over the administration of the NEP's Petroleum Incentive Payment (PIP) grants for activity within the province.

The two sides were now getting so close to an agreement that, in the words of one of the participants, they knew they were in for a "bad meeting". That meeting took place in Montreal on August 5. It was Alberta's turn to respond and Leitch's group were still hanging tough on high prices for conventional oil.

172

They refused to budge on royalties. They wanted the world price for new oil and they were still adamant that there would be no tax on gas exports. Lalonde and the federal bureaucrats thought the Albertans were being greedy, a view in fact that they had held all along, but now they allowed it to show. There was just a hint of acrimony. However, there were growing pressures on the federal side. In particular, they had a budget coming up, a budget that would be largely meaningless unless petroleum prices and revenue splits were known. The economy was deteriorating, interest rates were soaring and Jim Coutts, seen by many to be Pierre Trudeau's Crown Prince, had been stunningly defeated in the Spadina by-election in Toronto. The federal side now felt they could no longer be seen to be fiddling with Alberta while Canada burned.

It was time to settle.

## Ottawa Takes More and Finds It Needs More

The federal side appeared to have managed to shift revenues clearly in its own favour via the NEP. It had done this through massive new taxes on the industry but also at the expense of the consumer by transferring the subsidy on imported oil away from Treasury coffers and directly onto the price of oil via the Petroleum Compensation Charge (PCC). It had also allowed PetroCan to plug itself directly into the gasoline pump to pay for its acquisition of Petrofina. Moreover, both times Peter Lougheed had turned back the oil taps, on March 1 and June 1, Ottawa had simply imposed a special compensation charge on the price of crude. Since the NEP had been introduced, there had been two wellhead price increases of a dollar each. These had added just over 6¢ a gallon to the price of gasoline. However, the federal government had, through other charges, slapped on another 23¢ a gallon, none of which went to Alberta. Ottawa seemed to be winning the battle of the gas pumps hands down, and the wonderful thing for the feds was that the public had no clear idea where the increases were coming from. There was only a vague perception that they had "something to do with the federal-provincial squabble."

However, despite all this additional money that seemed to be flowing to Ottawa, EMR had discovered fairly soon after the announcement of the NEP that it had grossly underestimated the payments under the PIP grant system. Ottawa would need more revenue and, faced with staunch opposition to further concessions from their provincial counterparts, EMR convinced the Liberals that there was only one way to get the revenue they needed: slap higher price increases on the consumer and then cream off additional revenues to the industry by yet more punitive taxes. Although there were sound economic reasons for the higher prices, the Liberals' motivations seemed to be based on fiscal expediency. They were certainly impossible to reconcile with the 1980 election promise.

There was pressure, too, on Alberta to settle. The oil industry in general supported the principle of cutbacks, despite the fact that some of its members were badly hit by them. However, the weapon was proving nowhere near as effective as Lougheed had hoped. There were also rumbles of discontent about using non-conventional oil projects as a bargaining tool.

Alberta had run out of political options.

However, when the Albertans turned up at the Four Seasons Hotel in Montreal on Tuesday, August 25, some of them had misgivings about whether they were ready to make an agreement. The problem was that both sides were less ready than they knew. While the federal and Albertan computers had been running their numbers day and night, the world outside had been changing.

Because there were such long gaps between the two sides coming together and then returning to the suites where they had now installed their own computer terminals, the Montreal meeting proved to be an endurance test. The press, smelling agreement, also had the negotiating parties under siege. Meetings had to be shifted from the Four Seasons' mezzanine convention room because each time anybody emerged to answer the call of nature he was besieged by a news-hungry mob of reporters. The negotiations were eventually shifted to delegates' rooms but the media found their way up back staircases and fire escapes, and lingered in hallways with their ears cocked and their notebooks and cassettes at the ready. One day, Phelps and Lalonde managed to escape from the hotel for a walk up Mount Royal, but even there they were spotted by an old gentleman of Scottish extraction who homed-in on the pair and proceeded to berate Lalonde for the impact of the National Energy Program on his investments.

The psychological strain of the negotiations was beginning to tell. People were getting really tired. Meanwhile some of the logistic problems of the mammoth bargaining session were bordering on the farcical: the federal negotiators found themselves running out of socks and underwear.

Debbie Schertler, Lalonde's special assistant, was called in to organize the washing of Ottawa's dirty linen. She had to persuade the hotel manager to open up the hotel's washing machines and recruit several stalwarts to man the ironing boards. The final act saw the cream of the mandarinate sorting through their smalls on Schertler's bed. Perhaps there was a lesson to be learned: don't trust your economy to people who can't organize the washing of their socks.

## A Very Complicated Agreement

The first whiff of a settlement in Montreal came after four days, on the night of Friday, August 28, when Leitch emerged from a meeting to tell waiting reporters: "I'm calling the Premier. It looks like they've given up on the export tax. We may just have a deal."

Indeed, the clincher had been that the federal side had agreed to abandon their plan to tax gas exports, although, in fact, they actually maintained the tax but set it as zero, giving them the ability to impose a levy at some future date.

The following day, Peter Lougheed arrived in Montreal. During the critical stages of the negotiations, when it seemed that the federal side would not budge on the gas export tax, he had wanted to pull back the whole Albertan delegation. But Leitch had asked him not to and then had gone off to persuade Lalonde about the seriousness of the situation. It seemed therefore, that over the critical issue, Lougheed had had his way.

Nevertheless, for the moment, the overwhelming emotion among the negotiating parties was one of relief that a deal had been made. Earlier in the year, when the drilling rigs had been leaving the province, Barry Mellon had declared that the federal negotiators didn't know the difference between a drilling rig and a giraffe. When the agreement was concluded, Mickey Cohen, with whom Mellon had spent so many hours of negotiation, presented him with a picture of giraffes in flight. They had all spent so much time in hotel rooms with each other, occasionally drinking too much scotch in bars together, that they had developed a mutual admiration society.

On the Monday, Leitch, Lougheed, Trudeau and Lalonde appeared at the Ottawa press conference to sign what was effectively their peace treaty. The Prime Minister and the Premier sat in the middle dressed in light brown. Their energy ministers sat beside them decked in light blue. Then Mike Phelps, hovering in the background like the solicitous aide, began to pass the documents between the group for signature. When everything had been signed, the four stood up and began to shake hands across each other like combatants after a good game of mixed doubles.

And then Trudeau spoke. "I bet I know what's on your minds," he said. "Who won and who lost."

Trudeau went on to deliver a rambling monologue in his tired warrior mode, a slightly punchdrunk Muhammad Ali. "The victory," he told his inevitably skeptical audience of Ottawa pressmen, "is Canada's." The closeness with which the Prime Minister had been following the negotiations was indicated by his statement that he had been "told" that the agreement was for "something over $200 billion". Pierre Trudeau was obviously above all such petty, materialistic squabbling.

Peter Lougheed then followed with his own somewhat more upbeat, but equally vague assessment. "It's a very complicated agreement," he said. Like Trudeau, he congratulated the negotiating teams and finally, setting his jaw, said: "Let's get on with the job." And then the parties rose and left, without saying a word about the specifics of the deal. That thorny task was left to Mr. Lalonde.

Mr. Lalonde's press conference did not go well. The journalists wanted to get to the heart of the matter, or rather to the bottom line. What would this mean to the price of gasoline at the pump? But Mr. Lalonde claimed he couldn't say. How could he know what provincial taxes would be? But the media smelled obfuscation. Beads of sweat began to appear on Mr. Lalonde's upper lip. At last, Lalonde, with a bare face, was forced to say it. "We are significantly below the Tory price both in terms of the wellhead price and the blended price." In fact, the Liberals had already taken prices above those forecast in the 1979 Tory budget.

He was questioned, too, on how both governments could have so much more money. "The pie," he explained, "is much larger." The industry, he explained, although its share of the total had dropped from 43% in the NEP to 37% under the federal-provincial agreement, would, in fact, be getting $15 billion more than under the NEP. A prompting voice came from offstage. "I'm sorry," said Lalonde, "not $15 billion, $10 billion." The error was significant. It seemed to indicate that the industry's share was strictly a residual figure; that instead of being the first and most important number to be considered, it was in fact the last.

Lalonde was also closely questioned on how soon the "Lougheed levy", imposed to compensate for Albertan cutbacks, would be removed. Here again he seemed uncertain, pointing out that companies had made import contracts which they now had to honour. He said that the 120,000-barrel-a-day cutback might not be absorbed for "many weeks".

A journalist pointed out that the federal claim for a gas export tax had been based on Ottawa's claim that Canadians deserved a share of the fruits of exploration they had subsidized. Now that Ottawa had decided upon no export tax, did that mean that the principle no longer applied? "We have had a war," replied Lalonde, "and you have to be prepared to pay a price for peace."

Indeed there had been a war. It appeared at first sight that Peter Lougheed, by defeating the gas export tax proposal, might be able to claim some sort of victory. But that assessment was to prove short-lived. In fact, what the two sides had succeeded in doing was to create a fiscal desert and call it peace.

# 20
# Doubts about
# King Peter's Feet

*"They expected Ottawa to try to screw them, but
Lougheed had promised that he wouldn't be party
to any deal that would damage the province's
leading industry. And he had. Lougheed had been
seen toasting the perfidious Trudeau with champagne. The word began to spread that Peter
Lougheed had sold out."*

On September 3, in what became known as the "Pete and Merv Show",
Peter Lougheed appeared once more on the television screens along with his
faithful lieutenant Merv Leitch, to announce to Albertans the dimensions of the
victory. In a reference to his earlier statement about Ottawa occupying the
living room, he said that the peace pact meant that the previous enemy were
now "sitting on the front porch and we're serving them coffee".

But Lougheed's following comments were hardly conciliatory. He claimed
that only the oil cutback had allowed Albertans to win higher petroleum prices,
and that Albertans must continue their fight against Trudeau's plans for
unilateral patriation of the constitution.

Lougheed also pointed out the dangers of the federal-provincial agreement.
It could lead to the "overheating" of the Albertan economy, he said, adding that
he was confident that the province could "manage the problems of growth,
which are preferable to the economic downturn that occurred after Ottawa
unilaterally imposed its National Energy Program last October."

But the trouble was that the agreement had not eased the problems caused
by the NEP; it had exacerbated them.

Ottawa's obsession about the oil industry — that it should get enough to do
the job required, but only just enough — was to produce very damaging effects.

But Alberta, too, seemed to have little practical concern for the industry's
share of revenues. Despite great pressure, the province had maintained its
royalty levels. Moreover, although it so strongly disagreed with the NEP's
discrimination, it agreed to administer within Alberta the main instrument of
that discrimination, the PIP grant system. Its motivation, of course, was that it
did not want 400 federal bureaucrats operating in the heart of the industry, but
this aspect of the agreement was seen by the industry as a betrayal.

In other respects too, the Albertans seemed to have gone happily along with the fiscal pillage of the industry.

The agreement gave much higher prices for oil than those envisaged under the NEP, but it also imposed a correspondingly higher level of federal taxation to make sure that the "windfalls" didn't go to the oil companies.

Henceforth, there was to be a differentiated price in Alberta for oil discovered before and after January 1, 1981. Oil discovered before that date, "old" oil, consisting of the bulk of Canadian domestic supplies, would increase from $18.75 a barrel to $57.75 by July 1, 1986. However (and this "however" was to become extremely important within just months of the agreement's signing) the old oil price was subject to a ceiling. That ceiling was 75% of the delivered price of imported oil in Montreal, the terminal and refining centre of Canada's foreign oil supplies.

The price for "new" oil, which embraced not only discoveries made after January 1, 1981 but also synthetic oil and oil from enhanced recovery schemes like Imperial's proposal at Cold Lake, was to start at a much higher base of $47.30 a barrel (delivered at Montreal) on January 1, 1982, more than twice the old oil level. It was to rise by between $3.20 and $4 a barrel every six months until it reached $79.10 on July 1, 1986. Once again, however, there was to be a ceiling, in this case the actual international price. Even as the ink was drying on the documents in front of Lougheed and Trudeau, the prospects of the ceiling coming into effect were getting stronger.

Consumer prices of natural gas were due to increase from $3.20 to $7.35 over the life of the agreement, with Alberta agreeing to provide a discount for sales to new markets. The federal government also committed itself to authorize additional gas exports if the National Energy Board found that there was a surplus.

The agreement contained a declaration of intent by Alberta that it would grant "expeditious approval" for synthetic oil projects, and Alberta introduced a new royalty system for the projects and the promise of a $600 million "Canadianization" grant. The federal government, meanwhile, in the eternal quest to fetter oil companies' movements, declared that income from synthetics plants would be "ring-fenced", that is, would be completely separate from other income of partners when it came to calculation of taxes.

The most awe-inspiring aspect of the federal-provincial agreement was the numbers involved, which, as Mr. Trudeau had correctly been informed, theoretically totalled more than $200 billion. In fact, the computer pie of petroleum revenue for the five years and four months of the agreement totalled $212.8 billion, of which $54.3 billion would flow to the government of Canada, $64.3 billion to the government of Alberta and $94.2 billion to the industry. The figures were impressive not only for their size but for their accuracy. Just imagine, the government bureaucrats were able to calculate these figures right down to the nearest $100 million!

Unfortunately, the figures were based on assumptions that had been made invalid some time before the final carve-up was announced. Within just a few months they were to prove to be wildly off the mark.

## Running the Numbers on Disaster

When the federal and Alberta sides announced their agreement, there was an initial feeling of relief in the industry. If Peter Lougheed had concluded an agreement, they reasoned, it had to be a lot better than the arrangements of the NEP. Some, including Bill Daniel, the chief executive of Shell Canada, a company which as leader of the Alsands consortium had a vital interest in the new deal, came out publicly to praise the deal before examining it closely. But others were uneasy straight away. Gerry Henderson, the president of Chevron Standard — the enormously successful subsidiary of Standard Oil of California that had been responsible for the previous decades' two most significant oil finds in Canada, at West Pembina in Alberta and Hibernia offshore from Newfoundland — disliked the agreement as soon as he saw it. He immediately ordered his staff to run the numbers through the computer. Two days later he phoned Bill Daniel. "I've run the numbers," he said, "and the deal is a disaster."

Henderson wanted to get through to Merv Leitch to find out what had happened, but Leitch didn't want to say anything until the Premier had appeared on television to announce what a good deal it was. Henderson watched the Premier's TV performance with growing incredulity. He was expecting Lougheed to announce additional benefits for the industry. But Lougheed wasn't doing any such thing.

Soon the Calgary grapevine was buzzing. Company after company had put the agreement's numbers into their computers and came up with similar results. Far from returning the industry to a state of pre-NEP health, the deal didn't pan out to be much better than the NEP itself. In some cases it was worse. And as for all those billions of dollars that the bureaucrats had been playing with, they just didn't make sense. Nobody understood where they came from. Worst of all, the discriminatory, regulatory aspects of the NEP, far from being injured, were in fact now much strengthened because Alberta had actually agreed to administer the PIP program in the province.

The oil companies regarded the agreement's projection of world prices to be much too high. Since these world prices were critical for setting a ceiling on domestic prices, the oil companies believed that Canadian prices would bump up against the ceiling much sooner than the agreement predicted. This in turn meant that revenues would be considerably smaller. The Canadian Petroleum Association worked through the figures and calculated that, far from reaching the level of $57.75 a barrel predicted in the agreement by 1986, the price of old oil by that date would be $43.50 a barrel, a massive 36% difference.

The most onerous aspect of the NEP, the Petroleum and Gas Revenue Tax, far from being alleviated, had been effectively increased by 50%, from 8% to 12%, while a new tax, the Incremental Oil Revenue Tax (IORT) took 50% of the revenues, less Crown royalties, of higher-than-NEP prices. New oil prices looked attractive, but to receive them you first had to find new oil, and that could be a lengthy business.

As for natural gas, when the companies worked out the revenues flowing back to the producers, they were *worse* than under the NEP. This, ironically, would damage most severely the smaller Canadian companies that had led the way in gas discovery and development throughout the 1970s. And as for the commitment to examine additional natural gas exports, that proposal had effectively been dealt a kick in the teeth only days after the announcement of the agreement when the National Energy Board had indicated that no surplus gas was available for export.

Peter Lougheed, if never the industry's friend, had at least always been considered its ally. Now, it seemed to the oilmen, he had been cajoled, or conned, into a deal that fed the oil companies to the wolves.

The government officials and bureaucrats had emerged from their computer purdah thinking that they had recreated a new and better world of petroleum pricing and taxation. Somehow they managed to delude themselves into believing that such a result could emerge from a naked clash of political self-interest where the last — rather than the first — consideration had been the health of the oil industry.

There are those who believe that the federal side knew perfectly well what it was doing; that its priorities really were to hobble the oil business. Another theory is that the federal side knew that the figures of the agreement were unrealistic but realized that once the industry really began to suffer, the pressure would be exerted first and foremost on Alberta to provide relief, as was indeed the case.

However, the third, and perhaps the most plausible, theory was that the whole affair represented not simple, but highly complex incompetence.

The federal-provincial agreement was getting into a degree of fine-tuning and governmental regulation that is simply not possible in any society, let alone one where the oil sector is predominantly private. Any government can make a mess, but the potential for one served by enormously powerful computer-armed officials is correspondingly greater.

## Alberta's Image Crumbles

On a side table in Wayne Minion's office at the Alberta Petroleum Marketing Commission in Edmonton, sits a piece of parchment paper. Written on it in Gothic script is one of those joke notices so often seen around business offices. Only this one is too close to home to be really funny. It is titled "The five stages of a project." Stage one is "Excitement, euphoria"; stage 2 is "Disenchantment"; stage 3 is "Search for the guilty"; stage 4 is "Punishment of the innocent", and stage 5 is "Distinction for the uninvolved."

If the title were "The five stages of federal-provincial negotiations" we would now, in 1982, be between stages three and four. The euphoria of September 1 was quickly transformed into disenchantment as the premises of the agreement

180

fell apart in the face of industry analysis and world events. And now the finger was being pointed at Peter Lougheed and his officials rather than the federal negotiators. Whether Lougheed was innocent or not was a moot point, but there was a distinct whiff of electoral punishment in the air.

Minion and the other provincial bureaucrats were angry, angry with Ottawa but more angry with themselves for being part of what they now saw as a disastrous agreement.

The carefully cultivated image of the province's invincible administration was beginning to crumble. Just before the provincial Conservative convention in Edmonton in March, 1982, the Albertan bureaucrats were bringing up select groups of oilmen from Calgary and saying "We admit it, we screwed up. But now we're going to put it right for you. Just tell us how to do it. Tell us how much you want us to haul down royalties. But whatever you do, don't let it get out that we made such a damned *mess* of the whole thing."

But of course, that was not the public image being presented. Peter Lougheed was attempting, not surprisingly, to shift all the blame onto Ottawa.

Just six months after the declaration of peace, Lougheed appeared to be cranking up the old Albertan political war-machine once more. Only now, for the first time, he seemed to be cranking it up primarily for his own political motives rather than for the good of the province. For ten years Peter Lougheed's star had been inextricably linked to the fortunes of Alberta, but now, suddenly, there appeared to be a rift. Peter Lougheed had declared that he would not do a deal that would damage the industry. He had constantly asked Leitch, and Leitch had constantly checked with the Albertan officials, to make sure the industry would be all right after the agreement. They had told him yes, it would. But now it was obviously not all right with the industry. In fact, the industry was bleeding to death, and it didn't matter that it was significantly due to factors over which Lougheed had no control — like soaring interest rates and an arthritic federal policy of import compensation that was shutting cheap Albertan oil in while it was subsidizing expensive foreign imports. Albertans perceived that their problems sprang from the September agreement. They *expected* Ottawa to try to screw them, but Lougheed had promised that he wouldn't be party to any deal that would damage the province's leading industry. And he had. Lougheed had been seen toasting the perfidious Trudeau with champagne. The word began to spread that Peter Lougheed had sold out.

For some reason, Lougheed had always attracted the nation's finest writers of doggerel. Southam's Ottawa bureau chief, Charles Lynch, had written the classic "Sheik of Cal-gary" but during the 1981 negotiations, a new verse appeared. It was called "Peter Prayer," and went:

Our Peter who art in conflict,
Pricing be thine game,
Thy Day has come,
Thy Wrath be known,
in Hull as it is in Devon.

Give us this day our worldly price,
And forgive us our royalties
As we forgive them
who covet our trust fund.
Let us not into PetroCan
and deliver us from Trudeau,
For Cold Lake the ransom,
And the country will import,
For ever and ever.

The "Peter Prayer" was irreverent, but like all good humour, it hit the mark. Indeed, perhaps Lougheed quietly revelled in the image so portrayed. Over the decade of his power, he had become the idol of the Albertan religion of self-assertion. But now, in the wake of the federal-provincial agreement, even his closest acolytes were beginning to examine his feet.

Political diversion was called for.

## The Heritage Fund: Where's the Slot?

At the Edmonton convention in March, 1982, Lougheed said that he would be coming up with improvements in the agreement for the industry and that the federal side would have to make matching concessions, "agreement or no agreement".

He returned once more to the image of the homesteader being invaded by strangers from Ottawa. Six months before he had claimed that the federal-provincial agreement had moved them out of the living room onto the porch. Now, he said in a convincing cowboy drawl, "I'm beginning to think we ought to move them off the property." But despite the belligerent stance he was a worried man. For Albertans, whose chronic condition is one of frustration with a distant centralist government that does not understand them, a vote for Lougheed had always been a vote against Trudeau. Lougheed was always the champion who could give as good as he got in dealings with Ottawa. Alberta, through its Premier, had found identity in conflict. Edmonton, in the words of William Thorsell, deputy editor of the *Edmonton Journal*, had become a kind of "Western Tel Aviv", the centre of a province that saw itself constantly under financial siege from the cash-hungry federal government. But now, it appeared, the walls had been breached. Much worse, Lougheed seemed to have invited the enemy in. He had allowed Ottawa to impose massive new taxes on the industry and yet had refused to lower his own royalty take.

And now, the political heat generated by the Heritage Fund grew as never before. The fund, set up in 1976 to salt away non-renewable resource revenue against the distant day when such revenue ran out, had always been a political problem. But now, for the first time since the fund had been set up, Albertans were suffering financially; people were going bust, farmers were straining under high interest rates, the good citizens of Alberta were forced to refinance home mortgages at unprecedented rates. Never mind that future rainy day, grumbled the electorate, what about today?

The now almost defunct Albertan Social Credit party had, as its Parthian shot, run a series of ads portraying the fund as a giant piggy bank with no slot to retrieve the money. And the shot was effective. Nobody was arguing with the well-honed clichés and carefully-collected self-justifications assembled by the Albertan powers-that-be — that selling the province's oil and gas was like "selling the topsoil" or auctioning off "grandma's antiques," that what was being sold was irreplaceable. No, nobody in Alberta would argue with that. But what about a little piece of that great pot now? Previously, the enemy had always been Ottawa, the federal government trying to grab a chunk of Alberta's birthright, but now it seemed that the rival was none other than the province's unborn, represented by the humourless custodians in Edmonton.

Lou Hyndman, the province's Treasurer and one of Lougheed's old guard, the man, in fact, who nominated Lougheed when he began his rise to glory way back in March, 1965, held the increasingly uncomfortable job of sitting on the fund. Hyndman has been seen by many as Lougheed's potential successor, but political succession was not foremost in many Albertans' minds in 1982. What was foremost was personal economic survival, and what rankled was that piggy bank with no access to the cash.

In the Albertan orthodoxy, the Heritage Fund is the Tabernacle. Its defence is a catechism of arguments carefully collected over the years since the fund was set up in 1976. It begins with the portrayal of Alberta as just a poor province enjoying a temporary place in the sun; continues with emphasis on how cheaply Alberta is selling its birthright of non-renewable resources (that is, implying that the fund could and should be much larger); and ends with a declaration that the fund really is being well-managed, despite frequent assertions to the contrary. Hyndman, the lanky, bespectacled high priest in the immaculate, grey pin-striped suit, delivers the credo rapidly, almost breathlessly speaking of "unique opportunities", "God-given resources", and Alberta's "unexampled generosity" in selling its birthright so cheaply. He admitted, however, that there was a "communications challenge".

# 21
# Petroleum
# Pulls the Plug

*"Clearly, too, any country able to dissociate itself
from the world oil market of the 1980s should do
so, and quickly. Canada is one of the few that can."*
NATIONAL ENERGY PROGRAM, OCTOBER, 1980

*"The oil industry in North America is meeting
difficulties at present. We are living in a world
economy in this regard."*
MARC LALONDE,
FEDERAL ENERGY MINISTER, MAY, 1982

The first week of May, 1982 was not a good one for Liberal Federal Energy
Minister Marc Lalonde. In that week he had to deal both with the collapse of
the Alsands project — a proposed $13 billion, 140,000-barrel-a-day tar sands
plant — and a further two-year delay in the even more massive Alaska
Highway gas pipeline. The Opposition in the House of Commons was baying
for Lalonde's blood and for once his enormous self-confidence seemed in
danger of cracking.

Lalonde had good reason for discomfort. It had taken just eighteen months
for the Liberal government to realize that it was living in the whole energy
world, rather than its own nationalistic cocoon. Nothing brought the lesson
home more painfully than the difficulties that befell the country's petroleum
megaprojects, the multi-billion dollar schemes in which Canada was to lead the
world.

The collapse of the megaprojects in Canada was to a large degree due to the
collapse of world prices in 1981 and 1982. Both federal and provincial experts
failed to predict this trend. However, the implications of the OPEC price decline
for Canada go well beyond the issue of bureaucratic competence. An understanding of the economic forces of world oil is important not only in understanding where all those megaprojects went; it is important when assessing
whether they'll ever come back.

The fundamental question that arises from the events of the first two years
of the 1980s is: just how much power did OPEC ever have? Should OPEC be
seen as some sort of genie from an economic Arabian nights, springing from an
oil barrel and wielding awesome power? Or has it always been more like a
gold-plated cork bobbing on a tide of market forces?

184

Much of the wrangling about petroleum in the past decade has been about the extent to which world prices reflect the "real" state of economic affairs. In Canada, the issue has been a sideshow of Alberta's often bitter fight with Ottawa. Peter Lougheed claimed that the OPEC price was the right reference price for Albertan oil; Ottawa claimed that it was an unrealistically high price imposed by a powerful cartel.

In his famous Halifax speech during the 1980 election campaign, in which he promised lower prices over the ensuing four years than those announced by the Tories, Pierre Trudeau said: "The OPEC price for oil now has everything to do with politics, and almost nothing to do with economics . . . "

The authors of the National Energy Program continued to purvey this view of OPEC as a force capable of dictating world oil prices.

"By the mid-1970s," says the NEP, "the large multinational oil companies had lost their dominance over world oil production, and a new force emerged: the Organization of Petroleum Exporting Countries (OPEC), a cartel formed to obtain higher returns for its oil through supply management and decree. The cartel has succeeded. Oil prices that were $3 a barrel in 1960 — and still about $3 a barrel in 1970 — are now $38 or more."

The document is somewhat misleading. OPEC was actually formed not to impose higher oil prices but to stop the major oil companies from forcing them yet lower. Moreover, the organization first met in Baghdad in September, 1960. The NEP fails to explain why, if OPEC was such an effective cartel, the price of oil didn't move up at all for the first ten years of its existence.

Nevertheless, the NEP continues: "OPEC's effectiveness was proved by events after the 1978 Iranian revolution. There was more than enough oil available in the months following the revolution to meet the world's needs. Yet the price of oil more than doubled, due to OPEC's determination to raise prices — even if it meant restrained production, and panic buying by consumers fearing real shortages."

This paragraph presents a somewhat muddled view — deliberate or otherwise — of affairs. Saying that there was enough oil "to meet the world's needs" cannot possibly square with "panic buying", for if there really were sufficient oil, then panic buying would have no impact on prices whatsoever. The market makes no distinction between the emotional states of those making purchases. Prices on the spot market are not determined by the amount of sweat obvious on the brows of the trading partners, but on the supply and demand for oil. In the first half of 1979, there was indeed panic buying because supply had been curtailed. This cutback was not a result of any concerted action on the part of OPEC members, but was due to the shut-off of Iranian oil caused by the revolution.

Nevertheless, the NEP persists in attributing to OPEC the continuing ability to dictate prices. "It was once thought," it states, "that OPEC's power to set prices could be eroded significantly by consuming countries reducing their oil demands. While this is clearly the long-term solution, and while slackened

185

demand may moderate for a time the pace of price increases, the prospects are for a continuation of control by OPEC. Its members have demonstrated an ability and a willingness to adjust supplies in order to raise prices. In this vital sense, the oil market is not a free market. A market is not free if producers are able to manipulate prices by manipulating production . . . In short, the world is experiencing a major economic crisis brought on by decisions on the part of a small group of producing countries to raise the price of oil."

Like almost everything that happened in the world of petroleum in the two years after the publication of the NEP, events in the international oil market were to cast severe doubts on the document's line of reasoning. It had bestowed far too much power on OPEC. Within eighteen months, the organization was showing unprecedented signs of internal strain, even collapse. The greatest irony of the NEP was that Canada's self-sufficiency, based on petroleum megaprojects and expensive frontier exploration and development, was in fact *only* achievable if OPEC was actually as strong as the NEP claimed it was. The document, with its scant faith in the power of the market, gave no inkling that prices might actually *fall* significantly. "Clearly," concludes the NEP, " . . . any country able to dissociate itself from the world oil market of the 1980s should do so, and quickly. Canada is one of the few that can."

Within eighteen months of the NEP, the gigantic megaprojects on which this dissociation depended, had, like so many chimaeras, disappeared into thin air. Moreover, far from rejecting "artificial" and "arbitrary" OPEC prices as a reference point for Canadian oil, the federal government, once it had successfully negotiated for a greater share of the potential spoils, signed an agreement with Alberta that promised to take after world prices at a very rapid rate, while simultaneously slapping heavy new taxes on consumers. The further irony was that, even as the federal and Albertan governments signed the agreement divvying up the spoils, OPEC was crumbling. And as OPEC crumbled, the spoils, too, were disappearing.

## The Peculiarities of Petroleum

To put the events of the decade following the 1973 OPEC crisis into perspective, one should look both at the unique nature of petroleum as a commodity, and the impact of that nature on its pricing.

Man's history from cave-dweller to astronaut has been, in one critical respect, the history of his access to, and control of, energy — the power to do work. Muscle provided the only answer to man's earliest energy problems. In time, beasts were tamed and wind and water harnessed in order to help him grow crops, grind corn and sail the seas. Then came the quantum leap of the steam engine, the hissing clanking monster fueled by coal that shaped the nineteenth century's industrial revolution. The ox, the windmill and the locomotive marked the progression of man's constant striving for power but petroleum, and the technology it spawned, was to unleash power and economic growth of which the industrial revolution had never dreamed. It was one of the most powerful of nature's substances, but it was also one of the strangest.

Petroleum, literally from the Latin "rock oil" — a term embracing both crude oil and natural gas — has its origins in the sediments and reefs at the bottom of ancient seas. These became the graveyard for countless living creatures and plants that either inhabited the seas or were deposited in them by rivers. Over the immensity of geological time, in which, as H. G. Wells pointed out, the evolution of man represents but a tick of the clock, these subsea sedimentary layers turned into rock. Seas retreated and advanced as the earth was convulsed by hundreds of millions of years of growing pains, and the sedimentary layers became buried deeper and deeper below the surface. By a process still not fully understood, the enormous pressures on the organic material still within the rock — combined with heat, chemical, bacterial, and possibly even radioactive changes — caused the remains of prehistoric life to be changed into liquid and gaseous hydrocarbons which we now know as petroleum.

The sedimentary rocks also contained water, and since gas is lighter than oil, and oil lighter than water, the three substances migrated upwards — provided, that is, that the rocks were permeable enough. In some cases, the gas and oil were pushed all the way to the surface, after a journey that may have spanned a couple of miles and taken several million years. There they would seep into the atmosphere. In other cases, however, the oil and gas reached an impermeable rock layer that would not permit them to rise further. Hence a "trap" was formed where the oil and gas sat under enormous pressure, like some mythical monster imprisoned in the bowels of the earth.

Early exploration efforts were concentrated on areas where there was some visible sign of what lay beneath — gas bubbling up through a stagnant pool, or rainbow stains trickling down a stream. But gradually, oil explorers discovered that the greatest riches lay trapped in the less obvious reservoirs, often many miles beneath the earth's surface — enormous tantalizing pools of oil and gas that could bestow as much wealth and power as any gold strike.

The effort needed to release petroleum from its trap was relatively small. All that was required was to make a hole in the rock that bound it. It was almost as easy as rubbing a magic lamp. Once given an escape route, the oil and gas would surge to the surface under enormous pressure, bursting from its world of darkness.

However, because of this peculiar property — that to find it was simultaneously to produce it — it was able to wreak havoc on economic markets. In the very earliest days of the Oil Regions of Pennsylvania, in the 1860s, a barrel of oil could sell, within a matter of months, for a price ranging between 10 cents and $20 as new finds gushed onto the landscape and as quickly dried up. Within a few decades, the search for petroleum had spread over the globe. This sometimes obsessive search, combined with ever-improving technology, meant that, with a few wrinkles, the following hundred years were characterized by a supply which almost always stayed ahead of demand.

Even the explosion in petroleum demand during and after the Second World War was matched, and exceeded, by massive finds, primarily in the Middle East. Between 1880 and 1970, world oil prices moved in an astonishingly narrow range of between about 50 cents and U.S. $2.20. Throughout the 1960s, the official price was U.S. $1.80. But the 1950s and 1960s could be viewed either as a golden age or a fools' paradise. Sooner or later, with global demand doubling every ten years after the war, the world had to run out of $1.80 oil. The inevitable crunch came when U.S. domestic oil production — still the largest of any country in the world — peaked in the early 1970s. U.S. demand, however, continued to soar, leading to a massive thirst for imported oil. The signs of the shift in the market could be seen for a couple of years before the dramatic events of the winter of 1973-74. However, the 1973 Arab oil embargo is still widely seen as a watershed at which the OPEC nations learned to flex their economic muscles. But the embargo and the ensuing quadrupling of prices were really the tip of the market iceberg. Panic buying in spot markets had already driven prices to a seemingly astronomical U.S. $17 a barrel. The spot market held the key to what had really happened. Almost overnight, rocketing U.S. import demand had wrought a dramatic transformation on the world oil arena, changing it from a buyers' to a sellers' market. To that extent, OPEC did not force its will on the world, but merely took advantage of a dramatic shift in market conditions.

The scope for petroleum price increases was large for two reasons. On the one hand, oil was so much cheaper and so much more flexible than its alternative fuels. Moreover, the whole industrialized world — via its cars, its factories, its airlines — was firmly plugged into the huge petroleum network. This meant that demand for petroleum was, in economic terms, "inelastic"; that is, it would not drop proportionately anywhere near as far as the price could rise.

Although there was still lots of "cheap" — that is, cheap to produce — petroleum all over the world, from Saudi Arabia to Alberta, in order to satisfy projected demand, the search for new supplies had shifted to much more expensive areas. The oil companies were now looking for, and finding, oil offshore and in the Arctic. Big finds had been made in both the Arctic, at Prudhoe Bay on the North Slope of Alaska, and in the North Sea. However, this oil was expensive to produce, certainly too expensive to consider at $1.80 a barrel. This fact has been used by corporate conspiracy theorists to suggest that the oil companies may have in some way promoted the OPEC crisis, or at least egged on the producers to higher demands. However, from the point of view of market economics, if much higher prices had not been imposed in 1973-74, then Prudhoe Bay and the North Sea would not have added their supplies to the world and an even greater demand shortage would likely have occurred in the mid-1970s, with inevitably higher prices.

In any event, these frontier sources, combined with new supplies from Mexico, and a reduction in the growth of oil use because of worldwide recession, helped to keep OPEC prices down between 1974 and 1978. Sheik Yamani, the Saudi Arabian oil minister and the widely acknowledged spokesman for OPEC, made constant, well-reasoned appeals during this period for further gradual increases in the oil price to prevent large increases — with attendant economic disruption — later. His voice of reason was ignored. Western governments, with an eye on their balances of payments and the next election, could condone no such view.

What's more, they were busy loading their own taxes onto petroleum. For a revenue grab by governments was another key support for the upward movement of oil prices in the 1970s. Producing countries imposed royalties and taxes at the wellhead to cream off the windfalls of higher prices. Meanwhile, wholesale and retail taxes were added to petroleum products ostensibly in the name of conservation but equally in the name of increasing government revenues.

The Canadian federal government was very late getting into the game, but when it did get in, it got in with a vengeance. Unfortunately, the subsequent collapse of OPEC prices was to make its revenue projections a fantasy.

Even as the federal and Alberta governments were concluding the agreement in August, 1981 which painted a picture of continuously rising OPEC prices, slack demand for OPEC oil was pushing OPEC production to a thirteen-year low. Despite that, however, the Canadian bureaucratic wizards were telling the government that OPEC had the power, almost forever, to continue pushing up prices faster than the general rate of inflation. In fact, what the aftermath of the second OPEC price surge of the 1970s showed was exactly the opposite.

## What Goes Up, Can Come Down

The circumstances of the second OPEC crisis were remarkably similar to those of the first. A significant reduction in supply — caused by the revolution in Iran — combined with panic buying, created the circumstances for a major price increase. The word "circumstances" is used to highlight the fact that, as in the first crisis, OPEC may have subsequently increased official prices, but it did so against the background of rocketing spot-market prices. The repetition of this sequence of events led an increasing number of analysts to look at OPEC in a new light, not as a price leader but as a price follower. Among the foremost proponents of this view have been Herman Kahn and William M. Brown, respectively director of research and director of energy studies at the prestigious Hudson Institute. Examining the crisis of 1974 and 1980, they concluded in a 1980 joint paper: "The persistence with which spot prices exceeded the 'cartel price' in both periods is a dead giveaway that soaring demand, not the cartel's muscle, has been the prime mover of prices."

They also maintained that the latest round of OPEC prices would bring forth the surge of non-OPEC supplies that might break the cartel. Indeed, even before the NEP was published, downward market pressures on the world oil price were apparent. Two months after a general increase announced in July, 1980 — to a range between U.S. $32 and U.S. $37 — only a few OPEC members had made any attempt to push their prices to these "ceiling" levels. Even more important was the fact that, less than two weeks after the meeting in Algeria at which the increases were announced, both Algerian and Libyan oil was being offered on the spot market at below the official price. There was so much oil around, and stocks were so high, that cargoes were reportedly lying offshore the Gulf of Mexico because there were no storage facilities available for them.

As the National Energy Program was unveiled in October, Iran and Iraq went to war and the world market tightened up once more. At a meeting in Bali in December, 1980, the hawks appeared to prevail and new increased price ceilings in a range between U.S. $36 and U.S. $41 were announced. Sheik Yamani declared that Saudi Arabia would increase its output to more than 10 million barrels a day in order to exert downward pressure on prices. But whether Yamani was adopting his traditional pose as the West's friend, or whether he could see which way the market winds were blowing, is something we are never likely to know. The fact was that the market simply would not bear the December increases. Even the OPEC hawks had been seduced by the idea of their own power. That belief was soon to be rudely jolted.

Throughout the first half of 1981, the rout gathered momentum. By July, demand for the oil of the African hawks — Algeria, Libya, Nigeria and Gabon — was, at 2.7 million barrels a day, almost half what it had been at the beginning of the year. Secret meetings were held in Tripoli, but the hawks found they couldn't fight the market, particularly with Saudi Arabia on its side.

In August, Japanese refiners stopped taking delivery from five OPEC nations, while European and U.S. refiners were also reported to be walking away from contracts with the African producers. In October, the organization retreated from the high official prices of the previous year and accepted the unified benchmark price of U.S. $34 the Saudis had been trying to impose. By then, however, U.S. $34 was beginning to look expensive.

Overall OPEC production in 1981, in the face of declining markets, slumped by 16.4% to just under 22.5 million barrels a day, less than two-thirds of total estimated production capacity. And things were to get worse. By mid-January, 1982, even Saudi oil was being sold on the spot market for less than the official price, while Sheik Yamani was predicting little or no increase in real oil prices until the 1990s. Iran, attempting to finance its ongoing war with Iraq, was threatening to dump several million barrels of oil a day onto world markets.

By the beginning of March, it appeared that the oil weapon had once again switched hands. President Reagan announced that imports of Libyan oil would be banned, as would exports of U.S. oil and gas technology to that country. At the end of the first quarter of 1982, it was apparent that OPEC was facing the biggest crisis in its 21-year history. Iranian barter deals were being made at $12 below the world price; North Sea oil was going on the spot market for $27; demand for Libyan oil had dropped 70% from its peak.

These events formed the background to an emergency meeting at OPEC's Vienna headquarters. Ironically, it was at this meeting, in March, 1982, that OPEC attempted for the first time to act like the cartel that its critics had always claimed it was. In an attempt to maintain the U.S. $34 benchmark price, it set an overall production ceiling of 18 million barrels a day for the whole organization and, much more important, individual ceilings for its members. The overall ceiling was in fact almost irrelevant, because it was demand for OPEC oil that determined production levels. By mid-April, demand was below 16 million barrels, almost half the peak production level reached in 1977. Far more important, some countries, most notably Iran, were ignoring their own production ceilings and thus aggravating the position of other producers.

Some of the OPEC nations, meanwhile, were under severe financial strain. A common problem to many of them — particularly the more populous members — was the enormously expensive development programs they had entered into on the basis of optimistic oil demand and income projections. Nigeria in particular was felt to be very weak and was coming under pressure from the oil companies to lower its prices. OPEC meanwhile threatened sanctions against companies that stopped lifting oil from Nigeria at the official price. For the first time since 1973, the organization looked to be in real danger of collapse. But what would collapse mean?

## The OPEC Paradox

John D. Rockefeller, founder of the modern oil business and alternately remembered as one of the world's greatest businessmen and one of the world's greatest monopolists, reached to the heart of the matter more than a hundred years ago. Speaking of the small U.S. oil producers, he said: "The dear people, if they had produced less oil than the world wanted, would have got their full price; no combination in the world would have prevented that, if they had produced less oil than the world required."

The weakness of the small, fiercely independent oilman in the Pennsylvania Oil Regions of the 1860s and 1870s was exactly the same as that of the revolutionary government of Iran in the 1980s and, hence, of OPEC in general. He was strapped for cash, and since the oil was just flowing out of the ground, he sold it no matter what price he got. Obviously, the thirteen nations of OPEC are much more sophisticated than the old time wildcatter, but the key question is, can these "dear people" produce less oil than the world requires? For it is only then that they can get their "full price".

In this respect, Saudi Arabia is OPEC's critical member. It is not only the largest producer, with a capacity in excess of 10 million barrels a day, but its financial requirements — due to its very small population — give it the flexibility to produce at a lower level.

Nevertheless, Saudi Arabia has, since the first embargo of 1973, appeared reluctant to cut back production to the point at which it squeezes the market. Moreover, in the summer of 1982, other OPEC nations were demanding that

Saudi Arabia slash its output, not to increase prices but merely to maintain them.

As for future demand for OPEC oil, increased production from non-OPEC sources, drastic reductions in overall demand projections and the increased use of alternative fuels — most notably coal and natural gas — indicate that demand for OPEC oil will be below the organization's productive capacity until beyond the year 2000. Overall world oil demand is expected to grow by less than 1% per annum for the rest of this century, with no growth at all coming from the industrialized nations. Canada, for example, according to official estimates, is projected to use 18% less oil in 1990 than in 1982.

However, all projections are subject to instant defenestration, as events of the past decade all too clearly show. OPEC will remain the marginal supplier of oil, and Saudi Arabia will remain by far the most important marginal producer. The political uncertainties of the Middle East remain a constant question mark, and obviously one of the principal reasons for desiring a degree of insulation from the world market. However, related to this political problem is the thornier economic one, or what might be called the OPEC Paradox.

The problem was summed up in a speech given by Joel Bell in June, 1981. "OPEC production constraints and Middle East crises," he said, "have turned us all to the search of domestic self-sufficiency. Success in that effort around the world will produce a world of energy abundance — and maintain downward pressures on the so-called "world price" for oil. Projects which add indigenous supply in many countries might prove to be costly in relation to the pricing of lower cost international oil — and call for government "protection" of their viability. Paradoxically, if the world fails to respond with major investment efforts, the present oil exporting countries will be dealt a stronger hand and their deliberate pricing action or political crises will lead to higher "world prices" which would make many consumer country projects quite viable."

Canada is almost uniquely impaled on the horns of this dilemma, for its self-sufficiency depends critically on very expensive synthetic oil and frontier developments. To the extent that these projects are developed, and Canada, and other countries, succeed in weaning themselves away from OPEC oil, then OPEC oil will be in increasing surplus and its price will drop. This in turn will make the synthetic oil and frontier projects uneconomic. To the extent that these projects are *not* developed, then OPEC oil will be in increasing shortage and its price will rise. This in turn will make the synthetic oil and frontier projects economically attractive.

Bell concluded that this situation would call for " . . . policies which allocate risks . . . conducive to private investment and fair to resource-owners, taxpayers and consumers". The view, typical of the cream of Ottawa's rationalists, is a paradigm of policy logic. The realities of its administration, however — as events in Canada during 1982 showed — were somewhat less simple.

192

# 22
# The Mega-Mess

*"Sir, my need is sore.*
*Spirits that I've cited*
*My commands ignore."*
THE SORCERER'S APPRENTICE
GOETHE

For the Liberals, the collapse of Alsands was a political disaster. The breakup of the consortium, led by Shell Canada, not only dealt a seemingly fatal blow to the government's promise of oil self-sufficiency by 1990, it also killed its hastily botched-together industrial strategy, which had effectively put all of Ottawa's industrial eggs into the energy megaproject basket. At the time of the NEP, the basket had appeared full. By the spring of 1982 it was virtually empty. Imperial Oil's $12 billion-plus *in situ* heavy-oil recovery project at Cold Lake, Alberta, had been shelved; a planned $1.5 billion expansion of the Syncrude plant had, at least temporarily, been canned, while the $2.5 billion Arctic Pilot Project to bring liquefied natural gas from the Arctic Islands — sponsored by a consortium led by Petro-Canada — was beset by regulatory delays and other uncertainties. Myriad other, equally expensive schemes also seemed to be receding into the future, or oblivion.

For Peter Lougheed, too, the collapse of Alsands was an acute political embarrassment. He had been so confident of the future of Alsands and Cold Lake that he had used them as weapons in his fight with Ottawa. When, on April 30, Ed Czaja, the beleaguered head of Alsands, gazed grimly into the television cameras to announce that the consortium had disintegrated, a good deal of Peter Lougheed's precious political credibility disintegrated as well.

Within a remarkably short space of time, a slump in international oil prices and price projections, the prospect of further, massive cost escalations, and the unprecedented cost of borrowing money had all had a profound impact on the outlook for energy megaprojects worldwide. Both the federal and Albertan governments, in the wake of the Alsands collapse, were very eager to point out these adverse factors. But neither level of government should be let off the hook so easily. In Canada, the megaproject outlook had been darkened by federal-provincial wrangling, the nationalist and interventionist thrust of the Liberals' National Energy Program, and by the attitude of ministers and public servants who, imagining that they had the situation totally under control, paid little heed to the claims and demands of the oil companies or the exigencies of world oil. The federal government in particular had created a climate of distrust in which no company could be sure that an agreement made one day would be honoured the next. The whole Alsands exercise was characterized by an almost obsessive concern on the part of federal officials that profits on the venture should be regulated down to the very minimum at which the oil companies would consider it feasible. The Albertans, for their part, used Alsands as a club with which to beat their federal opponents, holding up approval until a "satisfactory" revenue-sharing arrangement was in place. When it became apparent that the project might really collapse, there was growing panic in both Ottawa and Edmonton. Large equity stakes were offered, loans were guaranteed, taxes were slashed. But by then it was too late.

There are perhaps three lessons to be learned from the collapse of Alsands. One is that such projects are uniquely sensitive to world prices and costs. The second is that the regulatory approval and control of such projects has become a far too inflexible and cumbersome process. The third is that bureaucrats are nowhere near as omniscient as they imagine themselves to be.

It was the proud boast of the NEP that Canada was one of the very few nations capable of dissociating itself from the world oil market. Such proved to be far from the case. Indeed, insofar as self-sufficiency depended on megaprojects, Canada was *uniquely* vulnerable to the world market.

The rapidly escalating price of oil in the 1970s was closely linked to a revolution in world petroleum supply. There were still huge amounts of oil to be found. The problem was that it was becoming both a more elusive and intractable beast — and that meant a more expensive one. The need to replenish reserves — and concerns about OPEC's political instability — led into the age of megaprojects.

## Canada Develops Mega-Fever

All over the world, energy developments were assuming staggering proportions — and staggering costs. In the North Sea, there were massive steel drilling and production platforms standing in 400 feet of water, capped by small service cities. In Alaska, an oil pipeline had been built in untested terrain with a price tag of $10 billion. In Canada, world leader in synthetic oil production, the $2.5 billion Syncrude plant featured 6,500-ton drag lines looming like prehistoric monsters out of the barren landscape.

Offshore and Arctic oil exploration was very expensive. However, if giant pools — the industry's "elephants" — could be found, then due to the huge volumes involved and the fact that the oil gushed under its own pressure, production costs were still relatively low. However, the schemes involving non-conventional oil — from tar sands, heavy oil deposits or oil shale — were different. These schemes — to produce synthetic oil — involved an ongoing process of either coaxing or forcing oil out of rock or away from sand.

It was a field in which Canada led the world, but it was an enormously expensive and technologically demanding one, as the histories of Canada's two tar sands plants, Great Canadian Oil Sands and Syncrude, had demonstrated. Great Canadian Oil Sands, built in 1967, had taken twelve years to show a profit. Syncrude had almost collapsed in 1975 when Atlantic Richfield Canada had suddenly and unexpectedly bailed out. Only the intervention of the federal government and the provincial governments of Alberta and Ontario had saved it. Both plants had been plagued by the problems of a technology that rested as much on brute strength as on scientific innovation.

Canada's non-conventional oil reserves, massive deposits of thick, bituminous crude that flowed sluggishly to the surface as heavy oil, or — stuck to sand — did not flow at all, had always held a fascination. Situated primarily in Alberta in the Athabasca and Cold Lake regions and in Saskatchewan around Lloydminster, their attraction was first and foremost their abundance. Estimates of their volume ranged up to 1 billion barrels of oil in place — more than the entire world's reserves of conventional oil. But there lay the rub. They were non-conventional. Because they didn't flow, or flowed only reluctantly, the cost of large-scale development was magnitudes greater than for the production of conventional oil. The Ayatollah, when he appeared on the world scene in 1978, may have seemed a baleful figure for some, but, insofar as he heralded higher international oil prices, his status for the oil sands was more like that of fairy godmother. Both Suncor and Syncrude, on the basis of their high costs, received world price for their output, so, as the world price escalated rapidly during 1979 and 1980, their profitability appeared to increase dramatically. The financial attractions of further such plants was also increased.

This further escalation of the world price appeared firmly to establish that the last two decades of the twentieth century would be the age of megaprojects, and that Canada would be in the vanguard. Producing studies on Canada's megaproject-dominated future — complete with comprehensive lists of solid-looking schemes and mind-numbing investment totals — became almost a growth industry by itself. Even before the Shah had fallen, a 1977 study by the Department of Energy, Mines and Resources produced a total energy investment estimate on such projects of $180 billion by 1990 ($275 billion in 1980 dollars). In the same year, the Toronto Dominion Bank produced an estimate of about $200 billion in 1980 dollars, while in 1979, the Royal Bank came up with an estimate of $225 billion in 1980 dollars. The latest, and glossiest, addition to the mega-literature came in the summer of 1981 with the report of the Mega Projects Task Force, a massive government-inspired study co-chaired by the politically sensitive Bob Blair and Shirley Carr, executive vice-president of the Canadian Labour Congress. This produced an inventory to the year 2000 of almost $440 billion. Within just one year of its publication, however, the Blair-Carr report was to appear grossly out of date, an exercise in counting unhatched chickens.

The Blair-Carr report was also typical of the nationalist and interventionist spirit of the times. There was scarcely any doubt that the oil companies would

195

build the petroleum megaprojects, so the report concerned itself with ensuring that there were bureaucratic structures to oversee activities and that maximum advantages went to Canadian companies, even if there were cost disadvantages to project sponsors. Seeking development of domestic talent and technology was of course laudable, but the fact that the report was considered to have gone too far in its interventionist stance was clear in the number of dissenting voices from its final draft.

The executives who had contributed to the report all seemed to object to the recommendation for a new interventionist Megaprojects Assessment Agency, discriminatory procurement programs, and to references to a "planned economy". Dr. John MacNamara, head of Algoma Steel, spoke for most of them when he wrote, in a dissenting addendum: " . . . I believe that major projects have to be viewed as business ventures first and job creating mechanisms second. While employment opportunities will be a primary benefit, these projects must continue to be justified on the basis of their economic viability."

However, the businessmen too, with their continuous references to unfettered "free market" forces, were perhaps failing to acknowledge the almost inevitably greater degree of overall government involvement in ventures as large as the megaprojects.

## The Uneasy Mega-Alliance

Part of the modern orthodoxy is that the largest corporations are simply too big. The specific evils of size are somewhat vague, but nevertheless, if one were to question the man in the street and ask him for examples of corporations that were "too big", the major oil companies might well spring to mind. However, when compared with the size and scope of the petroleum megaprojects, even the biggest oil companies appear small. Projects like tar sands plants have become so costly, and so risky, that even the largest corporations are financially frail by comparison. A group, or consortium, approach is almost essential, but even then, governments will be called upon to design special fiscal regimes and — as was the case with Syncrude — might still be called upon to bail companies out. Under these circumstances, therefore, government desire to be at least fully aware of what is going on is only reasonable. Moreover, given the impact of such projects on the environment and employment, and their need for infrastructure such as roads, it has become inevitable that governments at all levels would become increasingly involved at every stage of planning and development.

However, this situation, in which government involvement was almost essential, became confused with the notion that government involvement was *the most important* feature of megaproject development. Moreover, in the case of the consortia's dealings with the Liberal government and its officials, relationships were strained by Ottawa's antagonistic attitude towards the foreign-owned oil companies which dominated the megaprojects, and also by its basically negative approach to private corporations and business in general.

Indeed, there was at least one influential strain of Liberal academic advice that suggested that the foreign-owned oil companies should be kicked out and that Petro-Canada should undertake *all* megaprojects. It is interesting to note that Petro-Canada management regarded such suggestions with little short of horror.

It was assumed at the time of the NEP, and in the Blair-Carr report, that the oil companies would undertake the megaprojects regardless; that the federal government's job was to fine-tune the tax regime so that oil companies didn't earn too much money and the "public purpose" was served. All suggestions on the part of the oil companies that risks were too great or the tax regime not generous enough were treated either as transparent attempts to outsmart Ottawa or — if political points needed to be scored — as "blackmail".

That companies should attempt to get the best possible deal should come as no surprise. But their concern should be seen less as an attempt to make "excessive" profits as to ensure a financial cushion against the huge risks involved. The federal bureaucrats didn't like the concept of a cushion. They believed that cushions weren't so much unnecessary, as a thinly disguised attempt to gain windfall profits. Cushions should be fine-tuned out of the picture.

This line of reasoning was clearly apparent in the NEP, where under a section marked "The National Energy Program will Spur Oil Sands Development", and speaking of Alsands, it said: "Because the project — and others like it — are important to our energy objectives, the Government of Canada is concerned to provide a rate of return on this $8 billion project that is high enough to attract private investment." The rate of return was to be determined by government. It was to be "high enough", but obviously no higher, than that necessary to attract private investment.

The federal bureaucracy's anxiety about the elimination of cushions was also a symptom of its other, more basic concern, foreign ownership. This concern was outlined in documents prepared under the aegis of Ian Stewart and Ed Clark at Energy, Mines and Resources for the Conservative government. "The increasing importance of non-conventional oil," said one of these background papers, "advantages the big firms. Such projects can only be developed by large firms. Moreover, two firms, Shell and Imperial, hold some of the most attractive land. They thus have a strong say in the pace and terms for development. If non-conventional oil comes to dominate oil production as expected, the importance of their position will be even greater than it is today."

Given such statements, one might well wonder just how sorry the federal bureaucracy was when Alsands fell apart and Cold Lake was shelved, perhaps indefinitely.

The confidential discussion papers provided by EMR to the Tory federal government clearly indicated that the mandarins were at least as concerned with who built the non-conventional oil plants, and how they were financed, as they were with the building of the plants themselves.

What concerned Ed Clark most was that the tax system allowed companies to deduct outlays on future projects from current profits. Reinvestment of corporate profits had always been considered desirable, indeed laudable. For Clark, however, obsessed with foreign ownership and the concept of "equity", for such reinvestment to be tax deductible was blatantly unfair. It meant that companies without profits — a situation often taken as an indication of imprudence or incompetence — were at a disadvantage. An analysis by Clark of the Alsands scheme concluded that the existing tax system was "a potential barrier to entry and preserver of the status quo of corporate power."

This obsession with the "status quo of corporate power" meant that other, arguably more important, concerns were relegated to a secondary position. The Alsands plant was not seen as a project that would provide thousands of jobs directly and indirectly; it was not seen as a facility producing 137,000 barrels of oil a day and thus displacing that much imported oil with a corresponding benefit to the balance of payments. It was seen as a government-subsidized scheme to increase the stranglehold of foreign-owned oil companies in Canada.

Such thinking inevitably led to the discriminatory provisions of the NEP. But it was not only discrimination against them that concerned the foreign-owned companies so much as their subjection to the whim of government. In particular, they were deeply concerned by the implications of the treatment of Suncor's oil sands plant in the NEP. "The Suncor oil sands plant," said the NEP, " . . . has received the international price for its full production since April 1979, as part of an arrangement with the Government of Canada under which the company undertook to expand its plant. The revenues accruing under this agreement have more than covered the expected capital costs of the expansion, and *unwarranted windfall gains* would result if the arrangement were continued. [my italics] Therefore, the production from the existing plant will henceforth receive the conventional oil price. The expanded production will be entitled to the oil sands reference price."

Suncor's plant had operated for twelve years without making a profit. The government had signed an agreement to give it world prices and the subsequent increase in world prices had suddenly made it a very profitable operation. So the government, with a stroke of the pen, had reneged on its agreement.

Eventually, when the Federal-Alberta pricing agreement was settled — and following months of negotiations with Ottawa — Suncor received a new arrangement. Under this agreement it received the so-called New Oil Reference Price for all its tar sands plant's production. However, 75% of the revenue was subject to the new Incremental Oil Revenue Tax of 50%. The arrangement was a good deal better than that under the NEP. Nevertheless, the NEP, by shooting first and asking questions afterwards, had severely damaged the way in which Canada was viewed by foreign investors.

This seemed to be of little concern within EMR, where they believed they were acting in their own personal version of the national interest. In any case, they were used to the kicking and screaming of oil companies. The big oil companies, led by Imperial, had threatened to pull the plug on the Syncrude project but, the bureaucrats said to each other, look how profitable the Syncrude project was now. Moreover, Syncrude was another example in which Alberta appeared to have done much better out of the tax system than Ottawa. EMR's mandarins were determined that that would not happen again. As for the oil companies, Ottawa really didn't have too much faith in their figures. They believed that the oil companies had conned them before, but now they had the expertise at their disposal it wouldn't happen again. They knew the NEP would get the job done.

But the NEP didn't.

## Fine-Tuning a Mega-Fantasy

Even before the NEP, Peter Lougheed had said that he would hold up approval of both the Alsands and Cold Lake plants until a suitable revenue-sharing agreement was reached with Ottawa. Holding up agreements, however, didn't seem necessary after the NEP, because the oil companies were almost unanimous in declaring that, under those conditions, no further tar sands plants would be built. Under the NEP, oil sands plants were to receive the lower price of $38 a barrel, escalated annually by about 8% up to 1990, or the international price. At the time, EMR thought that the world price was running away, and they were determined that such an "arbitrary and artificial" price would not be received by the oil companies. Unless, that is, it was inexplicably to drop below the NEP's Oil Sands Reference Price.

The impact of this pricing regime on company intentions could be clearly seen in the energy supply-demand report of the National Energy Board issued in June, 1981, just eight months after the NEP came out. The National Energy Board had received twelve submissions on oil sands plants. Before the NEP, each of the twelve — from the Canadian Petroleum Association, Dome Petroleum, Gulf Canada, Imperial Oil, Norcen Energy Resources, Nova, the Government of Ontario, Petro-Canada, Shell Canada, Texaco Canada, Union Carbide, and the Alberta Energy Resources Conservation Board — anticipated that both Cold Lake and Alsands would begin production in the late 1980s. Most believed that fourth and fifth commercial tar sands plants would follow in the 1990s, along with a second, and possibly third, *in situ* heavy oil recovery plant similar to that proposed by Imperial.

After the NEP, only Petro-Canada, Texaco and Ontario projected that there would be further non-conventional oil plants built.

At least one of the oil companies had managed to persuade Marc Lalonde that the terms of the NEP were truly unsatisfactory. Shortly after the NEP was released, Jack Armstrong, the blunt chief executive of Imperial Oil, told Lalonde at a private meeting in New York's Park Plaza Hotel — where both were participating in an energy conference organized by the *Financial Post* — that unless the government carried the project's $40 million costs over the following

199

six months, Imperial would pull the plug on Cold Lake. Lalonde very quickly came up with the money, but some of the EMR officials believed he had "given in" to Imperial.

What really disturbed the mandarins at EMR were the rapid escalations in cost estimates for Cold Lake and Alsands. When the NEP had been released, Alsands was an $8 billion project. In less than a year, its cost estimate had risen to $13 billion. The bureaucrats believed they knew what the oil companies were up to. As world oil prices rose, the companies were working out what their revenues would be from these higher prices and *then* calculating what inflated level of costs they needed in order to "merely" make their target rate of return. It was outrageous, but the smart guys at EMR weren't going to fall for it.

In July, 1981, Imperial announced that Cold Lake was, for the moment at least, being shelved. That meant that Alsands assumed much greater importance. However, in the months leading up to the Federal-Alberta agreement, meetings with the Alsands consortium became less frequent. The bureaucrats retreated into their computer purdah to determine what, in their own upside-down world, was most important: how projected revenues would be divided. So intricately were they locked in their negotiations that they had no time to look outside and see that the projected revenues were disappearing into thin air.

But beyond the revenues for the five years of the agreement, Alsands, too, was looking less and less attractive to its sponsors, who, unlike the federal and Alberta bureaucrats, could see what was happening to world oil prices and interest costs. The September 1 agreement's New Oil Reference Price was considerably higher than that of the NEP, but it was really irrelevant for new oil megaprojects, since the agreement ran out in 1986, before any of them would come on stream. The agreement merely stated: "It is the intention of both governments that a NORP base price schedule for the period after 1986 will be established as part of any future agreement."

The agreement announced a new Alberta royalty structure for the Alsands and shelved Cold Lake projects, while Alberta agreed to donate $600 million to helping small Canadian companies become involved in the project. All that now remained was for the partners to sign on the dotted line.

But the partners, to the astonishment of both governments, were showing a certain reluctance to do so. The agreement, they said, was not adequate. This, thought the bureaucrats, was only to be expected. They were not dismayed, and when officials from the two levels of government came together before a meeting with the Alsands consortium members in Edmonton on December 18, they were, in the words of one of those present, "almost hugging each other". The bureaucrats from Ottawa and Alberta had battled long and hard, but now they had pulled it off. The problem was that the men from Alsands weren't smiling. Astonishingly, only then did the government officials for the first time appear to have any inkling that something was wrong.

When the Alsands project had received provisional approval in December, 1979, it had consisted of nine members. The leader was Shell Canada, subsidiary of the mighty Royal Dutch-Shell group, the world's second largest oil company. Shell Canada held 25% of the project. Its other members where Shell Explorer, a U.S. Royal Dutch-Shell subsidiary, with 20%; Amoco Canada, 10%; Chevron Standard, 8%; Gulf Canada, 8%; Petrofina Canada, 8%; Hudson's Bay Oil and Gas, 8%; Pacific Petroleums, 9%; and Dome Petroleum, 4%. Petro-Canada subsequently took over both Pacific and Petrofina, giving it 17% of the project, while Dome's acquisition of HBOG left it holding 12%, and left the group with seven members.

At the Edmonton meeting, Alberta agreed to provide a loan guarantee, while the federal government offered the project a reduced rate of its controversial Petroleum and Gas Revenue Tax. The consortium said that such moves were obviously in the right direction. But they still weren't smiling. Then the federal and Alberta governments became really worried.

When the parties met again in Ottawa on January 13, some consortium members noticed a new attitude on the part of the governments. For the first time, federal and provincial officials realized the project might collapse. Following up on the December meeting, Alberta committed to a loan guarantee of 20% of the private sector investment. Meanwhile, the federal side, suddenly aware that both self-sufficiency and its industrial strategy were on the line, declared that its Petroleum and Gas Revenue Tax would be reduced to zero on the project until the investors had recovered their investment. Then came the bombshell. Two of the companies, and two of the most financially sound, Amoco and Chevron, announced their withdrawal. Shortly afterwards Shell Explorer and Dome Petroleum also withdrew. That left just three companies in: Shell Canada, which had apparently found the April offer acceptable, Gulf Canada, and Petro-Canada.

Alberta and Ottawa now worked feverishly to come up with concessions that would attract other companies in. They also agreed to take up 50% of the equity — including Petro-Canada's 17% — and increase the level of loan guarantees. But there were no takers. On April 30, the project collapsed.

## A Murky Mega-Future

Government attitudes and policies cannot be regarded as the primary reason for the collapse of Alsands or the delay or abandonment of the other megaprojects. However, the NEP and its aftermath will certainly influence the willingness of private investors to undertake such projects if economic conditions improve. And the fact is that at some stage, these projects may well still be needed.

In 1981 and 1982 the basic financial prospects of such projects, based on falling international oil prices and escalating costs, deteriorated remarkably. At the beginning of 1981, international bankers, in assessing the financeability of major oil projects, were assuming a world oil price of about U.S. $71 a barrel by the end of this decade. By the end of 1981, financial analysts were forecasting a figure of less than U.S. $60. Such a change had enormous impact on the financial viability of megaprojects. All over the world, such projects were shelved or cancelled. However, the very fact that so many were being shelved revived the issue of the OPEC Paradox. If such projects are not developed, and worldwide economic growth resumes, then we could become vulnerable to another surge of OPEC prices due to insufficient supply before the end of the decade. And that, of course, ignores the issue of political instability as a source of supply disruption.

Canada is fortunate in that it also has major potential for increased oil supplies through East Coast offshore developments in and around the Hibernia field, and in the Beaufort Sea, both of which are felt to be superior economically to non-conventional production. However, both projects are subject to delay, and the more promising, that of Hibernia, is mired in an ongoing and increasingly bitter dispute between Ottawa and Newfoundland.

Given the fact that their costs appear to escalate faster than those of the world price of oil, there must be some doubt now whether large-scale, non-conventional oil development based on megaprojects will ever go ahead on the scale envisaged in the late 1970s and early 1980s. Smaller-scale, heavy oil development and upgrading is possible and the impact of much higher prices for new discoveries of conventional oil has yet to be felt. However, the oil supply picture for the rest of the decade looks extremely uncertain. What has happened, and is happening, is a change of emphasis. Perhaps, as Peter Lougheed said in the wake of the Alsands collapse, "This is not the era of large projects . . . maybe it's the era of 'small is beautiful'."

# 23
# The NEP Update:
# Toughing It Out

*"Occasionally words must serve to veil the facts.
But this must happen in such a way that no one become aware of it; or, if it should be noticed, excuses
must be at hand, to be produced immediately."*

THE PRINCE
MACHIAVELLI

By the spring of 1982 it became obvious even to Ottawa that the National
Energy Program had played a major part in the worst economic crisis in
postwar Canada. Virtually all its projections had turned out to be disastrously
wrong, as had the premises of the Federal-Alberta agreement of September,
1981. The front-running megaproject, Alsands, had collapsed; the chosen
instrument, Dome Petroleum, was on the point of bankruptcy; promises of
moderate price increases had been totally abandoned in a grab for more
revenue, but then these projected revenues — in the face of slumping world oil
prices and a low level of activity — had disappeared. This in turn had
contributed to an unprecedented worsening in the federal government's fiscal
deficit. In November, 1981, it had been projected at about $10 billion for the
coming year. Just six months later, that projection had risen to $16 billion. In
the June budget it was revealed to be $19.6 billion. Meanwhile, the whole oil
industry was suffering, capital budgets were being slashed and many of the
smaller companies were going out of business.

Peter Lougheed's government, in the face of provincial anger, and following
its consultations with the industry, demonstrated a readiness to eat humble pie.
In mid-April it announced a series of tax, royalty and grant measures designed
to give the industry an additional $5.4 billion over its five-year life. However,
Lougheed left the federal government in no doubt that he felt it, too, should
respond with additional incentives.

The federal government did indeed respond, with a much smaller package it
claimed to be worth about $2 billion. However, these concessions were con-
tained in a somewhat astonishing document entitled *The National Energy
Program, Update 1982.* The document was astonishing because its principal
assertion was that the NEP had been a rip-roaring success. Anyone who read it
might well ask himself if he had been living in the same country as its authors
for the preceding two years. To claim any success whatsoever for the NEP

seemed somewhat akin to pointing to the proverbial charred remains of the burned-down house and claiming optimistically that at least the supper had been cooked. The *Update*, however, strove against all plausibility to claim that some objectives had not only been achieved but had surpassed expectations.

According to the *Update*, the Cold Lake and Alsands projects were "victims of oil world price uncertainty". Referring to the slump in oil activity, the document continued: "There was a faltering of industry exploration and development efforts in the Western provinces. This region has major resource potential. It will be looked to for increasing amounts of new conventional oil to improve Canada's supply-demand balance. Yet drilling activity fell in 1981."

The last sentence was delivered almost with a tone of surprise, as if punitive taxes could have had nothing to do with the reduced level of exploration activity. "New taxes" were eventually admitted as a contributory factor towards the industry's problems. However, they appeared last on a long list of other difficulties. The new upbeat view of western Canada's conventional oil potential was, meanwhile, somewhat different from the gloomy view expressed in the NEP. "Production from established conventional oil reserves in western Canada," said the NEP, "will decline substantially over the decade. New discoveries of western conventional oil are expected, but are unlikely to be of sufficient size to offset this decline." Now, however, the region had "major resource potential".

Laying out the "progress" of the NEP, the *Update* continued with many pages of detail on the status of numerous bureaucratic initiatives, including those of such pressing national concern as the "821 solar hot water heating systems" being built in Canada. "A year and a half after the introduction of the NEP, over 70 per cent of the new programs launched are now fully operational. Many of the others only await the completion of industry studies, action by provincial governments, or the passage of legislation by Parliament. Hundreds of thousands of Canadians have already received direct benefits under these programs; millions have benefited indirectly through increased industrial opportunities and enhanced energy security. The effort and rewards are only beginning."

Moving on to Canadianization, the *Update* pointed out that Canadian control of the oil industry had increased from 22.3% to 33.1% since the NEP was announced, while ownership had risen from 28% to 34.7%.

Little hint of the enormous controversy surrounding Canadianization appeared in the *Update*. In his foreword, Marc Lalonde coyly declared: "The National Energy Program has been a central topic of debate. Much of the debate has been helpful." In its Canadianization section, the report maintained: "The Canadianization objectives of the National Energy Program have been widely endorsed. The Governments of Saskatchewan and British Columbia underscored their support of this part of the Program in the agreements reached last autumn. The Government of Alberta went even further, agreeing to administer and pay for the Petroleum Incentives Program in the province."

To state that Canadianization had been endorsed was of course true. It was a motherhood objective. The controversial feature not even alluded to in the *Update* was, of course, the NEP's approach towards achieving it. To suggest that Alberta was an enthusiastic supporter of the NEP took almost unprecedented gall. The government of Alberta just *hated* the NEP, and the sole reason it had agreed to administer PIP grants was to keep federal bureaucrats out of the province.

But the document was to strain its readers' credulity yet further.

Under a chapter entitled "Issues Requiring Action", the *Update* maintained: "It is important in economic and energy terms that Canada have a strong and growing oil and gas industry. The National Energy Program is designed to help this occur." After this somewhat improbable claim, the document once again outlined the industry's problems in terms of world economic slowdown, depressed natural gas markets, high interest rates, lower world prices, etc. Government action was nowhere acknowledged as a problem. Nevertheless, compared with the arrogant and punitive tones of the NEP, an amazingly solicitous attitude towards the industry was displayed. The NEP had clearly acknowledged the problem of shut-in gas in Alberta. "The producers' problem is markets," it had said. "Even with recent approvals of new gas exports, the industry will have substantial excess production capacity." Nevertheless, the NEP rejected the idea of "automatic recourse" to export markets. ". . . the export market must not drive our energy policies, or dominate corporate decisions. Our first priority must be to put our domestic energy house in order."

The *Update*, however, was full of concern for producers and their shut-in gas. "Having spent considerable time, effort, and money on gas exploration and development, many companies are constrained, by limited markets, from realizing a return on their investment . . . Therefore, it is essential to allow the gas producers every reasonable chance to market their product — first, on the domestic market . . . and second on the export market, under policies designed to protect future Canadian requirements for gas, and to meet the need of the gas industry for markets to sustain and, if possible, enhance their cashflow position."

Referring to the fact that much contracted export gas was in fact not being taken by U.S. utilities, the *Update* declared that such an arrangement was not fair "to other utilities in the United States, which seek additional supplies of Canadian gas but are prevented from doing so because the successful applicants are holding rights to more gas than they are willing or able to use." This concern for U.S. gas utilities indicated a truly amazing cross-border expansion in the NEP's obsession with fairness.

As for the one measure proposed by the NEP that might really have eased the pressure on smaller gas producers — the $440 million Gas Bank, under which gas would be bought but left in the ground until needed — the federal government somewhat uncomfortably slid out from under this promise, claiming as a justification: "Many have argued that the industry, working together in a voluntary way, can find ways to ensure that the small producers enjoy a share of new markets. . . . It believes that the programs now put in place should increase gas sales, and that, provided the industry ensures that the small producers benefit from these increased sales, the Gas Bank will not be needed."

The *Update* thus seemed to be suggesting that it was not unreasonable for larger oil companies to shoulder the burdens of their small competitors, acknowledgement of a generous spirit within the capitalist heart that had nowhere been hinted at in the NEP.

## Liberal Fairness: A Very Flexible Ideal

With the *Update*, the federal government changed its oil and gas regime for the third time in eighteen months. The specific measures proposed to help companies were: a reduction in the effective rate of the Petroleum and Gas Revenue Tax from 12 to 11%; suspension of the Incremental Oil Revenue Tax until May 31, 1983; an increase in the price of oil discovered since 1973 to 75% of the world price; an annual $250,000 credit against PGRT liability — a move designed for the proportionately greater benefit of smaller producers; and a number of more generous price and tax measures for oil from tertiary and experimental projects, and from suspended wells. PGRT for oil sands plants was also lowered from 12% to 8% for 1983 and 1984.

With self-confidence in its world of altruistic rationality the NEP had declared: "The Canadian energy situation is manageable and the Government of Canada is determined to see that it is well managed." Less than a year later, revealing a totally new set of prices, and a severely modified tax regime under the Federal-Alberta agreement, Marc Lalonde had declared: "This allows Canada to pursue even more vigorously the objectives of the National Energy Program — security, opportunity and fairness." The prices of the NEP had been "fair"; now the much higher prices envisaged by the Federal-Alberta agreement were fair too. Those baffled about a working definition of fairness now began to see that it was quite simply whatever the government decided it was. And now, with the *Update*, there was a new regime, yet another version of fairness. But not only were the projected prices and taxes once again different, there was apparently a belated realization that the critical factor in Canada's energy future was the health of the oil industry. Said the *Update*: "The fiscal arrangements of the National Energy Program, modified by the agreements with the provinces and reflecting the changes subsequently made by both the Government of Canada and the Government of Alberta, now provide sufficient cash flow and the necessary incentives to the industry to ensure the needed investment in this sector."

In other words, we've screwed it up the other two times but this time we really *have* got it right.

The *Update* — despite the fact that Alberta had made concessions almost three times as great as the federal government's — noting that industry's share

206

of revenue would now fall less than the shares of governments, stated: "This is a clear indication of a fundamentally fair fiscal regime: on the downside, as prices and profits fall, the burden falls on Government, not the industry. When prices begin to rise, however, a growing share will accrue to governments." After declaring its intention to grab a larger share of oil industry revenues eighteen months before, the government was now maintaining how fair its tax structure was in leaving revenues in the hands of the industry. The very fact that both governments had now stepped back from their tax grab showed how crippling the effects of both the NEP and the subsequent Federal-Alberta agreement had been.

The claim that the NEP's tax regime was flexible and "fair" was a total perversion of truth. The whole point about the Petroleum and Gas Revenue Tax, the Natural Gas and Gas Liquids Tax and the Incremental Oil Revenue Tax was that they were all taxes on revenue with few allowable deductions and thus largely *insensitive* to the financial condition of the industry. They were levied regardless of any company's profits position and were thus particularly onerous — indeed potentially ruinous — during an economic turndown. Indeed, the system was so inflexible that relief could only be provided by reducing and providing a basic exemption from the PGRT, and by suspending the IORT completely.

However, it was interesting to note the suggestion that taxes should fall in line with profits. This was treated almost as a revelation, an advance in fiscal theory, rather than a basic rule ignored by the NEP in pursuit of higher objectives. This practical education of the highly theoretical brains behind the Liberal government had been acquired at a heavy price for the people of Canada.

Nevertheless, the NEP's stance of industry bashing had now been reversed to one of industry coddling. "There has been some criticism," said the *Update*, "that the regime introduced in the NEP, and as subsequently modified, has improved the financial position of the governments at the expense of the industry. While there are pricing scenarios, including the one envisaged last September, in which governments would increase their share of petroleum revenues relative to the industry, this is not now the case. Industry received roughly 45 per cent of petroleum revenues in the period 1975-80. It can now expect to receive a marginally larger share, about 46 per cent, over the period 1981-86. Thus, the restructuring of Government revenue shares that took place as a result of the September 1 Memorandum of Agreement will reflect a more equitable sharing of revenues between governments. It will not be at the expense of the industry."

The revised projections of revenue shares that appeared in the *Update* indicated the massive miscalculations made by the federal and provincial bureaucracies during 1981. No less than $51 billion of projected revenue in the period up to 1986 had disappeared in less than eight months. After putting the oil business through two years of trauma, the federal government had, in its wisdom, "decided" to leave it with exactly the same share of revenues as it had taken before.

Now that the minor readjustments had been dealt with, the *Update* moved onto the NEP's successes. "On the demand side," it declared, "progress has substantially exceeded expectations." The document, inexplicably, failed to point out the importance of both much higher price increases and economic recession in achieving this "progress".

"On the supply side," said the *Update*, "the incentive for new oil in both the provinces and the Canada Lands, Canada's promising geology, and the certainty of federal-provincial accords, provide a combination that is very attractive by world standards. The onus is now on the petroleum industry to respond to the opportunity; to find enough reserves in the West and the frontiers to bring oil supply and demand into balance within the decade. The incentive framework is in place; an improved cash flow will be provided through measures outlined in this document."

To write of the "certainty of federal-provincial accords" when the fiscal system had been changed three times in eighteen months took considerable nerve. To suggest that the oil industry hold its nose and charge ahead "to respond to the opportunity" when everything the government had done since it returned to power indicated there was no guarantee that any opportunity present today would exist tomorrow, indicated a more profound belief in the industry's Pavlovian reactions than its reflective ability.

## Foreign Oil: Howdy Partner!

However, the government was only too well aware that if it was to get the industry to respond — and if it was to help halt the slide in the dollar and cool U.S. feelings — then it had to backtrack on the tough anti-foreign oil company stance of the NEP. The *Update* clearly did so. Suddenly, the big foreign oil companies weren't the predators of the NEP; they were partners. Suddenly a new, more cooperative version of Canada's petroleum future appeared. "Several of the major oil and gas companies, including Esso, Gulf and Shell, have announced wide farm-out arrangements. This will lay the groundwork for the situation that the Government of Canada wishes to see in 1990: a strong Canadian component, second to none in its capacity to explore and develop oil and gas, alongside a strong group of foreign-controlled companies."

This desire for a strong group of foreign-controlled companies had not been apparent in the NEP.

On prices, the *Update* maintained that "The Government of Canada has kept its promise to oil consumers". Having abandoned this promise in the Federal-Alberta agreement, the slump in world prices, meaning a corresponding slowing of domestic Canadian prices, had now returned the government to the path of virtue. These tergiversations, however, were not spelled out. Instead, the government called upon the consumer to reflect on how lucky he was relative to consumers in other industrial countries. A chart indicated the extent of this luck, ranging from a slim 3% advantage over gasoline prices south of the border to a massive 137% difference with Italy. However, the chart also demonstrated something else not dwelled upon in the text. The government that had rejected "the simplistic 'solution' of dramatic price increases for gasoline" had, between January 1981 and January 1982 forced those prices up by almost 30%, an increase which in less enlightened circles might well be classified as "dramatic". Moreover, the fact that the reason Canadian prices were so much lower was partly due to the low price paid to Alberta for its constitutionally-owned oil was not dwelled upon. Indeed, it was not even mentioned.

For its total lack of contrition, one can only marvel at the NEP *Update*. If it represented the genuine view of EMR, then of itself it would present a powerful case for the presence of mass psychosis within the department. However, we should perhaps regard its stance rather as an example of the inevitably ambivalent attitude towards reality demonstrated by governments that have made huge policy errors.

Like the NEP, the *Update* contained numerous informative boxes. At the end of one of these, which reviewed the progress of the NEP's fourteen associated acts through Parliament, there was an assurance that the program certainly wasn't the creation of any bureaucracy, or even really the Liberal party; it was the creation of *Parliament*. "The Government of Canada is held accountable to the citizenry of Canada through the proceedings of Parliament," it reassured its readers. "Since the NEP started, 718 questions about energy policy have been answered during the daily Question Periods. Another 111 questions from MPs have been answered in writing.

"The National Energy Program began as proposals — it is now a series of decisions by the Parliament of Canada."

As a description of the modern political process in Canada, and in particular, of the way the NEP had evolved, the summary left a great deal to be desired.

# PART FOUR

# Winners, Losers and Survivors

# 24
# Dome and Gloom

*"All day long the analyst punched the buttons and the bad news appeared, riffling down, line after line, in bright green letters. He spoke rapidly of Dome, with the kind of cliff-clawing oratory a depression banker might have been inspired to use when faced with an angry crowd, withdrawal slips at the ready."*

Dome Petroleum was the company that persuaded so many people — especially the banks — that it could defy the laws of economic and corporate gravity. Now, in the summer of 1982, Dome, like an elephant tottering on a forty-storey building, was an object of fascination. One thing was certain; if it came down it was going to create one hell of a mess.

When *The Blue-Eyed Sheiks* was written, Dome had been the *Wunderkind* of the Canadian stock market, its value increasing sixfold between the beginning of 1977 and the summer of 1979. It had become one of a triumvirate of Canadian companies — along with Alberta Gas Trunk Line and Petro-Canada — that promised to take Canadians into the big league previously dominated by the Canadian subsidiaries of the international oil giants.

Fuelled by the dream of its chairman, "Smilin'" Jack Gallagher, and guided by its brilliant and abrasive president, Bill Richards, Dome was both spearheading the world's most expensive exploration in the frozen depths of the Beaufort Sea, and growing through massive acquisitions, funded with a seemingly limitless supply of gratefully-donated money.

The arrival of the National Energy Program, far from slowing Dome down, had led it into a frenetic new round of activity. Discovering that it was not sufficiently "Canadian" under proposed NEP legislation, it created a subsidiary, Dome Canada, whose $460 million initial flotation was the largest ever in Canada. Seeking to outpace, rather than merely follow the thrust of the NEP, it launched the biggest takeover in Canadian history, assuming control of Hudson's Bay Oil and Gas from U.S. giant Conoco, in a deal eventually costing over $4 billion. Searching for cash, it obtained $400 million from Japanese investors under terms so generous to Dome that they almost denied belief.

Always the most accessible of men, it seemed back in 1979 that Gallagher would invite almost anyone into his office, or over to the Petroleum Club, to explain the enormous potential of the Beaufort Sea. Richards seemed to be the only senior executive in Canada who answered his own phone. And if Gallagher and Richards weren't available, it was only because they were paying court in Ottawa, or spreading the word in New York, or Europe, or Japan: Jack Gallagher giving his low-key, almost hypnotic presentations about how the Beaufort contained maybe "one or two Middle Easts" of oil reserves; Bill Richards delivering his punchy summaries of Dome's latest achievements and its future directions.

And indeed, after the Hudson's Bay Oil and Gas deal, it seemed that Dome had at last leapt into an undisputed lead in the three-way race for Canadian oil supremacy. I remembered visiting Bill Richards in June of 1981, just after Dome had wrested the controlling block of HBOG from Conoco, and he had been so pleased he was almost hugging himself, strutting like a bantam around his oversized office. Dome was now not only the largest Canadian-controlled oil company, in terms of assets it was the largest oil company in Canada, its balance-sheet numbers muscling mighty Imperial Oil out of top spot.

But for oil companies, balance sheet numbers can be deceptive, and Imperial's huge oil reserves meant that it was still in fact a more valuable company. There was also a much more significant point. In one key balance-sheet figure, Dome had Imperial beaten by a factor of ten. Unfortunately, that figure stood for debt.

Nevertheless, that June afternoon in 1981, Bill Richards hadn't been too concerned about debt-loads. And he had seemed to have every reason to be pleased with himself. Dome's president was dilating on the reasons for the ease with which Dome appeared to run rings around companies of similar, or indeed any, size. The difference, he said, was that everyone at Dome had a stake in the company. They held shares bought with interest-free, company money. They had pension plans stuffed with Dome stock. And that, said Richards — who after all held more than $20 million worth of Dome equity himself — was what made the difference with all those other "management-run" companies. Everybody you ran into in the hallway or on the elevator at Dome had stock in the company, so everywhere you went you met pressure to perform.

"Management-run companies don't give a shit for shareholders," he said. "You've got to have shareholders biting at your ass, that's what capitalism is all about. I sweat blood over our earnings per share. All they want to do is protect their ass."

A year later the words rang with irony. With interest rates still in the stratosphere, ass-protection didn't seem like such a bad policy after all. The alligators had arrived.

Suddenly, Dome was no longer the *Wunderkind*. Instead, Dome was a company very severely strapped for cash and in so deeply to the big five banks that it was suggested that if *it* went, then perhaps one of *them* would go too. And when you talked about one of Canada's big five going under, then suddenly the magnitude of the problem became apparent. Dome might well survive, but if it didn't, its collapse could amount to the greatest financial disaster in Canadian history.

There was no denying that although nobody in Calgary actually wanted Dome to founder, there was a certain ill-concealed delight about the company's discomfort, especially among some of those "managers" Bill Richards had been so fond of putting down. Indeed, these days, the managers were pushing around a few pointed "Dome jokes". "Bill Richards goes into Jack Gallagher's office," the president of a large U.S. oil subsidiary leans toward me with a conspiratorial smile, "and he says 'Jack, I've got some good news and some bad news.'

" 'Well,' says Jack, 'first tell me the good news.'

"And Bill says: 'Imperial Oil is going for just $8 billion.'

" 'Oh,' says Jack, 'that sounds pretty cheap. What's the bad news?'

" 'They want $50 down.' "

For years now the corporate men, the "managers", had heard everybody go on and on about Dome — what a wonderful Canadian company it was, how much smarter and quicker it was than they were. They had seen Richards staring down his hot little nostrils at them, and they had all been waiting for the classic come-uppance. Now it seemed to have arrived. They may have covered their rear ends, but Dome had finally fallen on its ass.

Another smile crossed the multinational president's face. "I hear that Bill Richards is calling for a cash projection *every fifteen minutes.*"

## The Chosen Instrument

Some of Calgary's corporate oilmen were also taking a scarcely-concealed delight in Dome's problems because of another aspect of the company with which they had never been happy: its relationship with Ottawa. Throughout the 1970s, the whole oil environment became much more politicized. Most of the large foreign-controlled companies found this a difficult environment to adapt to. Indeed, insofar as it was an increasingly nationalist environment, they found it virtually impossible. Until the first OPEC crisis, the big oil companies had given advice to the National Energy Board, and the NEB had pretty much taken that advice along to the cabinet, who had usually accepted it. But OPEC, and some suspiciously rapid turnarounds in reserve estimates by big oil at the beginning of the 1970s, had changed all that.

Gallagher had first sold the Liberals on his Beaufort dreams by pointing out that those massive supplies up there were *federal*, not provincial oil, with all its problems of constitutional ownership. Gallagher the lone wolf would appear in the corridors of Parliament and buttonhole Pierre Elliott himself. And of course, once Pierre Elliott stopped to listen, Gallagher had him. He sold his dream to Donald Macdonald, and he sold it to Jean Chrétien, and he sold it to Alastair Gillespie. He so convinced them of the abundance and political value of Beaufort oil that in the 1977 budget, Finance Minister Donald Macdonald introduced a "super-depletion" allowance giving uniquely generous tax write-offs to wells costing more than $5 million. Of course, the only company drilling holes costing more than $5 million at that time was Dome Petroleum. The measure became known as the "Gallagher amendment" in the "Dome budget".

Henceforth, whenever Dome thought that it had a good idea, Jack, and later on Bill, would slip down to Ottawa. And perhaps Alastair Gillespie when he was Energy Minister would explain through an aide to Jack that he was *really* busy and couldn't see him, but the next morning Alastair Gillespie would walk into his office at 8 A.M. and there, waiting for him, would be Jack Gallagher. Gillespie would just have to smile and think to himself what *moxie*, and invite old Jack in.

When the Tories had their brief reign in Ottawa in 1979, Jack and Bill had continued to turn up and do the rounds, plugging into the new network in record time. Jack would come in and see Jim Gillies, Joe Clark's senior policy advisor, and tell him the great job that super-depletion had done in terms of Arctic exploration, and Bill Richards would make a point of keeping Harry Near, Energy Minister Ray Hnatyshyn's executive assistant, up to date with what was going on. And any chance they had of "stroking" one of the senior mandarins, they took. But there was a little problem. The mandarins in the Department of Energy, Mines and Resources had been looking at the tax system and they had decided that it was just too generous to big, foreign-controlled companies. But they also decided that it was even more generous to Dome, whatever its national status.

Then the Liberals had returned, and Jack and Bill switched back to a revised Liberal network. This time Marc Lalonde was obviously the man to be courted among the politicians, and the new rising star of the bureaucracy at EMR, Dr. Edmund Clark, was the mandarin who rated top of the list of public servants to be stroked. However, for the first nine months of the new Liberal reign, the courting and stroking weren't easy. The reason became apparent on October 28, 1980, when the National Energy Program appeared. Apart from its general principles of low prices and high federal taxes, which nobody in the industry liked, Dome was also particularly hit by proposals for a 25% back-in on federal lands, which included all its Beaufort acreage. Moreover, although Dome was always considered to be the cream of Canadian companies, the legislation dubbed it as otherwise, since more than 50% of its shares were held by admirers south of the border. This meant that the company was not eligible for exploration grants of any sort on provincial lands, and only of the minimum 25% on Canada lands controlled by the federal government.

Jack Gallagher went straight to Ottawa to quietly explain the error of the policy's ways to Marc Lalonde, but Bill Richards was not quite able to contain himself. He said the government course was "mad" because they were intent on "taking over other people's property." Bill Richards went down to Ottawa and raised hell. And sure enough, within a couple of months, the National Energy Program began to look less like a club to Dome and more like a springboard for it. Although Dome wasn't able to change the 25% back-in, pressure from it and the other oil companies made the government relent sufficiently to agree to make an "*ex gratia*" payment for the back-in. But the master stroke was Dome Canada, a new company totally under Dome's control but through which it raised $460 million of risk capital to drill on its own lands, and which, at the same time, was 75% Canadian-owned and thus the recipient of maximum grants under the NEP's grant scheme.

A senior investment analyst at Goldman Sachs Co. in New York summed up one view of the transaction. "It is," he said, "the greatest deal I've ever seen." More than that, Marc Lalonde himself flew out to Calgary to be present at the announcement of the creation of Dome Canada.

The federal government had created a piece of legislation and now seemed to be applauding the skill with which Dome was circumventing it. But of course, Dome had only been the victim of the legislation's letter, not its spirit. Helping good Canadian companies was the legislation's principal aim and Dome was, of course, the best of Canadian companies. Lalonde had written a letter to Gallagher at the end of January, 1981, in which he had said that he would be exercising "the discretion which I expect the legislation to provide." Suddenly a new term entered the debate around the National Energy Program. The term was "chosen instrument".

The chosen instrument was Dome.

## The Bloom Fades

The grab for foreign-owned oil companies began soon after the announcement of the NEP. Typically, Dome bagged the biggest to date, seizing control of Hudson's Bay Oil and Gas from Conoco of Stamford, Connecticut with an ease that made most babies' defence of their candy look pretty stout.

There had been a few problems with Dome's follow-up offer to the remaining shareholders, which included the Hudson's Bay Company, but that had eventually been ironed out. The federal government had, once again making policy without consulting Dome, almost managed to screw up the arrangement with its infamous 1981 budget, with provisions for imposing capital gains tax on share swaps that would have killed the deal. However, as soon as the budget was announced, Dome went to work on its Ottawa network. One of the newer converts to the Dome religion had been Secretary of State Gerald Regan, so Bill Richards had Regan tracked down to the East Coast, found out when his plane was returning to Ottawa and, sure enough, when Regan's Jetstar hit the tarmac back in Ottawa, who was waiting there, limousine at the ready, but Bill Richards. And pretty soon, Dome had arranged for its deal to be "grandfathered", allowed to go through on the basis that it was already in the works.

But then, suddenly, the bloom had begun to come off Dome. People began to realize that this time it really might have overextended itself. In particular, that enormous debt load, when combined with the promise of continuing high interest rates, spelled more than a problem that could be charmed away, or talked around. It presented a problem that could be terminal.

Corporate discomfort was being painfully reflected in the stock market. As recently as June, 1981, Dome had been trading, at $25⅜, at three times the level of its stock price in the boom summer of 1979. Meanwhile, a whole raft of new investors, some 60,000 of them, had hitched themselves to the Dome star via the giant, $460 million equity issue of Dome Canada, of whose separate existence the only evidence was a specially-commissioned Arctic seascape displayed on the senior executive floor of the Dome Tower and donated jointly by Richards and Gallagher.

But as doubts about Dome had grown, so share prices had slumped. In the first three months of 1981, Dome hit $7⅞, as the Toronto Stock Exchange had its worst first quarter in recorded history. Meanwhile, all the unsophisticated investors — and some sophisticated big ones too — who had climbed aboard Dome Canada watched miserably as the shares slumped to $3.70, little more than a third of the price at which they had bought them.

This slump in Dome's share price was also denting the credibility of a lot of stockbrokers and analysts around town.

I visited an old acquaintance, an analyst and veteran Dome-watcher whose words had been faithfully quoted as petroleum gospel in the newspapers since the great oil boom began. He was looking a little grey. At one end of his office, sitting like a deity on a little pedestal, was the mandatory stock-price screen. All day long the analyst punched the buttons and the bad news appeared, riffling down, line after line, in bright green letters. He spoke rapidly of Dome, with the kind of cliff-clawing oratory a depression banker might be inspired to use when faced with an angry crowd, withdrawal slips at the ready.

"The problem with Dome," he said, "is that most analysts who look at the company tend to have an *accounting* background." (They would be better, I thought to myself, to have a degree in *cordon bleu* cookery?) "When they look at the balance sheet, they look at the *accountant*'s version of the story. All you have to do is look at the *business* rather than the accounting. The balance sheet of Dome does seem fantastically out of kilter, but when you look at some methods of valuation, Dome has $20 billion of assets."

"Well," I said, unable to avoid it although I knew it was a little cruel, "then perhaps it would be in the shareholders' interest to wind up the company."

His heart almost stopped.

"*God* no," he said, eyes widening at the awful thought, and moved quickly on to his cash flow analysis for Dome. His assumptions were, to say the least, optimistic. He allowed that things might be a *little* tight in the current year, but then, in a world of eased interest rates and renewed demand, the money would just gush in, each year bringing a new and higher mountain of cash. The problem was that, at that moment, not too many people saw the world turning out that way.

And there was another detail that somewhat undermined his analysis, albeit in an oblique way. It had been nagging at my mind since I had walked into his office. It was that, apart from the desk at which his receptionist sat and the fittings of his own room, all the furniture in the office had recently been moved.

## A Rude Awakening from the Beaufort Dream

But perhaps the most poignant feature of the Dome story was the fate of Jack Gallagher's dream — a huge oil find in the Beaufort.

Smilin' Jack had undoubtedly been one of the greatest promoters — in the best sense of the word — in the history of oil, persuading everybody from the smallest shareholder to the federal government to fund his exploration efforts.

A great promoter is like an artist. He paints alluring pictures of the future, adapting each one to his patron of the moment. For investors he painted pictures of financial gushers; for the federal government, a picture of oil on federal lands as a source of central strength and a counterweight against the vast wealth of Peter Lougheed's Alberta; for almost every business newspaper and magazine reader, a picture of excitement.

In *The Blue-Eyed Sheiks* Dome's performance was likened to the dance of the seven veils. Each year of exploration in the Beaufort had produced another titillating promise of financial joys to come, which each year brought back investors in droves. But, as with the dance, the final veil had eventually to come off. There was a natural limit to both the audience's budget, and its patience.

That limit, too, seemed in danger of approaching.

Each year since drilling had started in 1976, Dome's activities in the Beaufort Sea had injected increasing excitement into summer and fall stock markets. In 1979, with the discovery of Kopanoar, a well that flowed 12,000 barrels of oil a day, it seemed that the dream had been vindicated. In 1980, Bill Richards had said that the Tarsiut well was on the point of being declared commercial.

After the 1981 summer drilling season, Dome had released independent assessments of two of its most promising Beaufort wells, Kopanoar and Koakoak. These had been carried out by the world-famous Dallas consulting firm of DeGolyer and MacNaughton. They said that Kopanoar could contain between 1.8 billion and 4.5 billion barrels of oil and that Koakoak could contain between 2 and 5 billion barrels. Initially the numbers seemed enormous, but closer examination provided a far less optimistic picture. Once uncertainties about just how much there was, and how much could be recovered (between 15% and 40% according to DeGolyer and MacNaughton), had been considered, these "super" wells appeared only marginally economic.

There was undoubtedly oil there, and there was lots of it. If a 12,000-barrel-a-day well were to be discovered onshore virtually anywhere in continental North America, it would be the most significant since the giant Prudhoe Bay find in Alaska in 1968. But a 12,000-barrel-a-day well beneath an Arctic sea covered nine months of the year in ice and many thousands of miles away from major population areas was a different proposition.

And now, in 1982, Dome was coming into its seventh year of activity in the Beaufort Sea. Would this be the year of the seventh veil? Would this *have* to be the year of the seventh veil? And the point was, that even if massive discoveries were confirmed, the OPEC glut had cast a pall over Jack Gallagher's dream.

Jack Gallagher was still available to tell his story, but, with round-the-clock financial meetings going on in the spring and summer of 1982, it was a little more difficult to get to him personally. I had been leaving messages with his secretary and finally, out of the blue, he had called me at noon on a Sunday, recognizing, as he did in all journalists, that I was a potential conduit for spreading the word.

And this time, Jack Gallagher's tone was different from the times I'd spoken to him before. For the first time in many years, he was on the defensive. Gallagher felt that his relationship with the federal government was being misinterpreted, and he was intimating that he hadn't been too happy with a lot of the decisions that Dome had had to make in the wake of the NEP.

In particular, Gallagher's sensitivity to the term "chosen instrument" was almost painful. One could imagine him wincing. "We're just the same as any multinational operating in federal lands. The Canadian ownership rating system and the 25% retroactive back-in have hurt us worse than anyone."

But what about Dome Canada, "the greatest deal ever seen?" "We *had* to react by forming Dome Canada," said Gallagher. "It certainly wasn't my choice because we already had enough shareholders."

And certainly the new shareholders Dome had acquired through its new subsidiary weren't too happy to be in the Dome camp, now that their new equity was languishing 60% below the offer price. But of course, Gallagher had a message of hope for them, a nugget in fact from his own past. He had bought his first shares of Dome Petroleum in 1951, he had said, for $10 U.S. a share and then bought them all the way down to C $3.80. And look where they were now. In fact, where they were now, compared with that opening price of $10 U.S. and allowing for stock splits, was at around $600. The word from Smilin' Jack was: keep the faith.

Then Gallagher proceeded smoothly into the newest version of his "presentation", delivering the very latest from the armoury of impregnable arguments supporting free enterprise in general and the Dome cause in particular.

It was fascinating to hear the new wrinkles in old arguments, subtle air-brush work on the great promoter's constantly-changing canvas: a combination of self-promotion, self-justification and macroeconomic theory all rolled up into one.

"We've never really been *privy* in Ottawa," said Gallagher. "All we've tried to do is inform. We don't try to influence. Most people in government at the federal and provincial level would rebel if we were as influential as the papers think we are. We just persuaded the government that it was in the country's interest to get super-depletion."

And then came a new wrinkle. "And just look what super-depletion did for the country. *It found Hibernia.*"

Once again, a Gallagher masterstroke. And of course he was right. The

Hibernia well drilled 200 miles from St. John's, Newfoundland, at the end of 1979 had been perhaps the most significant find ever made in Canada. The company that had drilled it, Chevron Standard — a subsidiary of Standard Oil of California, one of the "Seven Sisters" — had admitted that it had only drilled such an expensive wildcat because of the uniquely generous tax benefits of super-depletion. Chevron might have actually drilled the hole, but it was the "Gallagher amendment" that had made the whole thing possible.

Then Gallagher shifted expertly from the detail to the more general background. He pointed out that studies showed that the average resource dollar was turned over 3.3 times, and that each time the dollar was turned over the government collected 35% in tax. And what that meant to anyone who could handle fairly simple arithmetic was that for each dollar spent in the resource industry, the government finished up with *more than a dollar in taxes*. Another masterstroke. "So there's no way the government can lose by giving a little bit of help in the exploration phase."

A little tax deferment never hurt anyone.

But what I really wanted to press Gallagher on was the government. In fact, Jack Gallagher had *always* been a critic of the political system in Canada. Not just a Calgary-conventional, kneejerk critic but a long-time, thoughtful critic about the problems that, under the existing Trudeau government, were assuming crisis proportions: the power of the bureaucracy; the lack of power of Parliament; the inevitable bias in the system towards the interests of the consumer and short-term expediency over long-term planning. Indeed, Jack Gallagher's magic lantern show to investment dealers — now almost a sacred ritual of the North American investment scene — had usually ended, at least in Canada, with a call for political reform: an upgrading of the Senate; more power to the producing provinces.

If you stood back and thought about it, it seemed pretty strange that a man who spent so much time in Ottawa successfully promoting Dome's interests should be such a staunch critic of the place. But Gallagher was just so charming and likeable that he could get away with it. He could even tell Pierre Trudeau somewhat pointedly that he believed no Prime Minister should serve more than two terms, and Pierre certainly didn't like it, but, coming from good old Jack, he took it.

And really, it was quite easy to imagine how Trudeau would admire Gallagher, a man who, although from a completely different world, reflected many of the attributes so prized by Trudeau: intellectual talent, wealth combined with personal asceticism, athletic ability, and perhaps above all, independence — the pursuit of an individual dream and the unswerving commitment to remaining one's own man despite the constraints of leadership.

It was pretty obvious that at times Gallagher almost despaired at the way Trudeau's thinking was influenced by his senior bureaucrats and advisors, none of whom seemed to know, or care about business and all of whom, in the classic Calgary phrase, always looked at the hole instead of the doughnut.

221

For example, Gallagher had made his point to Trudeau about super-depletion and the Hibernia well, and the P.M. had said, "Well, that means they really drilled and earned that interest for nothing." It was thinking like that that made Gallagher depressed. That wasn't the *point*, Jack explained patiently to the Prime Minister. And in any case super-depletion only meant that the tax was deferred, not foregone completely. The real point was that the measure had *got the hole drilled*. It had led Chevron to bring a whole new exploration approach to the basin and they had struck it big. For Canada. And the P.M. said, "Well Jack, all *I* heard is that they got it for nothing."

Of course, when Gallagher spoke of "the people in Ottawa" he was full of the highest admiration for their qualities. "There's a tremendous dedication of time and energy in Ottawa. The job of minister is a thankless task. They never have a moment to themselves. I think there's a tremendous amount of talent in the Civil Service."

But then came the sugar-coated barbs. "But the problem is that it's a lifetime career. They never get exposed to business. They tend to be academic."

And as for ministers never having a moment to themselves, what he really meant was that they had to spend so many hours preparing to answer damn-fool questions in Parliament that they just didn't have the time to do their jobs properly.

Gallagher's final touch to the canvas was one of pathos. "The terrible thing you realize at my age is that you can dedicate thirty-one years of your life to a tremendous effort in trying to open up the Canadian frontiers, and it doesn't matter how successful you are, it can all be ruined by government and government regulations that are not enlightened."

Of course, it was at this point that one needed to rein in one's credibility. It was one thing to admire Jack Gallagher for what he was and what he had done. It was quite another to swallow the Gallagher story hook, line and sinker. Dome's size and spectacular growth had been more than aided and abetted by Ottawa. You couldn't have it both ways. In the words of one Calgarian company man, "If you lie down with dogs, you're going to wake up with fleas." But perhaps a more appropriate axiom, somewhat adapted, was "He who lives by the government must be prepared to die by the government."

If anything was actually going to kill Dome, the government could be considered the murderer only in the broadest sense. They could, indeed, be held responsible for the policies that required such high interest rates. But the reason those interest rates were so crippling for Dome was that it had borrowed more than any company in Canadian history.

Nobody had forced such enormous ambitions upon it.

But if Dome and the rest of the Blue-Eyed Sheiks seemed to be hanging on for their corporate lives, there was one corporate entity that had few such problems. Apart from the Ottawa bureaucracy, it was the one clear winner from the NEP. Perhaps that was not surprising, for it was the child of the Ottawa bureaucracy.

# 25
# The Petro-Cat
# That Got
# the NEP Cream

*" . . . it is not the source but the limitation of power which prevents it from becoming arbitrary. Democratic control may prevent power from becoming arbitrary, but it does not do so by its mere existence. If democracy resolves on a task which necessarily involves the use of power which cannot be guided by fixed rules, it must become arbitrary power."*

THE ROAD TO SERFDOM
FRIEDRICH HAYEK

Joel Bell sweeps through the doorway of Centre Block committee room N.112 surrounded by his entourage of Petro-Canada underlings, leaving the CBC camera bobbing in his wake. Most super-mandarins have an aura of importance, but Bell's is almost one of celebrity. Some consider it a dangerously high profile for one of the chosen few to adopt. Considering that he is here to face the all-party committee on Energy Legislation, the group of MPs charged with examining the many and divers parts of the legislation implementing the National Energy Program, and knowing that the Tory members are likely to be hostile, Bell appears remarkably self-confident. This perhaps tells us something about the relative power and knowledge of Bell and the committee. The committee is a parliamentary watchdog, but for the next two hours, the animals that will spring to mind as the questions and answers unfold are not canine; they are cat and mouse. Bell is the cat.

Not only will Bell, executive vice-president of the national oil company, emerge as more than competent to deal with the slender challenges thrown at him by the committee, he will also exude a sense of supreme satisfaction, both with Petro-Canada and with himself.

The satisfaction springs from his key role as a leading architect in the only widely-acknowledged success of the Liberal government's energy policy of the previous ten years, and in particular of the past two. Since 1976, Joel Bell has been an employee of Petro-Canada, but he has also stayed close to the heart of Liberal policy-making. The dual role has proved not without its advantages for Petro-Canada. In particular, Petro-Canada has emerged from the National Energy Program, which Bell helped write, as the most blessed of Crown corporations. While oil companies sink under the weight of their balance sheets, megaprojects founder, and the whole economy threatens to collapse, Petro-Canada, almost uniquely, is sitting pretty. The NEP has achieved this "success" via the devastatingly simple method of plugging Petro-Canada directly into the cash register of every gasoline station in the country, thus granting it access to huge new public funds at no corporate cost. With these funds it has acquired the assets and resources of Petrofina Canada for $1.5 billion. Never before has there been such a sweet deal organized, and the man who helped organize it was Joel Bell.

Bell is facing the committee today specifically with regard to Bill C.101, which will increase Petro-Canada's authorized capital ceiling from $1.5 billion to $5.5 billion. The increase will greatly expand Petro-Canada's potential size and power, giving it the financial springboard to become possibly the largest oil company in Canada. Such a move, in terms of its implications both for the balance of power between the private and the public sector and for its potential cost to the taxpayer, should be considered of enormous importance. One would imagine that it would be subject to the most thorough-going scrutiny and analysis. What it gets instead is a couple of sessions of half-hearted and super-ficial probing of Bell and later his boss, Petro-Canada chairman Bill Hopper, by MPs with little support staff and many other problems on their minds.

With each MP's allotted time limited to 15 minutes on the first "round" of interrogation, and to 10 minutes on the second, Bell is easily able to filibuster any undesirable questions, in particular the now almost hoary issue raised by Conservative Jim Hawkes. The untenability of Bell's role as player and referee in the system bothers Hawkes who wants to know more about Bell's role as an advisor on the National Energy Program. Bell proceeds to give a long explana-tion of Petro-Canada's role as a "window on the industry" and "takes excep-tion" to the suggestion of the impropriety of wearing two hats. Why, claims Bell, he just "talks to government" like any other oil executive would. And then Hawkes' time is up.

The Liberal questions, not surprisingly, are hardly probing. Indeed, at least one Liberal MP is reported to have approached Petro-Canada to *provide him with questions* to ask the national oil company's executives. Such a suggestion is only mildly shocking when it is remembered that MPs place at least as high a priority on appearing well-informed in committee as on asking meaningful questions.

Bell comes across like an extremely articulate and self-confident corporate executive putting it over at the annual meeting.

He notes the "importance of control and accountability", speaks of Petro-Canada staff as being "second to none", points out that the company's record is "very comparable with the industry" and boasts that its frontier exploration performance has been "enviable". Bell's vision of nationally-sensitive capital-ism appears to offer the best of all possible worlds: "hard-nosed commercial standards while promoting Canadian interests".

Calgary Tory MP Harvie Andre, chain-smoking and interjecting barbed remarks about profiteering from takeover leaks, sit across from Bell and just obviously loathes him. But he just as obviously loathes the fact that Bell is so difficult to tie down. To the outside observer Andre, with his lantern jaw, his five o'clock shadow and his big, charmless bulky presence, comes across as the epitome of the unacceptable face of capitalism. Bell, by contrast, ascetic, smiling, concerned, emerges as the very model of the guardian of the public purpose.

There is no doubting Joel Bell's commitment to the "public purpose" but it is also extremely important to remember that it is the public purpose as defined by Joel Bell. Despite all his talk of accountability and his relatively high profile for a public servant, Joel Bell's real power is exercised well outside the reach of Parliament and its committees. It is exercised through his network of contacts and friends in the real seats of political power in Canada today — the Prime Minister's Office, the Privy Council Office, the Treasury Board and the Departments of Finance and Energy. Bell has worked the system for more than ten years. He knows how it operates and he knows how to use it. If he wants to influence a policy, he offers himself to the people who are writing it, and often helps write it. This is not an evil power but it is a dangerous power. For many years, Bell characterized the intellectual free-floaters that populated the Trudeaucracy. He was a firefighter, a problem solver, and what gave him his political purity was that he had no territory to protect. He was a hired intellectual gun, available at the drop of a hat to spread his "pragmatic idealism" wherever it was needed.

But now, after six years with Petro-Canada, Bell undoubtedly *does* have a territory to protect, and he appears to have done an outstanding job of protecting it — in the national interest, of course. From an energy program that has virtually crippled many of its rivals, Petro-Canada has emerged with a new ability to put its corporate hand straight into the consumer's pocket, and with a more than trebled capital ceiling.

But despite the fact that Petro-Canada did well because of the NEP, the fact that the NEP subsequently proved to be a policy disaster in virtually every other respect is the key issue. If Petro-Canada was created as a "window on the industry" — one of the most strongly promoted parts of its initial mandate — then one can only come to the conclusion that either the window presented an extremely distorted view of the realities of the oil business, or, more likely, that the newer, younger, more left-wing bureaucrats at EMR who framed the policy, led by Ed Clark, did not choose to look through it. They just wanted to increase federal power over the oil business. PetroCan was the principal beneficiary of that aim.

Arguing with Bell about the legitimacy and financial performance of Petro-Canada is a little like arguing with a theologian about the existence of God. The theologian, if he finds himself on the defensive, will retreat into the explanation: "It's a mystery". When Petro-Canada's financial performance is questioned,

Bell will explain that it's because the state oil company is pursuing its "public purpose". The characteristic businessmen and Tory MPs find most frustrating about Bell is his ability to switch ground in mid-argument. The feature they find most disquieting is the aforementioned dual role as player and referee.

By the end of his two-hour session with the Energy Legislation committee, Bell has achieved his unstated purpose. The Liberals are looking satisfied, the NDP man has disappeared, and Harvie Andre and Jim Hawkes sit looking sour.

Once again, as so often happens in Ottawa, the meeting calls to mind an image from *Alice in Wonderland*. It is of a charming smile whose corporeal essence remains absent. Joel Bell is the bureaucratic Cheshire Cat who got the NEP cream.

## A Protean Corporate Animal

Petro-Canada has always been a protean corporate animal, presenting different images to the public, the oil industry and its masters in Ottawa. Even within its own increasingly large organization, its mandate is viewed in very different ways. For the public, it is seen as a security blanket against international uncertainties and a rival to big, foreign-controlled oil — as a source, even, of national pride. For the oil industry, it has, from the start, represented the thin end of the socialist wedge. Such a view was believed by many observers to be an over-reaction from business to any form of government intervention. Since the introduction of the National Energy Program, however, the industry view is certainly no longer an exaggeration. Ottawa now clearly sees Petro-Canada less as an instrument to influence petroleum industry activity in the national interest, and more as the vanguard of growing state ownership and control.

Rather than an ideological move, the original creation of Petro-Canada should be viewed as part of a worldwide response to the politicization of oil supplies and the increased desire for domestic security. As such, it also formed part of the increasing growth of governments throughout the industrialized nations, part of a trend towards more bureaucratic, more centrally-controlled, less financially responsive, less efficient societies. Again, this latter trend seemed not so much the result of moral turpitude, or declining standards as it was a function of economic structure in wealthy societies where the greatest enemy, uncertainty, made the public call for more government control of the economy.

However, with the NEP, this quantitative shift in favour of government control seemed to have led to a qualitative change, a belief that further government control was desirable for its own sake.

But while the "thin end of the wedge" thesis seemed to be borne out, PetroCan had inevitably been evolving to an internal logic of its own. All large organizations seek their own purposes and want to avoid "interference" from

226

outside, be it from shareholders or governments. Moreover, such purposes tend to be remarkably similar. The fact is that while the public saw PetroCan as a counter to the vaguely defined evils of multinational oil, which Ottawa sought to supplant with state control, Petro-Canada was becoming more like the other big oil companies every day. Far from making it more acceptable within the Canadian-owned element of the oilpatch, this fact made it even less popular. In the wake of the NEP, antagonism towards Petro-Canada reached fever pitch in Calgary. The very obvious local symbol of an increasingly distrusted and despised central government had been given an even further-preferred position in the oil business. When Bill Hopper, delivering his Christmas address to the staff two months after the announcement of the NEP, said: "I want to thank you, and the government of Canada wants to thank you," it was reported that even PetroCan's own employees booed.

But one telling feature of the criticism made by Calgary's outspoken entrepreneurs was that it was couched in almost exactly the same terms they used to criticize *all* the larger oil companies.

The attitude was summed up for me — somewhat ironically in the light of subsequent events — by Bill Richards, the stocky and dynamic little president of Dome Petroleum, which had just pulled off the biggest corporate takeover in Canadian history. "I sweat blood over our earnings per share. All they want to do is keep their minister out of trouble."

Richards' statement was perhaps a clearer indication of the Canadian industry's attitude towards Petro-Canada than a consistent analysis, for the fact is that the minister whom the Crown corporation is concerned to keep out of trouble is the very same shareholder for which it is not meant, in Richards' words, to "give a shit".

However, Richards' remarks pinpoint one of the principal continuing causes of tension within Petro-Canada.

Nothing more clearly highlights the uneasy fit between PetroCan's political mandate and its internal logic than the differing views — and sometimes uneasy relationship — between Bill Hopper and Joel Bell. Bell is often described as the "intellectual", the "party theorist", even the "commissar", a man who is prepared to sit and argue political theory late into the night. Hopper has been known to go to great lengths to avoid participating in such philosophical speculations. Bell is keen to maintain close, two-way contact with Ottawa; Hopper wants a written mandate, an armslength relationship and the minimum of government "interference".

Hopper, in private — and occasionally in public — can be scathing about the competence of government, and almost always tends to be cynical about Ottawa. When he turns up at a parliamentary committee there tends to be a quite different atmosphere than when Bell attends. When Hopper appeared at the Energy Legislation Committee after Bell in April, 1982, he seemed to be far more popular with the Tory side of the committee. Before the session started, he sat joking with Tory MP Jim Hawkes about the French version of a PetroCan submission. Hawkes said that he had only two further lessons to go on his own French course. "Well, that's good," said Hopper, "then you'll be bilingual. You'll be able to be a bureaucrat."

Later in the session, when somebody made reference to testimony previously given by Bell, Hopper said that he hadn't read the transcript, noting, "I have to read enough of what Mr. Bell writes."

Because Bell believes in a far closer relationship with Ottawa than Hopper, he is the object of much more industry distrust. Bell had told me once before: "The industry says to me, 'Choose — are you part of the industry or part of the government?' As if we have to be one or the other. It is inherent in our mandate that we live on that bridge."

At an address by Bell to a group of corporate planners in Calgary in mid-1981, the attitude towards PetroCan's executive vice-president had been openly hostile. Bell was telling the group it was a fallacy to draw a distinction between national and corporate goals. The latter had to be fitted into the former. The responsibility for going behind public policies and understanding them, he said, lay with "us on the corporate side." But not too many people there went along with Bell as one of "us". Bell was one of "them".

Bell attempts to talk his way out of accusations of conflict in advising on the NEP by saying that he was "seconded" to Ottawa and that he wasn't allowed to talk to anyone in PetroCan about what he was doing during that period. He tries to portray himself as just another corporate executive called in during the consultation stage of a policy. Such a claim is hard to swallow.

Petro-Canada is not just another corporation and Bell is not just a corporate executive. Furthermore, there was virtually *no* consultation with the industry in the formulation of the NEP. Bell was in a uniquely advantageous position and, judging from the results, one has every right to assert that he used it to the full in Petro-Canada's favour. Moreover, if he was there at EMR as a "window on the industry", to educate the bureaucrats in the realities of the oil industry, then he plainly did a very poor job. The NEP was a disaster for virtually every other company except PetroCan.

Meanwhile, although Hopper may adopt the stance that Bell is "too close" to Ottawa, he certainly hasn't turned down any of the advantages offered to PetroCan under the NEP. Although the two men may not always see eye to eye, one thing they indisputably share is an almost proprietary interest in the growth and success of PetroCan and — as the more perceptive critics of the Crown corporation have said from the beginning — such a priority doesn't necessarily fit in with government policy objectives.

## Who Guards the Guardians?

The potential benefits to Petro-Canada from the NEP were enormous, in particular, the Canadian Ownership Account and the 25% interest in all Canada lands. There was a firm commitment to greater public ownership, but it was also obvious that some of the NEP's authors were a little concerned about the growth of Petro-Canada. The novel, and somewhat bizarre solution to this potential problem was seen as "more companies *like* Petro-Canada". [my italics] Ed Clark was firmly in favour of greater public — as opposed to private Canadian — ownership of the oil sector, but was obviously aware of the horrors of state monoliths around the world. The NEP boldly declared that it did not intend "to encourage monopoly in the public sector of the industry. To ensure competition in the public sector, the Government may establish one or more new Crown corporations to hold the assets acquired, rather than adding them all to Petro-Canada. Petro-Canada will remain a principal direct policy instrument of the Government of Canada in the energy sector, and it may be that some of the assets acquired will be transferred to Petro-Canada, to strengthen its capacity to perform this role. Nevertheless, it is the Government's view that if all the firms acquired were to be incorporated within Petro-Canada, its effectiveness as an instrument of Government policy would be reduced, rather than strengthened."

The concept of public sector competition was perhaps considered an ideological breakthrough by the authors of the NEP. It opened vistas of numerous state oil companies all vying with each other, not according to squalid capitalist yardsticks like efficiency or profits, but according to some altruistic definition of the public purpose.

Bill Hopper had a word for the idea of public sector competition, which he expressed to a magazine journalist. It was "shit".

The NEP assured that Petro-Canada would not be allowed to grow too large. "Petro-Canada will act as the agent of the Government of Canada to acquire the additional firms. Once significant progress has been made on the acquisition program, the Government will direct Petro-Canada as to the disposition of the assets acquired. There will likely be a small addition to Petro-Canada's asset base to round out the activities in which it is engaged, in order to ensure that Petro-Canada is involved in all aspects of Canada's oil and gas industry. Depending on the size and nature of the assets acquired, the remaining assets will form the basis for one or more new Crown corporations."

And all the while, the man who would be there advising on Petro-Canada not becoming too large and powerful would be Joel Bell, one of its senior executives, someone who undoubtedly believed that what PetroCan needed for the public good was — more power!

That is perhaps the irony of Joel Bell's situation. Although he is keen to maintain, and indeed stand on, the bridge between Ottawa and PetroCan, he has increasingly found himself putting forward views developed from his position within the Crown corporation that do not fit with the visions of the Liberal party's ideological mentors.

## On the Acquisitions Trail Again

Indeed, despite all the talk contained in the NEP of monitoring and controlling Petro-Canada's size, the company was already once again on the acquisitions trail, and had been ever since it became obvious that the Conservatives would fall. The new orientation established internally with the Pacific acquisition, that Petro-Canada should dive into the mainstream of the business in order to generate finance for its expensive frontier mandate, was extended. Now it became a fully-integrated oil company, present, and able to compete, throughout Canada. With the Pacific takeover, Petro-Canada had acquired service stations in the West. Now it decided it needed them in the East also, so Petro-Canada started looking at two of the smaller, Montreal-based multinationals, Petrofina Canada and BP Canada.

Petrofina Canada was headed by Pierre Nadeau, an ardent free-enterpriser and staunch opponent of government intervention. Some of his strongest public statements about the evils of political involvement in oil were delivered not long after the Liberals returned to power. He almost certainly could feel which general way the political winds were blowing, and perhaps felt a particularly keen chill in his own corporate suite.

However, when PetroCan, through agents Pitfield, Mackay, Ross, first approached Petrofina Canada's Brussels-based parent, Petrofina S.A., they received a very cool reception. The management wasn't interested in selling. It was then that Maurice Strong once more entered the fray. After leaving PetroCan's chairmanship, and following an abortive attempt to enter federal politics, Strong had returned once more to the full-time business of making money, although he assiduously maintained his enormous circle of political and bureaucratic contacts throughout the world. Joel Bell and Mike Phelps, Marc Lalonde's executive assistant, were all part of a carefully cultivated circle that included heads of state, chief executives of major corporations, Arab sheiks and senior OPEC and United Nations officials. Strong, as ever, was riding the wave of the future. Aware of the trend towards foreign assistance flowing into petroleum exploration in developing countries, Strong had masterminded a new Geneva-based corporation, the International Energy Development Corporation. The IEDC's mandate was "to help developing countries become self-reliant in meeting their own energy needs". It was, in its own words, "A private corporation with a public purpose". Its board included Franco Parra, one of the first Secretaries-General of OPEC; Pehr Gyllenhammar, the chief executive of Volvo; Keith Huff, former world exploration manager for Exxon, the largest oil company in the world; and Nordine Ait-Laoussine, former executive vice-president of Sonatrach, the Algerian state oil company. It also featured two Canadian oilmen, John Godfrey, a former Imperial Oil and Dome employee who had been a vice-president at Petro-Canada, and Gus Van Wielingen, the flying Dutchman who had parlayed his exploration and entrepreneurial skills into the then highly-successful Sulpetro.

However, with regard to PetroCan's desires for Petrofina, the most important board member was Léonard Hentsch of the Swiss bank, Hentsch & Co. Hentsch was also chairman of another company on whose board Strong sat, Société Générale pour l'Energie et les Ressources, SOGENER.

Strong, through Hentsch, knew that even if Petrofina's management was unenthusiastic about a takeover, two of its major shareholders, Belgian banks, Banque Lambert and Société Générale de Bruxelles, might be more interested. Hopper flew to Brussels but discovered that the banks wanted what he considered far too much, over $150 for shares then trading at around $70 (and which had been trading in the mid $50s in August). He walked away from the deal. However, within weeks of his abortive trip came the development that made all foreign oil companies less desirable investments, the National Energy Program.

After Christmas, 1980, Petrofina's management decided that it was willing to negotiate after all. Strong once again carried out preliminary discussions — for which SOGENER was eventually to receive a fee of $1 million — and then Hopper and Bell flew to Brussels, where, over a weekend centred on the Belgian company's boardroom, an intricate financial arrangement was worked out that would give Petro-Canada Petrofina Canada for $1.46 billion. The deal gave PetroCan control of Canada's 18th largest oil and gas producer, but it also gave it marine and pipeline terminals, 45 bulk plants in Ontario, Quebec and the Maritimes, another 5% of Syncrude and, perhaps what was most important, another 1,120 gasoline stations.

## Catalyst or Competitor?

Petro-Canada's internal logic was taking it to mammoth proportions in a timeframe never imagined in its original legislation. Moreover, internal corporate logic was also to look with annoyance on parts of its "political" mandate. Bill Hopper, for example, clearly regards such requirements as shepherding small Canadian companies into frontier exploration as a pain in the neck. It may look like a noble policy-objective from Ottawa, but when you actually have to implement it, then it suddenly becomes a royal nuisance.

He also regards the requirement to give preference to Canadian suppliers as a burden. This, again, was clear from Hopper's appearance before the Energy Legislation Committee. "Hardly a day goes by when I don't get a letter from someone complaining that I haven't given them work," he said. "Canadian businessmen are pretty much like other businessmen, they'll say anything or do anything just to make a buck. If they think they can charge me 25 or 30 per cent more by being Canadian, they'll try to get their hands on me and they'll try to rip me off."

To anybody who understands business mentality, Hopper's remarks would come as no revelation, although the observations might well come as a surprise to policy-makers in Ottawa. But what is really telling is that Hopper clearly indicates that he wants to — and thinks he ought to — behave like any other oil company.

Indeed, quite apart from being reluctant to favour Canadian companies, PetroCan has been quite willing to compete with them. In December, 1980, PetroCan snapped up a small chain of service stations in British Columbia against a counter-offer from Turbo Resources, a Canadian company. The rationale was given in terms of bolstering marketing on the West Coast and rounding out the national presence, but it marks a very different orientation from the original one of catalyst rather than competitor.

Moreover, the attitude within PetroCan towards the small independent Canadian gas companies who had in the early 1980s become strapped for cash and lacked gas markets was a far less sympathetic one than that expressed in Ottawa. Joel Bell has pointed out: "If you manufactured tractors and you stocked up too heavily, people would say you were a bad business-man. If you're in the oil and gas business and you stock up on gas with no market, then people say you're victimized." Again, for any businessman, such an observation is basic. However, it is plainly at odds with Ottawa's view that Canadian companies are to be encouraged whether they are competent or otherwise.

However, as the internal logic of the corporation — willingly promoted by the entrepreneurial leanings of Bill Hopper — has been moving towards a more "free-enterprise" view, that is, promoting PetroCan's interest above all else, Ottawa has been moving in the opposite direction. With the National Energy Program, there has been an enormous change in the way the state oil company is viewed by EMR's policy-makers. PetroCan was originally formed as a window, a catalyst and an instrument for broad policy objectives. With the NEP, it has suddenly become a resource rent collector and the main instrument of greater public ownership, a means of taking the industry out of the hands of the private sector and putting it under the control of the central bureaucracy. Said the NEP: " . . . direct public sector participation in this (petroleum) sector remains too low. By world standards, the degree of private sector investment in the Canadian oil industry is high. The industry owes much of its prosperity to cash flow and incentives provided by Canadian consumers and taxpayers, few of whom are in a position to share in the benefits of industry growth. For most Canadians, the only way to ensure that they do share in the wealth generated by oil, and to have a say in companies exploiting the resource, is to have more companies that are owned by all Canadians — more companies like Petro-Canada."

As with much of the NEP, these sentences should be examined closely, for they are filled with tendentious analysis. For a start, to point out that the level of "public ownership" in the oil industry is relatively low by global standards, and use this "fact" as an implicit justification for further state ownership, should be put in some perspective. The world's largest oil producer is the U.S.S.R. and the vast majority of OPEC production comes from state oil companies run by primitive monarchies, Islamic fundamentalist tyrannies or military dictator-ships. That is why Canadian levels of public ownership are relatively low. If it is by such standards of economic behaviour that we are to judge ourselves, then our level of private ownership is indeed too high.

The other rationale the NEP offers for public ownership seems to be that, although tax incentives have led to industry growth, only a few — presumably shareholders — have participated in the growth.

However, the notions that public ownership enables everybody to "share in the wealth" and "have a say" are ones that deserve much closer examination. Unless Petro-Canada were sold off, and the revenue used to reduce the federal government's enormous fiscal deficits, it is difficult to see just how the general "sharing in the wealth" would take place. Certainly the payment of dividends to the equity shareholder, the government, would be stoutly resisted by the management, and in any case does not fit in with the notion of expanding the state presence and carrying out expensive exploration in the frontiers. Given the Canadian Ownership Charge, public participation in Petro-Canada might be much more accurately described as a national "sharing in the cost".

As for "having a say" in companies, it is very difficult to see how this "say" is exercised. Petro-Canada has no annual meeting; its annual report certainly does not attempt to outdo other oil companies in terms of disclosure, and the public "owners" are not even able to find out how much its senior management earns, as they can, say, with Imperial Oil. The level of scrutiny in understaffed and overworked public committees is, as has already been pointed out, superficial, while the most critical relationship, that between Marc Lalonde's chief bureaucratic advisors and PetroCan's management, is open to no public scrutiny at all.

The formal control mechanism of prior approval of the capital budget each year means very little as long as someone like Joel Bell is presenting it to his close colleagues at the centre of power. Again, the company's board, packed with deputy ministers and Liberal patronage appointments, is an extremely dubious method of control and is totally inaccessible in any direct sense to the public.

What in fact "sharing in the wealth" and "having a say" means can only be appreciated by the realization that the NEP espouses a far more left-wing view of state ownership than anything perpetrated before by a peacetime government in Canada. When it talks about the "public" what it actually means is "the state". One of the central tenets of the socialist views behind the NEP is that the state, rather than acting as the servant of the people, is synonymous with the people. It is a surprisingly short step from such a "vanguard of the proletariat" view of the state — which gives all power to a central elite which acts in the "public interest" — to one which declares that all contrary thinking is regressive or deviationist. Fortunately, the potential dangers of such a system are very small in a multi-party democracy, since the practical deficiencies of a centrally-controlled socialist economy will soon become readily apparent and lead to the ejection of the offending government and — if the incoming government learns anything from history — the rapid ejection of the key members of the bureaucracy that advised, or possibly even led, it.

But to reject the much more interventionist stance of the NEP is not necessarily to reject the concept of PetroCan. First, one should examine what PetroCan has become and what it has done.

## Judging the Guardians

PetroCan has grown phenomenally since its creation on January 1, 1976. In 1981, its revenues were $2.7 billion, its book assets were $6.6 billion. It employed almost 6,000 people. But what had it done that could not have been done by the private sector? The answer is debatable. It has certainly pursued its mandate of promoting expensive frontier drilling. To the end of 1980, Petro-Canada participated in 72 of the 130 frontier wells drilled in Canada, spending 60% of its exploration budget — three times the industry average — in probing this expensive area. However, the point is that no company can afford to devote that much of its budget to projects with such long lead times without going bankrupt, or, in the case of PetroCan, continuously going back to the government for funds. The logic emanating from PetroCan management before the NEP, therefore, was that a high level of frontier exploration could be maintained only by making the whole company larger. The company could still spend as much on the frontier, but since it was imprudent to spend three times the industry average, the answer — the internal logic — was to be three times as big.

But in any case, to spend money in the frontiers is not difficult. Indeed, it is very easy. What has been found? Some PetroCan employees attempt to point to the company's role in the Hibernia field, which is projected to contain as much as 2 billion barrels of oil, the greatest discovery in Canadian history. The fact is, however, that PetroCan backed into the discovery well under federal legislation. Credit for the discovery, which would have been made with or without PetroCan's presence, belongs to Chevron Standard, the Canadian subsidiary of Standard Oil of California.

In the Arctic Islands, the Panarctic consortium had achieved significant success before the government's 45% share was given to PetroCan. Nevertheless, the dubious economics of the area have meant that PetroCan has, in fact, been carrying a much larger share of exploration budgets in recent years. Meanwhile, the only hope of any kind of payout from the Eastern Arctic surrounds the Arctic Pilot Project, an almost science-fiction scheme to liquefy natural gas aboard barge-mounted plants and then ship it south via super-reinforced ice-breaking tankers. The company's one clear success has occurred in the original farm-out taken from Mobil Canada off Sable Island — where drilling is now reckoned to have proved up a commercial-sized natural gas field.

It is very hard to make an objective judgment on this exploration performance. Given the large funds put at its disposal both by government directly and through government-backed takeovers, at least a degree of success could reasonably be expected. But what success has PetroCan enjoyed in its overall financial performance?

Both Bell and Hopper boasted to the Energy Legislation Committee in the spring of 1982 about how profitably they had performed and how efficient they were. Since the NEP, however, comparisons with the rest of the industry are no longer possible. While other oil companies have suffered under soaring interest rates, the unique benefit of the Canadian Ownership Account means that the public has provided money to PetroCan to take over Petrofina, in return for which non-interest-bearing, convertible notes have been issued to the government of Canada. It has been costless financing which has, in turn, made PetroCan's financial performance appear a good deal better than it really is.

No voluntary mention of this fact was made before the parliamentary committee by either Bell or Hopper.

However, if PetroCan were a private company, its financial results could hardly be considered outstanding. Its net earnings of $64.9 million in 1981 represented less than a 1% return on its total assets. If it had had to pay the interest on the debt to buy Petrofina, rather than charging it to the Canadian Ownership Account, earnings would have been even lower. Management, of course, points out that normal financial criteria cannot be applied to PetroCan because it concentrates its resources in long-term ventures that do not generate immediate returns. This, of course, is true. The problem is, how can the public differentiate between the cost of such long-term orientations and the costs of simple inefficiency? How can they tell if the management is doing a good job or not? The answer is that they can't.

Perhaps the worrying element about this situation is not so much the potential drain on the public purse as the fact that the public may not *care* about the situation. Most people have little knowledge of the role or importance of profits within the Canadian economic system. The important public perceptions about Petro-Canada have nothing to do with its economic efficiency. They tend to concentrate simply on its existence and so far they seem to have responded very positively to the Crown corporation's growth. It is obviously not perceived to be enough that foreign oil companies, like so many Gullivers, are held in place by myriad bands of red tape. What the national psyche seems to demand, and what PetroCan has given it, is a Gulliver of Canada's very own. As already indicated, however, once you force feed any entity to Gulliver size, then it perceives its own interests to lie not with the Lilliputians, but with the other Gullivers.

In this almost inevitable development may lie the seeds of the public's eventual disenchantment with Petro-Canada.

## It's Ours, Isn't It?

In particular, PetroCan's desire to be a fully-integrated oil company, operating side by side with the Imperials and the Shells and the Gulfs and the Texacos, could be potentially damaging to its glowing public image. Once PetroCan, which is supposed to act more in the public interest than the multinational subsidiaries, starts to appear alongside them, the public will very soon notice that it is, in fact, acting no differently from them. So far, the public has shown a very positive response to the switch from the "Pacific 66" and Petrofina signs to those of Petro-Canada's spiky maple leaf on 1,400 stations across Canada. Sales at PetroCan have shown average growth far above the rest of the marketing industry. The question that even PetroCan supporters now ask is whether these stations might provide the public familiarity that will inevitably breed contempt. These reservations are shared by the two energy ministers who presided over the companies' creation and growth, Donald Macdonald and Alastair Gillespie. Donald Macdonald told me quite flatly: "I don't think they should be in the downstream end of the business." Alastair Gillespie pointed out that retailing was "always at the bottom of the list. What's more," he said, "I wouldn't want to be energy minister when people started asking questions about the price of gasoline at such-and-such an intersection when there are so many major issues to be dealt with."

Nevertheless, far from shunning a high profile in the retail market, PetroCan, early in 1982, carried out a promotional burst featuring its service-station activity. An enormous multi-media binge was launched, the principal theme of which was the Canadian-ness of the Crown corporation. "Petro-Canada," came the slogan at the end of the 30- or 60-second TV commercials. "It's *Ours*!" Billboards with levitating gasoline nozzles recommended "Pump your money back into Canada."

Such an invitation might well lead the public to contemplate just how much more it seems to be pumping back into Canada since the Liberals returned to power in 1980. Nor will it take long to realize that prices are no cheaper at PetroCan stations, nor is service likely to be superior. Eventually the public might begin to ask: 'Just what *is* the difference?'

If it emerges that there really isn't much in terms of prices, performance and profitability — and if one believes that multinational oil corporations are useful, indeed critical, entities in the well-being of the country — then there might be some cause for joy. However, one might also ask why, exactly, we need it to be publicly owned. The answer might well be that PetroCan's value as a psychic balm to the national inferiority complex *vis-à-vis* U.S. oil is reason enough.

However, from an ideological view, the important thing to remember is that PetroCan is not "ours". It belongs to the state and the state under the Trudeau Liberals seems determined above all else to increase its own power and direct control over the economy at the expense of private initiative. Under these circumstances, and the heavy hand of bureaucratic inertia, what we might end up with is something the size of Imperial Oil with the efficiency levels of the Canadian Post Office.

Bill Hopper is only too aware of these problems. Privately, he has been reported to have remarked that PetroCan wouldn't be necessary if the federal government constructed the right tax regime, but the problem, he said, was that the federal government was *too dumb* to create the right regime. Hopper is widely believed to regard the NEP as being rooted in economic naiveté and he certainly doesn't see eye to eye with Ed Clark. Given their quite different orientations, it is difficult to see how Hopper and the men responsible for the NEP co-exist. Marc Lalonde reportedly tore a strip off Hopper when Petro-Canada's chairman openly criticized the wrangling between the federal and Albertan governments — mainly, perhaps because Bill Hopper was sounding for all the world like the chairman of Imperial Oil.

# 26
# Homo Imperialis:
# A Breed Apart

*"Their Imperial Oil is still the Imperial Oil of*
*'Hockey Night in Canada' and a 'Tiger in Your*
*Tank', of an age when corporate profit increases*
*were not emblazoned across front pages like some*
*Central American jungle atrocity, and gasoline*
*consumption could be a guilt-free, even enjoyable*
*activity."*

This tendency of Bill Hopper, however, leads us to a more basic question. It is of critical importance if we are to pass judgment on the wisdom or otherwise of the National Energy Program. The question is: what exactly is Imperial Oil?

At the very beginning of this book, distrust of major oil companies, both at a "gut" and supposedly analytical level, was indicated as an important factor in promoting the NEP and the popularity of Petro-Canada. Imperial Oil is the biggest major and a critical focus of such negative feelings. But does either the man in the street, or indeed the federal bureaucrat, understand what Imperial is all about? Perhaps an equally important question when it comes to understanding the "two solitudes" of business and public opinion is: does the Imperial executive understand the feelings and perspectives of those outside his all-embracing corporate world?

The average age in the great vault of the Royal York's Canadian Room must be at least sixty. There are more than a thousand people here and it's difficult to imagine a more venerable gathering. Widowed matrons, some introducing their daughters to the rite; sedate elderly couples who define the word "comfortable"; small pockets of retired professional men; a multitude of clipped moustaches and ramrod-straight backs; whole squadrons of former airforce and navy men.

Although some sit quietly as if waiting for a service to begin, the journey of these people here from Rosedale or London or Sarnia or Oakville or Kingston has obviously been more than a matter of duty. Some of the ladies crack little jokes in slightly quivering voices. The professional men josh each other like the boys from the Molson ad, *circa* 1935.

Less conspicuous are the younger men, the representatives of the financial establishment, the proxies, come to cast the votes of absent powers.

They are all here to play their part in the well-scripted 1982 meeting of

Imperial Oil, the nation's largest oil company and one of its oldest corporate institutions.

For many of these people, this gathering is less an audience than a congregation. Despite unprecedented attacks on their corporate faith in the past turbulent decade, most of those here return each year to have their belief reaffirmed by Imperial's management. Indeed, that is an important reason for being here today. They are to have their first public view of Donald McIvor as Imperial's new chairman and chief executive. McIvor recently assumed the mantle from Jack Armstrong, the big, blunt man who guided Imperial through most of the 1970s. It is one of the weightiest mantles in the Canadian business world.

Multinational oil companies are an unloved — and most would say, unlovely — group. That fact was at the root of much of the public support for the NEP. As was indicated earlier in this book, the problem wasn't just foreign ownership; it was that the general public perceived the large corporations to be callous rip-off merchants. They were seen as Adam Smith's atomistic tradesman writ large — driven by the same basic self-love, or greed. However, since they were much larger, it was felt they were all the more able to put their selfish economic designs into effect. This view is confirmed by the opinion polls. The public tends to characterize oil companies as callous and interprets their power as enabling them to secure "more than a fair share" of petroleum revenues.

That corporations fight for revenues with governments is not to be doubted. That they receive more than a "fair share", however, is a moot point. But where the public view seems to be widest of the mark is in the perception of executive motivations. The man on a large oil company's management committee is a very different creature from the self-loving, eighteenth-century brewer or baker, or indeed the equally self-loving, small businessman of today.

But even if one could perform the somewhat uphill, public-relations task of establishing to the public that the corporate manager was among the most worthy of Canadian citizens, that still leaves the problem of foreign control. Do not their foreign parents merely pull the corporate strings in line with their own non-Canadian interests? That issue indeed deserves some examination, as does the nature of the major oil corporations and the character and motivations of the men who run them. Imperial Oil is the biggest of the breed. What manner of men run it, and, perhaps more important, what is their relationship with Exxon, the majority shareholder and the biggest oil company in the world?

## Preaching to the Converted

Imperial is the largest oil company in Canada, both the largest producer of oil and the largest refiner and marketer of oil products. In 1981, it produced 180,000 barrels of oil and 272 million cubic feet of gas every day. Its five major refineries processed 427,000 barrels of crude oil, turning out 700 products that were marketed through 3,900 gas stations and 700 agencies. Its other operations include chemicals, fertilizers, building materials and mining. Last year, the company had revenues of $8.2 billion, earnings of $465 million and capital expenditures, for the first time in its history, of over $1 billion.

But Imperial is much more than just an enormous company. For many of the shareholders here today it is as much a link to a passing world of social consensus and stable money as it is a critical piece of their portfolio. Their Imperial Oil is still the Imperial Oil of "Hockey Night in Canada" and a "Tiger in Your Tank", of an age when corporate profit increases were not emblazoned across front pages like some Central American jungle atrocity, and gasoline consumption could be a guilt-free, even enjoyable activity.

In any case, there are few reasons for hysterical headlines in the *Toronto Star* today. The congregation is already aware of 1981's 37% drop in earnings per share to $2.96. They will hear from Jim Livingstone, Imperial's president, that earnings for the first quarter of 1982 slumped almost 60% vs. the first three months of 1981, to just 38¢ a share. Don McIvor, it seems, has not taken over the chairmanship at a propitious time, and these people have certainly not come here to make his task any harder. That will become obvious as the meeting progresses.

Shortly after eleven a.m. McIvor calls the meeting to order. He welcomes everyone, delivers a short panegyric to Armstrong, who is inexplicably absent, and gives a special welcome to a group of high-school students who are to meet afterwards with some of Imperial's management.

McIvor is a good-looking man with a firm set to his jaw. His delivery has a little of Gary Cooper's honest deliberation, a touch of Jimmy Stewart's sincere hesitation. It is the right tone. All of these people need a little Frank Capra in their lives these days.

After dispatching with the legal niceties, McIvor calls upon Jim Livingstone to give his report. Livingstone is an Imperial man of the old school. He is soon to be succeeded as president by Arden Haynes, who is this day to be elected to the board. Haynes is a man of charm and what is known in Ottawa as "sensitivity" — that is, he can play the political game.

Livingstone could not be accused of charm, at least in his public persona. He delivers his somewhat sombre financial report in a monotone, word-for-word from his set speech.

Imperial, like the industry, he says, has been hit by much higher government taxes and latterly by the economic downturn. Profits and cash flows are down; projects have had to be cancelled or shelved. Capital expenditures for 1982 are likely to remain at about $1 billion, but could be lower. Projected highlights are the planned $800 million expansion of the Norman Wells oil field in the Northwest Territories and further exploration in the far north and offshore from the East Coast. There will be "prudent" investments in coal and minerals and further investments in petrochemicals. These are difficult times but Imperial has responded quickly and accelerated growth should again be possible by 1984.

"When I look at Imperial right now," concludes Livingstone, "I see a company with an impressive inventory of strengths — a large resource base, a sound financial capability, diversified operations, industry-leading technical competence and — perhaps most important of all — an aggressive, flexible and responsive management team backed up by employees as dedicated and professional as any in Canada. With resources like these at our disposal, I believe we can face the future with confidence and optimism."

That's what the shareholders came to hear.

After Livingstone's speech, McIvor invites questions from the floor. They are delivered through microphones placed along the aisles of the great room. The first inquiry comes from microphone number five, a middle-aged lady who is concerned about the Falklands crisis and the fact that Imperial has a subsidiary in Venezuela. McIvor gently points out that Imperial doesn't actually have a Venezuelan subsidiary, and that he doubts that the Falklands affair would have any influence on Venezuelan supplies. "But I can see, Madam, how you have that concern with everything you read in the papers."

Microphone number three, a straight back and grey moustache, wants some comment on the "cloak and dagger" negotiations between Federal Energy Minister Marc Lalonde and his provincial counterpart Merv Leitch. McIvor patiently explains that they are discussing Alsands, a project in which Imperial is not involved.

An ancient microphone with a shaky voice in the centre aisle wants to know if France is interested in investing in Imperial's proposed Cold Lake heavy oil. McIvor says not as far as he knows. The old gentleman, who has become somewhat incoherent, then appears to want to know about Exxon's involvement in cosmetics. There is a slight pause of embarrassment as McIvor looks to his directors. "I'm not aware that they've been involved in the development of cosmetics." And then, after a further slight pause: "I'll chase that down."

Things appear to be about to liven up when microphone number four, a portly man with a Henry Kissinger accent, wants to know why some of the board members have so few shares. Don't they have enough confidence in the company? Are they just in it for the directors' fees? There is a slight rustle around the massive room. This appears daring stuff indeed, at least for an Imperial annual meeting. The question comes from one Mr. Goetz, a shareholder who has become something of a feature at Imperial meetings in recent years. McIvor's tone is somewhat affronted. "I won't speak to directors' motivations," he says, but "none of our directors are in it for the directors' fees."

As if to dispel the slightly discordant tone, the final question in this portion of the meeting comes from microphone number one, another middle-aged lady who has read somewhere of an Esso manager who has changed his home-heating system from oil to natural gas. The lady wants to know if she should do the same. Laughter breaks out. "No," says McIvor simply. "Stay as sweet as you are."

McIvor then asks for nominations of directors. The approved slate is read from the floor by a representative from Montreal's *Caisse de Dépôts et Place-*

*ments.* Other dignitaries rise on cue to propose and second that a vote be taken. Discussion of the nominations is requested and tacitly declined. There are no other nominations. A show of hands is invited. No contrary hands are raised. "It would appear," says McIvor, "to be carried unanimously." Auditors Price Waterhouse are similarly unanimously reappointed.

Then comes McIvor's own set-piece speech, a finely-crafted and well-delivered lament on the federal government's energy policies and their injurious consequences. McIvor's delivery is in marked contrast to the wooden recitation of Livingstone. It is the style of the fireside chat. "What I'd like to do now," he says, "is to share with you the ideas I've developed on the situation that Jim described."

There is no trace of anger at the government's misguided approach, just a quiet sadness as he outlines the policies' consequences. They will result in a massive $2.4 billion projected cutback in capital and exploration expenditures over the period 1982 to 1986 vs. the outlook in the summer of 1981, a reduction in research and development expenditure, and the disappearance of thousands of employment opportunities.

The National Energy Program's higher taxation, combined with economic recession, has created a "double-whammy", while the program has also severely damaged investor confidence.

Alberta has made some concessions to the industry on its part and now, McIvor says, it is important "for the health of the industry and the economy" that the federal government does likewise. He realizes, of course, the government's "serious fiscal problems" and that it has "very little room to manoeuvre."

McIvor, it seems, is at pains not to lay too great a blame on the federal government. Indeed, at times, he almost seems to be making excuses for them. "In fairness," he says, "it could not have foreseen that the first full year of the National Energy Program would coincide with one of the worst economic periods this country has experienced for a very long time." Nevertheless, if the government really wants energy security and improved economic performance then what it has to do is to cut its taxes and leave more funds in the hands of the industry.

The applause is long and appreciative.

Further questions are invited from the floor. None too demanding, they are deftly volleyed by McIvor or one of his management team. Close to the end, a young man called Glen Harper stands up, announcing that both his parents are Imperial shareholders and that his mother works in the audit department. He wants, he says, to thank the company for giving him a higher education award. This gesture receives the day's biggest round of applause. Don McIvor says: "Glen, you're welcome." Then a former employee stands up to thank Imperial for a recent increase to his pension. Further applause. The Imperial family juices are flowing.

Close to the end of the meeting, microphone number four, the Kissingervoiced Mr. Goetz, rises once more to express dissatisfaction with McIvor's answer on the directors' share-ownership. Is the day to end on a sour note? Mr. Goetz goes on to bring up a suggestion that he made at the Imperial meeting the previous year, that the company should place on all its gasoline pumps a sticker indicating just how much of the price of each gallon of gasoline goes to governments. McIvor says he'd like to hand that question over to Tom Thomson, a senior vice-president and the board's youngest director and most obvious rising star.

The painless *coup de grâce* is about to be delivered.

"I'm delighted you've raised that idea again," says Thomson, going on to announce that such notices are in fact to be affixed to pumps this very year.

"And now," says Thomson to Mr. Goetz, "we'd like to present you with a sticker that is framed."

There is further laughter and applause. Even the carping voice of Mr. Goetz is loved within the great Imperial family. Dissent has thus been not only rewarded but almost institutionalized. Mr. Goetz is obviously both pleased and flustered and repeats an earlier commitment that he will match purchases with those directors who, he feels, have too few shares, up to 250 shares each.

Soon afterwards, McIvor draws the meeting to a close. There is a film to be shown and then the shareholders will enjoy a buffet lunch of turkey à la king and have the opportunity to mingle with the directors. "We'd like to chat with you," says McIvor. The financial community will assemble at a private reception with the directors elsewhere in the Royal York. The schoolchildren will meet with other Imperial managers and then, after lunch, all will leave and the management of Imperial Oil will be able to devote itself for another year to the running of Canada's largest oil company.

Anyone arriving at the meeting from a foreign country would think that modern Canadian capitalism was a friendly and co-operative thing indeed. He would be aware that there was a somewhat difficult factor not present at the meeting — the federal government — that seemed for some perverse reason to want to discourage investment, employment and wealth. However, there would seem to be a very close fit between these honest shareholders and their sincere corporate management.

## The Empty Pew

But of course there is far more to the Imperial Oil story than is apparent from the mutual admiration society of the annual meeting. For a start, it would appear that certain decisions are made at the annual meeting — the nomination and appointment of the board of directors being the most significant. This, of course — as with virtually every annual meeting — is not the case. Should any shareholder be foolish enough to suggest a nominee who is not on the company's slate, Don McIvor would thank him or her and then quietly point out that they could certainly go ahead with their nomination but that he already holds sufficient proxies to ensure that the company's own slate is elected.

The observer, if inquisitive, might wonder on whose behalf these proxies are cast. Only one matters: the Exxon corporation, the largest oil company — indeed the largest industrial corporation — in the world. For a company that owns 70% of Imperial's shares, Exxon is not conspicuously present at the meeting. This is no accident. In any case, Exxon really has little need to be brought up to date with the present condition or future prospects of its Canadian subsidiary. It already knows. Does this mean, then, that this whole event has been a pointless charade, a mere legal requirement? Technically it might be, but what is presented at the Royal York appears less a charade than a paradox. How does this theoretical domination by the world's largest oil company fit in with Imperial's self-portrayal as a proponent of the national economic interest and, more than that, a great Canadian institution? Moreover, if there is a great conspiracy, then these very solid men on the board who also manage Imperial are conspirators.

Their allegiance is first to the edict of those who sit in the leather-bound hush of Exxon's corporate headquarters, fifty floors above the bustle of the Avenue of the Americas in Manhattan. The concerns of Imperial's 40,000 or so Canadian shareholders can come only a distant second; Canada's economic interests but a more distant third.

But if such is truly their list of priorities, then they are indeed the most accomplished group of liars and scoundrels on the face of God's earth. Not only do they attempt to convince you that they are not puppets, but they do so while giving the impression that — far from being devious — they are merely exceptionally well-trained Canadian businessmen, devoted to their company and their country before any dark foreign power. They even maintain this charade in their private lives, pretending to be pillars of the local community, giving freely of their time to charitable causes, attending church. This group has, indeed, to be part of a most dastardly and carefully-conceived plot.

There is, of course, an alternative explanation: that these men genuinely believe that it is possible to serve both their shareholders and their country, and that there is essentially no long-term difference between the interests of the Exxon Corp. and the widow from Sarnia.

In the public and political arena, however, that has not recently been the prevailing view. Those self-confident Imperial ads no longer appear during "Hockey Night in Canada". Instead, you are more likely during the 1982 Stanley Cup to have seen ads for another oil company, the state-owned Petro-Canada. The catch-line of these ads is "Petro-Canada. It's Ours." The implication is obvious.

Imperial Oil. It's *Theirs.*

# 27
# The Roots of
# Self-Righteousness:
# What's Good for Imperial . . .

*"The vast majority of employees never even reach the curve's launching pad. Some advance along it for a while and then, like rockets whose boosters have flared out, fall away to a flatter trajectory. The very few who climb to its peak have the power to overcome gravity's rainbow . . . "*

If one were to look at the relative sizes of Imperial and Exxon, then it would be easy to conclude that Exxon was the dominant partner. Imperial is big; Exxon is huge. It consists of more than 400 corporate entities operating in 100 countries. It has an ocean-going fleet as big as Britain's Royal Navy. Every day it moves between 4 and 5 million barrels of oil, equal to three times Canada's domestic consumption. Revenues of the U.S. giant in the first quarter of 1982, at $27 billion, were three times as large as Imperial's *total* revenues for 1981, and this year its income will be larger than the gross national product of several European countries. Exxon's assets at the end of 1981 totalled $63 billion, of which just over $7 billion was attributable to Imperial. It employs 180,000 people. It has 65,000 gas stations. And on and on.

For economic nationalists, however, size is obviously not the main consideration. It is simply that Exxon is not Canadian. This fact, and the somewhat ill-defined problems that are meant to flow from it, are considered sufficient cause for damnation by Canada's "new nationalists", men like Bob Blair. Sitting in his corporate suite high over Calgary — and staring across at the new headquarters of Imperial's resource arm that have recently spoiled his view — he says: "A branch office isn't as good as a main office, no matter how many Canadians it puts on its board."

When I suggest that Imperial seems to have considerable autonomy, Blair responds sharply: "That's bullshit. There is no such thing as a multinational. If they are anything, they are national. Imperial is an American company."

However, Imperial's relationship with Exxon is far too subtle to be expressed in terms either of financial clout or foreign domination. Such concepts are essentially arbitrary and as such an anathema for the Exxon empire. Within that empire, reason is meant to rule — and reason serves the interests of corporate growth through enlightened free enterprise. That is the common god that Exxon, and Imperial, and the twelve other large affiliates within Exxon's global empire, serve.

That concept can certainly be said to have flourished most freely in the American environment, but to say, as a result, that Imperial is an "American" company is to confuse — not entirely innocently — nationality, and hence nationalism, with an economic philosophy.

## An Affiliate with a Difference

Imperial is the oldest of the Exxon affiliates. Indeed, it is older than Exxon, which in 1982 celebrated its 100th anniversary (Imperial's 100th birthday was in 1980). It is also fundamentally different from the other affiliates in that it is the only one that is not 100%-owned.

Like the rest of the affiliates, Imperial's membership in the Exxon family gives it access to the technical and research expertise of the whole organization. It also gives it access to Exxon's international supply pool of oil. When it comes to the management relationship, Exxon operates much less like a control centre than a giant investment club. It examines proposals from all over the globe, and then allocates resources according to where it thinks it will make the best long-term return. This fact, of course, is one that makes all national governments nervous. Imperial is fundamentally different because, unlike the other affiliates, it raises its own capital. That does not mean, however, that its investment criteria are any different, or that it can make major investments without Exxon's approval.

Like those of the other affiliates, Imperial senior executives, led by the chief executive, have to make at least three trips a year to New York. In November, Imperial presents its long-term corporate plan to the eight-man Exxon management committee. In March it delivers a "stewardship" report, indicating its short-term profit position and the progress of its corporate plans, and in May it presents its "people" plan, its proposals for executive succession.

For Imperial, the issue of Exxon's power over decision-making is obviously a delicate one. Exxon's ultimate power is never denied. Jack Armstrong was fond of saying: "They can always fire me if they don't like what I'm doing." Don McIvor acknowledges that they would "lay their hands" on Imperial if Imperial management was to "dumb up". However, the whole point about Imperial management is that, in the eyes of Exxon at least, it is virtually incapable of "dumbing up".

Disagreements with Exxon are treated with the secrecy of the confessional, but it is widely understood within the organization that Exxon was much less keen than Jack Armstrong on going ahead with the giant Syncrude project. Bill Twaits, Armstrong's predecessor, acknowledges that, in his day, they had doubts about the wisdom and potential financing difficulties of the Interprovincial pipeline to bring oil from Alberta to the east. However, both projects went ahead because Exxon deferred to the wisdom and specialized knowledge of Imperial's management.

The suggestion that Exxon may in some way act as puppeteer causes indignation among Imperial management. "When the press looks at Exxon and Imperial," says Twaits, "they think of something like Roy Thomson running the show from top to bottom. Imperial just isn't like that. It's a self-competent affiliate."

Ron Ritchie, a former senior vice-president of Imperial who left to go into politics and now works with the Investment Dealers Association, stresses that when Imperial goes to Exxon it is not going for instructions, it is going for approval. "Imperial might sometimes have to fight for its budgets, but the Exxon people would have to have very serious reservations in order to stand in the way of something Imperial wanted to do." He also emphasizes that Imperial isn't like the other affiliates. "Sometimes you might run into middle management down at Exxon who would expect to treat Imperial the way other affiliates were treated. I never hesitated to tell them that I represented lots more shareholders than Exxon."

Says Tom Thomson: "People would make a hell of an assumption about me if they thought that I might do something against Imperial's interest."

The key point that every executive stresses is that the Exxon-Imperial relationship is a communications rather than a decision-making process. And it goes far beyond the formal visits to Exxon by Imperial's management group.

"It's almost impossible to explain to outsiders," says Thomson. "It takes place at so many levels. Say we were thinking about expanding a refinery. We'd be talking to people at Exxon Research and Engineering about the latest technology. Marketing people at junior levels would talk to their Exxon opposite numbers about market projections and the latest forecasting techniques. It's just a matter of picking up phones. Most of us have worked down there and some of them have worked up here. There are relatively formal systems whereby people in certain functions talk to others in similar functions, but it goes far beyond that. But in no way do I feel a sense of stewardship to Exxon."

Some observers believe that Imperial plays down disagreements with Exxon. For example, former Liberal Energy Minister Alastair Gillespie, when Jack Armstrong was still chairman, told me: "I believe Armstrong's cross is that he is having to fight Exxon privately and defend it publicly. You could call it the double cross of Exxon."

And indeed, a behind-the-scenes battle between Exxon and Imperial is not out of the question. But it is unlikely. There may always be different managerial assessments of any situation. However, large deviations are extremely unlikely because Imperial and Exxon management think the same way.

Having 30% of its shares held outside the Exxon system, mostly in Canada, does give a degree of autonomy to Imperial in its decisions which is not available to other affiliates. However, it would be a mistake to over-emphasize outside shareholdings as the root of Imperial's independent decision-making

247

ability. Autonomy *per se* is not a prime objective of Imperial management because the whole process is geared towards producing an almost perfectly parallel system of corporate analysis and management development. Imperial's management are not clones of Exxon's. It is nothing as sinister as the "Boys from Brazil". But they are close enough that the issue of "string-pulling" or "manipulation" by the parent is largely irrelevant. Why would you bother to try to manipulate anybody who thought exactly the same way that you did? The most compelling evidence for this view lies in the fact that Imperial and Exxon management are almost totally interchangeable. And frequently interchanged.

## The Men on the Curve: The Right Stuff

Perhaps the critical factor in understanding both the character of Imperial Oil and the nature of its relationship with Exxon is Imperial's executive development system, the process by which the great corporate organism regenerates itself. Not only does the system closely parallel that of Exxon, it is also closely integrated with that of Exxon, in that a key part of the development of any corporate high flier is at least one tour of duty with the parent company. Moreover, if Imperial sometimes seems to display both clannishness and a certain arrogance, these characteristics' roots almost certainly lie in the management development system.

Although Don McIvor comes across a little like Mr. Deeds newly arrived in Washington, the facts of his ascent, indeed any executive's ascent, to the pinnacle of Imperial have nothing whatsoever to do with a simple heart, good fortune or a lucky face. Those members of management who sit on Imperial's board and those who wait below to replace them, are a species not born, but selected and then constantly screened and developed through several decades of one of the most comprehensive management programs in the world. Beneath Don McIvor's personable, downhome exterior, lies the finely-tuned, analytical brain and the fiercely loyal heart of *Homo Imperialis*, a breed apart. Apart, that is, from every other except Exxon Man.

When an Imperial manager tells you that one of his prime concerns is the development of people, he isn't trying to hide a cold, calculating corporate heart behind a mask of humanity, or pretending that he cares more for his staff and his peers than for his job or Imperial. What he is doing is stating a simple but fundamental corporate philosophy: Imperial is not a separate entity from its staff. The quality of the company is synonymous with the talent and dedication of its employees. However, this orientation isn't merely some vague notion of commitment; it is a highly refined system which few companies — perhaps only IBM and General Electric — can match.

Don McIvor is both the ultimate product and now high priest and guardian of that system. "To my mind," he says, "people decisions are the most important decisions we make. We linger over them much more than over operating decisions."

Like all high priests, McIvor has had passed on to him certain sacred documents. But he has also brought a new symbol to the priesthood. It is a curve.

The axes of Don McIvor's own particular graph do not appear particularly dramatic. The X axis is Imperial's salary code; the Y axis is age. Somewhere on the graph, every Imperial employee has his own little dot. McIvor's curve, however, does not trace any mundane series of dots; it traces the ascent over time of the company's highest fliers. It shows what your salary should be at a particular age if you are to be considered on the fast-track for the biggest job in the company. It is not a theoretical curve, but an empirical curve, and can be plotted over time against the career of someone like McIvor, who has made it to the top, or at any point in time to embrace that select group of individuals aged between about 25 and 50, who are all on the flightpath to corporate stardom.

The personnel people at Imperial are at great pains to stress that the system is geared to the development needs of every individual within it, which is true, but the Men on the Curve are of paramount importance. They will one day control the company. Of course, just being on the curve is no guarantee of success. One thing is certain: to stay on it requires enormously hard work; to follow it to its apogee requires both enormous talent and a lifetime of commitment.

The vast majority of employees never even reach the curve's launching pad. Some advance along it for a while and then, like rockets whose boosters have flared out, fall away to a flatter trajectory. The very few who climb to its peak have the power to overcome gravity's rainbow, the will to stay on course when it would be so much easier to throttle back just a little bit, to take off the strain, to enjoy a little more relaxation, a little more time with the family. So although Don McIvor sometimes comes across as Mr. Deeds, it is well to remember that he is also a corporate astronaut. Don McIvor has Imperial's — and Exxon's — version of the Right Stuff.

Imperial rarely, if ever, recruits executives from outside the company, so it is highly probable that the man who will be chief executive in the year 2000, and probably the man who will preside in 2010, is now working somewhere within the Imperial system, or is on loan assignment with Exxon. What's more, Don McIvor already knows who he is. He not only has a curve, he has a list, in fact two lists, the sacred and secret documents passed on to him by Armstrong. One, the chief executive officer, or CEO list contains perhaps half a dozen names. The youngest might be in his early thirties, indeed, if he is exceptional, he may be in his late twenties. The oldest will be in his fifties. These are the men considered most likely to stay on the highest curve. They are never told who they are, but they have a pretty good idea. Almost certainly, a great many more executives than half a dozen believe they are on the list. McIvor's other, broader, list is the board list, 20 to 25 names within a similar age range who are considered to have the potential to make it to Imperial's board.

The CEO and board lists might never exactly be posted in the corridors, but an analysis of career paths would establish the likely candidates, the Men on the Curve. Those considered "high-potential" are selected sometime between five and twelve years after entering the company. They will almost certainly have joined with some form of technical degree — in geology or geophysics or engineering — or possibly one in commerce, most likely an MBA. The graduate net is spread over all Canadian universities, although it is perhaps worth noting that Jack Armstrong, Don McIvor, and Arden Haynes all attended the University of Manitoba.

The graduate entrant will spend his first ten years or so in a line organization "in the field", working in exploration, or refining or marketing. During that ten years he will have perhaps four separate jobs, one of which will be a specialist job and one of which will be in a supervisory position. Sometime during that period, he will have been spotted as the kind of man who looks as if he'll make it to vice-president in one of Imperial's three operating subsidiaries: Esso Resources Canada, the exploration and production arm; Esso Petroleum Canada, the re-fining and marketing group; or Esso Chemical Canada, the chemical subsidiary.

After this initial period, he is brought into corporate headquarters and given a staff assignment so that he can expand his knowledge of the commercial and economic side of management. He might come in as secretary to the manage-ment committee — the board's management directors, the men who run the company — or to analyze and work on a particular project. A couple of years later he may be moved to his old function somewhere within the Exxon organization or given a staff assignment with them. After another couple of years it may be decided that the individual has the ability to go all the way to the top, so he's brought back to Canada and given one of the top administrative jobs, as a vice-president with one of the operating companies. If he continues to perform there, then he will eventually make it as a senior vice-president and director of the main board, one of the heirs apparent. If the CEO looks as if he will still be there for some time, then the individual may be moved out again to Exxon or one of its affiliates round the world until it's time to be brought back as president or chief executive.

"The fast track," says McIvor, "means accelerating within the function, working outside the function and working in different geographical locations. You realize that you are expected to excel. Another factor is that you keep getting pushed into *terra incognita*, to see how you can cope with discomfort. Some people can't hack it, and there's no shame in that, but it's a pretty carefully thought-through process."

Concern for employee development is not something confined to selecting those with the right stuff for senior corporate management. Nor is the concern with succession restricted to that line-up of high fliers that represent the dots along McIvor's curve. Employee assessment and development is a pervasive process at Imperial. Moreover, the successful development of others' careers is perceived as a *sine qua non* for the Man on the Curve. To have failed to see the potential of a subordinate is almost as serious as having failed in one's own job. What's more, such a failure would become readily apparent, for at each management level of Imperial, employees are required to put a numerical ranking on those beneath them with whom they come into contact on a fairly regular basis. The ranking system is exactly the same as that in Exxon, and goes from 1 through 4. A 4 ranking indicates the individual is extremely sub-standard, indeed almost certainly on the way out. A 3.5 means that someone is performing below standard but has correctable deficiencies. A 3 is performing to expectation. Someone with a ranking of 2.5 is considered to have an edge, to be doing an above-average kind of job. A 2 is considered a performer and a 1 is operating in an outstanding fashion.

Due to the breadth of the ranking, each individual will be ranked by several superiors. That is where the pressure on the managers comes in. Each manager has to do a seriatim ranking — that is, setting in order, one-two-three etc. — as well as the straight numerical ranking. This seriatim ranking is then subjected to a forced distribution to make sure that numerical rankings are not lopsided. For example, 1s are meant to account for 10% of the workforce, 2s for 25% and so on.

For the rankers, the virtue is to hit the norm of others' rankings. Too great a deviation will mark you as a bad ranker, and bad rankers are suspected of not being good at employee development.

All this numerical ranking is supplemented by interviews between the employee and his manager, and by the manager's assessment of particular opportunities for the employee and particular forms of education and employment which may "round him out". One thing each manager is especially concerned about is the identification of one or more successors for his own job. The multi-layered effect and intent of this system on the great management structure is that anybody's promotion should leave no more of a hole than a boat passing through water.

It is important to remember that those with high potential do not get 1s all the time, nor are those who rate as 1s all high potential. A 1 could be a man who has, in the corporate geography, "plateaued", that is, gone as far as he is likely to go, but is nevertheless doing an outstanding job. A brilliant engineer on the fast track, by contrast, suddenly pushed into a staff job in strange territory, could have rankings of 2.5 or 3.

The executive development process, and the appraisal system, go all the way to the apex of the pyramid — indeed, beyond it. The highest review body in the company is the management Compensation and Organization Committee, consisting of all the employee directors headed by Don McIvor. Above that is the review carried out by McIvor, dealing with the replacements for CEO, president and the employee directors. McIvor takes this plan to the board's Compensation Committee, which consists of himself and the four outside directors, and then finally takes his review to New York for ratification by Exxon's management committee.

This enormous ongoing process, which is meant to encourage the feeling that someone, indeed several people, "up there" are looking out for you rather than merely looking over you, is a key part of Imperial's peculiar internal cohesion. Individualism is discouraged; emphasis is placed on performing as a "team player". Careers cannot be carved out; they have to be carefully built. The whole system creates an extremely effective loyalty to the company, helps mould the Imperial Man. Says Bill Moher manager of Imperial's Management Development and Organization Division, "We don't choose people because they are different behaviourally or attitudinally, but they may well become so after they join Imperial."

In fact, it seems at first rather perverse that one of the key goals of managers in the system is to make themselves expendable, although they hope that their own job will become vacant because they have been promoted. There is only one position where this rule cannot apply, and that, of course, is at the very top. It seems somewhat strange to hear Bill Moher say in front of Don McIvor, and with both of them smiling: "McIvor's totally expendable. If he had to be replaced tomorrow there would be several candidates."

Don McIvor has spent thirty hard years working to make himself virtually redundant. And he loves the idea.

## The Ultimate Flightpath

Imperial executives do not like talking about themselves and their private lives. This is partly a result of the team approach, partly due to the fact that they see their private lives as totally irrelevant to any inquiry about Imperial. Why would one look for clues to their character outside the office when the very fact that they are here, at the top of the curve, says everything about them that anyone could possibly want to know?

As for their youth, is there life before Imperial? Don McIvor acknowledges that he grew up in Winnipeg, where his father was a newspaperman on the *Free Press.* He went to the University of Manitoba on a scholarship in physics and chemistry having been bitten by the earth sciences bug — as other mortals might be bitten by jazz or tennis — while working in a gold mine between high school and university. He joined Imperial as a trainee in geophysics in 1950. He spent his eight years in the field before coming to Calgary in 1958. In 1961 he got first staff job, assistant to the exploration manager, and his first senior management job in 1965, when he became manager of exploration research. His specialist exploration knowledge led him to be sent on loan to Exxon and work in Angola and France during this time. He went from Calgary to another Exxon assignment, with the Jersey Production Research Company in Tulsa, Oklahoma, before moving to Toronto as assistant manager and then manager of Imperial's corporate planning department.

In 1970, he became exploration manager and in 1972 was sent to the elite one-year course at the National Defence College of Canada. When he returned he was named a senior vice-president and director. In 1975 he became executive vice-president, one short step from the summit. In 1977, Exxon needed a vice-president of oil and gas exploration and production, and McIvor once again moved into the Exxon system. Some observers wondered whether this indicated that McIvor had been moved out of the running to be Armstrong's successor. There was even a bizarre rumour that Maurice Strong, then chairman of Petro-Canada, had somehow had McIvor removed because he was too vociferous an opponent of the Crown corporation! However, speculation was ended in July, 1981, when McIvor returned to Imperial's board as deputy chairman.

This all-embracing system, with its emphasis on team-work and developing those around you, means also that naked ambition is a rarely displayed characteristic. The Imperial system, however, once an employee has absorbed its implications, allows ambition to be not so much suppressed as sublimated. *Homo Imperialis* does not have to keep staring at the pinnacle of the pyramid. He knows that as long as he is doing a good job in his present posting, then the system will be ambitious for him. This of course does not preclude normal corporate tactics like getting oneself attached to high-profile projects of high-flying superiors, or even the sort of more or less subtle back-stabbing that goes on in every corporate organization. But it does make it plausible that someone can reach the top of Imperial playing it perfectly straight all the way. Thus Bob Peterson, the stocky 44-year-old who at the beginning of 1982 assumed the presidency of Esso Resources, can say: "I'm not driven by a desire to be CEO," and it can be *just about* plausible, although to an outsider it looks a little like someone 50 feet from the top of Mount Everest asking: "How did I get here?"

You meet the same sort of statement again and again. In an interview a year or two ago Jack Armstrong had said: "I never expected to be here." Don McIvor, if he will not admit to ambition, at least acknowledges that the sense of competition increases the farther up the organization you go. But he, too, says: "I never programmed my life to be at a certain point at a certain age. I was always too busy to worry."

McIvor claims he received some insight recently when he made this point to the wife of a colleague and she replied: "Well, perhaps subconsciously you felt you never had to." The colleague's wife hit it right on the head. The true fast-tracker at Imperial, confident in his own skill and the quality of his work, just doesn't have to worry about the curve. That's plotted by mission control. And although he's not told, he knows he's on it.

Within the whole process, the stint with Exxon is considered *de rigeur.* As Bill Moher says: "There's no rule that says you have to work for Exxon, but if I was a young man starting out, then I'd certainly be looking for a couple of years with Exxon to get some world experience."

And of course, the tour with Exxon isn't just the U.S. parent doing its Canadian subsidiary a favour. Says Moher: "Exxon will come to us and say, we're having trouble filling this job in Kuala Lumpur. So we'll have a look at it and see if we find it a good fit for someone who needs some offshore experience, and if we have someone we'll let him go and restructure an entry point for him. Placements in Exxon are partly a matter of individual development and partly a matter of executive supply and demand."

The Exxon stint is also something else; it is the means by which the senior executives at Imperial establish powerful links with their counterparts at Exxon, and, more subtly, develop a common view of the world.

# 28
# Keeping the Faith

*"In truth, politics is an abstraction to self-made men, most of whom suspect party politics of being frivolous and who, deep down, remain unimpressed by the efficacy of universal suffrage. The presence of two different but indistinguishable parties involved in a constant struggle for office seems to many to be both inefficient and extravagant."*

POINTS OF DEPARTURE
DALTON CAMP

To those who have had to do business with them, the face presented by *Homo Imperialis* has not always been that of the kindly tolerance obvious at the annual meeting. At its best it was the face of supreme competence, the self-confident embodiment of solid business virtues; at its worst it was somewhat arrogant. Until the past decade, there was little suggestion either from inside or outside Imperial that Imperial men were anything but the best.

The company's enormous inner strength came from a profoundly held conviction that what it did was "right". It invested and reinvested in accordance with purely objective analytical criteria; it scrupulously obeyed the laws of the land; it provided excellent opportunities for its employees; and it produced an enormous range of goods and services at competitive prices. Until recently, the only mistake that it would ever freely acknowledge was that it had failed to take seriously enough the essentially irrational forces of public distrust of big oil and political expediency — which between them had given birth to the economic nationalism expressed in the National Energy Program of October, 1980.

In fact, Imperial has had undoubted corporate problems in the 1970s. Some outsiders, eager to attack Imperial's "perfect" self-image, maintain that these represent corporate errors that indicate Imperial has fallen from its position as industry leader.

The corporate problems were real, but rumours of Imperial's demise as industry leader may have been greatly exaggerated. Until the first OPEC crisis of 1973-74, Imperial Oil was the Canadian oil industry's undisputed technical leader and its most credible voice. Its origins went back virtually to the beginnings of the oil business itself, and its relationship with the Standard Oil - Trust, forerunner of Exxon, almost as far. Imperial's roots lay in the oilfields of southwestern Ontario. In 1880, a number of small Canadian refiners, faced with stiff competition both from Pennsylvania's sweeter and more abundant crude and from the spreading marketing and refining network of young John D. Rockefeller's Standard Oil, joined to form Imperial. Throwing the fixed assets of their refineries and a total of $25,000 into the pot, the sixteen operators rationalized their activities under the direction of Jacob Lewis Englehart, who had come to Canada from Cleveland, Rockefeller's power base, in 1866 to seek his fortune.

By 1883, Imperial had a single refinery at Petrolia, a huge smoky operation covering 50 acres, where kerosene, waxes and lubricating oils were produced. These products found their way not only to the Maritimes and the most outlying trading posts of the Hudson's Bay Company, but were also carried by the great sailing ships to markets as far away as Japan and Australia. Just three years after its founding, Imperial's distribution network spread from sea to shining sea, with 23 branch offices between Vancouver and Halifax.

The refiners had originally joined to combat the competition from the growing Rockefeller empire. In the end, what they had merely done was to form a more rational unit for Rockefeller to absorb.

## Rockefeller: Bringing Order to a Chaotic World

John D. Rockefeller was one of the most brilliant businessmen to ever live, but he was also, primarily due to his taciturn and secretive nature, one of the most widely feared and despised. He was considered the world's greatest monopolist and thus the direct cause of the great wave of anti-trust feeling that swept the United States around the turn of the century. Fundamentally, however, Rockefeller's tactics were largely dictated by the nature of the substance in which he dealt, petroleum. Never had there been a commodity that could wreak greater havoc with the market system, as the early days of the oil industry amply demonstrated. Petroleum would appear, suddenly and unexpectedly, like some powerful genie from the Arabian Nights, briefly spewing forth out of control and bringing enormous wealth to a few. Then, as the reservoir from which it came dried up it disappeared just as quickly. The price of oil shot up and down like a yo-yo, often rising or falling by a factor of ten in just a few months as one genie disappeared and another gushed all over its finders to create a new temporary glut.

Rockefeller observed such disorder with profound distaste, but he also saw the enormous potential for someone who could bend the genie to his will. He realized that the way to master oil was to control its transportation, refining and marketing rather than its production. Six years after the discovery of oil in Pennsylvania, when he was 26, he bought a refinery in Cleveland and soon managed to gain a dominant position in the nascent industry. He persuaded the railroads to give him secret rebates so he could undercut and then buy out his rivals. After only seven years in the business, in 1870, he formed the

Standard Oil Co. In 1873, having gobbled up most of his rivals — in most cases, secretly — he formed the Standard Oil Trust.

By the 1880s, Standard also controlled a third of the Canadian market and Imperial was eventually to be drawn into the Standard system by Rockefeller's competition and its own need for capital. In 1898, Imperial sold control to Standard and thus became part of Rockefeller's great scheme to bring order to the chaotic world of petroleum.

By that time, however, Rockefeller had stirred forces he could not control. The anti-trust movement found Rockefeller's vision distinctly at odds with its own ideas of the democratic spirit of free enterprise. The Sherman anti-trust act was passed in 1890, but it wasn't until 21 years later, following a massive lawsuit and an appeal to the Supreme Court, that Standard was ordered to divest itself of its subsidiaries. Of these subsidiaries, the largest was Standard Oil of New Jersey, later to become Exxon, which held onto Imperial as a subsidiary.

Imperial meanwhile was establishing itself as the dominant oil company in Canada. Between 1905 and 1915, the number of automobiles in Canada increased by a factor of a hundred, to more than 60,000. In the miraculous decade up to 1920, Imperial boosted its refining capacity from 900 to 23,000 barrels a day. Domestic Canadian supplies were totally inadequate to meet this demand so oil was brought from South America through an Imperial subsidiary, International Petroleum, which was highly successful in exploration and production, and eventually sold to Exxon in the late 1940s. Imperial meanwhile explored for oil and gas in Canada. It participated in the finds in Alberta's Turner Valley during the 1920s and 1930s, and found oil in the Northwest Territories at Norman Wells — a field which only in recent years has become commercially attractive. By 1947, however, Imperial had drilled 133 consecutive dry holes when it finally drilled the well at Leduc near Edmonton that was to herald the birth of the Canadian oil industry as a significant international force.

Thenceforth, Imperial clearly established itself as the leader of the Canadian oil industry in exploration as well as refining and marketing. The Albertan fields it either discovered or helped develop in the 1950s and 1960s, such as Redwater, Judy Creek and Golden Spike, still provide a large proportion of Canada's domestic oil supplies.

Moreover, when Imperial talked, government listened. If the National Energy Board, set up at the beginning of the 1960s both as a regulatory and advisory body to cabinet on energy, wanted advice, it turned first to Imperial. What was good for Imperial Oil was considered good for Canada. At the beginning of the 1970s, Joe Greene, first minister of the newly constituted federal Department of Energy, Mines and Resources formed a National Advisory Committee on Petroleum, NACOP, to get the industry's views. The body was low profile and its members, all heads of leading oil or pipeline companies, were sworn to the cabinet vow of secrecy. Their most vociferous member was Bill Twaits, Imperial's chief executive.

But then, in the early 1970s, with the OPEC crisis, Imperial's crown began to slip. For a number of years, the Canadian economic nationalists, chief among them Walter Gordon, the former Liberal cabinet minister, had been claiming that foreign domination of Canadian industry was dangerous. Suddenly, in 1973 and 1974, there seemed to be some firm grounds for suspicion. Bill Twaits and his colleagues at NACOP had taken a lot of time and trouble to educate Joe Greene. In June, 1971, Greene felt sufficiently educated to suggest that: "At 1970 rates of production, (Canada's) reserves represent 923 years' supply for oil and 392 years for gas."

Such "education" coincided with unprecedented demands from the U.S. market for Canadian oil. By 1973, just before the OPEC crisis, Canada was shipping over 1 million barrels a day south of the border, and its only concern was that it might simply have more oil than it conceivably knew what to do with. Then suddenly came the OPEC crisis and things changed rapidly. The National Energy Board now had submissions from the oil companies telling them that Canada's oil was running out, and that, in fact, we had less than ten years' supply.

This turnaround in the reserve picture triggered a more widespread fear that U.S.-owned companies like Imperial were being manipulated with blatant disregard for Canada's national economy. The NDP now constantly called for the nationalization of Imperial.

There were to be other problems with corporate strategy. After the discovery of Prudhoe Bay field on the North Slope of Alaska in the late 1960s — and believing that Alberta was largely "played out" in terms of Imperial's massive needs to replenish its petroleum reserves — Imperial shifted the bulk of its exploration efforts to the north, in particular the Mackenzie Delta. However, in the process it allowed much of its western exploration land to fall back into the hands of Alberta. At the time, the decision appeared rational. However, the company had not allowed for the enormous increase to come in Canadian domestic prices plus the very generous tax regime introduced in Alberta after the fierce dispute between the federal and provincial governments during 1974. The result was an upsurge in exploration activity, and discoveries, in the mid-1970s from which Imperial found itself embarrassingly absent. It was dealt another severe blow when the reserves it had developed in the Mackenzie Delta were effectively sterilized by the decision in 1977 to kill the proposal of the Arctic Gas consortium — of which Imperial was the leading Canadian company — to build a pipeline from Prudhoe Bay via the Mackenzie Delta to bring both American and Canadian natural gas to southern markets.

The result was that Imperial, its reserves dwindling, was forced to buy its way back into Alberta at very high prices. Ten years before, the smaller Canadian companies would scrabble around in Imperial's shadow, hoping to pick up a piece of the action by grabbing some fringe acreage where the giant was drilling. Now Imperial found itself approaching Canadian companies that had not existed ten years before in order to get a piece of their action. In particular, Imperial approached a company called Canadian Hunter, the brainchild of John Masters and Jim Gray, and agreed to carry out $179 million of exploration work in return for 12½% of Hunter's land in the Elmworth field, where they had discovered one of the most significant fields in North America, and a slightly larger percentage of other exploration lands. In Calgary, the farm-in was viewed as the most expensive piece of humble pie in Canadian oil history.

The fact, however, that Imperial was able to spend such a large amount of money was an indication of the enormous cash-generating machine that it had become over its hundred-year history. Moreover, there was also a tendency to exaggerate the importance of Imperial's absence from the Albertan finds of the mid-1970s — principally at West Pembina and Elmworth — because many in the industry took scarcely concealed delight in the fact that Imperial appeared to have made a mistake. The industry view — and also a little of the industry green eye — was apparent in a statement made by J. C. Phillips, chairman of Gulf Canada, another of the subsidiaries of the giant American multinationals. "There is a tendency in this business to follow Imperial Oil's lead," he said in an internal publication. "If Imperial jumped off a cliff, the others would follow. And when they hit the bottom and were hurting real bad they'd still say, 'It can't be all that bad because Imperial is down here with us.' There'll be none of that with Gulf Canada. We'll find our own way to profits and do it independently."

This desire to compete with, and outdo, Imperial amounted almost to a corporate Oedipus complex in the oilpatch. But Imperial did appear to be slipping. Dome Petroleum had seized the initiative in exploration in the Beaufort Sea; Imperial was absent from the huge find at Hibernia off the East Coast, while the superior political antennae of Bob Blair had enabled him to win regulatory approval for his Alaskan Highway pipeline to deliver Prudhoe Bay gas to southern markets.

And politically, there was worse to come. There was the National Energy Program. The NEP, moreover, appeared to be just one, if the most serious, aspect of a concerted attack on foreign-owned oil companies. The Petroleum Monitoring Agency purported to show that the foreign-owned companies were not acting as much in Canada's interest as the domestically-controlled ones. The Bertrand Report, produced by the Combines Investigation Branch of the Department of Consumer and Corporate Affairs, declared that the major oil companies had "ripped-off" the Canadian public to the tune of billions of dollars. The PMA report was tendentious to say the least. The Bertrand Report was a hotchpotch of dubious assumptions and slipshod analysis whose release was deliberately couched in sensational, indeed, almost hysterical tones.

The rationale for the Canadianization aspect of the National Energy Program was that foreign-controlled oil companies were implicitly a dangerous force in the Canadian economy; that companies like Imperial Oil could not be trusted. They were a potential Trojan horse. Little evidence was offered to support such a view, but there was no problem in selling it to an economically illiterate public with a profound mistrust of large institutions.

From Imperial's point of view, it had grossly underestimated the potential power of this antipathy towards it. In particular, it had never imagined that a government would use it to launch a discriminatory attack against foreign-controlled oil companies. It had underestimated it because the world of Imperial was a rational world. Corporate bogeymen and politically bankrupt governments clutching at any policy to survive were irrational. But they proved to be no less real.

## The World Falls Out of Step with Imperial

In the days when Imperial was actually in a position to exert powerful influence on public policy, its self-confidence appeared like true corporate championship. However, with the decline of its public clout, it has at times appeared on the point of drifting into self-righteousness. It is never a sound policy to hold an obvious conviction that everybody is out of step but yourself, even if it is true.

It certainly isn't the case that Imperial lacks the analytical equipment to examine what is going on.

If one was merely to examine the enormous sophisticated system of socio-political analysis within Imperial, then one could not fail to be impressed. Expensive public opinion surveys are carried out. The media is picked apart. Organized groups, academics and activists are studied and surveyed while, at the political level, issues and legislation are constantly reviewed and contacts made with politicians, bureaucrats and advisors.

But if, as the company itself declares, "external activities are directed towards government policies that permit the achievement of company objectives", then, in the words of one of the more percipient members of Imperial's corporate affairs department: "The whole program has been an unqualified disaster."

If Imperial appeared somewhat slow to realize the extent of the political problems facing it, it was not only because it was rational, but also because it was very big, a huge self-contained system that provided not just a place of work but a total environment. Suggestions that Imperial was engaged in reprehensible activities had always been treated not so much as a matter of concern within the organization as a cause for indignation, even outrage. Indeed, perhaps the most startling discrepancy between the internal and external views of Imperial Oil surrounds allegations that Imperial is capable of any form of corporate rip-off. Much of the public takes it as read. The staff of Imperial regards it as inconceivable.

Like employee development, Imperial has ethics built right into the system. It's drummed into the employee on his first day on the job. He's even given a booklet to absorb on the subject. Meanwhile, corporate headquarters has a whole floor of legal advisors who agonize over the legality of every move

259

Imperial makes. At first, when Imperial people talk so much about ethics, one can't suppress a suspicion that a corporate snow-job is being carried out. But eventually you realize that they actually mean it. Bill Moher, for example, says: "The reason people feel comfortable in Imperial is that they can function without having to worry about moral issues."

That outsiders fail to appreciate this is regarded as a constant source of frustration within Imperial. It spends huge amounts of money on advertising and public relations, but its problems seem to have sprung at least partly from its inflexible, somewhat self-righteous attitude.

Imperial's determination to play "by the rules" contrasts markedly with the sort of tactics used against them. The classic example was perhaps the Bertrand Report, named after Robert Bertrand, former director of investigation and research under the Combines Investigation Act. Issued just five months after the announcement of the National Energy Program, when criticism of the policy was at its height, the seven-volume report, entitled "The State of Competition in the Canadian Petroleum Industry" was released to the media late one afternoon, close to deadlines, accompanied by a sensational press-release that declared that the major oil companies, led by Imperial, had ripped off the public to the tune of $12.1 billion between 1958 and 1973.

It is debatable whether the Bertrand Report should be considered as an example of Ottawa's ignorance of corporate motivations, workings and re-lationships, as an example of outright antagonism towards big oil companies, or as an example of how easy it is to manipulate the press in an attempt to influence public opinion. The fact is that it was an example of all three. The report's allegations were subsequently spread across newspaper head-lines and featured top story status on television and radio news across the country.

Close examination of the $12.1 billion figure revealed it to be based on a number of quite unrealistic assumptions. In 1961, under the federal govern-ment's National Oil Policy, the Ottawa Valley Line was created as an artificial barrier to cheap imported oil so that more expensive Albertan oil would have a market in Ontario. The Bertrand Report suggested that the oil companies should have *ignored* the policy and supplied the Ontario market with cheaper imported crude. The fact that they didn't do so was alleged to account for $3.1 billion of the "rip-off". Another $3.2 billion was claimed to have been ripped off as the difference between the price paid under long-term contracts for offshore supplies and the cheaper price on the "spot" market. The desirabil-ity of long-term contracts for ensuring supplies, and the fact that import demand could not possibly have been supplied from spot-market sources on a day-to-day basis were not even considered. Finally, the largest component of the "overcharge", $5.2 billion, was allegedly due to "inefficiencies" in gasoline marketing. The figure was based on the greater costs of running full-service gasoline stations vs. the no-frills stations run by independent retailers. It was assumed that 50% of gasoline sold by major companies should have been marketed at the prices charged by small independents. From that highly arguable assumption, the $5.2 billion element of the rip-off emerged.

All the major oil companies, who tend to choose their words carefully, poured scorn on the report. Imperial said that it contained "errors and omissions" and in places showed either "complete ignorance" of oil industry realities or "a limitless willingness to distort fact and logic".

A rebuttal from Shell Canada said: "Unable to document any real evidence of illegal or unethical activity, the Bertrand Report describes general industry practices and performance and then compares this information to completely unrealistic criteria based on an idealistic description of the market devised by the report's authors . . . it . . . is distinctly unfair and biased. Its ill-founded conclusions are based entirely on its limited and selective 'analysis' of the evidence. The result has been to consider the industry guilty until proven innocent — a violation of all of the principles which protect the rights of individuals and corporations in our society."

J. C. Phillips, Gulf Canada's chairman, laid the blame fairly and squarely at 'the door of the man responsible for the report, Robert Bertrand. Phillips told the annual meeting: "He has long been known as a zealous advocate for change in Canadian competition law. As a public official, however, he has a duty to administer the law as it exists in an even-handed manner. The tone of the report and the method of its release clearly demonstrates that this perspective has been ignored completely. It has been supplanted by a desire to shock and inflame."

For the public at large, however, there was little interest in examining the detailed rebuttals of the big oil companies. What stuck was the headline — "$12 billion rip-off". The Bertrand case was a classic example of the oil companies' overwhelming tactical disadvantage in dealing with an Ottawa that knows how to manipulate the press. Imperial, for example, had known weeks before that a hostile report was coming. It had cranked up its huge public-affairs machine to set "communications objectives" and to prepare "position papers" and briefing kits for senior management. When the report was released, senior executives granted more than thirty interviews to the media. Letters were sent to shareholders, employees and agents. Brochures with "Not Guilty" on the front were stuffed into credit card bills. Within a few days, Jack Armstrong had shot a commercial denying the allegations and welcoming a public inquiry. However, the ad was turned down by the CBC and CTV as representing "advocacy", despite the fact that the networks' own newscasts had, without examination, featured the "$12 billion rip-off" as a lead item. But in any case, although Imperial was quicker than all the other majors, by the time it had its responses out, the whole issue was dead. Just the mud was left sticking to the oil companies' already tarnished image.

A great deal of the pressure for Jack Armstrong to appear on television to deny the allegations came from company employees. The day the report came out, according to a former employee, a kind of Dunkirk spirit pervaded

Imperial's headquarters. But of course, getting big, blunt Jack Armstrong to appear on television wasn't necessarily the right response, because that was where Imperial got into the difference between honesty and credibility. And the two, of course, are not necessarily synonymous. Big, blunt men don't necessarily go down well on television. Someone suggested to Jack Armstrong when he was shooting the Bertrand rebuttal that he might bring along a sports jacket. "I don't wear sports jackets," he snapped back.

Summing up how Armstrong came across, one observer said it reminded him a little of Richard Nixon. Not the looks or the character, just the implicit message: I am not a crook.

Jack Armstrong in a way summed up Imperial's whole problem in a new and devious political age where making plausible noises was more important than sticking to any set of principles. Bill Twaits, his outspoken predecessor, had never had any problem. He was the last of the Imperial CEOs to enjoy a measure of public esteem. In the 1970s, however, public esteem became a rare commodity for corporate chieftains, in particular the heads of multinational companies.

Like Twaits, Armstrong still had enormous clout, but the subtle change was that Imperial was becoming a less credible, public spokesman. In any case, Armstrong didn't come across as well as Twaits. He was a little too straight. Jack Armstrong had followed the curve. He had come up through the system, believed the system, administered the system. He worked 70-hour weeks and still found time, as a Mormon, to devote time to the church and the community.

He was never holier-than-thou, indeed, he had a reputation as a hell-raiser during his days as a young geologist, but he was sure as anything a fanatic devotee of the Imperial faith. But he could also never be accused of having been smooth, and he also had a mighty temper. "On some days," said a former employee, "going before Jack Armstrong was a little like going before the Ayatollah." But everybody respected Jack because Jack knew the business and he was devoted to Imperial.

Armstrong was described by a former colleague as a "western man with a western approach." What he liked to do was to get around the poker table and take people on. His greatest piece of poker playing will probably be remembered as his part in rescuing the Syncrude project in 1974.

Armstrong believed that sitting down one-on-one with government was the way to get things done. They might be politicians, he thought, but at heart surely they had to be reasonable men, interested, as he was, in economic growth and the good of Canada. In that view, however, he may have been somewhat naive. Indeed, one of the main difficulties of Imperial management in the past decade may have sprung from its difficulty in comprehending not only that the political world is far less rational than their own, but also that it can hurt them, and hurt them badly.

There was a very noticeable deterioration in Imperial-government relations under the three federal energy ministers who served during Armstrong's tenure as chief executive.

Donald Macdonald ran a tight ship. He, too, was a big, outspoken man and there was reportedly much table thumping between Armstrong and himself at NACOP meetings. However, Armstrong and Macdonald felt a mutual respect, not to mention a bond in the rescue of the Syncrude project. The rot really began to set in under Alastair Gillespie.

Alastair Gillespie, when he was federal energy minister, might have been a little intimidated by Jack Armstrong in private. He could hardly fail to be impressed by his technical grasp and his forthright approach. But when it came to saving the Liberals' political hide, Gillespie had no compunction about blowing the affair of the "Exxon diversion" in the winter of 1978-79 out of all proportion, knowing that it would strike a chord with the electorate's dark suspicions about big oil, and would also be useful if the country experienced shortages, as was at one time feared.

The worst thing that can be said about the so-called "Exxon diversion" was that it indicated insensitivity on the part of Exxon towards Imperial's delicate political position. What it amounted to was that, when global supplies were sharply curtailed during the Iranian revolution, Exxon cut back all its affiliates' imports.

Imperial informed Gillespie of Exxon's proposal and he immediately summoned Jack Armstrong to see him. Jack Armstrong's secretary phoned to say that he wouldn't be able to make it for a couple of weeks. He had to go to New York. This infuriated Gillespie. Armstrong was ordered to appear and did so, but Gillespie had by now decided to make a political issue of the affair, pointing out to the press that the source of Imperial's imports from Exxon was Venezuela, which was subject to no disruption in supplies. Why then, he asked, should Canada suffer any cutbacks at all? He demanded that Imperial sever its supply relationship with Exxon and deal with Venezuela directly.

Vainly did Jack Armstrong and other Imperial executives point out that the Exxon system was the height of rationality. What, they said, if all our oil came from Venezuela under contract and it was suddenly all cut off? Where would we turn then? Exxon's pooling arrangement was constructed to ensure that no affiliate should suffer unduly from oil disruptions. Eventually, Exxon agreed to cut back Imperial's import reduction. Politics had forced yet another "irrational" decision and Imperial had emerged as a company forced to act at the whim of its mighty parent.

Under Marc Lalonde, relationships with Imperial were to sink even further. Certainly Lalonde, the most powerful minister in Trudeau's Cabinet, and his team of super-technocrats, the brains behind the NEP, felt they had no need to consult with Imperial when they were formulating their policies during the summer of 1980. Indeed, they believed that part of the problem had been that governments had listened too many times to oil companies. Of course, Armstrong and Lalonde met, but there could have been little meeting of the minds. There was also a tendency for Lalonde and his team to downgrade the importance of Imperial, even the competence. When there was a rapid escalation in the costs of Imperial's proposed Cold Lake megaproject, Lalonde would greet Armstrong with his superior smile and ask "What is it today, Jack?".

However, Lalonde and his team weren't quite as smart as they thought they were. They grossly miscalculated the impact and consequences of the NEP in a depressed economic climate, while the Liberals' industrial strategy, based on energy megaproject development, has come tumbling around their ears. When both the Shell Canada-led Alsands consortium collapsed, and the Alaskan Highway gas pipeline was delayed yet another two years, Lalonde came in for a lambasting in the House of Commons and was visibly shaken. With perhaps ultimate irony, scrambling around for something, anything, positive to announce, he eventually came up with the first exploration agreement under the NEP's new frontier lands administration. It was an eleven-company drilling deal worth $600 million over five years. The lead company was Esso Resources Canada.

However, Imperial should not look for federal gratitude. Indeed, it is sometimes in such political embarrassment that a hardening of attitudes is born. As long as the present Liberal government endures — which in their present state of economic chaos may not be beyond the next election — Imperial has cause to be uneasy. But it also has to get much smarter about the whole devious nature of politics. Jim Livingstone sums up Imperial's problem exactly. "We're better," he says, "on how government works than on what motivates politicians." The old guard of Imperial can appreciate Ottawa as a rational process; they still can't entirely understand the means by which it seems to produce irrational results.

I interviewed Jack Armstrong just after his retirement. He had moved out of the chairman's office and was sitting in one much smaller, although still on the 20th floor of Imperial's Toronto headquarters. The smaller office didn't look very comfortable on him. Speaking to him of his period as chief executive I suggested, somewhat tentatively, that he might have considered perhaps *bending* a little more with the prevailing political winds of the 1970s. "I will not," he almost shouted, "prostitute my integrity." It could easily have been John Wayne speaking. But Jack Armstrong wasn't putting on any act.

Now, the almost inconceivable notion of Jack Armstrong prostituting his integrity, at least as chairman, is purely academic. He has acquired an office in the suite that Imperial maintains on Bay Street for its retired senior executives. There he has joined Bill Twaits and the others who are involved in their representative organizations, and their charitable works, and he, like them, will keep well plugged into the corporate establishment, and will move onto various company boards.

But for the rest of Jack Armstrong's days, the thing that will dominate his memory, as it dominated his life, will be Imperial Oil. And anyone who suggests to Jack Armstrong that he wasn't working all those long years in the best interests of Canada, too, will do so at his peril.

## A New Face but an Unchanging Heart

Don McIvor already appears to be far more aware than his predecessors of the importance of image. By nature, he seems like a much more publicly palatable figure: laid back, intellectually inquisitive, a man who says that what he enjoys most is just "trading ideas" with fellow executives.

In fact, the more subtle approach at Imperial was being installed before McIvor returned. The company was learning the virtue of not appearing too outspoken when schemes were being floated that were politically appealing but — in Imperial's opinion — made little economic sense. One example was the scheme to extend the TransCanada natural gas pipeline eastward beyond Montreal. Bill Twaits would have come right out and said the proposal was nonsense. However, Jack Armstrong and other senior management were advised not to oppose the scheme on the basis that they would have been in a no-win situation trying to fight political sentiment on economic grounds.

How well this new trend went down with Jack Armstrong is not certain.

The arrival of McIvor signals not just a less outspoken version of *Homo Imperialis*, however. It also signals another very fundamental change, the arrival of a *fallible Homo Imperialis*. One enormous difference between Don McIvor and his predecessors is that he is willing to admit that Imperial made a mistake. This is no light matter. In fact, McIvor takes personal responsibility for the mistake, the aforementioned abandonment of western exploration when Imperial moved to the far north at the beginning of the 1970s. The move had been common knowledge in the oilpatch for years, but to get either Bill Twaits or Jack Armstrong to admit to it was like drawing blood from a stone. Also, when I interviewed Jim Livingstone for this book I mentioned to him, while leaving his office, that I had seen him several years before about Imperial's "mistake". "You're entitled to your opinion," he said stiffly.

The attitude of Twaits, Armstrong and Livingstone is partly pure religion. Imperial doesn't make mistakes any more than Rolls Royces break down. But they also have a rationale, which is that if Imperial made any decision, then it was the most rational decision at the time, based on the best information and the most thorough analysis. If anything had subsequently gone astray, it hadn't been them. It had been the world.

It would be erroneous to say that Imperial man has failed to adapt to modern conditions. He has no intention of doing so. He sees nothing wrong with what he is. But he may at last be realizing that, in a politically sensitive age, he should also be concerned with what he *appears* to be.

Imperial was slow in realizing its diminishing influence over the environment in which it operated, but the resulting changes in the environment have — from Imperial's point of view — been both irrational and ultimately harmful.

As such it believes that the environment may have to change before it has to.

Imperial firmly believes that the federal government, with its National

265

Energy Program, has endangered the country's energy supply future, its economic efficiency and its international financial status. The consequences of this misguided policy must, it believes in the end, become evident to the public. Then the policy will be changed. Indeed, there are now signs that it *will* be changed.

As for the "new nationalists" who were meant to seize the corporate initiative from Imperial, the Bob Blairs of Nova and the Jack Gallaghers of Dome, Imperial never really regarded these men as rivals. They were playing a dangerous game, making noises that were politically appealing rather than economically sensible, or else engaging in rapid empire building at the expense of financial prudence. Imperial has been watching them as some great bird might have watched the attempts of Icarus. And now it watches as they plummet.

So now, as with all the cycles of life, Imperial's fortunes, even as they appear to be blackest, may in fact be picking up. The false gods are crumbling.

Of course, the purely corporate problems remain enormous — rationalizing a stagnant refining and marketing business; finding new sources of reserves as cash flows are slashed and projects are shelved. But in relative terms, Imperial remains one of the most financially sound and well-managed companies in Canada. Just one of the several short-term ironies of the National Energy Program is that, if anything, it has actually increased Imperial's relative strength vs. its more "Canadian" counterparts.

Don McIvor, as he showed at the annual meeting, may be more adept at appearing sensitive than his predecessors — or at least may have the wisdom of choosing more sensitive speechwriters — but it is important to remember that he is still not in the business of making politically attractive noises. He is, at heart, of the same stuff as Twaits and Livingstone and Armstrong — firmly in the business of making "sound" corporate decisions.

# Conclusion

*"That maze, I realized, is the liberal ideology itself — a hash of statism, collectivism, egalitarianism, and anti-capitalism, mixed with the desire for the results of capitalism. This murky conceptual mess renders even the most innately brilliant men stupid.*

*And I would stress sharply that by stupid I really mean stupidity . . . They are not conspirators; they are intellectual basket cases in the realm of basic economics."*

A TIME FOR TRUTH
WILLIAM SIMON

The story of the National Energy Program has so far been told largely in terms of men and events. It is now time to return to the larger issues of economic understanding and political philosophy touched on at the beginning of the book. Understanding these issues is important, because they involve nothing less than the future shape and well-being of Canada.

As noted in the introduction, the Liberal government of Pierre Trudeau has, as this book goes to press, retreated once more into one of its perennial bouts of "pragmatism", in which business advice is heeded once again as it struggles with *ad hoc* measures to shore up the economy. When the economy seems hell-bound, an obsession with the Canadian content of the handbasket does not seem most appropriate, hence economic nationalism and the NEP are once again out of the limelight. However, the fact that they have been temporarily removed from the stage makes it all the more important to reemphasize just what the NEP's policy objectives were in order to support the assertion that it was not only an inept, but dangerous policy.

The "hidden" purposes of the NEP, as a revenue grab and an attempt to put the oil industry under much greater direct government control, have been clearly spelled out. The damage, and counterproductiveness, of the revenue grab have also been demonstrated. It remains now to further examine the dubious rationalizations for, and dangers implicit in, greater government control of oil, or indeed, any business.

Economic nationalism of the kind espoused in the NEP has to justify discriminatory measures and a degree of expropriation by asserting, or at least implying, that not only has foreign control been gained unfairly, but that it is economically damaging. The economic nationalists seek a further shift in the balance of power from business to the state on the basis that control is better vested in the Canadian state than in a foreign-controlled private sector. As such, they inevitably play down the dangers of excessive government intervention and exaggerate the implications of foreign-control. Also as such, what they are espousing is less appropriately described as economic nationalism than as national socialism.

Refuting the spurious arguments of the NEP's brand of economic nationalism is less a defence of foreign companies than of a system which has made us one of the wealthiest — and most politically free — nations on earth.

It is important to note that the defence of a free-market system does not involve the defence of the cosmetic defects of its individual members. As was noted earlier in this book, Adam Smith pointed out long ago that the brewer and the baker may not have been necessarily very lovable creatures, but eighteenth-century consumers obtained beer and bread from them because these tradesmen loved *themselves*. It is just so with the much larger economic units in the modern economy. One does not have to love large corporations or the flinty men who have climbed their corporate ladders. Love or hate are inappropriate emotions. Indeed, *emotions* are inappropriate. What is important is an intellectual recognition of the fact that, by pursuing their "bottom line" objectives within the legal constraints of the state and the ethical constraints of society, corporations are promoting the wealth of society as a whole.

It cannot be stressed sufficiently that the theory of the free market is not a recommendation for individual action, but a description of the system that emerges when individuals act freely in the economic sphere. It is not necessary for the businessman to have ever heard of Adam Smith, or even be able to read and write, for the theory to be borne out. Again, the individual businessman himself will not always like the working of the free market. Indeed, when he is in difficulty, the businessman might well invoke state aid or intervention. This, however, is not a flaw in the theory of the market. A person who stumbles off a ten-storey building will almost certainly pray for something soft on which to land. He would be wiser to do so than to hope for the law of gravity to be revoked. It is not inconsistent to believe in a force and yet not wish to be a victim of its potentially adverse consequences. But the point is that the man falling off the building will fall at the same rate whether he has heard of the law of gravity or not.

It is possible to make all sorts of "cases" against individual oil companies, ranging from examples of insensitivity in dealing with their Canadian subsidiaries to accusations about the use of offshore tax havens. What one has to decide is whether such examples provide a *prima facie* case for the rejection of private corporations and the market system, and the centralization of economic power in the hands of the state.

The reason socialistic central direction of the economy is doomed to gross inefficiency can be easily summed up. If the economy is like a horse, the capitalist wants to ride it; the central planner wants to redesign it. This might seem less an analogy than a ludicrous parody, for if anyone were to suggest that

268

he planned to retire to the laboratory to make a horse from the molecules up, we should all break down laughing. The problem is that whereas most people comprehend the physiological complexity of a horse, many do not understand that the economy is similarly complex. What they also fail to understand is that, just like a horse, *nobody needs to intervene to make the economy work*. The flaws of a theory that suggested a horse might run faster with only three legs would, one would hope, be apparent without resort to surgery. The flaws of a theory that suggests that an economy could be much more rationally operated by a group of intelligent central planners are less immediately and intuitively obvious. They are, however, no less real and no less damaging should such social surgery be put into effect. Due to the amorphous nature of the economy, however, the damage they would wreak would be less easy to pinpoint. The central planners would almost certainly claim that the faults of their new system were merely temporary, or due to factors outside their control. Thence the economy would move to the equivalent of the theory of a two-legged horse. And so on into disaster.

Of course, to suggest as this book has that central economic planning and state control are dangerously counterproductive is not to say that government has no mandate to intervene in society. Government exists for that purpose. The present situation has arisen, however, because of a growing confusion in the public mind about what government can deliver, and just who creates wealth in society. Because of the central government's role in redistributing wealth and borrowing and printing money in the name of social justice and economic management, the impression has grown that it is government that is the most important player in the economy. Nothing could be further from the truth. Such a notion is similar to believing that the most important people at sporting matches are the referees or umpires. The economy is like a gigantic game where we only see the score, so a public confusion, encouraged by the political referees, has grown up. However, just as no umpire ever scored a home-run in baseball and nobody in boxing was ever knocked out by the Queensberry Rules, so the political regulators have never actually created anything. It is a critically important point.

Nevertheless, this confused view of the economy has led to public support for increased government intervention in the name of economic well-being. The advocates of interventionism are articulate and seem to display admirable public concern. The advocates of free enterprise seldom articulate their views at all. Part of the problem is that interventionist, socialist ideologies are explicit, whereas the philosophy of free-market capitalism is implicit. Adam Smith, the prophet of free enterprise, did not *create* the system. It was already there. He merely explained how it worked and noted what a marvellous self-regulating mechanism it was. Socialism, however, be it of a "democratic" or whatever stamp, is always a *projected* goal of "public good". Capitalists, when they speak in theoretical terms at all, seem merely to advocate the status quo and self-interest. Those of socialist inclination always speak of bigger and worthier-sounding goals. The idea of a self-correcting market does not have much appeal, particularly to someone who happens to be at the locus of any particular economic problem. It is far more intellectually appealing, when faced with any sort of economic glitch, to intervene and do something about it. Of course, there are cases where intervention is necessary. Under socialism, however, intervention becomes the general prescription rather than a particular tool, and that is where the problems start.

In Canada, the ideological picture has been further blurred because there *has* been a solid historical tradition of government involvement in the economy. Indeed, in a number of cases, such as the CPR, government intervention has appeared to form a noble part of the nation's historical fabric. Such ventures were not widely regarded as matters of ideology but of national necessity, the sort of "pragmatic" approach on which the Canadian people have traditionally prided themselves. This has, in turn, created a powerful precedent for the notion that government involvement is both necessary and workable. This historical feature, however, may be dangerous, for by regarding government intervention as non-ideological, Canadians may be less concerned about its inherent dangers and may be less discriminating between the *types* of government intervention.

The fact is that, historically, government involvement in Canada has been of the type *recommended* by free-enterprise philosophers: that is, to achieve objectives or build projects that could not be achieved by the private sector alone. The National Energy Program, however, preaches something quite different: that government should take over viable parts of the private sector merely because they are foreign-owned. It is possible to claim that such action *is* in the mainstream of Canadian government intervention because it is achieving something that the Canadian private sector cannot achieve by itself. Moreover, the policy claims to act in the national interest and towards the formation of a stronger national identity. However, there is a powerful case to be made that state-controlled economic nationalism is based on a spurious — and ultimately dangerous — vision of Canada's economic and political self-interest.

## Benign Intentions: Bad Results

The dangers of centralized state power — and the threats to individual freedom and initiative in such power — have been the subject of some of the best-known works of political philosophy of the past two-hundred years. The overwhelming theme of classical liberal philosophers such as Adam Smith and John Stuart Mill, and of writers like Alexis de Tocqueville, was that state power had to be constrained because the best of intentions, once funneled through centralized power, created the worst of results. Lord Acton summed up the underlying beliefs of such men in his classic statement that: "Power tends to corrupt, and absolute power corrupts absolutely." De Tocqueville brilliantly analyzed the threats lurking beneath the most high-sounding of principles. "The foremost, or indeed the sole, condition required in order to succeed in centralizing the supreme power in a democratic community is to love equality or to get men to believe that you love it. Thus, the science of despotism, which was once so complex, has been simplified and reduced, as it were, to a single principle." Within the past fifty years, the warnings of such men received their fullest justification with the two most glaring examples in history of the horrors and perversions capable of being performed in the name of the public good — in Hitler's Germany and Stalin's Russia.

Ironically, however, within the same period, public demands to provide economic security have meant that governments almost everywhere have grown and their power has increased. The intentions behind such growth have, of course, been benign.

Indeed, the role that governments have adopted is that of the state as good shepherd. The potential pitfalls of this role were spelled out in one of the greatest books on economic and political freedom ever written, Nobel-prizewinning economist Friedrich Hayek's *The Road to Serfdom*. First published towards the end of the Second World War, it warned of the dangers of the drive towards central economic control of the kind recommended by socialism.

Said Hayek: "Just because in the years ahead of us political ideology is not likely to aim at a clearly defined goal but toward piecemeal change, a full understanding of the process through which certain kinds of measures can destroy the bases of an economy based on the market and gradually smother the creative powers of a free civilization seems now of the greatest importance. Only if we understand why and how certain kinds of economic controls tend to paralyze the driving forces of a free society, and which kinds of measures are particularly dangerous in this respect, can we hope that social experimentation will not lead us into situations none of us want."

Hayek's argument, as with the classical liberal philosophers, was that central government planning and control was firstly inefficient, and secondly, politically dangerous. Writing at the time he did, of course, the political dangers were foremost in people's minds. However, despite numerous, largely unsuccessful, experiments in central planning throughout the Western world, and the growth of governments, totalitarianism did not break out in the Western democracies. The quarter of a century after the end of the Second World War was marked by enormous economic growth. This growth enabled governments to engage in large-scale redistribution of income as the spirit of liberalism underwent a massive change; in fact, it actually reversed its poles. Liberalism became synonymous with state power and intervention for the "public good". Instead of wanting to limit the reach of government, liberals or "democratic socialists" as they often styled themselves, wanted, in the 1960s and 1970s, to extend the healing hand of the government into every walk of life.

This was very much the orientation of Trudeau's Liberal government when it came to power in 1968. The wave that Trudeau was riding was clearly identified by Robert Heilbroner. "In the long run," he said, "the ascendant elites within capitalism are not themselves capitalist in mentality or outlook, and will

271

slowly incline society toward that deliberate application of intelligence to social problems that is characteristic of their professional commitment."

Trudeau and his government stood clearly for the "deliberate application of intelligence to social problems." A more praiseworthy goal could hardly be imagined.

Indeed, how could one argue *against* "the deliberate application of intelligence to social problems"? However, the key to the dangers inherent in such an approach lay in just what one meant by "social problems" and just how great one considered the scope for the "application of intelligence". Adam Smith had revealed the existence of the "invisible hand" which guided the individual towards a greater public good that was "no part of his intention", and had realized that the wonder of the market economy was that it *required* no "deliberate application of intelligence". Former U.S. Treasury Secretary William Simon put it succinctly: "The single most awe-inspiring thing about our economic system lies in what is *absent*, what is *not* perceivable to the naked eye. It is the fact that the flood of wealth emerges from the lack of government control, from the lack of state-imposed or 'national' purposes and goals." Modern-day liberal interventionists have found this an unsatisfactory state of affairs.

But perhaps what they disliked most of all was that the driving force for Adam Smith's invisible hand was "self-interest". To community-minded men and women consumed by a desire to be seen to be doing good, no motivation could appear more objectionable, whatever its results. They just knew that they had to be able to improve on a system driven by materialistic desires. They felt they could build a better horse.

Despite the fact that the Trudeau government's attempts at rational planning have been an abject failure, Ottawa's enlightened interventionists continue to believe in their ability to perpetrate a more efficient society. Blinded by their own fervent desire to rectify inequality and "do good" they do not consider for a second that gross inefficiency might result, and that the very health of society could be in danger from their very prescriptions. They are experts at the game of false logic: that supporting the health of corporations is in some way depriving the much-invoked "little man"; that because their intentions are good, the results cannot be bad. Danger from their recommendations? Do we really think the men in the brown uniforms will come next? they scoff. And as for opposing the NEP, well that just means, they say, that you don't support Canada!

## Loving the Wood but Hating the Trees

Appeals to our concern about the "little man" and the "national interest" are at the very root of the interventionists' conscious or unconscious false logic. By asserting that the National Energy Program is synonymous with both concepts, while the interests of foreign-owned oil companies are diametrically opposed to them, they seek to win their case by default. Unfortunately, in many cases they are successful. When they are forced to make their case explicitly, however, the cracks begin to appear.

Higher prices and tax incentives have been given in pursuit of the national objective of finding additional petroleum supplies. Their inevitable concomitant has been that the companies who have produced the largest supplies of oil and gas, do the bulk of exploration, and find the new reserves, get richer. One cannot stimulate the nation's resource wealth in a free-market economy such as Canada's without enriching the private sector in the process. That is the very basis of economic growth but, due to the dominant position of foreign companies in the industry, it is a fact that militant economic nationalists abhor. They struggle, therefore, to prove that the wealth of corporations and the wealth of society are not synonymous but contradictory. They yearn for the benefits of free enterprise without the corporate intermediaries that provide them. They display an inability to see the great Canadian economic wood for the foreign trees within it. More than that, they seem to seek — and indeed, to believe that it is possible to find — a system whereby we can have woods *without* trees.

Such a view means that features of capitalism previously considered praiseworthy, such as reinvestment, have to be condemned because they are the means whereby foreign-owned or controlled oil companies have grown. This argument is perverse because it takes the view that only the original cross-border flow of investment from a foreign country should be counted as investment at all. Reinvestment of domestically-generated profits, instead of being viewed as the admirable engine of job creation and economic growth, has, instead, to be treated as a sneaky and reprehensible method of gaining a stranglehold on the economy. Meanwhile, the fact that governments have allowed companies to write-off reinvestment against corporate taxes on their own profits is treated as tantamount to Canadian taxpayers financing the buy-out of their country.

In attacking the argument that corporate interest and national interest are largely synonymous, the economic nationalists are attacking nothing less than the whole theory of market economics. They assert that foreign companies, by acting in their "own interests" are *per se* acting against the interests of that great collectivist myth so beloved of economic nationalists, the "Canadian People". Adam Smith pointed out that the economic interests of all are best served by the units of the market pursuing — on a voluntary basis — their "own interests". Unless one espouses the Galbraithian view of a world of moronic consumers and all-powerful corporate manipulators — which, as I pointed out earlier on in this book, many bureaucratic interventionists do — then one is led to the conclusion that foreign-owned companies could never have grown to their present size *unless they had provided Canadian consumers with products they wanted.* They could never have provided these products unless they had been successful in searching for and finding oil and gas (and despite myriad takeovers, the major oil companies *did* find most of the oil and gas in Canada) and had employed — and indeed, in most cases been managed by — Canadians.

However, the determination, indeed the necessity, of not seeing the wood for the trees leads to a totally jaundiced view of the achievements of foreign-owned oil companies. For example, the discovery of the Hibernia field off Newfoundland by a consortium led by Chevron Standard, a wholly-owned subsidiary of Standard Oil of California, was viewed by the economic nationalists — and even, as I indicated earlier in this book, by Pierre Trudeau himself — as a "giveaway" because of the low cost of the well to the companies that drilled it. Blinded by their aversion to foreign oil companies, such people seem to take no joy in the billions of dollars of potential revenue to come to Canada from the field. All they see, and regret, is the inevitable increase in the value of the companies who discovered it. Sometimes, it seems as if they would prefer not to have the wealth if it has been created or discovered by a foreigner. There is a term for such highly-selective perception: it is called looking at a doughnut and seeing only the hole.

Because of their anticapitalist bias, whenever such people see a booming or profitable industry, such as oil in the latter half of the 1970s, they perceive it as a cause for sorrow rather than joy. The industry has plainly had "too much"; its tax allowances have been too great; its prices have been too high. In their profound commitment to perverse notions of equity, such conditions need to be "rectified". The question that haunts them when they look at the oil industry's financial performance is: couldn't we have got them to do all this for less? Hence, their eternal quest is to "fine-tune" windfall and "excess" profits out of the system. Of course, the very driving force of both the entrepreneur and the giant corporation is the making of profit, so what the fine-tuners in fact seek to achieve — whether they know it or not — is to rob the system of its motive force. As long as such men are in positions of power in Ottawa, seeking eternally to remove all traces of "excess" profit in the name of social equity, then the whole wealth generating process must slowly but surely be strangled. Capital will flee the country — as it did in the wake of the NEP — and we will be left with a spineless system based everywhere on publicly determined "utility" rates of return. The irony perhaps is that while giant corporations would continue to operate under such a system, smaller entrepreneurs *would not*.

Another spurious argument much loved by the economic nationalists is that the foreign-owned oil companies are involved in a process of bleeding the country dry. According to the National Energy Program, as indicated earlier, the total payout of dividends to non-residents in 1979 was $600 million. This, however, compares with an asset value for foreign-owned oil companies of $31.9 billion. Can a dividend payment of less than 2% of the value of book assets in a year represent a hemorrhage? If one really wants to witness a hemorrhage of capital, then one should examine the *aftermath* of the National Energy Program, clearly spelled out in figures provided by the government itself through the Petroleum Monitoring Agency's report for 1981. In 1981, Canada experienced a net outflow of $4.8 billion in the capital account related to the buy-out of foreign-owned oil companies, principally by the state and principally at public expense. Meanwhile, the net outflow of dividends, far from being reduced by the takeovers, continued to rise, to $528 million. Again, this latter figure can be considered far from excessive, but it indicates one of the most frightening aspects of economic nationalists' thinking — that their analysis represents a self-fulfilling prophecy. Nothing persuades an overseas investor in Canada that he should withdraw his money more than the prospect of being expropriated.

Thereupon, of course, the economic nationalists can all proceed to bleat that the overseas investors were never really "committed" to Canada in the first place, and that, in withdrawing their money, they have put their "own interests" first. But of course, major oil companies cannot physically withdraw from Canada. They cannot move their refineries, they cannot shift their petroleum reserves, they cannot transport their retailing outlets overseas. They *can* sell out, but the PMA figures — which show that to gain another 6.5% "control" of the industry cost Canada more than $5.6 billion in 1981 — indicate the horrendous costs of that buy-out. Most important, however, the notion that we *have* to buy them out is a canard, since outright purchase leads to a far worse drain on the balance of payments than overseas dividends are ever likely to.

The NEP has been not merely economically injurious but ideologically misguided. The former point is a matter of observation; the latter is inevitably more political and personal. By declaring that the government has gone too far in one political direction, this book, at least implicitly, recommends a move in the opposite direction. This, however, does not represent any simplistic call to "clear the decks" and let business get on with business. No attempt is made to deny the wide and legitimate role of government in society. What is called for is a recognition that a dangerous imbalance has grown up between the powers of government and of business.

Business may have been shortsighted about the extent of the political dangers facing it in recent years, but that does not mean that it has lost its legitimacy. Business still, critically, generates the bulk of wealth in society. The more the state assumes that function, the smaller will future wealth be. The potential damage of mismanagement at even the largest of private corporations is far smaller than the havoc that can be created by a bad decision in Ottawa.

Meanwhile, the conventional wisdom of the latter 1970s — that a smart corporation was one that aligned its activities with the aims of government — has been shown to deserve much closer examination. The fate of Dome Petroleum, in particular, demonstrates the grave dangers of such an approach. Any business that climbs into bed with a government such as the 1980 reincarnation of the Trudeau Liberals will find itself — like the black widow's mate — coupled with an unpredictable and possibly lethal partner.

This book, I believe, makes a powerful case for not allowing further economic control to fall into the hands of central government and the bureaucracy without examining closely its justifications and analyzing its likely results. It also, I believe, establishes that there is an urgent need for more experience of business in the bureaucracy and for a greater awareness of the limits of its own ability. Those limits should not be tested pragmatically and thus at the public expense. The experience of Joe Clark's 1979 Tory government indicates that real change requires more than merely the replacement of one party by another.

# Index

Axworthy, Lloyd, 128, 133n
Axworthy, Tom, 50, 128

Baker, Walter, 109
Bankenko Mines, 25
Basford, Ron, 62
Baxter, Clive, 65
Beaufort Sea, 202, 213, 215-16, 219, 258
Bell, Joel, 53, 62-3, 67, 71-2, 103, 140-1, 192, 223-9, 235
Bell, Max, 59
Bertrand Report, The, 258, 260-2
Bertrand, Robert, 260-1
*Birds of Prey, The* (Saul), 68
Blair, Bob, 19, 20-1, 70, 128, 157, 195, 245, 258
Blair-Carr report, 195
Blais, Jean-Jacques, 133n
*Blue-Eyed Sheiks, The* (Foster), 20, 26, 70n, 213, 219
Bow Valley Square, 20
BP Canada, 230
Brawn, Bob, 24-5, 113
British Columbia Resources Investment Corporation, 107
British Petroleum, 100
Broadbent, Ed, 113
Brown, Bobby, 59-61
Brown University, 88
Brown, William M., 189
Buckley, William F., 42
Bureaucracy: and Federal-Alberta pricing agreement, 168-79; and foreign ownership of oil industry, 197-200; growth of, under Trudeau, 45-7, 49-50, 54; in Energy, Mines and Resources, 61-4, 86; politicians' reliance on, 48, 53-5; power of, 16, 48, 52-57, structure of, 45, 50-2, 56; style of, 45, 52-4, 141; under Conservative party, 48, 83-124, 139-40

Burns, Fry, 111
Bussières, Pierre, 133n

Cabinet committees, 49, 52, 54, 130; Central Agencies, 50-2; Federal-Provincial Relations Office, 50; Prime Minister's Office, 50-1, 54, 66, 130, 225; Priorities and Planning Committee, 49; Privy Council Office, 47, 51-4, 77, 225
Cabinet ministers, 53-55
Caccia, Charles, 133n
Calgary, 19-27, 155-6, 215, 228, 258
*Calgary Herald*, 101
Camp, Dalton, 29, 88, 101, 104, 131
Canada Development Corporation, 113, 158
*Canadian Business*, 78, 157
Canadian Corporate Management, 128
Canadian Hunter, 96, 155, 258
Canadian International Development Agency, 67
Canadianization of oil industry: costs of, 15, 33, 159, 161; and the NEP, 14, 27
Canadian Labour Congress, 195
Canadian Oil and Gas Lands Administration (COGLA), 161
Canadian Ownership Account, 149-50, 228, 233. *see also* National Energy Program
Canadian Pacific Railway. *see* CPR
Canadian Petroleum Association, 32-4, 145, 157, 179, 199
Canadian Superior, 146
Canadian-US relations: and the NEP, 13, 15, 64, 156-7, 159-61
CanDel Oil Ltd., 25-6
Cantertech, 141
Canute, King, 99

279

Home Oil, 59-61
Hood, Bill, 91, 103
Hopper, Wilbert, 33, 61-3, 67,
    69-72, 102-3, 224, 227-9, 231-3,
    235-8
Hormats, Robert, 160
Howe, Pat, 93
Hudson Institute, 189
Hudson's Bay Company, 255
Hudson's Bay Oil & Gas, 159, 201,
    213-4, 217
Huff, Keith, 230
Husky Oil, 69-71, 158

Icarus, 19
Île Perrot, 130
Incremental Oil Revenue Tax, 150,
    198, 207. *see also* National
    Energy Program
Independent Petroleum Association
    of Canada, 155
Indiana University, 88
Imperial Oil, 52, 58, 61, 65, 72, 93,
    96-7, 112, 128, 193, 197, 199,
    200, 214, 237, 238-66
International Energy Development
    Agency, 230, 263
Investment Dealers Association,
    247
Iona Station (Ontario), 37
IPAC. *see* Independent Petroleum
    Association of Canada
Iran, 191
Iraqui National Oil Company, 84

Japan, 77
Jamieson, Don, 135
Jamieson, Nancy, 124
Janisch, Andy, 69
Jersey Production Research
    Company (Oklahoma), 252
Johnston, Don, 135
Joudrie, Earl, 155

Judy Creek oil field, 256

Kahanoff, Syd, 110-12
Kahn, Herman, 189
Kanik, Myron, 163, 170
Katz, Julius, 64
Keynes, John Maynard, 46
Khomeini, Ayatollah, 22, 73, 99,
    195
Kharg Island, 84
Koakoak, 219
Kopanoar, 219
Laing, Art, 57
Lalonde, Marc, 50-1, 55, 96n,
    130-7, 140, 145-7, 155-60, 162,
    165, 167-8, 172, 174-6, 184,
    199, 204, 206, 216-7, 241, 263-4
Lambert Royal Commission, 54
Lamond, Bobby, 26-7
LaSalle, Roch, 109
Lebel, Louis, 145-6
LeBlanc, Roméo, 133n, 137
Leduc, 20, 256
Leitch, Merv, 117-21, 162, 164-5,
    168, 174-5, 177, 179, 241
Lenin, 70
Lévesque, René, 129
Lewis, David, 65
Liberal Party: attitude to business
    community of, 35, 131, 267; and
    bureaucracy, 139-40; economic
    nationalism, 22, 128-9, 131;
    election campaign of, 127, 134-8;
    energy platform of, 134-41;
    ideology of, 16, 36, 43, 125-6;
    and National Energy Program,
    16, 147-51, 166-7, 171-4; in
    Opposition, 126-7
Little, Paul, 111-13
Livingstone, Jim, 240-1, 264-5
Loiselle, Bernard, 133n
Lougheed, Peter, 22-24, 26, 64,
    116-9, 121, 123-4, 164-7, 169,
    174-82, 185, 193, 199

Lynch, Charles, 181

Macdonald, Donald, 55, 62, 63, 66-7, 77, 131, 163-4, 215, 236, 263
MacDonald, Flora, 109
MacDougall, Grace, 51
MacEachen, Allan, 134-5, 147, 159
Mackenzie Delta, 65, 257
Mackenzie Valley, 30
Makenzie Valley pipeline, 65
Macleod, Dixon, 162
MacNamara, Dr. John, 196
Malmgren, Harald, 160
Mandarins. see Bureaucracy
Marcel, Ray, 133n
Marsden, Lorna, 134
Massé, Marcel, 118, 163
Masters, John, 96n, 155, 258
McCauley, Gary, 133n
McDougall, Donald, 110-12, 115
McGill University, 51, 62
McIvor, Donald, 239-50, 265-66
McLeod, Jack, 145
McLeod, Young, Weir, 111
McNabb, Gordon, 62
McRae, Paul, 133n
Megaprojects: attitude of bureau-cracy toward, 196-200; collapse of, 184, 193-4; costs of, 195-7; future of, 201-2
Mega Projects Task Force, 195-6
Mellon, Barry, 163, 166, 175
Merland Oil, 25
Mill, John Stuart, 270
Milner, Stan, 21
Mineral Lands Leasing Act (US), 161
Minion, Wayne, 163, 167, 180-1
Ministries: Energy, Mines and Resources, 47-8, 52-3, 55-6, 58, 61-5, 72-4, 76-7, 83-115, 118-23, 140, 142-8; External Affairs, 56, 159; Finance, 53, 63, 73-8, 168, 225; Federal-Provincial Relations office, 50; Industry, Trade and Commerce, 56, 74; Ministry of State for Economic Development, 56, 77; Treasury Board Secretariat, 50
Mobil Canada, 66, 68, 69, 100, 146, 234
Moher, Bill, 252-3
Multinational oil companies: attitude of public to, 27, 30-3, 238-9
Murray, Lowell, 90, 110

National Advisory Committee on Petroleum, 256
National Energy Board, 58-60, 62-3, 215, 256-7
National Energy Program: Alberta's reaction to, 22, 74, 205; and Canadian Ownership Account, 149; and Canadian ownership in oil industry, 27, 147-8, 150-1, 198-200; criticism of, 155-61, 242; evolution of, 52, 63-5; formulation of, 143-7; ideals behind, 16; introduction of, 13, 147, 216; objectives of, 14, 27, 147, 232-3, 267; and OPEC, 185-6; and opinion polls, 32-4; and Petroleum Compensation Charge, 149, 167, 173; and Petroleum Incentives Program, 150, 158, 172, 179, 204-5; and Progressive Incremental Royalty 150; public support for, 13-4, 27, 30, 32-3, 239; results of, 13-5, 203; roots of, 61-5, 85-7; under Conservatives, proposals for, 74-9, 117-24; under Liberals, pricing proposals for, 148-9, 166-7, 171-4; under Liberals, taxation and grant scheme of, 149-50, 171-4, 201, 207; and

283

Petro-Canada Task Force, 110-15
Petrofina Canada, 92, 173, 201,
    230-1
Petrolia, 255
Petroleum Administration Act, 122,
    167
Petroleum and Gas Revenue Tax,
    171, 179, 201, 207. see also
    National Energy Program
Petroleum Compensation Charge,
    149, 176, 173. see also
    National Energy Program
Petroleum Club, The, 24, 72, 75,
    213
Petroleum Incentives program,
    150-8, 172, 179, 204-5. see
    National Energy Program
Petroleum Monitoring Agency,
    144-5, 258, 274-5
Petroleum pricing and Auditing
    Agency, 138, 140
Phelps, Mike, 145, 156, 168, 171-2,
    230
Phillips, Art, 133n
Phillips, J. C., 258, 261
Phillips Petroleum, 71
PIP. see Petroleum Incentives
    program
Pitfield, Mackay Ross, 230
Pitfield, Michael, 50-2, 54, 74, 77,
    90, 130, 144
Pitfield, Ward C., 51
*Playboy*, 88
PMA. see Petroleum Monitoring
    Agency
PMO. see Prime Minister's Office
*Points of Departure* (Camp), 29, 104
Polar Gas project, 114
Pollock, Jackson, 40
Polls: 28-34, 239; Conservative
    polls, 32, 101-2; Goldfarb,
    Martin, 28-9; Gallup polls, 33,
    101, 107, 127
Polo Club, The, 64

Power Corporation, 67
*Practice and Theory of Federalism*
    (Trudeau), 45
Prime Minister's Office. see Cabinet
    committees
Priorities and Planning Committee.
    see Cabinet committees
*Privatization of Petro-Canada*
    (Scrim), 105
Privy Council Office. see Cabinet
    committees
Progressive Conservative Party:
    and bureaucracy, 83-104,
    139-40; energy policy of, 83-5,
    92, 94-5; and PetroCan, 99-115;
    relations with Alberta, 94-5,
    116-24
Prudhoe Bay field, 59, 65, 69, 128,
    188, 257
*Public Investment and Socialist*
    *Development in Tanzanania*
    (Clark), 75

Quebec, 44, 129
Qom (Iran), 73

Rabinovitch, Robert, 168
Radwanski, George, 36
Ranchmen's Club, The, 24
Rashish, Meyer, 160
Raymaker, Darryl, 145
Reagan, Ronald, 160, 190
"Red Square", 20, 68, 103
Redwater oil field, 256
Regan, Gerald, 217
Reisman, Simon, 60, 63, 163
Reuber, Grant, 103
Richards, Bill, 158, 213-16
Ritchie, Ron, 247
*Road to Serfdom, The* (Hayek), 271
Robertson, Gordon, 57
Robinson, Kathy, 135
Rockefeller, John D., 191, 255-6
Ross, Al, 145

University of Ottawa, 130
University of Prince Edward Island, 78
University of Toronto, 75, 134
University of Toronto Press, 75
University of Western Ontario, 78, 88
Uno-Tex Petroleum Corp., 158

Van Wielingen, Gus, 25-6, 230
Voyager Petroleums, 155

*Wall Street Journal*, 156
*Weekend*, 90
Wells, H. G., 187
Westcoast Transmission, 107-8

Western Development Fund, 151. *see also* National Energy Program
*When Business Fails* (Gillies), 34
Whitefish, 104
Widdrington, Peter, 110
Wilson, Michael, 115
Windsor, 130
*Winnipeg Free Press*, 252
Wolcott, Don, 68
Wood, Tom, 164, 168, 171
*Wordly Philosophers, The* (Heilbroner), 43
Yamanai, Sheik, 189-90
Yom Kippur war, 64
York University (Toronto), 88